Handbook of Public Policy in Europe

Also by Hugh Compston

THE NEW POLITICS OF UNEMPLOYMENT *(edited)*

SOCIAL PARTNERSHIP IN THE EUROPEAN UNION *(edited with Justin Greenwood)*

POLICY CONCERTATION AND SOCIAL PARTNERSHIP IN WESTERN EUROPE
(edited with Stefan Berger)

Handbook of Public Policy in Europe

Britain, France and Germany

Edited by Hugh Compston
Senior Lecturer in Public Policy
Cardiff University

Editorial Matter and Selection, Introduction
© Hugh Compston 2004
Chapters 1–34 © Palgrave Macmillan Ltd 2004

First published 2004 by
PALGRAVE MACMILLAN
Houndmills, Basingstoke, Hampshire RG21 6XS and
175 Fifth Avenue, New York, N.Y. 10010
Companies and representatives throughout the world

PALGRAVE MACMILLAN is the global academic imprint of the Palgrave
Macmillan division of St. Martin's Press, LLC and of Palgrave Macmillan Ltd.
Macmillan® is a registered trademark in the United States, United Kingdom
and other countries. Palgrave is a registered trademark in the European
Union and other countries.

ISBN 1–4039–0291–7

This book is printed on paper suitable for recycling and made from fully
managed and sustained forest sources.

A catalogue record for this book is available from the British Library.

Library of Congress Cataloging-in-Publication Data
Handbook of public policy in Europe : Britain, France and Germany / edited by
Hugh Compston
    p.   cm.
  Includes bibliographical references and index.
  ISBN 1–4039–0291–7
  1. Political planning—Great Britain.   2. Political planning—France.
  3. Political planning—Germany.   I. Compston, Hugh, 1955–

  JN318.H32 2004
  320.6′094—dc22
                                                              2004052590

10   9   8   7   6   5   4   3   2   1
13   12   11   10   09   08   07   06   05   04

Printed and bound in Great Britain by
Antony Rowe Ltd, Chippenham and Eastbourne

Contents

Part II Law and Order

Part III Economic Policy

List of Tables, Figure and Boxes

Tables

Figure

Boxes

Acknowledgements

The preparation of this volume has involved the coordinated efforts of no fewer than 52 contributors, whom I would like to thank not only for their work but also for their preparedness to step outside their normal frames of reference to put their chapters into the single common chapter format. In many cases this has not been easy. But the result is a picture of public policy as a whole in Britain, France and Germany that has never been seen before.

Hugh Compston

Currency Conversions

Except where otherwise indicated, all currency conversions between euros, pounds sterling and US dollars are calculated using 2002 Purchasing Power Parities as given in OECD, *Main Economic Indicators*: 245 (Paris: OECD, February 2003):
$1 = £0.654 = €0.889.

Abbreviations

bn   billion (thousand million)
m   million or metre, depending on context
Britain   United Kingdom of Great Britain and Northern Ireland

Notes on the Contributors

Hartmut Aden is a social scientist in the School of Law, University of Hannover.

Jane Ball is a solicitor and Lecturer in Law at Sheffield University. Recent publications include 'Renting homes, status and security in the UK and France – a comparison in the light of the Law Commission's proposals', *The Conveyancer and Property Lawyer*, Jan./Feb. 2003; and *Housing People on a Low or Middle Income in France: Planned Bias in the Law* (forthcoming).

Clare Bambra is a Lecturer in the Department of Sociology and Social Policy, Sheffield Hallam University. Recent publications include 'Worlds of welfare and the health care discrepancy', *Social Policy and Society*, 2004; and 'Welfare state convergence? The case of health care', *Social Policy and Society*, 2005.

Ian Bartle is a Research Officer at the Centre for the Study of Regulated Industries, School of Management, University of Bath. Major publications include 'When institutions no longer matter: reform of telecommunications and electricity in Germany, France and Britain', *Journal of Public Policy* 22(1), Jan.–Apr. 2002; *The Regulatory State. Britain and Germany Compared* (with Markus Müller, Roland Sturm and Stephen Wilks) (2002); and 'Transnational interests in the European Union: globalisation and changing organisation in telecommunications and electricity', *Journal of Common Market Studies* 37(3), Sep. 1999.

David Berry is a lecturer in the Department of Politics, International Relations and European Studies, Loughborough University. He has taught widely on issues relating to the political economy of contemporary France, and has published in journals including *Modern and Contemporary France, French Politics and Society*, and *The Journal of Contemporary European Studies*.

Hugh Compston is Senior Lecturer and Director of Politics in the School of European Studies, Cardiff University, and Convenor of the Standing Group on Comparative Political Economy of the European Consortium for Political Research. Major publications include 'Beyond corporatism: a configurational theory of policy concertation', *European Journal of Political Research* 42(6), Oct. 2003; *Social Partnership in the 1990s: The West European Experience in Historical Perspective* (ed. with Stefan Berger) (2002); and *The New Politics of Unemployment: Radical Policy Initiatives in Western Europe* (ed.) (1996).

Stéphane Cottin is Head Officer of the election service of the Constitutional Council of France. Publications include 'Purely bibliographic issues : the impact of the Internet on access to legal documentary material', *Revue Internationale de Droit Comparé*, 1998(2); and *La procédure devant le Conseil constitutionnel* (ed. with Jean-Pierre Camby) (2000).

Andrew Coyle CMG is Professor and Director of the International Centre for Prison Studies in the School of Law at King's College, University of London. He is adviser on prison issues to the UN High Commissioner on Human Rights, the UN Latin American Institute, the Council of Europe including its Committee for the Prevention of Torture, and the Organization for Security and Co-operation in Europe. He is also a member of the UK Secretary of State for Foreign Affairs' Committee against Torture. Relevant publications include *Human Rights and Prison Management: A Handbook for Prison Staff* (2002), available in Arabic, Chinese, English, Korean, Japanese, Portuguese, Russian, Spanish and Turkish; *Managing Prisons in a Time of Change* (2002); and *Capitalist Punishment* (2002).

Anne Daguerre is a Visiting Fellow at the Department of Social and Political Science, Royal Holloway, University of London. Publications include 'Policy networks in England and France: The case of child care policy 1980–1989', *Journal of European Public Policy* 7(2), 2000; 'La réforme de l'aide sociale aux Etats-Unis: modèle ou repoussoir?', *La Revue Française de Droit Sanitaire et Social* 3, 2001; and 'Neglecting Europe: explaining the predominance of American ideas in New Labour's welfare policies since 1997', *Journal of European Social Policy*, February 2004.

Mary Daly is Professor of Sociology at the School of Sociology and Social Policy at Queen's University, Belfast. Major publications include *Care Work: The Quest for Security* (2001); *Contemporary Family Policy* (2002); and 'The functioning family: Catholicism and social policy in Germany and the Republic of Ireland', *Comparative Social Research* 18, 1999.

Cecile Deer is a Research Fellow in the ESRC-funded Research Centre on Skills, Knowledge and Organizational Performance (SKOPE), Department of Economics, University of Oxford. Major publications include *Higher Education in England and France since the 1980s* (2002), and a number of articles on comparative educational policies.

Bruno Domingo is a researcher in the Centre d'Etudes et de Recherches sur la Police at Toulouse University, and directs the Toulouse observatory of delinquency. Major publications include *Douane et coproduction de sécurité, Rapport* *pour l'Institut des Hautes Etudes de la Sécurité Intérieure, Ministère de l'Intérieur*, 2000; and 'Partenariat et évaluation: le cas des contrats locaux de sécurité', *Revue internationale de criminologie et de police technique* 1, 2003.

Carl Emmerson is Programme Director of the pensions and public spending research sector at the Institute for Fiscal Studies, London, and has published on public finances and public spending, local government issues, the evaluation of government policy, pension provision and saving behaviour.

Hubert Ertl is Lecturer in Economic Pedagogy, University of Paderborn, Germany.

Martin Ferguson is Assistant Director of e-Government (Strategy and Research) at the Improvement and Development Agency for Local Government In England and Wales, and Senior Fellow in Information Management and e-Government at the Institute of Local Government Studies, University of Birmingham. He has led research culminating in the 'Local e-government now' series of publications (IDeA/Socitm). Other publications include 'Éstratégias de Governo-Eletrônica: O Cenário Internacional em Desenvolvimento', in *Internet e Política: a teoria e a prática da democracia eletrônica*, ed. José Eisenberg and Marco Cepik (2002) and British Council, *Developments in Electronic Governance* (1999).

C.H. Flockton is Professor of European Economic Studies in the LCIS Department at the University of Surrey, where he researches and teaches in the fields of European economic integration and the French and German economies. He has published widely in all these fields, but the focus in recent years has been on the transformation of the east German economy and the associated strains and policy changes induced in west Germany.

Carolyn Forestiere is a graduate student in Comparative Politics at Emory University in Atlanta, Georgia.

Andrew Flynn is Senior Lecturer in Environmental Policy and Planning, School of City and Regional Planning, Cardiff University. Recent publications include 'The National Assembly for Wales and the promotion of sustainable development: implications for collaborative government and governance' (with K. Bishop), *Public Policy and Administration* 14(2), 1999; 'The regulation of food in Britain in the 1990s' (with T. Marsden and M. Harrison), *Policy and Politics* 27(4), 1999; and *Consuming Interests* (with T. Marsden and M. Harrison) (2000).

L. Garside is a Research Assistant at the Leverhulme Centre for Market and Public Organisation, University of Bristol, and is co-author, with J-Ph. Terreaux, of 'Filière-bois: l'internationalisation confirmée', *Revue Forestière Française* 48(3), Mar. 1996.

P.A. Grout is Professor of Political Economy in the Department of Economics and the Leverhulme Centre for Market and Public Organisation, University of Bristol. Recent publications include 'Public and private sector discount rates in public–private partnerships', *Economic Journal* (2003); and 'Financing and managing public services – an assessment', *Oxford Review of Economic Policy* (2003) (with M. Stevens).

Wyn Grant is Professor of Politics at the University of Warwick and Chair of the Political Studies Association of the UK, 2002–05. Recent publications include *Economic Policy in Britain* (Basingstoke: Palgrave Macmillan, 2002); *Pressure Groups and British Politics* (Basingstoke: Palgrave Macmillan, 2002); and *The Common Agricultural Policy* (Basingstoke: Macmillan, 1997).

Clive Gray is a Principal Lecturer in Politics and Public Administration at De Montfort University, Leicester, and a member of the International Cultural Policy and Planning Unit of the University. Major publications include *The Politics of the Arts in Britain* (Macmillan, 2000); and 'Local government and the arts', *Local Government Studies* 28(1), Spring 2002.

Richard Giulianotti is Senior Lecturer in Sociology at the University of Aberdeen, Scotland. Major publications include *Football: A Sociology of the Global Game* (1999); and several co-edited books including (with Gary Armstrong) *Football in Africa* (Basingstoke: Palgrave Macmillan, 2004), and *Fear and Loathing in World Football* (2001).

Alan Greer is Reader in Politics and Public Policy, and Associate Head of Politics, at the University of the West of England, Bristol. Major publications include 'Countryside issues: a creeping crisis', *Parliamentary Affairs* 56, 2003; 'Policy networks and policy change in organic agriculture: a comparative analysis of the UK and Ireland', *Public Administration* 80, 2002; and *Rural Politics in Northern Ireland: Policy Networks and Agricultural Development Since Partition* (1996). Dr Greer is currently working on a book on European agricultural politics for Manchester University Press.

Graeme Hayes is Principal Lecturer in French and European Studies in the Department of Modern Languages, Nottingham Trent University. Publications include 'Exeunt chased by bear: discourse, action, and the environmental opposition to the Somport Tunnel', *Environmental Politics* 9(2), Summer 2000, and *Environmental Protest and the State in France* (Basingstoke: Palgrave Macmillan, 2002).

Thomas Heckelei is Professor of Economic and Agricultural Policy at the University of Bonn and Adjunct Professor of the Department of Agricultural and Resource Economics, Washington State University. Recent publications include *Agricultural Sector Modelling and Policy Information Systems* (ed. with H.P. Witzke and W. Henrichsmeyer); and 'Estimation of constrained optimisation models for agricultural supply analysis based on generalised maximum entropy', *European Review of Agricultural Economics*, Jan. 2003 (with H. Wolff).

Berkeley Hill is Professor of Policy Analysis at Imperial College London (Wye campus). His main area of research concerns economic statistics for informing agricultural and rural policy, and he has acted as an independent expert for UK government departments and international organizations including the OECD, UNECE and the European Commission. His book *Farm Incomes, Wealth and Agricultural Policy*, 3rd edn (2000) summarizes much of this activity.

Rolf Hugoson is Senior Lecturer in Political Science at Dalarna University College, Borlänge, Sweden. Recent publications include *Vad är kulturpolitik?: En fråga om retorik* (Umeå: Umeå University, 2000) and *Krig och retorik: En introduktion* (2004).

Uwe Hunger is Assistant Professor in the Department of Political Science, University of Münster, Germany. Recent publications include 'Temporary transnational labour migration in an integrating Europe: the challenge to the German welfare state', in *Migration and the Welfare State in Contemporary Europe*, eds Michael Bommes and Andrew Geddes (2000); and 'Party competition and inclusion of immigrants in Germany', *German Policy Studies* 3, 2001.

Majella Kilkey is Lecturer and Director of the Masters Programme in Social Policy in the Department of Comparative and Applied Social Sciences, University of Hull. Dr Kilkey conducts cross-national comparative social policy research around the themes of family policy, gender and citizenship. Her main publication in this area is *Lone Mothers Between Paid Work and Care: The Policy Regime in Twenty Countries* (2000).

Thomas Knorr-Siedow is Deputy Head of the Department for Structural Development of Settlements at the Institute for Regional Development and Structural Planning, Berlin. Recent publications include *Restructuring Large Housing Estates in Germany: The Berlin Case Studies* (2003) (with Christiane Droste); and 'Sustainable refurbishment in Europe: From simple toolbox to multilateral learning' (with E. van Bueren and F. Bougrain), in *The Theory and Practice of Institutional Transplantation*, ed. M. De Jong and K. Lalenis (2002).

Jeremy Leaman is Senior Lecturer in German in the Department of European Studies, Loughborough University. Major publications include *The Political Economy of West Germany 1945–1985* (London: Macmillan, 1988); *The Bundesbank Myth: Towards a Critique of Central Bank Independence* (2001); and 'Germany in the 1990s: the impact of reunification', in *Policy Concertation and Social Partnership in Western Europe: Lessons for the 21st Century*, eds S. Berger and H. Compston (2002).

Benjamin-Hugo LeBlanc is studying for a PhD in the Sociology of Religion at the Ecole Pratique des Hautes Etudes en Sorbonne, France, and Laval University, Canada.

Dirk Lehmkuhl is a Senior Research Fellow at the Center for Comparative and International Studies, University of Zurich. Recent publications include 'Harmonisation and convergence? Europe's differential impact on transport policies in the member states', *German Policy Studies/Politikfeldanalyse* 2(4), 2002; 'Europeanizing domestic regulatory policies', *European Journal of Political Research*, 41(2), 2002 (with Christoph Knill); *Differential Europe: European Impact on National Policymaking* (2001) (with Adrienne Héritier, Dieter Kerwer, Christoph Knill, Michael Teutsch and Anne-Cécile Douillet); and *The Importance of Small Differences. The Impact of European Integration on the Associations in the German and Dutch Road Haulage Industries* (1999).

Catherine Lloyd is a Senior Research Officer at QEH International Development Centre, University of Oxford. Recent publications include *Discourses of Antiracism in France* (1998); *Rethinking Antiracism: From Theory to Practice* (2002) (with F. Anthias); and 'Antiracism, racism and asylum seekers in France', *Patterns of Prejudice* 37(3), 2003.

Thomas D. Lancaster is Senior Associate Dean for Undergraduate Education and Associate Professor of Political Science at Emory University, Atlanta, Georgia. Major publications include *Policy Stability and Democratic Change*; and *Compounded Representation In Western Europe*.

John Madeley is a Lecturer in Government at the London School of Economics and Political Science. Major publications include *Church and State in Contemporary Europe: The Chimera of Neutrality* (ed. with Z. Enyedi) (London: Frank Cass, 2003); *Religion and Politics: A Reader* (ed.) (2003); and 'Reading the runes: the religious factor in Scandinavian electoral politics', in *Religion and Mass Electoral Behaviour in Europe*, eds D. Broughton and H-M. ten Napel (2000).

Azilis Maguer is a Post-Doctoral Researcher in Political Science at the Max Planck Institute for Foreign and International Criminal Law in Freiburg, Germany. Recent publications include 'Der neue Kontrollraum der grenzüberschreitenden polizeilichen Kooperation. Eine politikwissenschaftliche Untersuchung zur deutsch-französischen Grenzregion,' *Zeitschrift für europäischen Studien*, 2003, 3; and 'La coopération policière transfrontalière, moteur de transformations dans l'appareil de sécurité français,' *Cultures et Conflits*, 2003.

William A. Maloney is a Reader in Politics and International Relations, University of Aberdeen. Major publications include *Managing Policy Change in Britain: The Politics of Water Policy* (1996) (with Jeremy Richardson); *The Protest Business: Mobilizing Campaign Groups* (1997) (with Grant Jordan); and *Governing the European Motor Industry in a Global Economy* (1999) (with Andrew McLaughlin).

Francois Nectoux is Professor of Contemporary European Studies at Kingston University. Major publications include 'Between conformity and heterodoxy: recent trends in French economics', in *Contemporary Trends in French Economics*, eds N. Hewlett and C. Floyd (London: Macmillan, 2000); and 'The French welfare state: the crisis of solidarity', in *Postwar Trends in French and North American Industrial Societies*, ed. M. Borrell (2002).

John Preston is the University of Oxford's Reader in Transport Studies, Director of the Transport Studies Unit and a Fellow of St Anne's College. He is also editor of the journal *Transport Policy*. Major publications include *Integrated Futures and Transport Choices* (ed. with Julian Hine) (2003); and *Integrated Transport: Implications for Regulation and Competition*, eds with Helen Lawton Smith and David Starkie (2000).

Philip Raines is a policy advisor in the Scottish Executive working in the European Stuctural Funds Division. Until 2003 he was a Senior Research Fellow at the European Policies Research Centre at the University of Strathclyde, specialising in UK regional policy and foreign investment. Books he has edited on these topics include *The New Competition for Inward Investment: Companies, Institutions and Territorial Development* (2003) (with Nicholas Phelps); *Cluster Development and Policy* (2002); and *Policy Competition and Foreign Direct Investment in Europe* (1999) (with Ross Brown).

Luca Ratti is an Associate Lecturer in the School of European Studies, Cardiff University. He has also taught at the Istituto Universitario Orientale in Naples and is a Research Associate in History of International Relations at the University of Rome III. Publications include 'Italy in the NATO enlargement debate', *Mediterranean Politics* 6(1), Spring 2001; and 'National security and globalisation in post-Cold War Europe', *International History, Politics and Co-operation* 1(4), 2001.

Martin Rhisiart is Research Co-ordinator at the Observatory of Innovation, Cardiff Business School. Publications include 'Innovative Wales' (with M. Thomas) in *Wales in the 21st Century: An Economic Future*, eds J. Bryan and C. Jones (Basingstoke: Macmillan Business, 2000); 'Technology Clinics' (with G. Roberts and M. Thomas) in *Innovation Development Technologies*, eds Komninos *et al.* (published in Greek) (2001); and *Sustainable Regions: Making Sustainable Development Work in Regional Economies* (ed. with M. Thomas) (2004).

Uwe Richter is Principal Lecturer and Field Leader (German) in the School of Languages, Law and Social Sciences, Anglia Polytechnic University. Publications include 'Portfolio assessment in web-site design and development', in *Learning from Languages*, ed. Mike Fay (2003); and 'Foreign languages: using the internet for teaching and learning: A model of in-class delivery,' in *Towards the Virtual University*, eds Nistor, English and Wheeler (2003).

Peter J. Sloane is Director of WELMERC, Department of Economics, University of Wales, Swansea, and Professor Emeritus at the University of Aberdeen. He is also Vice President of the International Association of Sports Economists. Relevant publications include 'The economics of professional football. The football club as a utility maximiser,' *Scottish Journal of Political Economy* 18(2), 1971, reprinted in *The Economics of Sport*, ed. A Zimbalist, *The International Library of Critical Writings in Economics* (2001); and *The Economics of Sport: An International Perspective* (with R. Sandy and M. Rosentraub) (Basingstoke: Palgrave Macmillan, 2004).

Mike Stephens is a Senior Lecturer in Criminology and Social Policy in the Department of Social Sciences, Loughborough University. Major publications include *Policing: The Critical Issues* (1988); *Police Force, Police Service: Care and Control in Britain* (Basingstoke: Macmillan, 1994) (ed. with S. Becker); and *Crime and Social Policy* (2000). He has also conducted a major Home Office study of police training.

Andrew Street is a Senior Research Fellow in the Centre for Health Economics, University of York. Recent journal articles include 'Comparing the efficiency of national health systems: a sensitivity analysis of the WHO approach', *Applied Health Economics and Health Policy*, 2004; and 'Should general practitioners purchase health care for their patients? The total purchasing experiment in Britain', *Health Policy*, 2003.

Catherine Wihtol de Wenden is Director of Research at CNRS (CERI: Center for the Study of International Relations), Paris, and has been an expert in international migration in France and in Europe for the Council of Europe, OECD, UNHCR and European Commission. Recent publications include *L'immigration en Europe* (1999); *L'Europe des migrations* (2001); and *Police et discriminations: Le tabou français* (with Pr. Body-Gendrot, 2003).

Stephanie Wilde teaches in the Englisches Seminar at the University of Hannover. Publications include *Citizenship Education in Germany* (forthcoming); and 'A study of teachers' perceptions in Brandenburg *Gesamtschulen'*, *Oxford Studies in Comparative Education* 10(1), 2000.

Peter Witzke is Senior Researcher at EuroCARE, a consulting enterprise for policy related economic analysis. Recent publications include 'Impact analysis of the European Commission's proposal under the Mid-Term Review of the CAP using the CAPSIM model', in the European Commission's *Mid Term Review of the Common Agricultural Policy, July 2002 Proposals, Impact Analyses* (2003); and *Study to Assess the Impact of Options for the Future Reform of the Sugar Common Market Organisation: Main report by Eurocare* (2003) (with W. Henrichsmeyer, M. Adenäuer, A. Kuhn, J. Zeddies and B. Zimmermann). He has also written the two-volume textbook *Agrarpolitik* (with W. Henrichsmeyer and T. Heckelei) (1991 and 1994).

Eckhard Wurzel is Senior Economist and Head of Desk for Germany at the Organization for Economic Co-operation and Development (OECD), and has co-authored several *OECD Economic Surveys* on Germany. Other publications include: 'Consolidating Germany's finances – issues in public sector spending reform', *OECD Economics Department Working Paper* 366, September 2003; and 'The economic integration of Germany's new Länder', *OECD Economics Department Working Paper* 307, September 2001.

M.J. Yong is a graduate student at Oxford University and was previously a Research Assistant at the Leverhulme Centre for Market and Public Organization, University of Bristol. Her publications are 'The role of donated labour and not-for-profit at the public/private interface', *CMPO Working Paper* 032/074 (with Paul Grout); and 'Going the extra mile: Can "not-for-profits" deliver better public services?', *Market and Public Organisation* 9 (2003).

Introduction: the Nature of Public Policy in Britain, France and Germany

Hugh Compston

This book provides authoritative information on the nature and content of public policy in Britain, France and Germany across the full range of policy areas. By 'content of public policy' is meant the activities of government as they affect those to whom they are directed, as distinct from government intentions, how policies are implemented and what their effects are. Regarding pensions, for example, the focus is on pension rates rather than the aims of the pension system, how it is administered or the effects of pensions on the distribution of income. As a whole the book provides a synoptic view of public policy in Britain, France and Germany at the turn of the 21st century.

Nothing like this exists at present, so it should be of use to a wide range of readers. Students can use it as an introduction to areas of public policy relevant to their studies in public policy, politics, economics, sociology and/or social policy. Researchers and professionals can use it as a point of entry into policy areas or countries outside their own area of expertise, or as the vantage point for a look across the broad sweep of public policy for comparative or analytical purposes. And journalists can use it to provide the public policy context for the events they are reporting.

For reasons of space the focus is on public policy at the national level, but the activities of the European Union (EU) and sub-national levels of government are also taken into account. All three countries are members of the EU and therefore subject to policies made at EU level, especially in areas such as monetary policy and agriculture. Below the national level, various kinds of local authorities are important in areas such as social services. In between there are regional tiers of government. In Germany the powers of the 16 *Land* (regional or state) governments are constitutionally guaranteed. In Britain the Scottish Parliament, Welsh Assembly and Northern Ireland Assembly (when the province is not under direct rule from London) have independent policy-making powers. In France there are two intermediate tiers of government: 22 regions and 96 *départements*. Because in any given area public policy can be affected by

1

Table 1   Policy areas

Policy area	Policy sector	
Defence and foreign affairs	Foreign policy	Defence
Law and order	Police and internal security	Penal policy
	Judicial policy	Immigration
Economic policy	Macroeconomic policy	Business regulation
	Taxation	Financial regulation
	Competition	Research and development
	Employment	Regional policy
	Investment	
Sectoral policies	Agriculture, forestry and fisheries	Information Society
	Energy	Water
	Transport	Media
	Communications	Environmental policy
Social policy	Health	Housing and urban affairs
	Social security	Women
	Social services	Minorities
	Education	Family policy
Other policies	Culture	Religion
	Sport	

the actions of all these levels of government, it is often necessary to include descriptions of EU and subnational public policy in order to make national-level public policy intelligible.

To make the book easy to use, policy areas are defined in terms of the areas characteristically covered by individual government ministries in Western Europe. The classification of policy areas, each of which is covered by a separate chapter, is set out in Table 1.

Each chapter consists of five main components:

1. *Introduction*
   A paragraph or two to give you a taste of the nature of public policy in the particular policy area covered.
2. *The Nature of X Policy*
   A short but exhaustive classification of the types of activities undertaken by British, French and German governments in the policy area, putting these in context as necessary and drawing attention to similarities and differences between the three countries. This gives you the essence of what public policy is in each area. The main departments and agencies involved in each policy area are then identified, along with the extent of central government involvement compared to that of the EU and sub-national levels of government.

3. *Specific comparisons*

   Here the values of a limited number of representative indicators of public policy in the relevant area are described and compared to give you the flavour of its reality, as space considerations preclude a comprehensive account of all policy activities. For example, payment of pensions is a typical government activity in the area of social security, so typical pension rates are set out and compared in the chapter on social security.

4. *Recent developments*

   A brief account of recent issues and policy changes in each policy area, to give you an idea of what is topical and the direction in which public policy is moving.

5. *Sources*

   A list of references and other sources of information. A particular feature is the inclusion of web references to enable the reader to investigate further and update the information given in the chapter.

In order to make the book as accessible as possible to readers from as wide a range of countries as possible, all monetary figures are given in three currencies: euros, pounds sterling and US dollars. To ensure that the exchange rate reflects equivalent buying power rather than the judgement of financial markets (the two do not always coincide), all currency conversions, except where indicated otherwise, are calculated using OECD Purchasing Power Parities for 2002 (OECD 2003: 245). These specify that US\$1 = £0.654 = €0.889.

To get a detailed picture of public policy in any particular area you will need to read the relevant chapter, but because one of the aims of the book is to provide a synoptic view across the full range of policy areas, the remainder of this Introduction consists of a summary of the activities that constitute public policy as a whole in Britain, France and Germany, based on the accounts given in the relevant chapters.

The 34 policy areas are grouped under five main headings: foreign affairs and defence, economic policy, sectoral policies, social policy, and other policies.

Foreign policy and defence

To survive at all, a state needs a secure defence and an effective foreign policy, so these policy areas come first. The question is, what exactly do governments do in these areas?

Foreign policy

- Diplomacy: diplomats conduct negotiations, gather information and intelligence, perform public relations functions and serve as administrative representatives.

- Provision of consular services: passport and visa services, protection of the interests of nationals.
- Trade policy: imposition of tariffs and/or legal limits on the value or volume of particular imports, granting of export subsidies, voluntary export restraints.
- Provision of assistance: state-to-state loans and grants; donations in kind; instructors, teachers, doctors, nurses; study grants and apprenticeships; subsidies to local authorities and other promoters of cooperation projects.
- Military intervention.

Defence policy

- Maintenance of armed forces to defend national territory, maintain a military presence in priority areas, secure control of key strategic sites and facilities, gather intelligence via surveillance, provide assistance to civil society in areas such as disaster relief, and provide crisis management and peacekeeping.
- Participation in regional security structures such as NATO.
- Imposition and enforcement of economic and trade sanctions.
- Protection of environmental and national resources.
- Protection of the national language, customs and values.

Law and order

Securing law and order has long been recognized as a core function of the state, which means police (and internal security), courts and punishments. It also means control of entry to the country: immigration policy. What do governments do in these areas?

Police and internal security

- The police are responsible for preserving law and order, detecting crime, gathering evidence in relation to offences, and crime prevention and reduction activities via, among other things, mounting foot and motor patrols, using trained detectives, employing specialist serious crime and drug squads, and riot control.
- Internal security agencies gather intelligence on internal threats to national security using open and secret methods, and act against these threats.
- Customs and immigration agencies assist in these tasks.

Judicial policy

- Criminal courts judge whether individuals or organizations have broken the law on the basis of evidence beyond all reasonable doubt, and set sanctions where guilt is established.

- Civil courts adjudicate in matters of contractual and other disputed events on the basis of the balance of probabilities, and award appropriate damages or provide certain relief for the party that wins the case.

Penal policy

- Imposition of sanctions (mainly fines, imprisonment, community service).
- Formulation of guidelines for their use.
- Administration of early release and social reintegration.

Immigration policy

First, the regulation of the movement of people into and out of a given territory using:

- External controls implemented in other countries, in particular visas.
- Frontier passport and other controls.
- Internal controls: registration with police, passport checks.
- Exit visa and passport controls on leaving the country.
- Setting and enforcement of penalties for non-compliance with immigration rules.

Secondly, immigration policy involves the setting and enforcement of rights and conditions of residence for foreigners:

- Eligibility conditions for long-term residence and citizenship.
- Provision of economic and social support, and of legal support.

Economic policy

Economic policy consists of macroeconomic policy, taxation policy, competition policy, employment policy, investment policy, business regulation, financial regulation, research and technology policy and regional policy. What national governments do in these areas is integral to the workings of their economies.

Macroeconomic policy

- Monetary policy: manipulation of interest rates to control the quantity of money in use or its growth or the demand for money; and management of currency value via buying and selling of national currency.
- Fiscal policy: provision of public infrastructure, goods and services; and use of taxation and spending to affect the level and composition of demand in the economy.

Taxation

Imposition and collection of financial levies, the main types of which are personal income tax, corporation tax on profit income, Value Added Tax on each stage of the production of goods and services, capital gains tax, and excise duties on specific products and services.

Competition policy

- Regulation (and mostly prohibition) of anti-competitive agreements.
- Regulation (and mostly prohibition) of the use of a dominant position to restrict competition.
- Regulation of mergers, acquisitions and joint ventures.

Employment policy

- Regulation of employment relations between employer and employee via the establishment and policing of framework rules for wage negotiations, trade union rights, working conditions, working hours, holiday entitlement, employment protection and dismissal, minimum wages, conflict avoidance and conflict resolution, and the formal institutions of workers' participation.
- Promotion of employment opportunities via the regulation and coordination of career training in conjunction with employers, trade unions and educational institutions; and expenditure measures designed to influence demand in the labour market, either indirectly through the tax system (tax credits) or directly through financial support for schemes of job-creation.

Investment policy

- Marketing of locations to investors.
- Provision of financial and fiscal incentives for investors.
- Discriminatory regulation of foreign investment.
- General regulation of investment.

Business regulation

- Company law: regulation of incorporation, financing, takeover, sale, insolvency and liquidation.
- Consumer protection: complaints mechanisms, product safety regulation.
- Regulation of public procurement.
- Regulation of retailing: business authorization, opening hours.

Financial regulation

Authorization, regulation and supervision of financial activities as they pertain to:

- Banks: existence, organization and operation of banks and credit institutions.
- Securities: management of stock exchanges, supporting infrastructures, market participants and financial products.
- Insurance: existence, organization and operation of insurers.
- Accounting: preparation and disclosure of financial statements and verification by audit.

Research and technology

- Public funding of research and development (R&D) (level, distribution, selectivity).
- Regulation of R&D (scientific and professional ethics and safety).
- Planning and implementation of R&D (priority areas, action plans and budgeting, government bodies employing researchers).
- Evaluation of research.
- Recruitment and training of researchers.

Regional policy

- Financing of subnational government by national government, including fiscal equalization.
- Regulation of subnational government spending.

Sectoral policies

Sectoral policies are aimed at influencing specific economic sectors rather than the economy as a whole, and comprise agriculture, forestry and fisheries policies, energy policy, transport policy, communications policy, policies concerning the information society, water policy, media policy and environmental policy.

Agriculture, forestry and fisheries

National policies relating to agriculture are dominated by the European Union's Common Agricultural Policy (CAP), which provides:

- Product-specific support linked to production via (i) intervention in commodity markets to enhance prices, using instruments such as import taxes, quotas and support buying; and (ii) direct payments to producers based on farm area and other criteria.
- Support for rural development to improve the structure of the industry, preserve the environment and stimulate the rural economy, using instruments such as contracts with farmers to engage in environmental improvements.

The role of national governments is restricted to:

- Inflecting the application of the CAP in areas in which they are involved in implementing CAP policies, such as rural development and the environment.
- Acting in policy areas not covered by the CAP, including non-CAP commodities, such as potatoes, as well as land tenure, taxation, research, education, technical advice, maintenance of traditional landscapes, hygiene and animal welfare.

Energy

- Determination of ownership and of rights and privileges in the market.
- Provision of subsidies and tax incentives (or disincentives) in order to achieve policy objectives such as energy security, environmental protection, economic efficiency and social welfare.
- Regulation of operations including price control, licensing and authorization, environmental standards and public service obligations.
- Direct provision of research and development.
- Promotion of new technology, energy efficiency and conservation by means such as provision of information, coordination and funding.

Transport

First, the setting of the broad policy parameters in relation to:

- Transport operations and planning, including investment procedures and levels, vehicle and driver licensing, and safety standards.
- Fiscal measures such as fuel tax and road tax.
- Environmental standards such as exhaust controls.
- Planning standards such as the prohibition of certain land-uses because of adverse transport impacts.
- Regulatory standards, including those related to competition policy.

Secondly, the direct provision of transport operations and infrastructure for air, rail, road, water and urban transport.

Communications

- Determination of basic industry organization: ownership, competition and government services.
- Provision of postal services.
- Regulation: licensing and authorization for technical and public interest reasons; economic regulation, especially price control and regulation of access and interconnection to promote market entry and competition; regulation

of radio spectrum, satellite communications and numbering conventions; environmental regulation, especially in relation to location of infrastructure; and regulation of rights of way, rights to install on public and private land, and rights to share facilities of other operators.
- Representation and protection of interests of domestic and business consumers.
- Measures to ensure security of transmitted information and protection of personal data and privacy.
- Promotion of new technology, national industry and competitiveness by means such as provision of information, establishment of priorities, coordination and funding.

Information society
- Measures to improve access to electronic information and to overcome the 'digital divide' by providing public Internet access points and ensuring that IT skills are integral to education and training.
- Legislative and regulatory action to provide service providers and citizens with secure means for electronic identification, and to adapt existing regulation to take account of e-business.
- Provision of national and local government services online where appropriate, including services relating to health, social security, education, employment, police, business activities, permits, personal documents such as passports, and libraries.
- Measures to improve citizen participation in decision-making by means such as online consultation, online participation in meetings, and electronic voting (e-democracy).

Water policy
- Economic and environmental regulation.
- Setting and collection of taxes and charges, and redistribution of revenue through grants, loans etc.
- Inspection and monitoring of water quality.
- Funding of key resource improvement and protection programmes.
- Information and education.

Media policy
- Determination of ownership and industry organization.
- Direct provision of media, especially state-owned broadcasting.
- Content regulation: content specification such as programme quotas; restrictions on content such as advertising; prohibition of content, for example sexual acts.

- Imposition of taxes and/or provision of subsidies and other public funding, for example to assist the press.
- Regulation of mobile media communication systems.

Environmental policy

Environmental policy is aimed at (i) preserving habitats, species and landscapes, and (ii) reducing chemical, industrial and domestic pollution and waste in the air, water and soil, by means of:

- Regulation.
- Imposition of taxes and charges.
- Funding and regulation of parapublic agencies.
- Monitoring of standards and quality.
- Grants.
- Sponsoring of research.

Social policy

Social policy consists of health policy, social security, social services, education, housing and urban affairs, policies relating to women, policies relating to minorities and ethnicity, and family policy.

Health policy

Provision, financing and regulation of:

- Doctors and other health professionals.
- Organizations that deliver health care, such as hospitals and nursing homes.
- Pharmaceuticals and medical devices.
- Preventive services such as occupational health and safety, consumer protection in areas such as food safety, and control of environmental health hazards.
- Research into health and health services.

Social security

Provision of cash benefits to those whose resources fall below certain levels and to compensate parents for child expenses: old-age benefits, disability benefits, benefits in relation to occupational injury and disease, sickness benefits, benefits for carers, maternity benefits, widows'/survivors' benefits, unemployment benefits, social assistance and other means-tested benefits, family allowances and child supplements to other benefits.

Social services

Definition and regulation of local government provision of services (plus cash payments in France and Germany) for older people, children and families, people with disabilities and illnesses, young people, addicts, and the socially excluded in general.

Education

Provision, financing and regulation of education at pre-primary, primary, secondary and higher levels, with particular reference to access policy, evaluation, curricula, examinations, and teacher recruitment and training.

Housing and urban affairs

- Intervention to secure the health and safety of buildings.
- Regulation of newbuild and improvement and planning control.
- Urban development, for example demolition and urban renewal in designated zones.
- Action in relation to the environment, such as the preservation of green spaces.
- Measures to facilitate access to housing by people on modest incomes by means of aids to construction (grants, loans), housing benefits and tax incentives.
- Provision of access to housing for the homeless and poorly housed, for example by funding or direct provision of hostels.
- Protection of occupants of housing by means of regulation of tenancy agreements; property law including the law relating to squatters; regulation of mortgages and financial services; requisition of property for social homes (France); consumer law; regulation of eviction; regulation in relation to over-indebtedness and insolvency; laws regulating misbehaviour by landlords, neighbours and outsiders; provision and regulation of sewerage, domestic waste and utilities; provision of roads and other infrastructure; family law (for division on dispute); and inheritance law.
- Provision of housing or adaptation for special groups such as the aged, the disabled, travellers, asylum seekers, and women suffering from domestic violence.

Policies in relation to women

- Employment: maternity leave, health and safety regulations specific to pregnancy and nursing mothers, anti-discrimination regulation, funding and/or direct provision of childcare, parental leave, re-organization of working time to allow flexible working (France and Germany).
- Social security: maternity leave benefits, parental leave benefits (France and Germany), childcare benefits, financial and childcare support for women returning to the labour market.

- Health: funding and/or direct provision of ante-natal and post-natal care, screening services for women-specific cancers, funding and/or direct provision of contraceptive and abortion services.
- Social services: funding and/or direct provision of women's shelters and refuges, survivor support groups, and/or mother and infant health services (France and Germany).
- Legislation on rape and domestic violence.
- Legislation on the rights to abortion.

Minorities policy

Establishment and enforcement of:

- Political rights to equal representation and to be safeguarded against discrimination.
- Cultural rights (language, religion).
- Social and economic rights which take specific cultures into account.

Family policy

- Cash payments to families.
- Tax allowances for families.
- Employment leaves.

Other policies

Three additional policies are difficult to fit into the categories so far used: cultural policy, sports policy, and policies relating to religion.

Cultural policy

- Support for performing arts: production subsidies, investment in new works, maintenance of performance spaces, direct funding of artists and companies, encouragement of private sector funding by means such as tax incentives.
- Funding and direct provision of support for museums and national heritages.
- Protection of national cultures, for example regulation of the national language (France and Germany) and regulation of media output (France).
- Promotion of national culture throughout the world.

Sports policy

- Regulation of sports administrative bodies, commercial activities and televising of sport.
- Enforcement of prohibition of doping and violence.

- Funding for major capital projects.
- Sports lotteries.
- Planning in collaboration with sports organizations.
- Provision and/or funding of publicity and education.

Policies relating to religion

- Protection of religious freedom.
- Regulation of religious organizations eligible for state aid.
- Tax concessions for religious organizations plus, in Germany only, raising of taxes for churches.
- Funding and maintenance of church property.
- Regulation and funding of religious schools and welfare organizations.
- Employment of chaplains in public organizations.
- Grants of legal powers to religious organizations (Britain and Germany).
- Provision of religious education in state schools (Britain and Germany).

References

OECD (Organization for Economic Cooperation and Development), *Main Economic Indicators* (Paris: OECD, February 2003).

Part I
Defence and Foreign Affairs

1
Foreign Policy

Luca Ratti

Introduction

Foreign policy is usually defined as the activities a state undertakes in order to accomplish its objectives as they relate to other states or political entities external to the state. In its broadest sense, this definition could be taken to mean that foreign policy includes all policies having an external dimension. This means that there is often a considerable overlap between a country's foreign policy and its domestic policies. On most issues decision-makers and diplomats must understand and work well not only with foreign counterparts but also with legislators, nongovernmental organizations, outside experts and representatives from the private sector, both business and labour.

The nature of foreign policy

The basic goal of foreign policy is the preservation and continuation of the state and its sovereignty, and the expansion of its influence abroad. Foreign policy activities comprise diplomacy, trade policy, economic aid, technical assistance and military intervention.

Diplomacy is the process by which sovereign states conduct their mutual relations through accredited officials. The diplomatic service is an organized body of agents which represents the state abroad and is accredited to the central government of the foreign country in question. Diplomats are also accredited to international organizations where they represent their countries in conferences and meetings. The functions of diplomats are to conduct negotiations, gather information and intelligence, perform public relations functions and serve as administrative representatives. Diplomats enjoy diplomatic immunity: they are exempt from search, arrest and prosecution. This immunity is deemed necessary for diplomats to carry out their official duties properly.

Diplomatic activities are generally conducted according to forms long established by custom, including memorandums, informal oral or written notes, and formal notes. If two countries have no diplomatic relations, their interests may be represented by diplomats of other powers, and when two states are at war their interests are usually represented by neutral states.

The diplomatic service comprises secretaries; military, cultural, and commercial attachés; clerical workers; and various experts and advisers. The consular staff, far more numerous than the diplomatic one, is stationed in major ports and other commercial centres abroad and is accredited to the local authorities. Its tasks comprise providing passport and visa services and protecting the interests of private nationals living, travelling, or doing business in that region (Kennan 1997).

While the political elements of external relations are normally the responsibility of a Ministry of Foreign Affairs, some aspects of foreign relations, such as the defence of national sovereignty, trade policy, and technical and cultural co-operation, are sometimes placed under the charge of other ministries. In most European countries, subject to the overall direction of the Government, the Ministry for Foreign Affairs has responsibility for external political affairs, the co-ordination of policy in the European Union (EU), policy with regard to the United Nations (UN) and other international organizations, development co-operation, consular affairs, and cultural relations (Government of Ireland 1996). Other Ministries have responsibilities in relation to other aspects of foreign relations, for example Trade Ministries in respect to external trade and Finance Ministries in the field of external financial policy.

Trade Ministries are responsible for commercial relations with other political entities. The instruments of trade policy comprise taxes on certain international transactions, subsidies for other transactions, and legal limits on the value or volume of particular imports. Other instruments of trade policy are export subsidies and voluntary export restraints. Borderline cases such as the sale or gift of military hardware can be classified either as trade or as military policy, depending on the particular case in question.

States provide technical, civil and military assistance to other political entities in order to achieve one or more of at least three totally different objectives: rehabilitating the economies of war-devastated countries, strengthening the military defences of allies, and promoting economic growth in under-developed areas. Aid may be given as a grant, with no repayment obligation, or as a loan. Assistance is given by state officials or volunteers, or through contracts with private consultants and experts. Other forms of assistance are state-to-state loans; donations in kind; the sending of instructors, teachers, doctors and nursing staff; the awarding of study grants and apprenticeships; and subsidies to local authorities and other promoters of cooperation projects.

Military interventions can serve to deter infiltration and aggression; maintain territorial integrity and political independence; secure the withdrawal of foreign forces, advisers, mercenaries and paramilitaries; liberate seized territory and restore government; remove 'rogue' leaders and locate and detain war criminals; enforce economic and arms embargoes; dismantle or destroy arms inventories and production facilities; and protect relief operations and provide emergency relief from natural disasters (Goodpaster 1996).

There are important institutional differences in the way in which different countries implement foreign policy. In Britain this process is tightly organized and highly centralized. Although the Queen has the power to conclude treaties, declare war and make peace, recognize foreign states and governments, and annex and cede territory, the legal powers of the Monarch are primarily of a formal nature and are mostly exercised by the Prime Minister and the government (James 1985: 122). As a result the Cabinet Office rather than the Foreign and Commonwealth Office has the lead role in the co-ordination of Britain's foreign policy.

In France the strong constitutional position of the President ensures that nothing can be done without his consent and limits the role of the Prime Minister and other Ministers, although his task can be fraught with difficulty in periods of cohabitation, when the Prime Minister is from the other side of politics. Between 1993 and 1995, for example, the authority of Socialist President François Mitterand was challenged by Gaullist Prime Minister Eduard Balladur, who tried to establish that Article 20 of the French constitution gives the leading role in foreign policy to the Prime Minister rather than to the President (Blunden 2000: 29).

The German constitution, the Basic Law, does not clearly stipulate who or what is the actual vehicle for the implementation of foreign policy. Article 59 of the constitution establishes that the Federal President represents the Federal Republic in its international relations, but in the first years of the Federal Republic Konrad Adenauer was able to strengthen considerably the role of the Chancellor in German foreign policy. Otherwise these powers have long been decentralized among many other units within the various ministries involved with foreign policy, with some 250 ministerial units currently involved in the foreign policy process (Siwert-Probst 2001: 19–37).

One distinctive aspect of foreign policy in Germany is the autonomy of the *Länder*, which can sign international treaties in such areas as culture, education and science. However to enter into these treaties they need the approval of the central government, which decides whether such treaties touch upon the German national interest or not. Decentralization in foreign policy has created confusion between the competences of the national government and those of the *Länder*, with most issues having to be resolved by the Chancellor.

Specific comparisons

A clearer picture of the orientation of foreign policy in Britain, France and Germany can be obtained by looking at their role in the UN, their relations with the United States, and policies in relation to European integration. Each of the three countries also has specific areas of foreign policy interest.

UN

As two of the victorious allies in World War II, Britain and France have permanent seats on the UN Security Council, which gives them a veto over any policy they do not like. Britain has used its veto on 32 occasions since 1945, while France has used it 18 times, 13 of those alongside the United States and Britain.

While on some occasions Britain has bypassed the authority of the Security Council, as during the build-up for the invasion of Iraq in 2003, France has attempted to preserve the Security Council's strong position and has encouraged all reforms designed to improve the effectiveness of UN peacekeeping operations. France has also spared no effort within the organization to secure the establishment of an international judicial system: it was among the instigators of the Security Council resolutions setting up the international criminal tribunals for the former Yugoslavia (1993) and Rwanda (1995). France took also an active role in the negotiations which led to the creation in 1998 of the International Criminal Court (Permanent Mission of France to the United Nations 2003).

The two states of divided Germany gained membership of the UN in September 1973, but neither was made a permanent member of the Security Council. This did not change on reunification, so Germany cannot veto Security Council resolutions.

After the United States and Japan, Germany, France and Britain in that order are the largest financial contributors to the United Nations (see Table 1.1).

Relations with the United States

While the 'special relationship' with the United States constitutes a long-standing and core feature of British foreign policy, and retains a status of primary

Table 1.1   Contributions to the UN's regular budget, 2003

	Britain	*France*	*Germany*
Gross contributions	€76.5 m (£55.9 m, $86 m)	€89 m (£65 m, $100 m)	€134 m (£98 m, $151 m)
Net contributions	€66.8 m (£48.8 m, $75 m)	€77.4 m (£56.6 m, $87 m)	€117.5 m (£85.8 m, $132 m)
Share of financing	5.54%	6.46%	9.77%

Sources: Permanent Mission of France to the United Nations 2003; United Nations Information Centre for the Nordic Countries 2003.

importance for Germany on matters of security, French relations with the United States have been marked on the one hand by shared security interests and, on the other, by resistance to US supremacy in world politics.

The sceptics' view is that Britain is the junior partner in its 'special relationship' with the US: it needs to prove its usefulness to its more powerful friend. One example of the importance of this relationship for Britain is the fact that Britain has used its power of veto in the UN Security Council 23 out of 32 times alongside the United States.

By contrast, France has attempted to resist the increasing American influence on the international stage. Accordingly, France promotes those international organisations within which French influence is greatest, such as the EU, and resists any increase in the power of those dominated by the Americans, such as NATO. The French government also sees itself as a bridge between the United States and those nations US decision-makers have deemed to be threats to the new world order, such as Serbia, Iraq, Libya and Iran. In 1999 France endeavoured to forestall military action against the Serbs, while in 2003 it voiced strong criticism of the Anglo-American intervention in Iraq. Other differences between the positions of France and the United States have arisen in relation to European defence, world trade, climate change, and the International Criminal Court.

Relations between Germany and the United States remain strong despite some recent friction between the Bush administration and the German government due to German calls for the US to adhere to the statute of the International Criminal Court and Germany's vehement opposition, alongside France and Russia, to the use of military force against Iraq in 2003. During the 45 years in which Germany was divided, the US role in Berlin and the large American military presence in West Germany served as symbols of the US commitment to West German defence. German reunification was possible only with the strong support of the United States, and even in 2003 more than 71,000 US military personnel were still stationed in Germany. Economic interests have helped consolidate this relationship: the United States is the second largest market, behind France, for German exports and the third largest source of imports into Germany (German Embassy in the United States 2003). The two countries are also important to each other as locations for foreign investment (US Department of State 2003).

Europe

While France and Germany have played a leading role in European integration, the 'special relationship' with the United States has deterred Britain from playing a similar role. As a result, Britain has favoured an intergovernmental approach to European co-operation instead of supranational models that involve loss of national sovereignty. Although it signed the Maastricht Treaty in 1992, Britain has not become a member of the European Monetary Union (EMU) and has not adhered to the Schengen agreement, which abolishes border controls among several of the European Union's member states.

Table 1.2 Contributions to the EU budget, 2003

	Britain	France	Germany
Initial proposal	€13.5 bn	€16.6 bn	€22.0 bn
	(£9.9 bn, $15.2 bn)	(£12.2 bn, $18.7 bn)	(£12.2 bn, $18.7 bn)
Updated	€11.5 bn	€15.9 bn	€20.4 bn
contributions	(£8.5 bn, $12.9 bn)	(£11.7 bn, $17.9 bn)	(£15.0 bn, $23.0 bn)
Share of financing	12.90%	17.87%	22.96%

Source: European Parliament 2003.

As well as supporting European integration, French decision-makers have developed a certain idea of Europe as an amplifier of French power and have tried to use the European Union as a vehicle for doing things that France alone cannot do, such as promoting French interests in areas of the world where French influence is limited, and where the scale of resources required are beyond the capacity of France alone to provide.

France attaches particular importance to the development of the EU external action – *L'Europe Puissance* – and staunchly promotes the development of a Common European Security and Defence Policy (CFSP) at the expense of the American alliance. The Convention charged with the task of preparing the draft of a new European constitution is chaired by former French President Giscard d'Estaing. As a result of its historical links with the countries of the Balkans, France is also an active player in this part of the continent, and was one of the instigators of the Stability Pact for South-Eastern Europe.

Support for European integration was part of Chancellor Adenauer's *Westpolitik* ('Policy towards the West'), the political blueprint aimed at promoting the integration of the Federal Republic into the Western bloc during the Cold War, and remained a feature of German foreign policy after reunification. The most notable manifestation of this commitment has been participation in the European Monetary Union, as this has meant the loss of the *Deutschmark*, a symbol of the country's economic strength. In exchange for giving up its monetary sovereignty, however, Germany ensured that the new European Central Bank (ECB) adopted the philosophy of the *Bundesbank*, that is, a tight monetary policy aimed at preserving price stability and a strong currency. As the EU's largest and economically strongest state, Germany is the main contributor to the institution's budget (see Table 1.2) and retains considerable influence over its policies: major policy initiatives rarely survive without German support.

Special areas of interest

As a consequence of their colonial past, Britain and France retain a special interest in relations with their former colonies. Germany, by contrast, as a consequence of its geographical position has a particular interest in relations with the countries of Eastern Europe.

The Commonwealth is the main expression of Britain's strong ties with its former colonies and bears witness of Britain's global interests. Britain's main regional focuses are the Near and Middle East, sub-Saharan Africa (especially South Africa and Zimbabwe), the Indian subcontinent and the Far East. In China and in Asia as a whole, Britain is the largest source of European direct investment. In 2002–03 direct contributions by the Foreign and Common-wealth Office to the Commonwealth Secretariat, Commonwealth Foundation and Joint Office for Small States in New York was expected to amount to £4 million (€5.4 million, $6.1 million) (Foreign and Commonwealth Office 2003).

Successive French governments have sought to maintain their *domain privé*: those areas of the world, such as francophone Africa, in which France has been able to retain a leadership role as a former colonial power. Ties with North Africa are strengthened by the fact that there are about 4.5 million people of North African descent in France. Relations with former African colonies guar-antee France an important source of international support and are vital to sus-taining France's claim to be a world power. There are regular summits between the Heads of State of France and those of African countries. Its ties with Africa provide France with significant support in the United Nations and in other international organizations. In exchange for this support France has interceded in all the centres of financial power, including the Group of Seven (G7), the International Monetary Fund (IMF) and the World Bank, to argue for more international aid for African countries (Blunden 2000: 35). Coordination with Britain on policy towards Africa has been strengthened during the 1990s.

Germany's special area of interest is its relations with the countries of Eastern Europe: *Ostpolitik* ('Policy towards the East'). One important reason for this is its trade relations with the countries of this region: Germany is the largest trading partner of Eastern Europe, and over 40 per cent of East European exports go to Germany (Berend 1997: 12). Accordingly, Germany is particularly concerned about the political and economic stability of these countries. It has provided 40 per cent of total Western financial aid and has concluded numerous investment protection and promotion agreements with them (Auswärtiges Amt 2003). Germany has also supported the expansion of the European Union to Eastern Europe. While reflecting a desire to reunite these countries with the European family of nations, this support can also be attributed to the interests of German business-men and investors in ensuring political and economic stability in these states.

Recent developments

'Foreign policy' has traditionally been defined in terms of states in the inter-national system: it is the boundary of the nation-state that determines what is domestic and what is foreign. Simple observation suggests that in practice this traditional convention does not hold any longer. Today the number and variety of actors involved in politically significant activities crossing state borders is far larger than it was even 50 years ago and includes international agencies, such as the Red Cross, that 'conduct' a form of foreign policy either under the tutelage of states or as independent actors; multinational corporations and private organisations able to conduct business around governments; and mass movements, such as the anti-globalization movement, that influence foreign policy through their ideologies and interests. As a consequence of the steady increase in the number of activities crossing state boundaries, today's diplomats have to tackle issues such as conflict prevention, the promotion of human rights, sustainable development, climate change, biodiversity, and the fight against terrorism, drugs and international crime.

Britain has continued to assume that the United States, rather than EU member states, is its preferred partner: on all the main issues that have shaped the current international political situation, from the Balkan conflicts in the early 1990s to the military ousting of the Iraqi regime in 2003, British decision-makers have stood close to their American allies.

France has continued its efforts to maintain an international role commensurate with the global rank that it claims, and has increased efforts to develop the European CFSP as an alternative to American hegemony.

Continuity has also been the main feature of the foreign policy of the reunified German state. During the 1990s the German authorities confirmed the ties with the United States and European integration as the twin pillars of the Federal Republic's foreign policy, but since reunification Germany has nevertheless gradually developed a more assertive approach to foreign policy, as demonstrated by its conduct during the Yugoslav crisis at the beginning of the 1990s and during the second Gulf War in 2003.

Sources

Auswärtiges Amt (2003), <www.auswaertiges-amt.de/www/en/laenderinfos/laender> [24 July 2003].

Auswärtiges Amt (2003), <www.auswaertiges-amt.de/www/en/aussenpolitik/vn/vereinte_nationen/finanz-deutsch_html> [25 July 2003].

I.T. Berend, 'Germany and Central Europe: Geopolitical Destiny of Interrelationship', in *Germany and Southeastern Europe – Aspects of Relations in the Twentieth Century*, ed. R. Schönfeld (Munich: Südosteuropa-Gesellschaft, 1997).

M. Blunden, 'France', in *The Foreign Policies of European Union Member States*, eds I. Manners and Richard G. Whitman (Manchester: Manchester University Press, 2000).

European Parliament (2003), <www.europarl.eu.int/meetdocs/committees/budg/20030616/10b_EN.pdf> [21 November 2003].

Foreign and Commonwealth Office (2003), <www.fco.gov.uk> [24 July 2003].

German Embassy in the United States (2003), <www.germany info.org/relaunch/info/facts/facts_about/07_06.html> [22 July 2003].

A.J. Goodpaster, 'When Diplomacy Is Not Enough: Managing Multinational Military Interventions', *A Report to the Carnegie Commission on Preventing Deadly Conflict* (New York: Carnegie Corporation, 1996) <wwics.si.edu/subsites/ccpdc/pubs/dip/dip.htm> [3 September 2003].

Government of Ireland (2003), *The White Paper on Foreign Policy 1996*, <www.gov.ie/iveagh/information/publications/whitepaper/default.htm> [20 July 2003].

Grundgesetz (Basic Law) (2003), <www.lib.byu.edu/~rdh/eurodocs/germ/ggeng.html> [25 July 2003].

P.S. James, *Introduction to English Law* (London: Butterworth, 1985).

G. Kennan, 'Diplomacy Without Diplomats?', *Foreign Affairs*, September/October 1997, <www.foreignaffairs.org/19970901faessay3805/george-f-kennan/diplomacy-without- diplomats.html> [3 September 2003].

Permanent Mission of France to the United Nations (2003), <www.un.int/france> [24 July 2003].

Permanent Mission of France to the United Nations (2003), <www.un.int/france/frame_anglais/france_and_un/france_contribution_to_un_budget/contribution_to_un_budget.html> [25 July 2003].

J. Siwert-Probst, 'Traditional Institutions of Foreign Policy', in *Germany's New Foreign Policy. Decision-Making in an Interdependent World*, eds W.D. Eberwein and K. Kaiser (Basingstoke: Palgrave Macmillan, 2001), pp19–37.

United Nations (2003), <www.un.org/aboutun/charter/> [31 July 2003].

United Nations Information Centre for the Nordic Countries (2003), <http//www.un.dk/danish/Budget/ST.ADM.SER.B.597.pdf> [31 July 2003].

US Department of State (2003), <www.usembassy.de/usa/garelations.htm> [21 July 2003].

2
Defence

Luca Ratti

Introduction

Defence policy sets the framework for a nation's defence. While the defence policies of Britain, France and Germany are all based on the North Atlantic alliance with the United States, their defence stances are far from identical. Britain and France are nuclear powers whereas Germany isn't. Furthermore, Britain is very close to the United States while France takes a more independent line, with Germany somewhere in the middle. Conversely, France and Germany are more supportive of a separate European defence identity than is Britain.

The nature of defence policy

The aim of defence policy is to ensure that national independence, sovereignty and territorial integrity are protected. It comprises the political, economic, military, social, legal and environmental measures which have been developed by the state in order to safeguard the security of its inhabitants and its territorial integrity. Defence policy is also concerned with the process of preparation, decision-making and political guidance necessary for the general and specific tasks of military defence. One innovative aspect of this policy is participation in operations to maintain international security and stability. Participation in the defence of the state is usually regarded as the duty of every citizen and of the nation as a whole, as well as of institutions, commercial enterprises and other organizations.

The armed forces represent the principal instrument for the implementation of defence policy. Their tasks comprise:

- defending the national territory against external aggression;
- maintaining a military presence in priority areas of the globe;

- securing the control of key strategic sites and facilities, such as communication lines and production sites;
- intelligence gathering through surveillance;
- providing assistance to civil society by carrying out activities such as limited provision of housing, disaster relief missions, communications and transportation, and engineering repair; and
- crisis management and peacekeeping activities, for example restoring law and order, providing security for elections, and supporting the rebuilding of infrastructures in conflict-ridden countries.

However defence policy is not limited purely to political and military aspects of security, but also includes implementation of economic sanctions and trade restrictions as well as protection of the environment and of the country's natural resources.

In addition to this, defence policy can involve a series of relations with other political entities involving defence and military components. The decision to join a regional security structure such as the North Atlantic Alliance (NATO) or the Western European Union (WEU), and the management of this membership once it has been achieved, is an area of government policy in which both the foreign and defence ministries have a major interest and responsibility.

Finally, defence policy also has economic and social implications: disarmament and rearmament have an impact on economic indicators such as growth and employment, for example, while an increase in arms procurement may lead to a reduction in social spending.

In principle defence policy depends on foreign policy in that it is one of the practical ways in which foreign policy is given effect. However defence policy is partly also a subset of domestic policy, as in the internal security area, and occasionally the defence policy establishment can influence aspects of foreign policy, for example by enabling certain courses of action, such as military intervention.

Most defence policy structures in European countries feature a strong central staff of some kind, although its ability to initiate policy, as opposed to blocking initiatives, is fairly limited.

In Britain defence policy is centralized in the hands of the government which, with the advice of the Foreign and Commonwealth Office, decides what sort of military role Britain ought to play in the world: the Ministry of Defence is relegated to a secondary role.

In France defence policy, even more than foreign policy, is centralized in the hands of the President. Power is exercised through the *Secrétariat Général de la Défense Nationale*, which is subject to little supervision or external influence even from Parliament. However, although the President has a lead role in defence policy and is the commander in chief of the armed forces, the government led by the Prime Minister has acquired increasing influence in defence matters.

As far as Germany is concerned, during the Cold War there was no proper national military staff for planning or developing a national military strategic or operational concept. This task was left to the North Atlantic Alliance, and German forces and planning processes were more closely integrated into the structure and goals of NATO than those of any other member state (Rohde and Von Sandrart 1994: 29–31). Since the end of the Cold War Germany has developed a defence planning system characterized by political control and co-operation between the Bundestag, the government and the Ministry of Defence. This approach ensures that the system does not develop into a self-contained, independent process.

Specific comparisons

The similarities and differences between the defence policies operated by Britain, France and Germany can be illustrated by examining their military personnel, defence budgets, the role of nuclear weapons, armed forces deployment, and orientations towards NATO and the idea of a separate European defence identity.

Military personnel

There are over twice as many military personnel in the armies of France and Germany than in the British army, while the British navy, along with the French navy, has about twice as many personnel as the German navy, and there are more air personnel in France than in Britain or Germany (see Table 2.1).

Defence budgets

Table 2.2 shows that in 2002 defence expenditures were highest in France and lowest in Germany.

During the 1990s France eschewed budget-led reforms and chose not to make the kind of 'peace dividend' cuts evident elsewhere amongst NATO members. French defence spending actually increased in real terms between 1985 and

Table 2.1 Military personnel and structure of the armed forces, 2003

	Britain	*France*	*Germany*
Army	114 800	220 000	280 120
Navy	42 400	55 000	24 660
Air force	53 300	76 422	66 580

Sources: National Statistics 2003; Bundeswehr 2003; Ministère de la Défense 2003.

Table 2.2 Defence expenditures 2002 (estimated)

	Britain	*France*	*Germany*
Percentage of GDP	2.4	2.5	1.5
Per capita	$536 (£348, €477)	$771 (£501, €686)	$490 (£319, €436)
Percentage annual variation	−1.9	−0.1	0.6

Source: NATO 2002.

1995 by 2 per cent while over the same period spending fell by 20 per cent in Britain and by 21 per cent in Germany (Couvrat 1996: 3).

Nuclear weapons

The main difference between British, French and German defence policy centres around the role of nuclear weapons: Britain and France have nuclear power status, but Germany has not developed its own nuclear arsenal. Although France was a founder member of NATO and of the WEU, it has not systematically relied upon these alliances to defend French interests but instead has sought to achieve self-sufficiency in arms procurement, retaining large conventional forces and developing its own nuclear arsenal – the *force de frappe*. While allowing France to take a more independent stance from the United States, the development of a nuclear arsenal has also preserved its standing as a 'world power', a status which French leadership is loth to abandon. France currently maintains about 470 deployed nuclear warheads, a number which is expected to decline to around 400 by 2005 (Global Security Institute 2003). Britain currently has a stockpile of fewer than 200 operationally available warheads.

Armed forces deployment

Naval power has traditionally been paramount in British defence policy, but in recent years British naval assets have been scaled back, although in 1982 the Falklands did create a temporary sense of renewed naval grandeur. Since 1969 a significant proportion of British armed forces has been engaged in policing Northern Ireland, which has become the main theatre for training and deployment of British combat troops at a cost of up to £2 billion (€2.7 billion, $3.1 billion) per year. During the 1990s British troops were deployed in various policing and peacekeeping roles across the world: in 1991 Britain deployed some 40,000 troops in the US-led coalition force of 550,000 that liberated Kuwait from Iraqi occupation, the second largest contingent in the first Gulf War; in 1994 around 3000 British troops joined the UN forces in Bosnia; in 1999 more than 10,000 British troops went to Kosovo, where they constituted the largest single national contribution to the NATO Kosovo force (KFOR); 800 British paratroopers were sent to the

West African state of Sierra Leone in 2000 to evacuate British citizens and help UN peacekeepers secure the airport; in August 2001 British troops were again deployed for peacekeeping duties in Macedonia, with the task of overseeing the collection of weapons from ethnic Albanian rebels; and 2000 British troops were deployed to Afghanistan just before Christmas 2001 in the wake of the defeat of the Taleban (Ministry of Defence 2002). Britain also provides peacekeeping forces for the UN operations in Cyprus and retains specific if dwindling responsibilities for some overseas territories, such as the Falklands and Gibraltar. More recently it contributed significantly to the US-led invasion of Iraq in 2003.

Before 1990 German armed forces had taken part in over 120 humanitarian aid missions but were never employed in any peacekeeping operations under the UN flag, as the participation of the *Bundeswehr* in military actions outside German territory was prohibited by the most common interpretation of the Basic Law. German troops did not participate in the first Gulf War in 1991, although the German government contributed $10 billion (£6.5 billion, €8.9 billion). Throughout the 1990s, however, it became increasingly difficult for Germany to back away from its partners' expectations: German helicopters flew UN disarmament inspectors on control missions in Iraq between 1991 and 1996; marine troops took part in monitoring the arms and trade embargo against Yugoslavia between 1992 and 1996; and around 1800 German soldiers were stationed in Somalia from 1992 to 1994 to give the UN troops logistic support.

The deployment of French troops in the world reflects this country's attempt to retain a prominent international role. About 40,000 troops are currently deployed outside metropolitan France. The most numerous concentration is in Africa. In Ivory Coast 4000 French troops enforce a buffer zone between the government and rebels. About 3500 troops remain on the Indian Ocean islands of Réunion and Mayotte, 2500 in Djibouti and 1100 in Senegal. French troops are also deployed in the Central African Republic, Gabon, Cameroon and Chad. France also retains more than 4000 troops in its Pacific territories of New Caledonia, French Polynesia and the Wallis and Futuna Islands.

Although France, like Germany, did not contribute troops to the invasion of Iraq in 2003, it has given a significant contribution to international peacekeeping missions in the Balkans. Almost 5000 French soldiers are currently operating in this region: 3200 troops in the KFOR mission in Kosovo and 1200 in Bosnia. France also has 4000 troops deployed in the Antilles, while almost 1000 French troops are deployed in Afghanistan and neighbouring Tajikistan as part of the International Security Assistance Forces (ISAF). Finally, around 3300 French military personnel are based in Germany.

In July 1994 the Federal Constitutional Court ruled that the participation of German forces in military operations outside NATO territory was permissible as long as such operations were conducted under United Nations auspices and with the consent of the German Parliament, the *Bundestag* (Auswärtiges Amt 2003). Accordingly, in 1995 a contingent of around 3600 German soldiers was employed to support the NATO-led implementation force (IFOR) in Croatia. Since late 1996 the *Bundeswehr* has participated in the NATO stabilization force (SFOR) in Bosnia and Herzegovina, and in 1999 the German air force took part in the bombing operations conducted by NATO against Serbia. Since the withdrawal of the Yugoslav Federal Army from Kosovo, German troops have been administering a section of this region as part of the NATO Kosovo Force (KFOR), and in 2001 the *Bundeswehr* assumed the command of operation 'Amber Fox' in Macedonia, which is aimed at helping Slavs and Albanians to live peacefully together. Finally, Germany is currently contributing a contingent of more than 2000 troops to the International Security Assistance Forces (ISAF) in Afghanistan.

North Atlantic Alliance

Co-operation with the North Atlantic Alliance represents a common feature of British, French and German defence policy. However while Britain and Germany have made NATO the cornerstone of their defence policy, France's relationship with the alliance has at times been difficult.

Since the end of the Second World War, British defence planning has been underpinned by the perception that British security would be threatened if the United States was to turn away from Europe. In the early 1990s Britain's commitment to NATO was strengthened by its difficult experience in former Yugoslavia, where British troops played a major peacekeeping role alongside the French but were eventually obliged to call in US forces – especially air power – in order to put an end to the fighting. The 1998 Strategic Defence Review continued to recognize NATO as the principal security apparatus for Western Europe. Britain also remains one of the main contributors to the alliance (see Table 2.3). Around 5000 British troops are currently committed to NATO operations in Bosnia and Kosovo (Ministry of Defence 2003).

Although France had been among the founding members of NATO in 1949, it left the NATO integrated command in 1966 in protest over what President

Table 2.3 Contributions to NATO's Common Budgets, 1999

	Britain	*France*	*Germany*
Infrastructures	$53.6 m	$34.3 m	$108 m
	(£34.8 m, €47.7 m)	(£22.3 m, €30.5 m)	(£70.2 m, €96.1 m)
Military	$91.3 m	$29.3 m	$85.5 m
	(£59.3 m, €81.3 m)	(£19.0 m, €26.1 m)	(£55.6 m, €76.1 m)
Civil	$27.9 m	$24.7 m	$25.0 m
	(£18.1 m, €24.8 m)	(£16.1 m, €22.0 m)	(£16.3 m, €22.3 m)

Sources: Congressional Budget Office 2003.

De Gaulle alleged was US domination of the alliance, forcing NATO to move its headquarters from Paris to Brussels. France's decision meant that the country with the largest land area in Western Europe was withdrawing from the military organization, leaving NATO's Southern flank cut off from the Centre and the North. The relative isolation of the French military and defence communities from the NATO command structure began to decrease only in the second half of the 1980s, due in large part to French anxiety about the prospect of German reunification. During the 1990s France moved towards closer military cooperation with the alliance (Gordon 1995: 85). A large French contingent is currently serving in the NATO stabilization force (SFOR) in Bosnia and Herzegovina and in the NATO Kosovo force (KFOR).

West Germany was not admitted to NATO membership until 1955 with the signing of the Paris Treaty. As well as reassuring West Germany, membership of NATO contained the Federal Republic, binding it to the West while laying the foundations for a concerted Western containment effort against the Soviet Union (Hanrieder 1989: 31). Germany's commitment to NATO remained strong throughout the Cold War, although at the beginning of the 1980s the alliance's decision to deploy nuclear missiles on West German territory was met with strong resistance by part of West German public opinion. German membership of NATO was also a condition for US and European consent to reunification, which further increased Germany's importance for the alliance. During the 1990s Germany has played an important role in the transformation of NATO, lobbying in favour of the admission of former Warsaw Pact states, especially Poland, Hungary and the Czech Republic, which gained NATO membership in 1999.

The European security and defence identity (ESDI)

While France and Germany support the development of an autonomous European capability in security and defence issues, viewing it as an important aspect of the integration process, British decision-makers continue to perceive the 'special relationship' with the United States as the cornerstone of Britain's defence policy and refuse to support the creation of a European defence structure independent of NATO.

However Britain's military commitments have recently shifted away from complete association with the United States towards a more balanced relationship with the European Union. At the beginning of the 1990s Prime Minister Major agreed to an increased but limited role for the WEU, which was later incorporated into the original Treaty of the European Union.

The Saint Malo agreement with France in December 1998 commits the two countries to creating a significant European capacity to deal with crisis management. A similar pledge was made at the British-Italian Summit in 1999. The British government has committed 12,500 troops to the new force. Nevertheless, the British political establishment has been reluctant to push West European defence co-operation to the point where the United States may feel that it was neither wanted nor needed in Europe. The British viewpoint remains unchanged: European defence co-operation must be conducted in close and direct liaison with NATO.

By contrast, France has developed a strong partnership with Germany to counterbalance US influence in European security issues. The signing of the Elysée Treaty in 1963 laid the basis for Franco-German military co-operation and can be regarded as the beginning of the establishment of a ESDI. On French initiative, a 5000-strong Franco-German brigade was formed in November 1987. This brigade constituted the original nucleus of the *Eurocorps*, which the French consider as the embryo of a future European army. All the WEU member states were invited to give a contribution to the *Eurocorps*. The *Eurocorps* are based in the French city of Strasbourg and can call on 60,000 troops for operations. In 1993 Spain, Belgium and Luxembourg became members of this new defence structure. Nearly 13,000 French troops are currently assigned to the *Eurocorps*. In 1999, the *Eurocorps* was officially made available to the European Union. One of their units was activated during the Bosnian war but was not engaged in any major activities. *Eurocorps* headquarters held command of KFOR troops in Kosovo from March to October 2000.

After the end of the East–West division, the German authorities also gradually came to recognize the importance of developing an autonomous European military capacity to avoid the risk of excessive subordination to the United States. As early as 1987 German Chancellor Helmut Kohl agreed to the formation of the Franco-German brigade. As a result of this decision, Germany started developing the *Eurocorps* with France, providing the basis for a European defence structure and assuaging French concerns about reunification. The creation of the *Eurocorps* marked the return of German troops to French territory for the first time since World War II. However Germany insisted that the creation of a European defence capacity must not undermine NATO. As a result of German pressures, in 1992 France and Germany announced that the *Eurocorps* could be placed under NATO command, in the case of an attack on the alliance or of a decision by NATO governments to dispatch a peacekeeping force outside alliance territory. In 1999 Germany set up another international force: the Multinational Corps Northeast, a Danish–German–Polish force. German support for the construction of a European defence structure also has great symbolic importance: on 14 July 2003, France's traditional Bastille Day military parade was opened by a German general leading 120 troops from the *Eurocorps*.

Recent developments

The transformation of the international strategic environment and the emergence of new threats to state security, such as international terrorism, drug trafficking and organized crime, are global concerns that transcend national borders and raise fundamental questions in regard to defence policy.

As a result of the evolving international political situation, Britain, France and Germany have endeavoured to achieve greater professionalisation of the armed forces and to improve force projection for crisis management.

At the strategic level, British decision-makers appear to be convinced that Britain can continue to combine its relationships with the United States and Europe, although in several areas of the world, as in the Gulf and in the Middle East, American and European strategic thinking is far from identical. In 2003 Britain sent some 45,000 members of its armed forces to the Gulf during the military operations to topple the Iraqi regime. British troops were then deployed to restore order to Iraq's second city, Basra.

The new guidelines for French defence policy were laid down by a major presidential initiative, *Une Défense Nouvelle*, which was unveiled by President Chirac in February 1996 and addresses defence issues for the period between 1997 and 2015 (Ministère de la Défense 2003). Among the planned reforms was the phased abolition of conscription by 2002, ending more than 200 years of continuity in the recruitment of military personnel, and a far-reaching restructuring and down-sizing of the French armed forces. However there has not been a radical revision of French defence policy, the core feature of which continues to be the maintenance of an independent defence capability.

The German government is also drawing up plans for fully professional armed forces like those of Britain and France. Germany is one of the last countries in Europe to practise conscription, with recruits each having to serve for nine months. Conscripts performing obligatory service still make up one third of the total German armed forces. The abolition of conscription remains, however, a delicate issue in the German debate on defence, and the German authorities are also considering the possibility of a reduction of national service to only six months.

Sources

Auswärtiges Amt, <www.germany-info.org/relaunch/info/archives/background/bundeswehr. html> [23 July 2003].

Auswärtiges Amt, <www.germany-info.org/relaunch/info/archives/background/armedforces. html> [24 July 2003].

Bundeswehr, <www.bundeswehr.de/forces/personalstaerke.php> [4 September 2003].

Congressional Budget Office, <www.cbo.gov/showdoc.cfm?index=2665&sequence=4> [3 September 2003].

J.F. Couvrat, 'Le Défense Coûte 52 Milliards en Trop au Budget', *La Tribune*, 27 June 1996.

French Defence Ministry, <www.defense.gouv.fr/ema/index.htm> [30 October 2003].

Global Security Institute, <www.gsinstitute.org/resources/countries/france.shtml> [31 July 2003].

P.H. Gordon, *France, Germany and the Western Alliance* (Boulder: Westview Press, 1995).

Greenpeace, <www.greenpeaceusa.org/nuclear/historytext.htm> [27 July 2003].

W.F. Hanrieder, *Forty Years of German Foreign Policy* (New Haven: Yale University Press, 1989).

International Institute for Strategic Studies, <www.iiss.org/iraqCrisis.htm> [26 July 2003].

Ministère de la Défense/SIRPA, *Une Défense Nouvelle 1997–2015*, February 1996.

Ministère de la Défense (2003), <www.defense.gouv.fr/english/defence_and_citizens/armies_in_a_nutshell/> [2 September 2003].

Ministry of Defence, <www.mod.uk/issues/investment_strategy/02/intro.htm> [26 July 2003].

Ministry of Defence (2002), <www.official-documents.co.uk/document/cm56/56u/Chap01.htm> [31 July 2003].

Ministry of Defence, <www.mod.uk/aboutus/defence_matters/info_pages/cont_to_un.html> [31 July 2003].

Ministry of Defence, <www.official-documents.co.uk/document/cm56/5661/chap01.htm>

National Statistics, <www.statistics.gov.uk/downloads/theme_compendia/UK2003/UK2003.pdf> [3 September 2003].

NATO, <www.nato.int/docu/pr/2002/p02-139e.htm> [31 July 2003].

J. Rohde and H.H. Von Sandrart, 'German Defence and Force Structure Planning', in T. Taylor (ed.), *Reshaping European Defence* (London: Royal Institute of International Affairs, 1994).

Part II
Law and Order

3
Policing and Internal Security

Mike Stephens, Hartmut Aden, Bruno Domingo and Azilis Maguer

Introduction

All societies require mechanisms for preserving social order and control. Among the most prominent of these are the police and the security or intelligence services. This chapter concentrates on the work of the police, as it is the police that have the higher public profile and the greater impact in the majority of instances relating to the normal social activities of a country. Furthermore, given that within Britain there are distinct police organizational structures in Northern Ireland, Scotland, and England and Wales, this chapter will focus on the largest police body in England and Wales.

The nature of policing and internal security policy

The functions of the police are to preserve law and order (and to restore it where it has broken down), to detect crime, to gather evidence in relation to actual offences, and to engage in crime prevention and reduction activities. Many varied police activities are required in order to fulfil these functions, and the personnel involved include officers who patrol on foot and by car throughout all parts of a police force's area of control, specialist motor patrols for high-speed roads, trained detectives to detect and arrest offenders, specialist serious crime and drug offences squads, dog handlers, officers trained to look after individuals held for questioning in police cells, training officers, and riot control squads.

Internal security agencies are designed to protect the security of the nation from actual and potential threats from within their national borders. The precise focus of these agencies varies over time and between countries according to the nature of perceived and actual threats, but all aim to counter terrorist threats, gather intelligence on subversive people and organizations both openly and by secret methods such as phone tapping and infiltration, and act against those who would seek to undermine the interests of the nation through illegal

Table 3.1   Police and internal security

	Britain	France	Germany
Police	43 regional constabularies National Criminal Intelligence Service	*Gendarmerie* National Police	*Land* police forces *Bundeskriminalant* *Verfassungsschutz*
Internal security	Special Branch MI5	National Police Central Direction for General Intelligence, and Direction for Territorial Surveillance	

or violent means. On occasion the activities of internal security agencies become controversial, for example when they investigate the activities of trade unionists and other prominent left-wingers who are acting legally but are nevertheless seen as 'subversive' by security personnel. In all three countries the respective customs and immigration agencies also play a role in combating terrorism and serious crime.

Table 3.1 sets out the main policing and internal security agencies in Britain, France and Germany.

The 43 separate police constabularies covering England and Wales range markedly in geographical size, numbers of officers, rates of crime, financial budgets, and so on. Each constabulary is subject to a tripartite system of control in which responsibilities for the work of the police are shared by the chief constable, the local police authority and the Home Office, and comprises not only officers who conduct general patrol duties either on foot or by car but also a range of specialist officers such as plain clothed criminal investigation officers (Criminal Investigation Department or CID), traffic officers, firearms units, drug squads and serious crime squads. The constabularies cooperate a great deal via regional crime squads, the work of the Association of Chief Police Officers (ACPO) acting as a central pressure group working on behalf of all constabularies, and the sharing of information with the National Criminal Intelligence Service (NCIS 2003). ACPO now acts as a central policy-making forum alongside the Home Office and has a great deal of influence on the nature of future police activities and on the format of inter-agency cooperation. A Police National Computer also allows all officers anywhere in the country to access a central database on crime-related issues and suspected individuals.

While the ordinary police throughout the country have a role to play in countering terrorism and threats to the realm, especially through the work of the Special Branch, it is the security service in the shape of MI5 that is mainly responsible for such matters. This agency is under the authority of the Home

Secretary. With the reduction in terrorist threat and activities in Northern Ireland, the MI5 security service has partially reinvented itself by gaining a new remit to work more closely with the police to counter serious crime. As a consequence its current role is to protect national security and economic well-being and support the police in preventing and detecting serious crime (MI5 2003).

Most German police officers are employed by the *Länder*, which have the authority to define priorities for internal security strategies and for the recruitment of new police officers. The *Länder* police organisations vary to a certain degree, as do regional police laws, but all *Länder* have central criminal investigation units *(Landeskriminalämter)* and specialized units for criminal investigation *(Kriminalpolizei)* that are more or less interconnected with other branches responsible for traffic on public roads, etc. *(Schutzpolizei)* (Polizeiportal 2003). Federal authority for policing is limited to coordination of *Länder* activities for criminal investigation, and management of international cooperation by the *Bundeskriminalamt* (BKA), the federal criminal police office located at Wiesbaden (Aden 1999; Bundeskriminalamt 2003). However the various police forces have used a common computer system (INPOL) for criminal investigation since the 1970s, and intensive coordination is also carried out by the permanent conferences of the regional and federal interior and justice ministers plus numerous coordination circles at the administrative level, especially of the police.

The federal polity has three secret services but only one, the *Verfassungsschutz*, which comes under the Ministry of Interior, is responsible for domestic political matters (Bundesamt für Verfassungsschutz 2003). This agency observes extremist political opposition forces and has offices at the federal level and in each *Land*. The *Verfassungsschutz* gathers intelligence openly and by secret means such as telephone tapping and infiltration, but has no executive powers.

The activities of the police in France can be divided into five main areas: public security, organized and serious crime, border police/control, intelligence services and public order. Three major control organizations participate in internal security: the two police forces of the national gendarmerie and the national police, and the customs services. The gendarmerie is under the authority of the Ministry of Defence and works under a military statute. The national police are a civil force under the Ministry of Interior. Although the police and gendarmerie have similar areas of activity, they are different in two important respects. First, the police have the general competence in relation to large scale and organized crime as well as for international cooperation. Highly specialized national agencies for the fight against organized crime are located within the Ministry of Interior (General Direction of the National Police) where the staff are composed of both police and gendarmerie officers. Second, the gendarmerie traditionally operate in rural territories, whereas the national police are mostly active in urban areas (Dieu 2002). In 2002 the Ministry of Interior took over the operational direction of both the police and gendarmerie and some new forms of integrated work were implemented.

The Police Nationale's Central Direction for General Intelligence and its services at regional and departmental level collect information on political, economic and social issues for the government. The Direction for Territorial Surveillance of the Police Nationale is a counterspy service which collects information on activities of foreign governments within French territory that might endanger the security of the state. The Central Direction for Border Police and its departmental services focus on cross-border traffic, illegal immigration and foreigners residing in the country.

Specific comparisons

This section examines in more detail police numbers, police powers and procedures, public accountability and strategies for fighting crime.

Police numbers

Although fully internationally comparable figures are not available, national figures suggest that police and internal security personnel are most numerous in Germany.

In France, the gendarmerie employed 81,030 agents in 1998 (Ministère de la Défense 2003; RMCC 2003), while in 2001 the Police Nationale employed 144,997 (Ministère de l'Intérieur 2003).

In England and Wales police officer numbers reached record levels in March 2002 with a total of 129,603 officers, an increase of 4000 on the year before and the largest increase for 26 years (Police Strength 2003).

In Germany the *Bundeskriminalamt* has around 5000 permanent staff, the *Bundesgrenzschutz* (Federal Border Police) around 35,000 and the *Zollkriminalamt* (Customs Investigation Authority) around 400 (Bundeskriminalamt 2003, Bundesgrenzschutz 2003 Geheimdienste 2003; Statistisches Bundesamt 2003). The 16 *Länder* employ around 300,000 people for internal security matters in total, while the political secret service officially employs a permanent staff of 2300 people at the federal level.

Police powers and procedures

In all three countries the police possess considerable powers to enable them to carry out their duties, but their use of these powers is constrained by legal safeguards in areas such as phone tapping, searches of premises and detention of suspects.

One significant difference between the three countries is that while police are routinely armed in France and Germany, in England and Wales they normally do not carry firearms, although at certain locations, such as airports and other places at greatest risk of terrorist attack, gun carrying police officers are a common sight, and each of the 43 constabularies in England and Wales has its own specialist squad which undergoes intensive training in the use of firearms.

In England and Wales the police have wide powers to stop and search people, search private premises and seize property found there, and detain and question those suspected of criminal acts. Normally a person can only be detained by the police for questioning for 24 hours, at the end of which time they must either be released or charged with a crime. However, senior police officers may authorize a further period of detention of up to 36 hours in total, and magistrates may grant a total period of detention of up to 96 hours.

The legal powers of the criminal police in Germany have been considerably enlarged in recent years, especially for secret gathering of intelligence by telephone tapping, direct listening, undercover agents, and co-operation with informants from criminal milieux. For most of these activities the police need the authorisation of a judge prior to starting the investigations, except in urgent cases. Authorization is also necessary to search private homes, business premises and offices. Constitutionally the police power to keep someone in custody is limited until the end of the day that follows the arrest. For any prolongation, an authorisation by a judge is required.

Police officers in France can conduct four kinds of inquiries in respect of criminal matters. The first is an inquiry into 'flagrant offences' (*flagrant délit*), which is carried out under the control and direction of the public prosecutor but allows the police officer to choose what kinds of action to pursue, including the use of police custody. Secondly, the preliminary inquiry is an unofficial police inquiry and is the mode of inquiry most used by criminal police officers, but its simple procedural form is counterbalanced by the very limited powers it gives to the police, who can interview anyone but cannot use custody. Thirdly, inquiries can also be made under the authority of an instructing magistrate (instructing judge or president of a penal court) who delivers to the police service a letter of request (*commission rogatoire*) specifying all acts that are to be carried out for the purposes of the inquiry. Lastly, police may conduct inquiries in order to search for the causes of a questionable death. In addition, police officers may undertake identity checks and, under judicial control, intercept communications via telecommunication means. They are also responsible for executing arrest warrants, summons to appear, and committal orders.

Public accountability

All police authorities and internal security agencies must account for their actions to some extent, but in general the institutional means of enforcing accountability are mainly internal and hierarchical, and for internal security agencies in particular public accountability is weak.

In England and Wales the police are publicly accountable to the local police authority composed of elected local councillors, Justices of the Peace and independent local citizens. However in practice police authorities are weak and it is the Home Secretary and the Association of Chief Police Officers (ACPO) that have the greatest influence over the work and future direction of the police. Deviant acts committed by the police may be investigated internally by specialist departments or by the Police Complaints Authority, whose officers supervise police-led investigations into more serious allegations of police wrong-doing. The activities of MI5 are regulated by various acts of Parliament and by coming under the authority of the Home Secretary but, for the most part, remain secret, with only information of a general nature made available. The budget of MI5 is paid from a single account that funds all the security services, so we do not know the precise costs of MI5 operations. Without a more open discussion of its duties we cannot know either whether it is truly being held accountable for its actions.

In France public accountability is internal and hierarchical in nature. The Police Nationale controls its services in two ways. The *Inspection Générale des Services* (IGS) is responsible for the control of the Parisian police services and for preventing police deviance (Labrousse 2001). The *Inspection Générale de la Police Nationale* (IGPN) is responsible for controlling and preventing police deviance in the rest of the country (Razafindranaly 2001). The gendarmerie is also controlled by an internal inspection service. In addition, a new *Commission Nationale de Déontologie de la Sécurité* (CNDS) was created in 2000 to conduct inquiries on behalf of any Parliamentary deputies or government members who receive a complaint from a victim or witness what might be police deviance, but this authority cannot oblige police officers to respond and has only recommendatory powers regarding cases and parties. However, it does deliver a yearly activity report to the President of the Republic (Le Roux 2001). While the Central Direction of General Intelligence and Direction for Territorial Surveillance are both part of the Police Nationale, only the former is subject to the accountability mechanisms sketched above.

Public accountability of German police and internal security agencies is comparatively weak. There are no specialized monitoring bodies for policing and only weak ones for secret services to compensate for very limited parliamentary control. Hierarchical control predominates for all internal security institutions. For criminal investigations, police officers are supervised by the public prosecutors (*Staatsanwalt*). Police action outside criminal investigation can be individually challenged before an administrative court, but only by those to whom this action is addressed. Members of parliament have the authority to make inquiries of the government in policing matters. In cases of major scandals, parliaments at the *Land* and federal level have the right to set up commissions of inquiry, and this has been done from time to time for internal security matters. For the secret services German parliaments have very little rights of control. Even the budgets are secret. Small groups of members of parliaments are elected to supervise the secret services and their telephone tapping but do not have the right to inform the public or even other members of parliament if they discover actions that might be illegal or inefficient.

Strategies for fighting crime

In all three countries new developments and political pressures are leading to changes in police priorities and strategies.

The way the police in France fight crime depends partly on the nature of the crime and partly on central government priorities. One major priority is the so-called 'weekday security', which involves combating urban violence and public order offences as well as the fight against the public's fear of crime (Body-Gendrot and Duprez 2001) by means of increasing the number of police officers in uniform and implementing community policing policies. In addition, greater use is being made of police auxiliaries and temporary assistants and there is a general improvement in public access to the police and in the treatment of victims.

A second major priority deals with organized crime, terrorism, illegal immigration and drug trafficking. Since 2002 new tools to fight against illegal traffic networks have been created, including all-services inquiry and intervention groups (GIR), cross border inquiry and surveillance teams, growing participation in international and European cooperation, and the widening of operational police powers such as shared intelligence-gathering and cross-border powers of arrest. These reforms have been accompanied by new political and administrative pressures to improve police results, such as the monthly publication of levels of recorded crime in each police jurisdiction.

In England and Wales the police are under similar public and political pressure, and in addition to regular publication of local crime trends and figures are subject to a number of central government targets intended to encourage them to reduce crime and the fear of crime. There has been a long tradition in England and Wales of 'bobbies on the beat', but the ever growing demand on police resources has seen greater attention to specialist duties, often at the expense of this more community-oriented style of policing. One example of specialized activity is 'targeted' policing, which involves subjecting known and suspected burglars to surveillance and other forms of undercover work in an attempt to reduce significantly the number of offences carried out by such people. These strategies often require increased use of various forms of technology. But while targeted policing, zero tolerance policing and problem oriented policing may be effective in many ways, the public still yearns to see more and more officers in uniform on the beat, a desire that the police are struggling to meet (Stephens 2000).

In Germany too there has been a clear trend towards the greater use of technology in the fight against crime. In 2003 the central BKA database was replaced by a more efficient version integrating federal and *Land* systems into a single system architecture (*INPOL-neu*). Another trend is the legalisation of 'operative' investigation methods such as cooperation with informants from criminal milieux and the use of undercover agents and direct listening in private houses in 'organized crime' cases (Aden 1998: 367–92). Criminal investigation units are using telephone tapping so often – more than 21,000 instances in 2002 – that this practice has been the subject of repeated public criticism.

Recent developments

Successive French governments have been concerned at the growing social division between the population (especially French youths of foreign origin living in poor neighbourhoods) and the police (Mouhanna 2003), especially as this has been linked to the increase in recorded delinquency. To bridge this gap the police have been developing a new police model: the *police de proximité*, which is a French version of community policing (Monjardet 2002). The model (*Guide pratique de la police de proximité 2000*) is designed to produce a police force that is better able to anticipate and prevent difficulties, more familiar with its own territory and its inhabitants, and better able to respond effectively to the demands of the population. The aim is to bring the police and the population closer together by encouraging the police to take better account of social demands. This model of policing favours 'neighbourhood logic' (Dieu 2001) and 'problem solving logic' rather than logics related to public order and the fight against criminality. It spread rapidly throughout the whole Police Nationale urban services between 1999 and 2002, but while this change in the professional culture of the police has been welcomed by the public, many police officers see it as a deflection from their traditional activity and have yet to embrace it fully (Mouhanna 2003). After the presidential elections in May 2002 its philosophy was changed to reflect a greater focus on 'order policing', and a series of new laws were passed which increased the powers of police officers.

In Germany there has been a greater emphasis on crime prevention, and internal security policy shows a trend towards crime prevention at all levels. For 'organized crime' cases the starting point for criminal investigation has been moved to an earlier moment when no concrete crime has been committed and there is only suspicion (Pütter 1998: 32–57). For 'low level' crime, social prevention in various forms has been established (Aden 2002).

Recent developments in England and Wales have seen increasing public and political concern, followed by new or greater police action, in several areas. Some of these concerns have come close to being 'moral panics', such has been the demand for police action. Examples of these include the 'grooming' of young children via on-line chat rooms by paedophiles, the significant increase in street robberies involving the theft of mobile phones, the incidence of 'black on black' crimes and the associated rise in the number of firearms offences. Government has reacted in a variety of ways to these concerns, but it is always the police who have been urged to act more firmly and decisively at the so-called 'sharp end' of policing. Child pornography, for instance, is now the subject of intensive investigation by specialist police teams, as it is in Germany. The police operate in a frustrating public arena, for while recorded crime has actually been falling in recent years, the public are still fearful of crime.

Finally, there have also been significant developments in another area. In 1999 all constabularies in England and Wales were set government targets in respect of the recruitment, retention and progression of ethnic minority officers to ensure that by 2009 all police forces reflect their respective ethnic minority populations. By 31 March 2002 over 3300 police officers in England and Wales were from an ethnic minority background, representing 2.6 per cent of the total strength (Police Strength 2003).

Sources

H. Aden, *Polizeipolitik in Europa: Eine interdisziplinäre Studie über die Polizeiarbeit in Europa am Beispiel Deutschlands, Frankreichs und der Niederlande* (Opladen: Westdeutscher Verlag 1998).

H. Aden, 'Das Bundeskriminalamt. Intelligence-Zentrale oder Schaltstelle des bundesdeutschen Polizeisystems?', *Bürgerrechte & Polizei/CILIP* Vol. 62(1) 1999, 6–17, <www.infolinks.de/cilip/ausgabe/62/bka.htm>

H. Aden, 'Preventing crime, mobilizing new actors and tendencies towards a repressive roll-back: German security and crime prevention policies in the 1990s', in *The Prevention and Security Policies in Europe*, eds D. Duprez and P. Hebberecht (Brussels: VUB Press, 2002): 133–62.

S. Body-Gendrot and D. Duprez, 'Les politiques de sécurité et de prévention dans les années 1990 en France: Les villes en France et la sécurité', *Déviance et société*, vol 25/4 (2001): 377–402.

Bundesgrenzschutz, <www.bundesgrenzschutz.de/> [12 November 2003].

Bundesamt für Verfassungsschutz, <www.verfassungsschutz.de/> [12 November 2003].

Bundeskriminalamt, <www.bka.de/> [12 November 2003].

F. Dieu, 'Aperçu sur les expériences françaises de police de proximité', *Revue internationale de criminologie et de police technique et scientifique*, Vol. 3 (2001): 259–70.

F. Dieu, *La Gendarmerie, secrets d'un corps* (Bruxelles: éditions Complexe, 2002).

Commission nationale de déontologie de la sécurité <www.cnds.fr> [12 November 2003].

Geheimdienste, <www.geheimdienste.org/> [14 November 2003].

Guide pratique de la police de proximité (Paris: IHESI la documentation Française, 2000).

F. Labrousse, 'L'IGS, la légitimité d'un service de contrôle interne et judiciaire', *Les Cahiers de la sécurité intérieure*, Vol. 44 (2001): 171–88.

B. Le Roux, 'Sécurité et déontologie : la création d'une autorité administrative indépendante', *Les Cahiers de la sécurité intérieure*, Vol. 44 (2001): 143–52.

MI5, The Security Service, <www.mi5.gov.uk/purpose_values/purpose_values.htm> [29 October 2003].

Ministère de la Défense <www.defense.gouv.fr> [12 November 2003].

Ministère de l'Intérieur <www.interieur.gouv.fr> [12 November 2003].

D. Monjardet, 'La réforme de la police nationale', *Cahiers français* 308 (2002): 79–85.

C. Mouhanna, 'Le policier face au public: le cas des banlieues', in *En quête de sécurité: causes de la délinquance et nouvelles réponses*, eds S. Roché et al. (Paris: Armand Colin, 2003): 241–54.

NCIS (National Criminal Intelligence Service), <www.ncis.co.uk/> [29 October 2003].

Polizei-portal (central internet domain of German police organizations), <www.polizei.de> [13 November 2003].

Police Strength, <www.statistics.gov.uk/STATBASE/ssdataset.asp?vlnk=6377> [29 October 2003].

N. Pütter, *Der OK-Komplex: Organisierte Kriminalität und ihre Folgen für die Polizei in Deutschland* (Münster: Westfälisches Dampfboot, 1998).

J.R. Razafindranaly, 'L'IGPN, entre discipline et prévention', *Les Cahiers de la sécurité intérieure*, Vol. 44 (2001): 153–70.

RMCC (Royal Military College of Canada), <www.rmc.ca/academic/conference/iuscanada/papers/sorin_femmespaper.pdf> [12 November 2003].

Statistisches Bundesamt <www-genesis.destatis.de/genesis/online/logon> [10 November 2003].

M. Stephens, *Crime and Social Policy* (Eastbourne: Gildredge Press, 2000).

4
Judicial Policy

Mike Stephens, Hartmut Aden and Stéphane Cottin

Introduction

In mature democracies one should not be surprised to see that the court system and the judiciary are granted 'special' powers, powers which often make then largely or completely independent of government. Governments come and go, and while they may change the nature of their respective judicial systems, there is a strong public expectation that the quality of justice dispensed by these systems should not be undermined by government. Despite the differences between Britain, France and Germany, all three countries have well-established and respected legal systems that enjoy high levels of independence. In Britain there are significant differences between the separate jurisdictions of Northern Ireland, Scotland, and England and Wales. Since England and Wales is much larger than the other two jurisdictions, it is this judicial system which will be described here. Moreover, while the civil justice system is obviously of major importance in the lives of citizens, for reasons of space the bulk of the chapter will focus on the criminal courts.

The nature of judicial policy

Civil courts adjudicate in matters of contractual and other disputed events between citizens and various organizations, and award appropriate damages or provide certain relief for the party that wins the case. Whereas in criminal cases a defendant must be found guilty on the evidence beyond all reasonable doubt, in civil cases the lesser proof is used, namely the balance of probabilities.

The function of the criminal courts is to judge whether individuals or organisations have broken the law and, if so, to set appropriate sanctions. Equally important are the functions of protecting the rights of the defendant and providing a public forum in which justice can be seen to be done. In all three countries those accused of crimes are entitled to legal representation, although some defendants are unable to afford to exercise this right. Court proceedings consist largely of lawyers for the prosecution and defence (where there is a defence lawyer) competing to convince judge(s) and/or jury of the accused person's guilt or innocence – although at times negotiations take place between the prosecution and the accused (or their lawyer), for example with the aim of exchanging information for a lighter sentence.

In all three countries there is a general separation of powers between the courts (the judiciary), the executive (the government) and the legislature (the parliament or law making body). In Germany and in England and Wales the separation of powers and judicial independence are constitutionally guaranteed, whereas in France the Constitution of 1958 does not establish 'Justice' as a 'Power' co-equal to the executive and legislature but relegates it to the lower status of 'Authority'. Even so the independence of the courts is formally guaranteed even though the government retains some leverage in respect of judicial appointments and the financing of the court system. In fact it is the President of the Republic who acts as the guarantor of the independence of the French judicial authority, under which judges cannot be removed from office. Similarly, in Germany and in England and Wales judges are independent and it is very rare for any to be removed from office.

In England and Wales criminal cases are brought in the name of the Queen, a formal and constitutional device for bringing prosecutions in the public interest, and are conducted by a central agency – the Crown Prosecution Service. In Germany, public prosecution in criminal matters (*Staatsanwaltschaften*) depends on decisions taken at regional or federal justice ministries, but these ministries rarely exert any influence on actual investigations. In France the judicial system is a public service performed in the name of the French people. The equivalent of the Crown Prosecution Service is *la chambre de l'instruction*, which is a panel of judges in each court of appeal, but the decision to prosecute is generally taken by just one person: *le juge d'instruction*. Recently a new system has been set up whereby a second judge (*juge des libertés et de la détention*) decides whether the prosecuted person can remain free or is remanded in custody (Prosecution 2003).

Specific comparisons

A clearer picture of the similarities and differences between judicial policy in France, Germany, and England and Wales can be obtained by looking in more detail at court structures and procedures, the role of judges and juries, the treatment of juvenile offenders, and policies in relation to delays in the court process.

Court structure and procedures

French judicial organization is strictly separated into two branches: the judicial (civil and criminal issues) and the administrative. Each branch is hierarchical, with the *Court of Cassation* being the apex of the judicial branch and the Council of State the highest administrative court. The *Tribunal des Conflits* is in charge when a rare conflict of jurisdiction occurs. The judicial authority includes both judges and prosecutors (*magistrats du siège et magistrats du parquet*). Prosecutors are directly under the control of the Minister of Justice, in the sense that it is the minister who sets out the main directions of policy. However there are also a number of constitutional guarantees in respect of the judicial authority. The civil courts are governed by the Code of Civil Procedure (CCP1 2003) and the criminal courts are ruled by the Code of Criminal Procedure (CCP2 2003).

This is similar to the position in England and Wales, where the courts are essentially divided between criminal and civil matters. The vast majority of civil cases are handled in the County Court, while the equivalent legal workhorse in the criminal sphere is the Magistrates' Court, where 96 per cent of criminal cases are handled summarily. Above the County Court is the High Court, and above the Magistrates' Court is the Crown Court where more serious criminal matters are handled, such as murder, rape and robbery. The supreme adjudicating body is the House of Lords (Court Structure 2003). There are 218 County Courts within England and Wales, and 78 centres for Crown Courts. There is also a system of tribunals for civil matters relating to immigration, social security, child support, pensions, and taxation matters among others.

The German judiciary is somewhat different, largely because its judicial policy is closely connected to the federal nature of the country's political structures. In Germany the judiciary is organized into five relatively independent substantive legal branches. Each branch has its own hierarchy, with a federal-level court as the highest court on substantive legal questions within the branch (Alter 2001: 66–7). Criminal and civil courts form the main branch with three instances (levels) at the local and sub-regional (*Amtsgericht* and *Landgericht*), regional (*Oberlandesgericht*) and federal level; the highest instance is the *Bundesgerichtshof* (Federal High Court) (BGH 2003) at Karlsruhe. Besides these 'general' courts, four specialized branches exist for administrative law, labour law, social law and tax law. Another specialized branch is the *Bundespatentgericht* at Munich for matters concerning patents, which only exists at the federal level. Each judicial branch has its own procedural law. The distribution of tasks inside the specialized hierarchies follows similar principles.

With the *Bundesverfassungsgericht* (BverfG) located at Karlsruhe the German court system has a comparatively powerful constitutional court (Schlaich and Korioth 2001; Säcker 2003). It is not an appeal court, but has the authority to check the constitutionality of state acts, laws and court decisions. The BVerfG can also rule on *Verfassungsbeschwerden*, constitutional complaints against violations of fundamental rights that individuals can raise before the BVerfG. In 2002 4 692 new cases were registered by the BVerfG (BMJ 2003b; BVerfG 2003).

The role of judges and juries

The most striking difference here is that while juries are central to the court process in France and in England and Wales, there is no role for juries in Germany.

In England and Wales, Magistrates' Courts, which deal with lower-level criminal matters or 'summary' offences, are normally staffed by volunteer non-lawyers or Justices of the Peace who sit in groups of three and both decide guilt or innocence and carry out sentencing. Magistrates can normally only imprison someone for a maximum period of six months. Convicted defendants whose cases may warrant longer terms of imprisonment are referred to the Crown Court for sentencing (Magistrates 2003).

In the higher criminal courts in England and Wales, and in France, it is juries who decide on guilt or innocence and legally qualified judges who decide on sentences. In both countries juries are drawn at random either from the electoral roll (England and Wales) or the electoral list in the area of each assize (*département*) court (France).

The trial jury in France is composed of nine jurors when the court of assize rules at first instance (initial trial), and twelve jurors when it rules on appeal. The jurors may put questions to the accused and to the witnesses after asking the presiding judge for leave to speak. After the hearings, the judges of the court and the jurors retire to the discussion room. The court and the jury deliberate, then vote in writing and by separate and successive ballots, first on the principal offence and, where necessary, on the grounds of criminal irresponsibility, on each one of any aggravating circumstances, on subsidiary questions and on each one of any elements that constitute a cause for legal exemption or reduction of the penalty.

In England and Wales the jury is always composed of twelve individuals who rarely ask questions in the court room itself. Moreover, when they retire to consider their verdict, they do so alone with no judge or other legal official present. Their main duty is to deliver a verdict on guilt or innocence; it is the judge who may consider a reduction in the penalty, depending on the individual circumstances of the offence, when he or she comes to give the sentence.

In Germany there are no juries at all. Instead, 'low-impact' cases are handled by a single judge. More complex and more important cases are heard by chambers of three or, in some higher instances, five or more judges. In a number of cases, chambers comprise two volunteer non-lawyers *(Schöffen)*, who always sit with one or more professional judges.

Treatment of juvenile offenders

In all three countries, young offenders are treated differently to adult offenders.

In Germany there has been increasing concern at the rising number of offences being committed by young people over the past decade (BKA 2003:

74, 76). For criminal matters, the German court system has special judges and chambers for juveniles. The *Jugendgerichtsgesetz* is a special criminal procedure for juveniles. For some years education of offenders has generally been given priority over repression and imprisonment (DVJJ 2003), with imprisonment of juveniles in special prisons reserved for major cases, although this approach has been contested during recent years under the influence of the debates on 'zero tolerance' strategies for 'low level crime'. In 2002 there were 6949 prisoners below 21 years, 268 of them female (BMJ 2003b: 10).

In England and Wales persistent young offenders are now 'fast tracked' to appear before the Youth Court, which is a specialized chamber for dealing with children and young persons. The history of the Youth Court and of juvenile justice policy in England and Wales has been characterized by a debate over the merits of the welfare versus the punishment approach to youth crime. The Youth Court has at its disposal sentences that reflect both approaches, but the court is legally bound to have regard for the welfare of the child. However the welfare principle is not an overriding imperative, for it must be balanced against the 'just deserts' or punishment approach, as set out in the Criminal Justice Act 1991. Any welfare needs that an individual juvenile offender may have are communicated to the court through a pre-sentence report compiled (depending on the age of the defendant) by a social worker or a probation officer. The three magistrates who serve in the Youth Court, and who decide on guilt and on sentencing, are specially trained in youth-related issues, and the bench of magistrates must always contain at least one member of each gender.

In France the treatment of juvenile offenders is governed by an ordinance of 2 February 1945, which sets out the principle of the primacy of educational issues in applying sanctions for illegal behaviour. This ordinance led to the creation in each *département* of one or more juvenile courts (*Tribunal pour enfants*) and to the institution of a specialized judge, the judge of the children. Educational measures have to take precedence over any penal sanction when dealing with juvenile delinquents, and no penal sanction can be pronounced against a young person of less than 13 years (Youth Court 2003).

Delays in the court process

All judicial systems have procedural and due process safeguards in order to protect the rights of litigants and, especially, the rights of defendants who may lose their liberty if found guilty of a crime. However such safeguards and the pressing demands on the courts inevitably lead to varying levels of delay. Thus it is not surprising that attempting to ease these delays has been a continuing concern in all three countries in recent years. Another agenda-setting factor for initiatives to accelerate judicial work is the European Court of Human Rights' case law, according to which an excessive length of proceedings violates the European Convention on Human Rights.

In Germany the average length of first instance proceedings in 2000 was 5.5 months for criminal cases, 6.9 months for civil cases, 18.7 months for administrative cases and 17 months for tax cases (BMJ 2003b: 5–8). Governments and pressure groups have repeatedly developed initiatives aimed at cutting down the delays. In penal cases, defendants normally have to be released from preliminary detention if their process has not started six months after imprisonment. In some cases even murderers had to be released when public prosecutors did not respect this deadline, which led to considerable public protest.

In France the government passed an institutional act in February 2003 to create *juges de proximité*, essentially retired judges and former legal professionals, to try petty crimes and small matters of civil litigation in an attempt to ease the problems in the other courts (Proximity Judges 2003). The French have also altered their system of appeal, in part to speed up proceedings. Until 2000, criminal cases were only re-examined by the country's highest court, the Court of Cassation, and only on legal issues, not on the facts, but now when a criminal case in an assize court is appealed, it is now re-examined on appeal by another assize court.

In England and Wales the government has set targets for reducing the time it takes for a case to come to a criminal court, and has instructed the Crown Prosecution Service to work more closely with the police in the gathering of evidence to ensure fewer delays and fewer discontinuations of cases when they do come to court.

Recent developments

We have already see that in France there have been efforts recently to reduce delays by introducing *juges de proximité* and reforms to the appeal process.

In Germany 'modernization' of the courts has been a major topic of judicial policy since the 1990s. Measures under this heading have ranged from the introduction of computer techniques to administer the courts' daily work to the reduction of the number of cases to be heard via introducing new forms of mediation (BMJ 2003a). As with other areas of public administration, the courts have been more and more obliged to apply new managerial strategies in order to cut their costs during periods of budgetary restrictions (Schultze-Fielitz and Schütz 2002).

In England and Wales there has been a notable increase in custodial sentencing by the Magistrates' and Crown Courts over the past 12 years. Accordingly, the prison population has increased from 36,000 in 1991 to over 74,000 in 2003. This more than doubling of the prison population within a short span has been caused by two factors: the imprisonment of offenders who would previously have received a non-custodial sentence such as a community penalty, and the willingness of the Magistrates' and Crown Courts to hand down longer prison sentences. Between 1991 and 2001 both courts showed marked increases in their rates of custody, rising from 5 per cent to 16 per cent of sentences in the Magistrates' Court and from 46 per cent to 64 per cent of sentences in the Crown Court. Ironically, all of this happened during a period of falling crime rates and is a reflection of the widespread political, public and media pressure on magistrates and judges to be seen to be tougher on crime (Hough 2003).

Sources

K.J. Alter, *Establishing the Supremacy of European Law: The Making of an International Rule of Law in Europe* (Oxford: Oxford University Press, 2001).

Bundesgerichtshof (BGH), <www.bundesgerichtshof.de/> [2003].

Bundeskriminalamt (BKA), *Polizeiliche Kriminalstatistik 2002* (Wiesbaden: BKA 2003), also available at <www.bundeskriminalamt.de/pks/pks2002/index.html>

Bundesministerium der Justiz (BMJ), <www.bmj.bund.de> [12 November 2003a].

Bundesministerium der Justiz (BMJ), 'Zahlen aus der Justiz', <www.bmj.bund.de/images/11572.pdf> [12 November 2003b].

Bundesverfassungsgericht (BVerfG), <www.bverfg.de> [18 November 2003].

CCP1 (Code of Civil Procedure), <www.legifrance.gouv.fr/html/codes_traduits/ somncpca. htm> [21 October 2003].

CCP2 (Code of Criminal Procedure), <www.legifrance.gouv.fr/html/codes_traduits/ cppsomA. htm> [21 October 2003].

Court Service, <www.courtservice.gov.uk/> [11 November 2003].

Court Structure, <www.courtservice.gov.uk/about_us/structure/index.htm> [28 October 2003].

Deutsche Vereinigung für Jugendgerichte und Jugendgerichtshilfen e.V. (DVJJ), <www.dvjj.de/> [12 November 2003].

French Ministry of Justice (2003), <www.justice.gouv.fr> and especially <www.justice.gouv.fr/anglais/europe/aaqueltr.htm> and <www.justice.gouv.fr/anglais/justorg/justorga3.htm> [12 November 2003].

M. Hough, *The Decision to Imprison: Sentencing and the Prison Population* (London: Prison Reform Trust, 2003).

Magistrates, <www.magistrates-association.org.uk/> [28 October 2003].

Prosecution, <www.justice.gouv.fr/publicat/igsj150600c.htm> [11 November 2003].

Proximity Judges, <www.justice.gouv.fr/presse/conf020403.htm> [21 October 2003].

R. Perrot, *Institutions judiciaires* (Paris: Montchrestien, 2002).

J.-P. Royer, *Histoire de la justice en France* (Paris: PUF, 2001).

H. Säcker, *Das Bundesverfassungsgericht*, 6th edn (Bonn: Bundeszentrale für politische Bildung, 2003).

K. Schlaich and S. Korioth, *Das Bundesverfassungsgericht. Stellung, Verfahren, Entscheidungen*, 5th edn (Munich: Beck, 2001).

H. Schulze-Fielitz and C. Schütz (eds), *Justiz und Justizverwaltung zwischen ökonomisierungsdruck und Unabhängigkeit* (Die Verwaltung, Beiheft 5, Berlin: Duncker & Humblot 2002).

Statistisches Bundesamt, *Rechtspflege: Ausgewählte Zahlen für die Rechtspflege 2001, Fachserie 10, Reihe 1* (Wiesbaden: Metzler-Poeschel 2003a).

Statistisches Bundesamt, *Rechtspflege: Gerichte und Staatsanwaltschaften 2001, Fachserie 10, Reihe 2* (Wiesbaden: Metzler-Poeschel 2003b).

Statistisches Bundesamt, *Rechtspflege: Strafvollzug 2002, Fachserie 10, Reihe 4.1*, (Wiesbaden: Metzler-Poeschel 2003c).

Statistisches Bundesamt, <www-genesis.destatis.de/genesis/online/> [12 November 2003d].

M. Stephens, *Crime and Social Policy* (Eastbourne, Gildredge Press, 2000).

P. Truche, *Justice et institutions judiciaires* (Paris: La documentation française, 2001).

J. Vincent, G. Montagnier, A. Varinard and S. Guinchard, *Institutions judiciaires. Organisation, juridictions, gens de justice* (Paris: Dalloz, 2003).

Youth Court, <www.justice.gouv.fr/justorg/justorg9.htm> [11 November 2003].

5
Penal Policy

Andrew Coyle

Introduction

Comparing the penal policies of France, Germany, and England and Wales is not straightforward. There are large differences between the common law system in England and continental legal systems. The role played by the prosecution is much greater in France and Germany than in England and Wales. Definitions of criminal offences and methods of collecting sentencing statistics are not strictly comparable. Yet it is possible to make comparisons that are sound enough to reach some conclusions about different approaches in the different countries. For example, use of the most severe penal sanction, imprisonment, varies markedly between France, Germany, and England and Wales. Non-custodial sanctions are provided very differently, with more options in England and Wales than in either France or Germany. Policies towards juvenile defendants and offenders reflect a much higher level of belief in the efficacy and social benefits of punishment in England and Wales than in Germany or France.

The nature of penal policy

Penal policy deals with the system of convicting and imposing sanctions on people accused and found guilty of offences against the criminal law. It embraces the setting of sanctions (mainly fines, actual or suspended imprisonment, and community service), drawing up policies for their use (the age at which a person can be imprisoned, the offences for which imprisonment can be imposed, what happens to those who fail to pay their fines or carry out the conditions of supervision). It also covers responsibility for services that administer the sanctions (the prison service, an organisation to collect fines, a service to administer community supervision) as well as systems of early release and the social re-integration of former prisoners.

In general, penal policy is a function of the national government although some aspects, such as non-custodial supervision and post-prison social re-integration, may be contracted out to non-state bodies.

In Britain criminal justice policy is devolved. There are three separate juris-dictions – England and Wales, Scotland, and Northern Ireland – with significant differences between them in legal system and in organisation. This chapter concentrates on England and Wales, which is by far the largest of the three. In England and Wales there is no Ministry of Justice and the responsible Ministry is the Home Office, the equivalent of a Ministry of the Interior. The Home Office runs the prison service from the centre and the prison service is an executive agency of the government. Following the implementation of the Criminal Justice and Court Services Act of 2001, the probation service, which administers non-custodial sanctions and supervises offenders, lost its local base and devolved character to become also a centrally administered department of the Home Office.

In France penal policy is the responsibility of the Ministry of Justice. The Ministry directly administers the prison system and also the probation and rehabilitation service. Unlike England and Wales, where regional management of prison and probation services is separate, in France the regional director of the prison service is also the regional director of probation and rehabilitation.

In Germany, Ministries or Departments of Justice in each of the federal states are responsible for penal matters but policy is co-ordinated at the centre by the Federal Ministry of Justice. Criminal law is federal as is the law governing the administration of prisons. So as to avoid major inequalities in the application of law enforcement, Ministers of Justice from the federal states meet regularly and administrative rules which serve as guidelines have been issued on subjects such as the implementation of federal prison law (Albrecht and Teske 2000).

Specific comparisons

A more detailed idea of the content of penal policy in Britain, France and Germany can be gained by looking more closely at the use of imprisonment, sentencing practices, and penal policy in relation to young people.

The use of imprisonment
Since the death penalty has been abolished in all countries of the European Union the most severe penalty available in all three countries is imprisonment. Information on the number of persons incarcerated is readily available for all three countries and can easily be compared. Comparisons of world impris-onment rates are normally made by looking at the number of individuals incarcerated per 100,000 of the general population in the country. The EU average is 99 per 100,000.

Table 5.1 shows that the imprisonment rate in England and Wales is much higher than in Germany and France. The England and Wales figure is the highest in the EU. The overall British figure is 134 since Scotland is also high. The figure for Northern Ireland is low but the prison situation there has been linked to the political events and is not strictly comparable (World Prison Brief – all figures for 2002).

Imprisonment is used both for sentenced offenders and for people waiting for their trial or their sentence (sentencing is sometimes postponed while reports are prepared and considered). The proportion of the prison population that is awaiting trial for final sentence in France is much higher than in either Germany or England and Wales. It is a feature of both Germany and England and Wales that a proportion of those incarcerated pre-trial do not subsequently receive a prison sentence. In Germany 50 per cent of pre-trial detainees are not given a prison sentence (Ministries of the Interior and Justice). In England and Wales the proportion is 52 per cent of men and 64 per cent of women (Home Office 2001). Thus people whom the court do not regard as meriting custody serve some time in prison.

Women prisoners are always a very small proportion of the overall number of prisoners in any country but in England and Wales the proportion is nearly two-thirds higher than the proportion in France and one third higher than the proportion in Germany.

Life imprisonment is the most severe sanction available in all the jurisdictions. Life imprisonment does not usually mean imprisonment for the whole of the offender's natural life. Instead, the length of the sentence to be served is indeterminate, with the time of release based on various assessments of continuing dangerousness and other factors. England and Wales had 5150 prisoners serving life in June 2002 (Home Office 2002). The figure for Germany is proportionately much lower at 1300 (Dünkel and Rössner 2001) and in France on

Table 5.1 Rates of imprisonment

	England and Wales	*France*	*Germany*
No. of prisoners	71,894 (2002)	50,714 (2002)	78,707 (2000)
Prison population rate per 100,000 of the general population	137	85	96
Pre-trial detainees (%)	18.1 (2002)	33.6 (2002)	22.6 (2000)
Women prisoners (%)	6.0 (2002)	3.7 (2002)	4.5 (2000)
Foreign prisoners (%)	8.6 (2000)	21.6 (2000)	34.1 (1999)
Official capacity of prison system	64,147 (2002)	47,434 (2002)	76,725 (2000)
Occupancy level (based on official capacity)	112.1% (2002)	106.9% (2002)	102.6% (2000)

Sources: World Prison Brief (2002), Home Office (2001/02), Ministère de la Justice (2002).

1 January 1999 it was 551 (Combessie 2001). In Germany the life sentence is only imposed for murder whereas in England and Wales life sentences can be given for a wider range of offences. In France life sentences can be imposed for murder and for certain offences against the state.

All three prison systems were holding more prisoners than they were designed for but Germany was only slightly overcrowded, whereas the relevant level of overcrowding in France was over three times as high and that in England and Wales almost five times as high.

Differences in the size of a country's prison population can be accounted for by a number of factors. Research suggests that differences in crime rates do not account for most of the variance. The penal policies in place are more likely to be the significant factor. How much use is made of pre-trial detention and the length of such detention will affect the final incarceration level. The number of convicted offenders sentenced to prison rather than to an alternative sentence, the length of the prison terms imposed and the amount of the term that is required to be served before early release is granted, all play a part.

The three countries vary on all these indicators. France has an accepted policy of controlling the prison population and the President grants annual amnesties on 14 July which reduce prison numbers. In Germany there are great variations in the use of prison between the federal states. The highest imprisoning states are in the south of the country. In England and Wales any new penal policy measures tend to increase the use of imprisonment.

Sentencing

Comparing sentencing outcomes between jurisdictions is fraught with pitfalls and difficulties in trying to set like against like. For example, the population of offenders being sentenced may not be comparable if those facing the less serious charges are diverted from the criminal process and are dealt with another way, leaving only the more serious to be sentenced. In Germany the prosecution has considerable discretion to discontinue a prosecution with or without conditions and in 1998 47 per cent of charges were dealt with in this way (Ministries of the Interior and Justice). With these caveats in mind it is possible to look at sentencing practices in the three jurisdictions and construct some parameters for a comparative discussion (see Table 5.2).

Although comparisons must be made with caution it is clear that the three countries have very different sentencing patterns, with the fine playing a smaller part in the system of England and Wales and the suspended prison sentence occupying a central position in France and Germany.

It is also clear from the figures that having a wide range of non-custodial sanctions and a high level of use of them, as is the case in England and Wales, does not mean that there is less use of imprisonment. Non-custodial sanctions are not necessarily alternatives to prison.

Table 5.2 Proportionate use of imprisonment and non-custodial sanctions (%)

	England and Wales	*France*	*Germany*
Imprisonment	30.8 (men over 21)	18	6
Fine	28	33	80
Community service and supervision	23	6	
Suspended sentence	1	33	14
Loss of driving licence		6	
Discharge	13	2	

Sources: Home Office 2001; Ministry of Justice 2002; Ministries of the Interior and Justice 2002.

In all three jurisdictions the same non-custodial sanctions, namely fines, community service work and supervision or educational measures, are to be found, although their legal basis differs. As Table 5.2 shows, the monetary penalty, that is, the fine, is used in all three jurisdictions, though Germany has by far the highest use. Germany operates the 'day fine' system, whereby the amount of the fine is related very closely to the means of the offender. The fine is awarded in terms of a number of days, according to the seriousness of the offence, for up to a maximum of 360 days for one offence. A 'day' is then valued in monetary terms after an assessment is made of the means of the offender. Thus a wealthy and a poverty-stricken person might each be fined the same number of days for a similar offence, but the wealthy person would pay more up to a pre-determined limit. When an offender does not pay the fine that has been imposed the ultimate enforcement mechanism in Germany is imprisonment. Around seven per cent of fines are unpaid and 60,000 fine defaulters were imprisoned in Germany in 1999. One 'day-fine' is deemed to equal one day of imprisonment.

In England and Wales the 'day fine' was introduced for a brief period in 1991 but rapidly abandoned by the Government in 1993 after some high-profile cases had led to a media campaign against it. The use of the fine in England and Wales has declined steadily over the past 20 years.

The sanction of carrying out unpaid work for the benefit of the community is to be found in all three jurisdictions but in Germany it is not a sentence in its own right. Since the early 1980s it has been used when an offender who is fined fails to pay the fine. The fine is converted into community service and one day-fine is regarded as equal to six or eight hours of community service work.

In France on 1 January 2000 nearly 150,000 offenders were being dealt with by non-custodial sanctions, of whom three-quarters were under probation supervision, 16.7 per cent doing community service work (*travail d'intérêt général*) and 7.4 per cent on conditional release and other measures. A community service sentence in France involves unpaid work for a public authority or association for between 40 and 240 hours.

In England and Wales in 2000, 155,000 offenders (of all ages) were given non-prison sentences. Probation (officially called a 'community rehabilitation order') and supervision accounted for 44 per cent of these. Community service orders (called 'community punishment orders') made up 32 per cent. Attendance centre orders (for young people only) made up 4.5 per cent. Combination orders (combining supervision and community service) made up 12 per cent. A curfew order, requiring a person to stay at home within certain hours, accounted for 1.7 per cent and reparation and action plan orders (for young people) made up 5.4 per cent. Three thousand people were given a new penalty, a drug treatment and testing order (Home Office 2002).

In Germany more than two-thirds of the prison sentences imposed are suspended, that is, a sentence of imprisonment is imposed but not actually served unless the convicted person commits another offence. Instead the offender is placed on probation, sometimes under supervision by a probation officer. Where the convicted offender is unlikely to commit another crime and the prison sentence is one year or less the court is required to suspend the sentence.

The young

A major determinant of policy in dealing with juvenile offenders is the age of criminal responsibility, that is, the age at which the criminal law rather than a welfare or other response can be invoked in response to any act committed by a young person. England and Wales leans most towards penal sanctions in this regard too, with an age of criminal responsibility of 10, compared with 13 in France and 14 in Germany. International legal instruments stress that imprisoning those aged under 18 should be an act of last resort.

The number of juveniles in prison or in penal establishments (prisons for children are often given other titles such as reformatories or training centres) varies considerably. It is particularly difficult to make comparisons in respect of Germany because of the different statistics available for the former West and East Germany. However some broad comparisons are set out in Table 5.3.

In Germany children under the age of criminal responsibility who commit acts that could be classified as crimes if they were committed by someone over 14 are dealt with by the child welfare laws. Juveniles aged 14–17 are dealt with under the Youth Court Law which makes it clear that the exclusive aim is rehabilitation. The Youth Court is required to choose from among a range of sanctions specifically for juveniles. Courts may decide to treat young adults, aged between 18 and 20, as if they were juveniles and use the juveniles sentencing measures. More than 60 per cent of young adults are sentenced as juveniles.

Table 5.3 Juvenile offenders

	England and Wales	*France*	*Germany*
Age of criminal responsibility	10	13	14
Consideration of educational measures rather than penal measures	Up to age 12	Up to age 18	Up to age 20
No. of juveniles in prison	2600 (2002)	800 (2000)	841 (2001)*

Note * Germany, sentenced only.
Sources: Home Office, Ministère de la Justice, Ministries of the Interior Justice.

In France the law applying to juveniles emphasizes measures of protection, help, supervision and education. Educational measures take priority over penal measures. Children under the age of 13 can never be subject to penal measures. Juveniles can only be remanded in custody before a trial for one month and this period can only be renewed once (Combessie 2001).

In England and Wales penal measures are applied to children from the age of 10 years. From 12 a child may be held in a secure establishment before his or her trial. From 12 a child may be given a 'detention and training order' which can be for up to two years. Half of the time must be served in custody and half under supervision in the community. In England and Wales in June 2002 there were 2600 juveniles in prison, 2090 sentenced and 500 unconvicted or unsentenced. There were also several hundred 12–14 year olds held in 'secure training centres' outside the prison system but within the penal system.

Recent developments

All three jurisdictions have seen changes in their use of imprisonment over the past decade (see Table 5.4). In line with their policy of using prison sparingly, the trend in France has been towards stability, whereas in Germany the rate has increased by 37 per cent and in England and Wales by 52 per cent (World Prison Brief).

Table 5.4 Imprisonment rate per 100,000 people

	England and Wales	*France*	*Germany*
1992	90	84	71
1995	99	89	81
1998	125	86	96
2002	137	85	96 (2000)

Source: World Prison Brief 2002.

Increasing concern about the control of sex offenders has been expressed in new measures in all three countries. In Germany a new law came into force in 1998 which made longer prison sentences available in sexual abuse cases. Those sentenced to prison for two years or more are required to undertake treatment. Parole or suspended sentences must be accompanied by treatment (Albrecht and Teske 2000). In England and Wales the Sex Offenders Act of 1997 required specified sex offenders to register with the police and the Crime and Disorder Act of 1998 gave the police powers to monitor those subject to them.

The search for new sanctions has led all three countries to experiment with or to introduce a system of electronic monitoring under which offenders are fitted with an electronic bracelet or anklet, which enables their movements to be monitored by the authorities. This was introduced In France in 1997 to enable prisoners to be released early (Combessie 2001). In Germany a similar scheme for prisoners in the last three months of their sentence was introduced in a few federal states in 2000. In England and Wales the 'home detention curfew' is a form of electronic monitoring for prisoners released early. In June 2002 it was being used for 2330 prisoners.

More attention is being shown to the victims of crime in all three countries and the involvement of victims in some process of reconciliation and mediation with the offender is part of the law in Germany and in England and Wales. In both jurisdictions it is still little used.

The major difference between England and Wales and France and Germany is the belief in England and Wales that criminal punishment can be a tool of social policy and that it has a part to play in reducing crime. This is not just because of its incapacitation effects but also through the measures undertaken in prison or in the community sanctions. The White Paper 'Justice for All' (Home Office July 2002) is premised on the idea of 'punishments that work' and proposes a new sentencing structure that combines considerations of a punishment proportionate to the offence with aspects that aim to reform the convicted offender. In both Germany and France the more traditional European philosophy that imprisonment should be used as a last resort holds more sway. This is shown, for instance, in the more sparing use of imprisonment for women and young people, for whom the experience of imprisonment can be particularly damaging.

Sources

H.J. Albrecht, and R. Teske, 'Crime and Criminal Justice in Germany – Trends and Developments' in *Crime and Crime Control – A Global View*, ed. G. Barak (Greenwood Press: 2000).

P. Combessie, 'France' in *Imprisonment Today and Tomorrow*, eds. D. Van Zyl Smit and F. Dünkel (The Hague: Kluwer Law International, 2001).

F. Dünkel and D. Rössner, 'Germany' in *Imprisonment Today and Tomorrow*, eds. D. Van Zyl Smit and F. Dünkel (The Hague: Kluwer Law International, 2001).

Home Office (2001), <www.homeoffice.gov.uk>
Home Office (2002), <www.homeoffice.gov.uk>
Ministry of Justice (Ministère de la Justice) (2002), <www.justice.gouv.fr>
Ministries of the Interior and Justice, *First Periodical Report on Crime and Crime Control in Germany*, <www.bmi.bund.de> and <www.bmj.bund.de>
World Prison Brief (2002), <www.prisonstudies.org>

6
Immigration

Catherine Lloyd, Uwe Hunger and Catherine Wihtol de Wenden

Introduction

Immigration policy in Britain, France and Germany offers comparative material on several levels: the French model of republican assimilation, the British multicultural agenda, and in Germany a growing realization of the social importance of immigration. In all three countries there have been many policy changes in recent years in terms of the way in which they conceive of nationality rights, the control of immigration and policies towards asylum seekers.

The propensity to enter a given country depends on national policies, general attitudes towards the nationals of foreign countries, and whether there are existing networks of people from the same country of origin (migratory chains). Patterns of migration have changed over the past century in all three countries. At the beginning of the twentieth century labour migrants to France came mainly from Southern Europe and Poland, while most migrants to Britain were from Ireland. After 1945 new groups of migrants came to France from the ex-colonies of the Maghreb, while Germany recruited workers from Turkey, Yugoslavia, Greece, Italy, Spain and Morocco. Britain turned to the New Commonwealth, especially India, Pakistan, Bangladesh and the Caribbean, to help with its labour shortage. All three countries began to see family reunification during the 1970s. During the 1990s the emphasis shifted from labour migration to asylum seekers, although Germany signed bilateral contracts for workers from the countries of Central and Eastern Europe and introduced a 'green card' to attract specialists in information technology. Germany also had the special category of ethnic Germans from Eastern Europe born before 1992. Since 1950 more than 4 million ethnic Germans have come to Germany, aided by the fact that the constitution provides for them to have automatic citizenship. Since 1993 the number entering the country under these provisions has been limited to 103,000 a year, and only ethnic Germans from the territories of the former Soviet Union are now allowed to immigrate.

The nature of immigration policy

Immigration policy regulates the movement of people into and out of a given territory and the rights and conditions of their residence before and after they have been legally accepted into the society. The specific policy instruments of immigration policy are set out in Table 6.1.

These policies relate to different categories of migration, including labour migration, the reunification of families and the entry of asylum seekers and refugees, and are distinct from, but related to, policies that manage the integration of migrants.

In the past two decades the European Union has produced a number of regulations which have attempted to standardize national legislation, but significant national differences remain.

The main government departments and agencies involved in immigration report to different areas of state responsibility: immigration, nationality and asylum is a responsibility of the Home Office in Britain, but in France and Germany the Ministry of Labour also has an important role.

In Britain the Immigration and Nationality Directorate is part of the Home Office. The Directorate's purpose, as set out by the Home Office, is 'to regulate

Table 6.1 Immigration policy

Controls on movement	External controls implemented in other countries, in particular the provision of visas
	Frontier passport and other controls such as health checks, finger-printing and verbal examinations
	Internal controls: registration with police, passport checks either ad hoc by police or when the person involved applies for services or employment
	Exit visa and passport controls on leaving the country
	Setting and enforcement of penalties for non-compliance with immigration rules
Setting and enforcement of rights and conditions of residence	Setting and implementing eligibility conditions for long-term residence for employment, training and other reasons
	Setting and implementing eligibility conditions for citizenship (nationality policy), based on descent (the traditional German model) and/or residence (the French republican model)
	Provision of legal support for immigrants
	Provision of economic and social support, such as cash payments and services, for immigrants both before and after they are accepted, and pending deportation for those whose applications are refused

entry to, and settlement in, Britain effectively in the interests of sustainable growth, and social inclusion.' The UK Immigration Service, the visible face of the Directorate, operates chiefly in ports and airports, and undertakes casework and functions in British diplomatic posts around the world.

In France the *Office des Migrations Internationales* operates within the Ministry of Labour and is the only body legally charged with the recruitment of foreign workers and the return of French expatriates. Applications for asylum are processed by the Office for the Protection of Refugees and Stateless Persons (OFPRA) and, in the case of territorial protection for asylum seekers without refugee status, by the Ministry of the Interior. The treatment of asylum cases has been increasingly decentralized and much responsibility has been devolved onto non-governmental organizations, in particular the *Centre d'Accueil des Demandeurs d'Asile* (CADA) managed by *France Terre D'Asile*.

In Germany the responsibility for immigration policies is divided among various levels of government. At the Federal level, the Ministry of the Interior regulates immigration and settlement, the Ministry of Labour in collaboration with the Federal Labour Agency administers work permits, and the Ministry of Foreign Affairs issues visas. At the *Land* level the execution of immigration policies varies. Rates of naturalization and details of procedures vary tremendously both between and within *Länder*. Local authorities are responsible for many social services applicable to immigrants, such as the provision of social aid and kindergartens. At the Federal level, as well as at *Land* and local levels, there are a number of ombudsman institutions for immigrants. The most important of these is the Federal Commissioner for Migration, Refugees and Integration (*Beauftragte der Bundesregierung für Migration, Flüchtlinge und Integration*).

Specific comparisons

In this section we compare policy stances in relation to immigration control, nationality, and asylum.

Control policies

The general orientation of contemporary immigration policies in all three countries has changed in recent years. Britain was the first country in Western Europe to introduce immigration control policies in the post-war period, while France managed immigration for many years through a liberal policy of encouraging illegal immigrants, some of whom were subsequently 'legalized'. Until recently Germany managed immigration through labour immigration programmes combined with restrictive nationality policies. Since the 1980s all three countries have made provisions for families to join migrant workers and have seen major debates about nationality and citizenship as migrants have started to settle.

In Britain the Immigration and Asylum Act 1999 regulates practices such as the conditions for the granting of visas, which apply to persons before they come to Britain; how they are dealt with at ports when arriving in Britain; and how they are dealt with once they are in the country. It increased the penalties for carrying clandestine entrants to Britain, increased carriers' liability for inadequately documented passengers, created powers for immigration officers to arrest, search and take fingerprints, and funded more liaison officers to limit the numbers of people travelling on forged papers.

Some 88.1 million passengers arrived in Britain in 2001, the majority of whom were British or EEA nationals not subject to immigration control. Citizens of the Republic of Ireland are generally able to travel freely within Britain. British citizens, and those Commonwealth citizens who also have the right of abode, are not subject to immigration control and may freely enter and leave Britain. All others are subject to immigration control and must obtain a visa prior to travel to Britain.

More than half of the 12.8 million non-EEA nationals were temporary visitors. In 2001, 339,000 short- and long-term students and 109,000 work permit holders were admitted, and both figures are increasing. Some 37,865 passengers were refused entry. Family reunification remains an important factor: 8,855 husbands and 17,860 wives were admitted for a probationary year prior to settlement in 2001, mainly from the Indian sub-continent, the Americas and Africa. The number of female fiancées admitted fell by 695 to 1,775 in 2001 but there was an increase in the number of children admitted for a probationary year with a parent from 1195 to 4015. After the preliminary year, spouses can be given permanent leave to remain provided that they can prove that the marriage is bona fide (usually letters such as bills for utilities such as gas or electricity addressed to the couple at their normal abode is sufficient proof) and they must be able to show that they have not had, and will not need to have, recourse to public funds.

The number of work permit holders and dependants admitted to Britain was 108,825 in 2001, an increase of 16,995 over 2000, while 51,415 extensions of stay as a work permit holder or trainee (excluding dependants) were granted. In 2001 10,635 Commonwealth citizens with a grandparent born in Britain were admitted for four years to take or seek employment, and a further 1575 were granted an extension of stay on this basis (Mallourides and Turner 2001).

Just as in Britain, entry to France generally depends on the possession of a valid visa, which has to be followed up by a request for a residence permit within three months following arrival. Procedures vary according to the three main categories of immigrants: citizens of the European Union, who have free access to France on production of identification; people from countries which have bilateral agreements with France, such as African countries which are ex-possessions of France; and foreigners from a 'general' regime.

These categories give rise to three main types of residence cards. These are issued either for one year (temporary residence for specific groups of people such as students, artists and professional people) or for a renewable ten years (residence card). There is also a permanent residence card for citizens of Germany, Britain, Denmark, Netherlands, Finland and Austria, which is granted on the first renewal of the ten year permit. The only other category eligible for this card are political refugees. Approximately 85 per cent of foreigners who are legally in France have a ten year card. These residence cards require proof that the person can support themselves and will not require state benefits. A third type of card is for temporary visitors who come to France for private and family reasons. This is available not only for the relatives of people with residence and temporary cards but also for people with territorial asylum (see below). Of the total number of residence cards (all categories) 666,780 were given to foreigners in 2001, 197,339 of these for the first time.

Entry into Germany is only freely permitted to Germans, EU citizens and non-EU citizens with a permanent residence permit in Germany. All other non-EU citizens require special permission to enter the country. There are currently four main channels of immigration. Controlled labour migration occurs under the auspices of bilateral contracts with countries of Central and Eastern Europe relating to temporary contract workers (especially for the construction sector) and seasonal workers (mainly in agriculture). The 'green card' introduced in 2002 was an effort to attract highly qualified specialists in information technology to the country. Under this programme the government will allow up to 20,000 specialists to enter the German labour market within a period of three years. The second channel, family unification, which is open to all spouses and children of immigrants under the age of 16 who have obtained a permanent residence permit, enabled more than 326,000 immigrants to enter Germany between 1990 and 2002. The third channel is the immigration of asylum seekers and ethnic Germans (see below). Finally, the German constitution grants automatic citizenship to people of German descent living in Eastern Europe who wish to migrate to Germany. Since 1993 the number of immigrants under these provisions has been limited to 103,000 per year, and now only ethnic Germans from the territories of the former Soviet Union are allowed to immigrate.

New measures have reduced the different types of permits to two: a temporary permit and a permanent residence permit. Conversion from one to the other is possible after five years subject to conditions, in particular contributions to the obligatory pension fund and the ability to speak German (SOPEMI 2002).

Nationality policy

Nationality policy defines the boundaries of full membership of a community through citizenship. In the past the relevant rights have been based on descendance rights (law of blood) or residence (law of the soil). Germany was seen as a classic example of the former and France of the latter, while Britain tended to be seen as a mix of the two. In recent years, however, there has been some convergence between these models.

In Britain there are three types of citizenships: British citizenship, for people closely connected with Britain, the Channel Islands and the Isle of Man; British Dependent Territories citizenship, for people connected with the British overseas territories; and British Overseas citizenship, for those citizens of Britain and Colonies without connections with either Britain or the British overseas territories. Applicants for British nationality by birth or descent are not required to renounce the citizenship which they already hold, in 'recognition of their affinity to the country of their roots' (HMSO 1998). Of 110,000 applications in 2001, 90,000 persons were granted British citizenship, 45 per cent on the basis of residence, 30 per cent on account of marriage, and nearly 25 per cent as minor children. These were high numbers in view of the introduction under the Nationality, Immigration and Asylum Act (2002) of an English language test together with powers to remove citizenship from a person who has done anything prejudicial to the vital interests of Britain.

The French approach to nationality is based on Republican ideology, which holds that all citizens are equal irrespective of their origins, so there is only one category of French citizen. People born and subsequently living in France have the right to apply for French citizenship once they reach the age of majority. Otherwise access to citizenship depends on a residence test: the person applying needs to have lived in France for five consecutive years at the time they apply. Acquisitions of French nationality increased from 35,988 in 1993 to 59,836 in 1999. Acquisitions of nationality through marriage rose from 15,246 in 1993 to 24,088 in 1999.

In 1991 and 2000 the German law on naturalisation was modified from an earlier position largely based on blood rights to a more mixed provision. Every child born in Germany automatically receives citizenship on condition that at least one parent has been living legally in the country for at least three years. There are also provisions for children to take the citizenship of their parents, but those with dual citizenship must opt for one between the ages of 18 to 23. Adults are eligible for naturalization provided they have lived in the country for at least eight years, accept German basic law, do not have a criminal record and have 'sufficient' knowledge of the German language. The naturalization of foreigners under these new provisions has increased since the beginning of the 1990s, and in 2000 more than 185,000 foreigners were naturalized, mostly from Turkey, Iran and the former republic of Yugoslavia.

One significant difference between the three countries is the right to participate in elections. While in France and Germany one has to be a citizen to have the right to vote or stand in Parliamentary or national elections, in Britain this right is also given to all residents who are citizens of the Commonwealth or the Republic of Ireland.

Asylum policy

The specific issue of asylum seekers began to be posed in the early 1980s as wars and conflict in many parts of the world produced a growing number of displaced people and European countries systematically closed their frontiers to economic migrants. Across Europe, asylum became an important issue with the Schengen agreement (1985) and convention (1990) and the Dublin agreement of June 1990. The latter introduced common European criteria for asylum cases, such as a 'white' list to designate certain countries as essentially safe. Each country has adjusted in different ways to European harmonisation, and now experience similar problems relating to delays in the granting of asylum, which has meant a growing number of destitute people and pressure on voluntary organisations who are expected to fill the service gap.

Recent legislation in Britain has focused on making Britain unattractive to asylum seekers compared with her near neighbour France. The 'Fairer, Faster, Firmer' scheme gave the Immigration and Nationality Directorate a target of ensuring that 60 per cent of new asylum applicants receive their initial decision within two months. The National Asylum Support Service, a department of the Home Office, was set up in 2000 to coordinate the dispersal of asylum seekers throughout the country. This department also funds the voluntary sector to provide emergency support services. Local authorities support unaccompanied children and new asylum seekers who have special needs. Since the legislation of 2002, asylum applicants have not been permitted to work or undertake vocational training until they are given a positive decision on their asylum application. While induction centres are being set up throughout the country to screen and prepare asylum seekers for their dispersal, more controversial 'removal' centres have been organized to detain applicants, including children. All economic support is now given either in kind (housing, utility bills) or in cash. It can be given in cash only if the recipient can arrange to stay with friends or relations. Otherwise they are given a 'support package' in a designated dispersal area. The cash given amounts to 70 per cent of basic income support for adults and 100 per cent for children under 18 years of age. There are other exceptional payments, such as clothing or maternity benefits, but these are well below the level given to people normally living in the country (IPPR 2003). Applicants who cannot prove that they applied for asylum as soon as reasonably practical on arrival in Britain are not eligible for support.

The numbers of people seeking asylum in France increased from 31,000 in 1999 to more than 47,000 in 2001. There are several coexisting statuses for asylum seekers in France: conventional asylum as provided for by the Geneva Convention, territorial asylum for a fixed period and dependent on administrative discretion, and constitutional asylum for people who are

Table 6.2 Asylum applications, 1987–2001

	Britain	France	Germany
1987	5 900	27 300	74 600
1992	32 300	31 800	569 600
1999	71 160	30 830	85 113
2000	76 040	38 747	78 564
2001	71 700	47 291	88 287

Source: Adapted from HMSO 1998; ECRE 2002 and UK Immigration Directorate 2003.

'defending liberty'. The major problems in France are connected with the growing numbers of destitute asylum seekers who are either awaiting a verdict on their case or have been refused but cannot be deported. Asylum seekers are not permitted to work, but are entitled to an 'integration allowance' of €9.41 (£7, $10.60) per day if they are not housed in a reception centre. There is a serious shortage of places in these centres: by the end of 2002 there was only room for 7,500 people, and the system was forced to use other emergency hostel places. This has given rise to destitution, and voluntary humanitarian organisations have stepped in to help asylum seekers meet their basic needs

Germany claims to have received more asylum seekers than any other country in the world – more than two million since 1990, peaking at over 569,600 in 1992, compared to 250,000 applications in all other European Union countries. The combination of these high numbers of applications, together with the exploit-ation of the issue by right wing extremists, led the two major political parties to attempt to reduce the number of asylum seekers and to reform key aspects of asylum law. Table 6.2, which sets out the recent history of asylum applications in our three countries, shows that the most recent figures for Germany are well down on the 1992 levels.

Germany distinguishes between different types of asylum seekers. Recognized victims of political persecution, who are entitled to asylum under Article 16a of the Basic Law, and refugees recognized under the terms of the Geneva Convention of 1951, are entitled to bring their family members to Germany with them. Quota refugees are accepted in the course of humanitarian aid campaigns and are entitled to stay in the country without having to apply for asylum, as are refugees from war or civil war. The largest group in Germany today are de facto refugees: those who have not applied for asylum or whose application has been refused. Their deportation is deferred because they face serious and real danger to their lives in their own country. There are also other categories of foreigners who hold a residence permit under the exceptional provisions of the Aliens and Stateless Persons Act.

Recent developments

The Nationality, Immigration and Asylum Act 2002, the fourth piece of legislation to modify the British asylum system in the last ten years, has put added emphasis on the control and removal of unsuccessful asylum applicants and has replaced the voucher system by a cash voucher system. In the past, asylum seekers had to buy essential food items at designated supermarkets with vouchers and could not keep any change from their purchases. However the government has ended the assumption that all destitute asylum applicants should receive support from the National Asylum Support Service. It also announced that asylum applications from certain 'safe countries', such as the ten EU accession countries, should be automatically certified as 'clearly unfounded'. This list can be extended as the Home Secretary sees fit.

In France the present government plans controversial new legislation which will extend the length of time foreigners can be placed in a detention centre from 12 to 30 days. It will also become more difficult to obtain proof of residence for entry permits of less than three months, and non-EU visitors will be required to furnish digital fingerprints to be stored electronically. Foreigners already living in the country with a temporary residence card will have to wait five years, rather than the three at present, before they can apply for a ten year residence card. Measures against 'fraudulent marriages' are being intensified, and for the spouse to obtain residence papers a couple must live together for two years rather than one.

In 2002 the German government proposed new legislation, based on economic arguments, to facilitate the immigration of trainees, students, self-employed people and highly skilled workers to Germany, while more strictly regulating other forms of immigration such as family reunification and the entry of asylum seekers and refugees, including making it easier to deport rejected asylum seekers. For the first time the law proposed that immigrants take courses in the German language and the structure of the political system, culture and society, with the aim of helping them integrate into society. Although this law was ruled unconstitutional, the debate is expected to continue.

Sources

Asylum Aid, <www.asylumaid.org.uk/AA%20pages/policy.htm> [February 2003].

Commission for Racial Equality, <www.cre.gov.uk/about/about.html> [February 2003].

Bundesamt für die Anerkennung ausländischer Flüchtlinge (Federal Office for the Reception of Foreign Refugees), <www.bafl.de> [September 2002].

Bundesministerium des Innern (Ministry of Interior), <www.bmi.bund.de> [September 2002].

U. Davy, Das neue Zuwanderungsrecht: Vom Ausländergesetz zum Aufenthaltsgesetz', *Zeitschrift für Ausländerrecht und Ausländerpolitik*, 5/6 (2002): 171–9.

ECRE (European Council on Refugees and Exiles), *Synthesis of the ECRE Country Reports for 2001*(ECRE, 2002), <www.ecre.org/publications/countryrpt01.shtml>

Einbuergerung (Naturalization) <www.einbuergerung.de> [September 2002].

The Federal Government's Commissioner for Foreigners' Issues, *Facts and Figures on the Situation of Foreigners in the Federal Republic of Germany*, 19th edn (Berlin 2000).

The Federal Government's Commissioner for Foreigners' Issues, *Migrationsbericht der Ausländerbeauftragten im Auftrag der Bundesregierung* (Bonn 2001).

The Federal Government's Commissioner for Foreigners' Issues, *Bericht der Beauftragten der Bundesregierung für Ausländerfragen über die Lage der Ausländer in der Bundesrepublik Deutschland* (Berlin and Bonn, August 2002).

T. Hammar (ed.), *European Immigration Policy: A Comparative Study* (London, New York: Cambridge University Press, 1985): 1–13.

HMSO, 'Fairer, Faster and Firmer – A Modern Approach to Immigration and Asylum' (London: HMSO Cm 4018, 1998), <www.archive.official-documents.co.uk/document/cm40/4018/> [April 2003].

Home Office code of practice for carriers, <www.ind.homeoffice.gov.uk/default.asp?PageId=95>

Integrationsbeauftragte (Integration Ombudsman), <www.integrationsbeauftragte.de> [September 2002].

IPPR, *Asylum in the UK: An IPPR Fact File* (London: IPPR, 2003).

E. Mallourides and G. Turner, *Control of Immigration: Statistics United Kingdom* (London: Home Office, 2001).

Ministere de l'interieur, <www.interieur.gouv.fr/> [April 2003].

Office des migrations internationales, <www.omi.social.fr/omi/> [April 2003].

SOPEMI, *Trends in International Migration* (Paris : SOPEMI, 2002).

UK Immigration Directorate, <www.ind.homeoffice.gov.uk/> [February 2003].

Part III
Economic Policy

7
Macroeconomic Policy

Wyn Grant, Francois Nectoux and Eckhard Wurzel

Introduction

Britain, France and Germany face different challenges in the area of macro-economic policy. France and Germany are now part of the Eurozone, curtailing the range of macroeconomic policies and tools that can be utilised at the national level. There is thus a significant transfer of decision-making authority away from the national level. Britain has not yet made a policy decision about whether to join the euro, but has in any case shifted decision-making in macro-economic policy away from politicians and towards the central bank. Germany faces two challenges that are distinctive from those of France. First, unlike Britain and France, it has a federal system of government. Secondly, it still has to deal with the problems of assimilating the new states (*Länder*) that formed part of the former Communist regime in eastern Germany.

The nature of macroeconomic policy

Macroeconomic policy is designed to influence the economy as a whole to achieve such objectives as stable growth, high levels of employment and low inflation. The main instruments used are fiscal policy concerned with taxation and spending, and monetary policy concerned with interest rates and currency exchange rates.

Monetary policy seeks to control the quantity of money in use or its rate of growth through money supply or the demand for money by using the instru-ment of variations in the prevailing interest rate. France and Germany are now subject to the decisions of the European Central Bank (ECB) about interest rates. This has involved the transfer to the EU of responsibility for most credit and exchange matters, especially Euro exchange rate policies and determin-ation of interest rates. In addition, the EU has implemented deregulatory and open market policies across sectors that were crucial to the implementation of traditional macroeconomic policies such as price controls and regulation of monetary and financial markets. This development has limited to a great extent the scope of the macroeconomic policy measures available to the French and German authorities.

Since 1997 monetary policy in Britain has been the responsibility of the Monetary Policy Committee of the Bank of England, which sets interest rates. The decision to move the control of such an important policy instrument from the Government to the central bank represented a fundamental change in the conduct of economic policy. It was intended to shelter interest rate decisions from short-term political pressures and hence to make them more credible in the markets.

Both the euro and the pound are floating currencies whose value responds to transactions on the foreign exchange markets. Governments still have a capacity to intervene on the markets by buying or selling currency to increase or reduce its value. Exchange rate policy is used less actively than it was in the past, but there is still a role for the management of currency values.

Fiscal policy is concerned with providing public infrastructure and goods and services. This might involve the use of government spending and taxation to affect the level and composition of aggregate demand in the economy. Another way to see it is in terms of the manipulation of the relationship between expenditure and receipts to achieve economic objectives. Thus, if the economy is growing too fast, taxes might be increased and government spending reduced.

Any discussion of fiscal policy in Germany has to take account of the country's federal structure. The Minister of Finance has overall responsibility for the conduct of fiscal policy, but within certain limits the federal government and the *Länder* are autonomous in their budgetary policies. This requires complex institutional arrangements to promote inter-governmental co-operation, co-ordination and revenue sharing. The federal government is in principle responsible for matters considered to be of relevance to the whole country, as well as for the redistribution of income across the federation. Major responsibilities at the *Länder* level comprise the university and education systems and the health service.

German fiscal policy attaches considerable importance to realizing broadly equal living conditions across the country. This is reflected in a high degree of co-operation and revenue sharing between the different levels of government. About three-quarters of overall tax revenues are split by formula between the federal government, the *Länder* and the communes (local government), the remainder going exclusively to a particular tier of government. In order to secure roughly equal conditions across the country there is a fiscal equalization system based on the principle of burden sharing. Thus, a financially weaker *Land* receives both vertical transfers from the federal government and horizontal transfers from financially stronger *Länder*. In the equalization system the financial endowment of each *Land* is compared with its financial needs.

Britain does not have fiscal federalism like Germany. The Treasury and its chief minister, the Chancellor of the Exchequer, has overall responsibility for fiscal policy. The way in which fiscal policy operates has been affected by the introduction of devolved government, especially in Scotland. Since 1978 public expenditure has been allocated between England, Wales, Scotland and Northern Ireland using the Barnett Formula devised by the then Chief Secretary to the Treasury. The formula was developed as a means of depoliticizing decisions about the territorial sharing out of public expenditure, given that Scotland, Wales and Northern Ireland have historically received more public spending per capita than England. The formula is based on population and the importance of particular programmes to the devolved administrations. Because of a diminishing population and the way in which the formula fractionally diminishes Scotland's share each time public spending is increased, per capita spending levels are converging. For example, the health spending gap has traditionally been 22 per cent, but is likely to shrink to 11 per cent by 2007.

The Scottish Executive can decide to levy an extra 3p in the pound on income tax, although it has promised not to use that power until after the 2003 elections. In the meantime, the Scottish Parliament has undertaken ambitious spending plans in areas for which it is responsible, for example providing free nursing care for elderly people and absorbing higher education tuition fees.

France has highly centralized mechanisms for making policy, with the Prime Minister made directly responsible for economic policies, according to the Constitution of the Fifth Republic, although the President of the Republic may intervene. Within the government it is the Minister for Economy and Finances who in practice shapes and implements macroeconomic policies. The Parliament plays a very limited role, as its powers have been severely curtailed by the Constitution.

Specific comparisons

In this section the two main components of macroeconomic policy in Britain, France and Germany – monetary policy and fiscal policy – are compared in more detail.

Monetary policy

Responsibility for monetary policy in Britain has been delegated to the central bank, the Bank of England. The government specifies the inflation target, which was set in 1997 at 2.5 per cent. If inflation deviates from that target by more than one per cent (upwards or downwards) the Governor of the Bank has to send an open letter to the Chancellor. This is required to explain why the undershoot or overshoot has happened, what it is proposed to do about it and how long the remedial action will take to have effect. The 1998 Bank of England

Act provides that if, in extreme circumstances, the national interest demands it, the Government will have power to give instructions to the Bank on interest rates for a limited period.

The Monetary Policy Committee (MPC) has nine members. The Governor (who has a casting vote) and the two Deputy Governors of the Bank serve five-year terms of office. The Governor appoints the two other Bank members after consultation with the Chancellor. In practice they are the Bank officials responsible for monetary policy analysis and monetary policy operations. The Chancellor appoints the four external members, initially for terms of three years. A representative of the Treasury is allowed to attend the meetings and to speak, but cannot vote. The principal function of this representative is to introduce any relevant fiscal or other economic policy considerations into the discussion.

The MPC meets monthly to decide whether interest rates should be lowered, increased or remain unchanged. Typically, the rate will be left unchanged. For example, rates remained unchanged between February 2000 and February 2001. When changes are made they are typically small.

Professional research staff are available to assist the MPC in its work. It is required to consider regional and sectoral issues and makes use of a network of 12 regional agents for this purpose. Before coming to a decision the MPC might review such factors as the state of the world economy; money, credit and asset prices; demand and output; the labour market; and prices and costs.

Inflation has been lower and more stable since the transfer of interest rate-setting powers to the Bank. This may, however, reflect a generally benign economic policy setting rather than the merits of the framework. Its real test would be in a period of greater instability.

Monetary policy in France and Germany is now primarily the responsibility of the ECB. The transfer of responsibility has led to considerable changes in the conduct of policy. Previously, France had pursued a policy of *Franc fort* or the strong Franc as the centrepiece of French economic policies. This consisted of sustaining the value of the Franc in relation to strong currencies, especially the Deutschmark. The aim of this policy was to force improvements in the competitiveness of French firms as well as to reduce prices of imported inputs. A consequence of this approach was a rigorous policy of interest rate pegging in comparison with Germany.

The conduct of German monetary policy was based around the independence of the Bundesbank. Like other central banks in countries that have adopted the euro it is now part of the 'Eurosystem' that has the ECB at its head.

The primary objective of the 'Eurosystem' is to promote price stability, with the target of keeping price rises below 2 per cent. The main tasks of this system of banks are to define and implement the monetary policy of the euro area, conduct foreign exchange operations, hold and manage the official foreign reserves of the member states, and promote the smooth operation of payment systems.

Table 7.1 Frequency of variations in interest rates

Year	Britain (Bank of England)	France and Germany (ECB)
1999	6	2
2000	2	6
2001	7	4
2002	1	1
2003	3	2
Totals	19	15

Sources: Bank of England 1999–2003; European Central Bank 2003.

A key body is the Executive Board, which is made up of the President, the Vice-President and four other bankers each of whom serves a term of eight years. The Executive Board is joined by the governors of each of the national central banks which adopted the euro to form the Governing Council. This body formulates the monetary policy of the euro area, including decisions about interest rates and the supply of reserves in the Eurosystem. The ECB has been criticized for failing to cut rates sufficiently quickly in response to changing economic conditions. However, when one compares the frequency of interest rate changes made by the Bank of England and the ECB there is not a great deal of difference (see Table 7.1).

Following Economic and Monetary Union and the adoption of the euro in 1999, interest rates remained broadly stable up to early 2000, at which point they started to increase, peaking at 4.75 per cent in the autumn of 2000. As economic growth slackened, they fell back to 2.5 per cent in early 2003 (see Figure 7.1).

Fiscal policy

Fiscal policy is the other main instrument of macroeconomic policy. The reforms that the 1997 Labour Government in Britain introduced in relation to monetary policy were complemented by reforms in the conduct and implementation of fiscal policy. Fiscal policy has become more rules based as a means of enhancing the credibility of policy, that is, ensuring that economic agents such as firms and households believe that government will deliver on its policy commitments. Fiscal policy is seen as contributing to the Government's wider objectives of providing high quality public services and financial assistance to those in need. However, these goals must be pursued in a way that is consistent with the overall objective of economic stability. Emphasis is thus placed on ensuring sound public finances and that spending and taxation should impact fairly both within and across generations. Policy priorities must be met without a rise in the burden of public debt. Current generations should meet the cost of the services they consume.

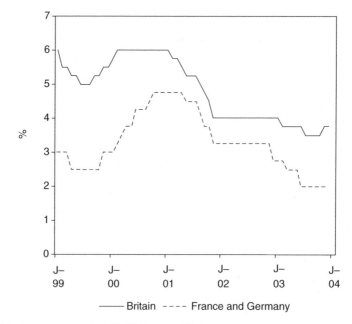

Figure 7.1 Interest rates since EMU January 1999
Source: Bank of England 1999–2003; ECB 2003 (refinancing rate).

Fiscal policy has been made more rules-based by establishing a Code of Fiscal Stability. This code is seen as embodying five key principles: transparency, stability, responsibility, fairness and efficiency. One of its requirements is the publication of a Pre-Budget Report. This is normally done in the autumn, but it can be argued that it has diminished the significance of the spring Budget.

Two key fiscal rules have been specified by the Government:

1. The golden rule. Over the economic cycle, the Government will borrow only to invest and not to fund current spending.
2. The sustainable investment rule. Over the economic cycle, public debt as a proportion of GDP will be held at a stable and prudent level. The Government's view is that net public debt should be reduced to below 40 per cent of GDP.

OECD estimates suggest that Britain's cyclically adjusted fiscal balance has improved substantially since the 1990s. A deficit of 5.5 per cent of GDP in 1994 moved to a 1.5 per cent surplus in 2000, although there is a deterioration thereafter. During this period, government expenditure as a percentage of GDP fell back, although by the millennium it was growing again.

Fiscal stabilization policy in Germany is confined to accepting the operation of the 'automatic stabilizers'. These denote spending and revenue items that 'automatically' fluctuate counter-cyclically with the business cycle, thereby dampening the temporal swings in macroeconomic activity. For example, tax receipts from private households and enterprises decline and unemployment related social transfers increase in periods of weak economic activity, stabilizing incomes and increasing demand. OECD estimates suggest that automatic stabilizers have a larger impact in smoothing the business cycle than in several other OECD countries. In contrast, discretionary variation in public sector spending or taxation for the purpose of influencing the business cycle has not played any significant role in German fiscal policy for more than twenty years.

The current fiscal policy agenda is increasingly being shaped by action to reduce the deficit and debt levels of all layers of government and the social security system. Under the Maastricht treaty, to avoid excessive deficits of the EU the government is obliged to keep the general government deficit below three per cent of GDP and to balance the general government budget in the medium term. However there have been growing expenditure and deficit levels over most of the 1990s. The boost in public sector spending, notably in terms of transfers associated with reunification, large inflows into early retirement, a secular trend to increase health care and social spending and persistently high unemployment rates were all major factors putting fiscal balances under stress. The substantial ageing of the German population implies further pressure in the medium term from both the spending side, in terms of higher outlays for pensions, health care services and long-term care, and the revenue side, via a shrinking tax base.

Policies to secure the sustainability of government finances are being taken on both the spending and the revenue sides of the budget. In particular, employment in the government sector is being continuously reduced. All layers of government are also cutting down their outlays for investment. On the revenue side, various indirect taxes and social security charges are being increased. These measures have not yet sufficed, however, to relieve government finances in a sustainable way, given the continuing spending pressure in other fields and recent income tax reductions. Indeed the 'structural' general government deficit as measured by the OECD, which adjusts the fiscal balance for the cyclical impact of the business cycle, has drifted above the level prevailing in the mid 1990s.

To strengthen fiscal consolidation policies, all layers of government have agreed on annual spending targets. For 2003 and 2004 the *Länder* agreed to limiting expenditure growth to one per cent annually, while the Federal government agreed to reduce expenditures by 0.5 per cent.

In France, the Eurozone's Stability and Growth Pact (which has more to do with stability than growth due to its emphasis on budgetary rigour) has also changed the nature of the macroeconomic policy framework by the restrictions it imposes on the scope for counter cyclical macroeconomic policies through budgetary and fiscal strategies, although France experienced increasing difficulty in adhering to its requirements in 2003. Eventually, in conjunction with Germany, it secured the removal of the sanctions element of the Pact.

In any case, the tradition of using budget deficits for reflation and the smoothing of economic cycles was abandoned in France in the early 1980s. This was not a straightforward process, however, because of the size of the public sector in France and the continuing problems of funding social security and pensions. As a result much public expenditure is 'incompressible', whereas receipts follow downturns of the economy. A reduction of fiscal pressure has been a more recent policy objective. The left of centre Jospin government implemented a reduction of income tax for lower earners, as well as a lowering of VAT from 1999. This policy has been pursued with renewed vigour by the right of centre Raffarin government from 2002.

Despite a shift towards a more liberal approach to macroeconomic policy, abandon completely opportunities for economic cycle control, in particular through the use of one of the few tools still available to national government, fiscal policy. Indeed the government appears quite ready to consider a reflationary policy consisting of a reduction of taxes accompanied by a stable level of public expenditure at a time when receipts are stagnating, similar to recipes used by the Reagan and Bush governments in the US, and the conservative government did not hesitate in the autumn of 2002 to refuse to acknowledge the warning of the European Commission about the risk of allowing a French budget deficit higher than that authorised by the Stability Pact.

Looking at the three countries comparatively, it is not surprising that France has higher levels of taxation, government expenditure, net lending and central government debt as percentages of GDP than either Britain or Germany (see Table 7.2). General government expenditure is more similar in France and Germany, although the British figure moved upwards after 2001. British net lending figures are also lower. When it comes to the composition of public expenditure, France is the biggest spender as a proportion of GDP on public education, and Germany on health.

Recent developments

Establishment of the euro as a single currency proved less difficult than many had forecast, although there have been complaints about upward inflationary pressures, particularly for small everyday items. As the dollar weakened, the

Table 7.2 Taxation, expenditure and debt as a % of GDP, 2000

	Britain	France	Germany
Total tax receipts	37.4	45.3	37.9
Current government expenditure	37.7	47.5	44.5
Central government debt (marketable plus non-marketable)	44.8	48.2	34.7
Net government borrowing	–2.0	1.2	0.1
Expenditure on public education	4.7	5.9	4.4
Public expenditure on health	5.7	7.1	7.8

Sources: OECD 2002a, b.

euro increased in value and achieved parity with the dollar. Nevertheless, the economic strength of the eurozone, and particularly its flexibility in response to economic shocks and challenges, has remained open to question. Growth rates in continental Europe have remained relatively low.

All three countries are under pressure from the EU to keep levels of debt and budget deficits under control. The EU controls monetary policy, but only has influence over fiscal policy in France and Germany, a situation that is likely to lead to recurrent tensions. It seems unlikely that Britain will adopt the euro in the immediate feature, meaning that its conduct of macroeconomic policy will continue to be distinctive. British membership of the euro would one of the most fundamental changes that could occur in relation to the arrangements and policies discussed here.

Sources

E. Aeschimann and P. Riché, *La Guerre de sept ans: histoire secrète du franc fort* (Paris: Calmann-Lévy, 1996).

E. Balls and G. O'Donnell, *Reforming Britain's Economic and Financial Policy: Towards Greater Economic Stability* (Basingstoke: Palgrave Macmillan for HM Treasury, 2002).

Bank of England (1999–2003), 'Monetary Policy Committee decisions', <www.bankofengland.co.uk/mpc/decisions.htm> [15 May 2003].

ECB (European Central Bank), (2003), 'Key ECB Interest Rates', <www.ecb.int/home/ecbinterestrates.htm> [15 May 2003].

W. Grant, *Economic Policy in Britain* (Basingstoke: Palgrave Macmillan, 2002).

D. Lipsey, *The Secret Treasury: How Britain's Economy Is Really Run* (London: Viking, 2000).

OECD (Organisation for Economic Cooperation and Development), <www.oecd.org>

OECD (Organisation for Economic Cooperation and Development), 'Basic Structural Statistics', *Main Economic Indicators* (Paris: OECD, 2002a).

OECD (Organisation for Economic Cooperation and Development), *The OECD in Figures* (Paris: OECD, 2002b).

Treasury (Britain),

E. Wurzel, *Towards More Efficient Government: Reforming Federal Fiscal Policy in Germany* (Paris: OECD Economics Department Working Paper 209, 1999), <www.oecd.org/pdf/ M00001000/M00001486.pdf>

E. Wurzel, *The Economic Integration of Germany's New Länder* (Paris: OECD Economics Department Working Paper 307, 2001), <www.oecd.org/pdf/M00017000/ M00017197.pdf>

8
Taxation

Jeremy Leaman, David Berry and Carl Emmerson

Introduction

There are few other policy areas that have the public resonance of taxation policy, as tax is central to government and to popular perceptions of policy success. Governments in the representative capitalist democracies of Europe are predominantly judged by their ability to maintain stable growth in levels of individual and collective consumption. The deployment of tax revenues and the use of tax incentives are long acknowledged vehicles for maintaining that growth.

Under the relatively stable conditions of the long post-war boom, different tax cultures in Britain, France and Germany operated effectively and with a minimum of social conflict, while taxation in earlier and subsequent periods was the source of strife between different social groups concerning the distribution of tax burdens and benefits. The repoliticization of taxation policy in the last quarter of the 20th century took varied forms, including the costly spat over the Poll Tax in Britain and the wave of neo-liberal reforms to national tax systems across the OECD.

The nature of taxation policy

Taxation can be defined as a financial contribution levied by one or more levels of government within a given territory on individuals or companies/organizations in order to fund the expenditure of government bodies. There is a wide variety of taxes in the countries compared here, but most state revenue is derived from the core of tax types listed in Table 8.1.

The administration of the major sources of taxation is centralized in the form of the Inland Revenue under the auspices of the Exchequer in Britain, and *Les administrations fiscales/trésors publics* under the control of the *Ministère de l'Économie, des Finances et de l'Industrie* (Ministry of the Economy, Finance

89

Table 8.1   Categories of taxation

Type of tax	Description
Income tax *(Einkommenssteuer, Impôt sur le revenu)*	Tax levied on individuals for earned income from work or 'unearned' income from savings and investments. Income tax generally operates on the basis of a 'curve of progression', where higher earners pay a higher percentage of their taxable income than lower earners.
– Pay-as-you-earn Income Tax *(Lohnsteuer)*	Tax levied weekly or monthly at source by employer on employees and transferred to relevant tax authorities (Britain and Germany only).
– Assessed income tax *(Veranlagte Einkommenssteuer, Impôt sur le revenu)*	Tax levied retrospectively by tax authorities on individuals or non-incorporated companies on the basis of annual returns by the individual taxpayer; this applies to all payers of income tax in France, but only to the self-employed, non-incorporated firms and employees with additional income in Britain and Germany.
Social security contributions	Statutory payments levied at source by one or more social insurance funds to cover risks to employees and their families such as unemployment, sickness, disability and debility in old age.
Corporation tax *(Körperschaftssteuer, Impôt sur les societés)*	Tax paid retrospectively (normally) on the profit income of incorporated firms after subtraction of allowances.
Value Added Tax *(Mehrwertsteuer, Taxe sur la valeur ajoutée)*	Tax paid on most products and services at each stage of their production and exchange according to the value added at that stage.
Capital Gains Tax *(Kapitalertragssteuer, Impôt sur les revenus des capitaux)*	Tax on the increased value of a capital asset (property or paper).
Excise duties	Purchase tax levies on specific products and services such as alcohol, tobacco and petroleum products.
Withholding tax *(Quellensteuer, retenue à source)*	Tax levied at source on financial holdings such as bank savings accounts.

and Industry) in France. Both systems involve a national network of regional and local branches. Revenue from all major direct and indirect taxes is collected centrally and apportioned either according to centrally defined and variable criteria (Britain) or to legally fixed but indexed distribution ratios (France).

Table 8.2 Taxation by level of government, % of total tax revenue, 2000

	Britain	*France*	*Germany*
Supranational (EU)	1.3	1.1	0.0
National	78.2	42.4	30.8
State	–	–	22.5
Local	4.0	9.6	7.5
Social security funds	15.5	46.9	39.2
Total	100	100	100

Sources: OECD 2002; Table E.

In Germany, only customs and excise duties on specific goods and services, such as mineral oil, tobacco, spirits, insurance and electricity, are levied centrally. Otherwise the administration of all taxes is conducted at regional (*Land*) level. Joint taxes (income tax, corporation tax and turnover tax or VAT) are collected by the Finance Offices within the regional Finance Ministries, along with the exclusive taxes of the *Länder* such as property tax, inheritance tax, motor-vehicle tax, beer tax, gaming taxes and other 'bagatelle taxes'.

Another difference between the three countries is that social security funds are relatively more important in France and Germany than in Britain.

In consequence, the relative tax revenue received by each level of government differs markedly, with central government being most dominant in Britain and least dominant in Germany (Table 8.2).

Table 8.3 lists the main national and subnational institutions involved in the making and implementing of taxation policy, along with the most prominent consultative bodies.

Specific comparisons

Four especially salient aspects of taxation policy are overall levels of tax revenue, the relative importance of different types of tax in revenue-raising, tax rates, and the use of income tax not only for revenue-raising but also for other economic and social purposes.

Levels of taxation

Aggregate levels of taxation as a percentage of GDP are significantly higher in France than in Britain or Germany (see Table 8.4). When non-tax income such as net revenues from public corporations, fees and charges, voluntary social security contributions and the pension contributions of public sector workers are taken into account, total government revenue exceeds 50 per cent of GDP

Table 8.3 Taxation policy-making and administration

	Britain	France	Germany
National	Parliament (House of Commons and the HM Treasury Select Committee) HM Treasury – Inland Revenue – Customs and Excise	National Assembly (Standing Committees) National Ministry of the Economy, Finance and Industry – *Administrations fiscales* – *Les trésors publics*	Federal Parliament (*Bundestag* and *Bundesrat*, Standing Committee) Federal Finance Ministry – Federal Monopolies (Customs and Excise) Federal Constitutional Court
Subnational	Scottish Parliament Local councils	Regions *Départements* Local councils	*Land* Assemblies (Standing Committees) *Land* Ministries of Finance (Finance Offices)
Consultative bodies	No formal bodies, but many groups contribute to debate	*Conseil Économique et Social*	Academic Advisory Committee to the Finance Ministry Council of Economic Experts 'Social Partners': employer and union umbrella organizations Federation of German Taxpayers

Table 8.4 General government receipts and outlays as a % of GDP, 2002

	Britain	*France*	*Germany*
Total tax and non-tax receipts	39.6	50.9	45.0
Total Government outlays	40.9	54.0	48.6

Sources: OECD 2003. For more details see International Monetary Fund's (IMF) *Government Finance Statistics Yearbook*. The term 'general government' refers to all levels of government taken together.

Table 8.5 Individual taxes as a % of total tax revenue, 1999

	Britain	*France*	*Germany*
Personal income tax	28.8	17.6	25.1
Corporate income tax	10.4	6.4	4.8
Social security contributions: employees	7.3	8.8	17.3
Social security contributions: employers	9.7	25.0	19.3
Taxes on goods and services	32.3	26.8	28.0
Other taxes	11.5	15.4	5.5
Total	100	100	100

Source: OECD 2001.

in France but is significantly lower in Britain, with Germany in the middle. Total government outlays vary accordingly, being highest in France and lowest in Britain. This has clear implications for the relative level and quality of public services in the three countries.

Composition of tax revenue

There are also considerable differences in the composition of tax revenues (Table 8.5). France derives a much lower proportion of its revenues from personal income tax than either Britain or Germany, although this is now rising. Germany derives a small and falling proportion of its revenues from corporation tax, while Britain is significantly more dependent on indirect taxes than its neighbours. Britain derives a much lower proportion of its revenues from social security contributions than France or Germany because the British 'Beveridge' system with its flat-rate benefits is much cheaper than the 'Bismarckian' systems used in France and Germany with their earnings-related benefits.

Tax rates

Table 8.6 shows a number of indicative tax rates. This reveals that although in 2003 the highest marginal rate of income tax was significantly lower in Britain than in France or Germany, the British system takes more from single people

Table 8.6 Indicative tax rates (%)

	Britain	France	Germany
Highest rate of personal income tax, 2003	40.0	52.75	48.5
Average income tax rates of a single person on average production wage, 2002	15.7	13.3	20.5
Main rate of corporate income tax, 2003	30.0	33.33	26.5
Average employee social security contribution rate of single person on average production wage, 2002	7.7	13.3	20.7

Sources: Highest rate of income tax: Inland Revenue 2003; Direction Generale Des Impôts 2002; German Embassy 2003; average income tax rates and social security rates: OECD 2003; main rate of corporate income tax: KPMG 2003.

on average wages than does the French system. This illustrates the fact that tax rates are not necessarily closely related to the importance of these taxes in overall tax revenues. This is because the overall tax yield depends not only on the rate of tax paid but also on the size of the overall tax base to which the tax applies. Revenue raised is also affected by incentives for individuals to change behaviour as a result of marginal tax rates. Reforms in Britain and more recently in Germany and France have reduced marginal tax rates while expanding the overall tax base. In Britain the main marginal income tax rates have not been increased for a quarter of a century but several reforms have increased the size of the overall tax base, for example the removal of dividend tax credits on pension funds and the abolition of tax relief for mortgage interest payments.

Although for a number of years corporate tax rates were lowest in Britain, recent reforms in France and Germany have drastically cut corporation tax rates – in the case of Germany to below the British rate.

Table 8.6 also reveals that social security contributions for single people on average wages are highest in Germany and lowest in Britain.

Non-revenue uses of income tax

As well as using income tax to obtain revenue, there is evidence in all three countries of attempts to use income tax instruments as levers to achieve other social and economic policy objectives. These include reintegration into the labour market (Working Tax Credits in Britain), and reconciliation of work and family formation (increased tax allowances for families with children in France and Germany, and Child Tax Credits in Britain). Tax allowances and grants are used to help reduce child poverty (Child Tax Credits in Britain), encourage top-up pensions (Britain, France, Germany) and facilitate investment by small business (Britain, France, Germany).

The effectiveness of such incentives seems to vary considerably. The greatest success has arguably been achieved in reducing child poverty in Britain with targeted measures of redistribution. In contrast, the tax allowances provided to encourage top-up pensions in all three countries have been disappointingly ineffective, most surprisingly in Britain where statutory pension benefits are considerably lower than in the other two countries and where additional coverage by supplementary pensions is more obviously needed.

In the medium term, tax incentives to stimulate self-help in relation to social security will tend to reduce burdens on employers and on the state and increase those on individual wage- and salary-earners. The reduction of the share of wages and salaries in national income over the last 20 years throughout the OECD, and including the three countries in this comparison, arguably confirms that economic policy makers are deliberately reducing taxation on business as a means of stimulating profits, investment and employment. However while foreign direct investment has been clearly influenced by levels of tax relief, the overall investment ratio has, if anything, continued to decline in all countries providing such relief: the virtuous loop – tax relief, higher profits, higher investment, higher employment – has so far proved unobtainable.

Recent developments

The three countries in this study manifest significant differences in their tax cultures, even though over time there has been clear convergence in the patterns of taxation. B. Guy Peters (1991: 67 ff), using four clusters of countries with similar patterns of taxation, notes a shift towards 'broad-based taxation' where 'the countries of the OECD are becoming much more alike in tax policies than they have been', so that the disproportionate reliance on one source of taxation has given way to the use of most forms as a 'means of reducing the visibility of taxation in an era of tax revolts'.

It is also the case that the policy process in all three countries is increasingly constrained by the effects of international tax competition and the new mobility of capital. Direct investment flows have been strongly influenced by percep-tions of the advantages of benign tax regimes in destination locations.

While the structure of the tax system in Britain has seen few fundamental changes, there were several important qualitative/ideological shifts in taxation policy between 1979 and 1990 aimed at reducing marginal tax rates, expanding the tax base by reducing allowances, and shifting the balance from direct to indirect forms of taxation. However while the first two aims have been success-fully implemented, there has been no marked shift towards indirect taxation, despite the doubling of VAT to 17.5 per cent, because yields from other taxes on consumption have fallen in relative terms. Recent years have seen changes to the taxation of income from different assets, which have reduced or removed unwelcome distortions such as the preferential tax treatment of housing. However the frequent reforms to capital gains tax are expected to considerably reduce future revenues. In addition, the policy of large real year on year increases in the tax rates on fuel and tobacco, which were in place from 1993 to 1999, now seem to have been abandoned. The success of the new traffic congestion charge in London may be an important factor as to whether this replaces the petrol duty as the Government's main instrument aimed at reducing pollution caused by cars.

Changes in the French taxation system since the beginning of the 1980s have been less fundamental than in either Britain or Germany. There has been little rationalization of the notorious complexity of both income tax and property taxation. With an historically higher dependence on indirect taxes, there has been less scope for tapping consumption taxes and a greater proclivity to maintain the complex set of taxes and levies on French businesses. In both qualitative and quantitative terms the French system offers greater ground for complaint than either the British or the German system, the latter being much more generous towards enterprises than the campaigns of German employers would have us believe: German corporate tax burdens, even before the latest reforms, were in the middle ground of OECD countries (Bach *et al.* 2002).

A factor unique to Germany has been the significant constraints on tax policy deriving from the massive fiscal burden of German unification in 1990, as this created a need to deploy around 4 per cent of total GDP on fiscal transfers to the East, which in turn led to the imposition of hefty surcharges on income tax in the 1990s (initially 7.5 per cent, reduced later to 5 per cent). The introduction of an 'eco-tax' on electricity by the Red-Green coalition in Germany has given new impetus to Europe-wide environmental levies, although it has also aroused stiff opposition from the business community on the grounds that it creates cost disadvantages for Germany as a location for investment. The use of the eco-tax (*ökosteuer*) to reduce contribution rates to the statutory pension funds, rather than to finance environmental initiatives, matches the ambiguity of British fuel taxation policy, which claims association with the international Climate Change Levy but, like its German counterpart, would seem to be more strongly driven by its general potential for generating revenue.

On a broader scale the advent of European Monetary Union in 1999 has generated an increasingly fierce debate about the fiscal commitments of the 1997 Stability and Growth Pact, which are aimed at eliminating the structural dependence of member states on debt. The Pact has implications for both the expenditure side of state budgets, encouraging in part severe reductions in state spending, and for the revenue side, discouraging borrowing and implicitly encouraging the imposition of tax levels which ensure the full funding of expenditure.

The political asymmetry of European Monetary Union without political union has generated an intense debate about the need (or otherwise) for a harmonization of tax systems and major tax rates within Member States. With Germany ostensibly the victim of taxation competition and of capital flight – in particular to Luxembourg, Ireland and Britain – both the Schröder and the earlier Kohl administrations expressed a preference for greater convergence of both key rates of taxation and the bases upon which taxes are assessed (thresholds, allowances etc.). However the establishment of EU-wide programmes of tax harmonization requires unanimous approval by Member States, so proposals to introduce harmonized rates of VAT, corporation tax or fuel taxes, or to establish a common bank withholding tax or a tax on aircraft fuel, run little risk of immediate realization. Although there have been several EU initiatives in the direction of the harmonization of VAT and excise duties, as part of the programme to complete the 'internal market', the only notable agreement has been on the exchange of information in relation to income from financial assets (Bach *et al.* 2002). Resistance to profound tax harmonization is particularly strong in Britain, even under Labour, because of its dependence on capital imports to offset the effects of a persistent balance of payments deficit.

With the recent reduction of German corporation tax to below the British rate, and increasing evidence of negligible corporation tax burdens on major German companies, international competition in the field of income taxation continues its potentially destructive path. On the other hand, in the face of the ongoing unpredictability of global capital markets and the fickleness of financial investments, the idea of a 'Tobin Tax' on short-term international capital transactions has had some resonance within political and academic circles in Europe.

References

S. Adam and C. Frayne, 'A survey of the UK tax system', *Briefing Note* No. 9 (London: Institute for Fiscal Studies, 2001), <www.ifs.org.uk/taxsystem/taxsurvey.pdf> [27 August 2003].

Stefan Bach, Bernhard Seidel and Dieter Teichmann, 'Entwicklung der Steuersysteme im internationalen Vergleich', *DIW-Wochenbericht* 40 (2002).

T. Clark and A. Dilnot, 'Long-term trends in British taxation and spending', *Briefing Note* 25 (London: Institute for Fiscal Studies, 2001), <www.ifs.org.uk/public/bn25.pdf> [27 August 2003].

A. Dilnot, C. Emmerson and H. Simpson, 'The IFS Green Budget: January 2001', *Commentary* No. 83 (London: Institute for Fiscal Studies, 2001), <www.ifs.org.uk/gbfiles/gb2001.shtml> [August 2003].

Direction Generale Des Impôts (2002), *French Taxation*, <www.impots.gouv.fr/deploiement/p1/fichedescriptive_1006/fich> [21 August 2003].

C. Emmerson and C. Frayne, 'Overall tax and spending', in T. Clark and A. Dilnot (eds), *Election Briefing 2001*, Commentary No. 84 (London: Institute for Fiscal Studies, 2001), <www.ifs.org.uk/election/index.shtml> [27 August 2003].

J. Fender and P.A. Watt, 'Should central government seek to control the level of local authority expenditures?', *Fiscal Studies* 23(2), June 2002.

German Embassy Economics Department (2003), *Taxation Fact Sheet 2003* (based on information from German Finance Ministry).

Inland Revenue (2003), 'Rates and allowances', <www.inlandrevenue.gov.uk/rates/> [21 August 2003].

Institute for Fiscal Studies, <www.ifs.org.uk/election/index.shtml> [27 August 2003].

IMF (International Monetary Fund), *Government Finance Statistics Yearbook 2003*, vol. 27 (Washington, DC: IMF, 2003).

European Commission, *Tax Policy in the European Union* (Luxembourg, 2000).

Isabelle Journard, 'Tax systems in European countries', *OECD Economic Studies* 34, 2002/1.

KPMG (2003), *KPMG's Corporate Tax Rate Survey – January 2003*, <www.kpmg.lu/download/surveys/cts2003.pdf > [21 August 2003].

OECD (Organization for Economic Cooperation and Development) (2001), 'Tax and the economy: a comparative assessment of OECD countries', *OECD Tax Policy Studies* 6.

OECD (Organization for Economic Cooperation and Development), *Revenue Statistics 1965–2001* (Paris: OECD, 2002), <www.sourceoecd> [10 September 2003].

OECD (Organization for Economic Cooperation and Development), *Economic Outlook* 73, June (Paris: OECD, 2003), <www.sourceoecd> [10 September 2003].

B. Guy Peters, *The Politics of Taxation. A Comparative Perspective* (Oxford, 1991).

SourceOECD (2003), *Taxing Wages Database*, <oecdnt.ingenta.com/OECD/eng/Table Viewer/wdsview/print.asp> [21 August 2003].

9
Competition

Ian Bartle

Introduction

The purpose of competition policy is to promote and protect competition in the economy and thus to enhance economic efficiency and consumer welfare. In the late twentieth century competition policy became increasingly salient, reflecting a dominant view that competition is an essential requirement for innovation, economic growth and prosperity. Competition policy is necessary because the economists' concept of 'perfect competition' is not encountered in the real world and firms often behave in ways which are harmful to competition.

One of the most striking features of competition policy in the 1980s and 1990s is cross-national convergence (Dumez and Jeunemaitre 1996). There is increasing salience of competition in economic policy, delegation of administration to independent agencies, and increasingly stringent processes of enforcement (Wilks with Bartle 2002). The decline of nationally based interventionist industrial policies and their replacement with a pervasive belief in competition and the free market is a significant factor in this convergence.

Competition policy in Britain, France and Germany is increasingly influenced by the EU and the competition directorate of the European Commission (Cini and McGowan 1998). The EU not only has authority over many aspects of competition policy but also has another type of competition policy, the control of state aids, which impacts directly on the governments of Britain, France and Germany.

The nature of competition policy

There are three main areas of competition policy. First, restrictive practices policy regulates and mostly prohibits anti-competitive agreements, or cartels, between firms which are detrimental to competition (Cini and McGowan 1998: 5).

These agreements can be formal or informal, written or unwritten and can involve setting of prices above the market level and/or market sharing, in which each firm acts as a monopolist in its part of the market. Agreements can involve firms producing similar products (horizontal agreements) or firms in different stages of the production process (vertical agreements).

Secondly, monopoly policy regulates and mostly prohibits the use of a dominant position by a firm to restrict competition. This can occur when one firm dominates the market or in an oligopoly where a very small number of firms dominate. Monopoly and oligopoly market structures are a pole apart from the idea of perfect competition and can allow firms to abuse their dominant position. The abuse can involve behaviour such as cutting prices below their market level to force out competitors (predatory pricing), or pricing or other behaviour to prevent new firms entering the market. Abuse of a dominant position might also involve charging high prices to consumers who have little other choice. A dominant position means that a firm is not subject to competition or is in a strong market position, which can mean that smaller firms are economically dependent on it. A dominant position can also result from an oligopoly, in which a small number of firms dominate the market and there is little competition between them.

Thirdly, merger policy regulates and mostly prohibits mergers, acquisitions and joint ventures that increase the concentration of a market sector to an extent harmful to competition. Merger includes the fusion of two companies into one whether by mutual agreement between the firms or by a takeover by one firm against the wishes of the other, as well as joint ventures in which two or more firms agree to work together. Mergers can have a negative impact on competition by increasing the level of concentration in an economic sector possibly leading to oligopoly or monopoly. Mergers, however, do not necessarily have a negative impact on economic performance, as they can involve the transfer of firms to more efficient management. Efficiencies can also develop from economies of scale (in which specialisation leads to the reduction of unit costs of output) and from the pooling of resources for research and development. Merger policy is therefore subject to more economic and political judgement than restrictive practices and monopoly policy.

In each country a government ministry has overall responsibility for competition policy: the Department of Trade and Industry (DTI) in Britain; the *Ministère de l'Economie, des Finances et de l'Industrie* (Ministry of the Economy, Finance and Industry) in France; and the *Bundesministerium für Wirtschaft und Arbeit* (Federal Ministry of Economics and Labour) in Germany.

There has been a distinctive tendency across Europe and elsewhere for governments to delegate the operation of competition policy to independent agencies. The roles, responsibilities, powers and levels of independence of the competition agencies vary significantly.

In Britain the Office of Fair Trading (OFT) is the institution which initiates the competition policy process, investigates markets and enforces competition law (DTI 2002e). It initiates the competition policy process by considering whether an agreement, abuse of dominant position, or merger qualifies for examination, and can carry out an examination itself or advise the Secretary of State for Trade and Industry to refer the case to the Competition Commission for examination. OFT has the power to impose fines of up to 10 per cent of a firm's British turnover. The Competition Commission investigates and reports on cases referred to it by the Secretary of State or OFT. There is an independent Competition Appeal Tribunal in which appeals by parties affected by decisions taken by the OFT can be heard (OFT 2003).

In France the *Conseil de la Concurrence* (Competition Council) has an advisory capacity and legal powers in all economic sectors (CdelaC 2002). It can have cases referred to it by the government, parliament, trade organisations, firms and industry regulators, although the minister only refers merger cases (Souam 1998: 223). It can receive requests for opinions on any competition matter. As well as the power of investigation, the Competition Council also has the power to make legal judgements. Within the council there is a clear separation of investigation and judgement. The head of investigation (*rapporteur generaux*) has full responsibility for investigation while not taking part in the final judgement, which is the responsibility of the Chair of the Council. The penalties for breaching competition law are 10 per cent of annual turnover.

In Germany the *Bundeskartellamt* (Federal Cartel Office) is responsible for investigating and enforcing the law on cartels, mergers and abusive practices (BKA 2002). For breaches of competition law the *Bundeskartellamt* may impose fines of up to €500 000 (£368 000, $562 500) or three times the proceeds obtained from the infringement. The federal office is responsible for all merger control in Germany, but it is only responsible for enforcing bans on cartels and abusive practices if the effect on competition extends beyond one regional state (*Land*). Each of the *Länder* has its own cartel office which is responsible for cartel and monopoly policy in its *Land*. At federal level there is also the *Monopolkommission* (Monopoly Commission) which, in an advisory capacity and initiated either by itself or by the Economics Minister, monitors concentration in industry and investigates special merger cases (Sturm 1996).

Specific comparisons

Clear cross-national convergence is apparent in many of the key aspects of competition policy. However it should be noted that much competition policy and law is steeped in complex and arcane legal and economic technicalities and decision-making is subject to economic and political judgement, all of which can vary substantially.

Restrictive practices policy

The basic approach to anti-competitive agreements in Britain, France and Germany is one of prohibition: all agreements covered by the policy and not subject to exemptions are deemed to be illegal.

In all three countries the definition of an agreement is quite wide. As well as legal and formal agreements it includes informal agreements (so called 'gentleman's agreements') even when the consensus is based only on an oral agreement such as a telephone call.

The types of agreement considered for prohibition are similar in all three countries and include price fixing and the fixing of other trading conditions; exchanging of price information; limiting production, markets, technical development and investment; sharing markets or supply sources; applying different conditions to equivalent transactions with other parties; and impeding market access. Agreements considered for prohibition are generally those between competing firms (horizontal agreements). In Britain and Germany, with the exception of most cases of price fixing and retail price maintenance, there is not a general prohibition on vertical agreements. In France, vertical agreements deemed to be anti-competitive are subject to prohibition.

In all three countries agreements are generally prohibited when their object or effect is judged by the competition authorities to be detrimental to competition. In Britain an agreement is seen not to have an appreciable effect on competition if the combined market share of the parties to the agreement is less than 25 per cent. However certain types of agreement – price fixing, market sharing, setting of minimum prices and being part of a network of similar agreements – can have an appreciable effect even if the market share is less than 25 per cent. In France and Germany there are no similar guidelines on the permitted market share of parties to an agreement.

In all three countries certain kinds of agreements are exempt from prohibition by the national competition authorities. Agreements covered by other national law or by EC law may be exempted. Agreements can also be exempted by the competition authorities or the minister responsible can exclude an agreement for reasons of compelling public policy. A key exemption criterion which applies to all countries is that agreements are permitted when they are judged to improve production and promote technical and economic progress, provided they do not eliminate competition. In Germany, agreements which help small firms in competition with large firms may be permitted, and similarly in France agreements may be permitted the purpose of which is to improve the management of small and medium-sized enterprises (SMEs). In Britain SMEs are not targeted per se but are likely to be exempt by virtue of the 25 per cent market share requirement noted above. In all three countries there can be an 'individual exemption', which is applied in individual cases, and a 'block exemption', which exempts specific categories of agreement. A third category

Table 9.1 Restrictive practices

	Britain	*France*	*Germany*
Agreements not normally included	Combined market share less than 25% (except price fixing and market sharing) Vertical agreements (except price fixing)	–	Vertical agreements (except price fixing)
Exemptions	Compelling public policy Economic and technical progress	Agreements which improve management of SMEs Compelling public policy Economic and technical progress	Agreements which help SMEs compete with large firms Compelling public policy Economic and technical progress
Covered by other laws	Financial services, broadcasting Agreements with EU dimension	Financial services, press and broadcasting Agreements with EU dimension	Credit and insurance industries, copyright collecting societies and sports Agreements with EU dimension

Sources: DTI 2002a; OFT 1998a; BKA 2002; CdelaC 2002; Ministry of the Economy, Finance and Industry 2002a; Maitland-Walker 1995.

of exemption applies when an agreement is already covered by EU individual or block exemptions.

In Britain there are areas such as financial services and broadcasting which are covered by other laws. In Germany certain areas of the economy, such as the credit and insurance industries, copyright collecting societies and sports, are exempted, and the transport, agriculture and forestry industries are covered by other laws (BKA 2002: 20). In France there are specific rules for financial services, and the press and broadcasting are exempted.

Table 9.1 summarises the main features of competition policy in Britain, France and Germany as they relate to restrictive practices.

Monopoly policy

All three countries adopt a prohibition approach to monopolies similar to the policy on restrictive practices. A dominant position per se is not prohibited but certain kinds of conduct deemed to be abusive by firms in a dominant position are illegal, unless specifically excluded.

In all three countries market share is the main criterion examined by the competition authorities to judge whether a firm holds a dominant position, although there is no fixed definition of market share deemed to be dominant and other market structural characteristics are also examined.

In Britain and Germany, nevertheless, guidelines are given on when a firm is presumed by the authorities to be in a dominant position. In Britain, a firm is unlikely to be considered dominant if it has a market share of less than 40 per cent. However a firm with a lower market share may be considered dominant if, for example, the structure of the market enables it to act independently of its competitors. The number and size of existing competitors, as well as the potential for new competitors to enter the market, are also key criteria. In Germany a single firm is presumed to be dominant if it holds one third of the market share. If three or fewer firms have a combined market share of 50 per cent they are also presumed to be dominant. In France no specific market shares are specified and a firm is judged to be dominant if it is able to play a leading role in the market and avoid the constraints of competition.

In all three countries examples of specific types of conduct that are likely to be considered as abuse of a dominant position include imposing unfair purchase or selling prices and terms and conditions of sales; limiting production, markets or technical development to the prejudice of consumers; applying different trading conditions to equivalent transactions; refusing to supply; tie-in sales; and attaching unrelated supplementary conditions to contracts.

In German law, abuse can occur in competition law when a firm refuses to allow access by competitors to an essential network. This applies in cases such as telecommunications, energy, and the railways where networks cannot easily be duplicated. In Britain and France network access is covered by the law and regulations of specific sectors.

In Britain no exemptions are possible from monopoly policy and the general exclusions are the same as for restrictive practices. In Germany and France the exemptions are the same as for restrictive practices.

Table 9.2 sets out the main provisions of monopoly policy.

Merger policy

A key aspect of merger policy is the determination of whether a merger is to be examined by the competition authorities. Large transnational mergers may be considered by the EU and large national mergers by the national authorities, while smaller mergers may not be examined at all.

In all three countries large mergers with a European dimension may be examined by the European Commission under the European Union Merger Regulation. Broadly, this covers the largest mergers, that is, those involving firms with a total world turnover of over €5 billion (£3.68 billion, $5.63 billion) where at least two of the firms have a total EU turnover of over €250 million (£184 million, $281.25 million). When covered by this provision they are not subject to examination by the national authorities unless referred back by the European Commission.

Table 9.2   Monopoly policy

	Britain	France	Germany
Guidelines on dominant position	Market share greater than 40%	Market share greater than 33%	Firm plays leading market role and can avoid competition
		Three or fewer firms with combined share greater than 50%	
Exemptions	No specific exemptions possible. Areas excluded same as for restrictive practices	As restrictive practices	As restrictive practices

Sources: DTI 2002a; OFT 1998a; BKA 2002; CdelaC 2002; Ministry of the Economy, Finance and Industry 2002b; Maitland-Walker 1995.

In Britain, mergers which qualify for examination are normally those where the worldwide assets taken over amount to more than £70 million (€95.1 million, $107 million), or a 25 per cent market share or more is created in Britain. In France, the conditions for examination are a combined worldwide turnover of €150 million (£110 million, $169 million) and a domestic turnover by at least two of the parties of €15 million (£11 million, $17 million). In Germany, mergers subject to scrutiny by the authorities are those where the firms have a combined aggregate annual worldwide turnover of €500 million (£368 million, $562 million), or at least one of the firms has a domestic turnover of €25 million (£18.4 million, $28 million).

Separate conditions often apply to media companies. In Britain there is a separate regime for certain media mergers for which the consent of the relevant Secretary of State (Minister) is required. In France the press and broadcasting are excluded from merger law and examination is subject to ministerial discretion (Souam 1998: 223). In Germany there are lower thresholds for the examination of mergers in the press and broadcasting industries.

In Britain the competition authorities base their decisions on mergers on a public interest test. This consists of a range of factors including competition, the interests of consumers and the regional balance of industry and employment (Gardner 2000: 30). If the public interest is harmed the merger can be blocked or the divestment of assets can be demanded. In France the Ministry of the Economy, Finance and Industry considers and makes decisions on merger cases and may refer to the Competition Council for advice. The criteria for the decision are competition and economic progress. In Germany the Federal Cartel Office decides on merger cases on competition grounds only. Firms can appeal against decisions in the courts and put non competition reasons to the Minister of Economics who can override the decision of the Cartel Office on public interest grounds.

Table 9.3   Merger policy

	Britain	France	Germany
Mergers examined when not considered by the EU	Worldwide assets taken over more than £70m (€95.3m, $107m) or a 25 per cent market share or more is created in Britain	Combined worldwide turnover of €150m (£110.4m, $168.8m) and a domestic turnover by at least two of the parties of €15m (£11m, $16.9m)	Combined aggregate annual world-wide turnover of €500m (£368m, $563m) or at least one of the firms has a domestic turn-over of €25m (£18.4m, $28m)
Variations	Media	Press and broadcasting	Press and broadcasting
Decision making	Public interest	Competition and economic progress	Competition grounds
	Secretary of State decides on advice from Office of Fair Trading and Competition Commission	Ministry of the Economy, Finance and Industry decides	Federal Cartel Office decides

Sources: DTI 2002c; DTI 2002d; OFT 2003; CdelaC 2002; Ministry of the Economy, Finance and Industry 2002c; BKA 2000, 2002.

Table 9.3 summarises the main features of national mergers policies.

Recent developments

In 2002 a significant reform to EU competition policy was agreed which directly affects competition policy in all EU member states (Commission 2003). The reform aims to improve implementation and involves a degree of decentralisation, in particular the abolition of 'Regulation 17' which required all restrictive practice agreements to be notified to the Commission. Policy has been reformed to enable closer cooperation between the Commission and national competition authorities and better targeting of resources to improve enforcement. The reform recognizes that despite the convergence of many basic aspects of competition policy, the effectiveness and enforcement of competition policy have not similarly converged. A survey undertaken by the Global Competition Review (Financial Times 2000, GCR 2000), for example, rated the German competition authorities as the best in the world and the British and French as much less effective. Criteria of importance are independence (normally from ministers), expertise and speed of decision making. Some of the recent changes and proposals for change, particularly in Britain and France, reflect these concerns.

In Britain the 1998 Competition Act included the creation of the Competition Commission (formerly the Monopolies and Mergers Commission) (DTI 2002a) with a separate appeals tribunal which became the Competition Appeal Tribunal, an independent body created by the Enterprise Act 2002. The approach to restrictive practices and monopoly policy was changed from one of permissiveness to prohibition, and the OFT was given a clearer and more powerful role to investigate, decide whether prohibited conduct has occurred, and impose. The Enterprise Act 2002 tightened up the merger policy regime with a competition test and gave competition authorities more independence in relation to merger decisions, and the Communications Act 2003 changed the regime for media mergers (DTI 2002b, OFT 2003).

In France the New Economic Regulations Act of 2001 included measures to improve independence and enforcement (CdelaC 2002). A clear separation of the investigation and judgement functions of the Competition Council has been adopted. The penalties for breaching competition law have been increased and the Competition Council has been given greater powers to take interim action against breaches of the law. Merger control has also been made more systematic by introducing compulsory merger notification to the Ministry of the Economy, Finance and Industry plus substantial fines for non-compliance.

In Germany in recent years the exemptions on the ban on cartels and the approach to monopolies are being viewed more critically (BKA 2002). The Energy Act 1998, for example, abolished the monopoly of energy supply via networks, and in utility industries generally the refusal to grant access to essential networks can be prohibited on the grounds of abuse of dominant position. There is also a greater tendency to subsume the regulation of the liberalized utility industries under general competition law and administration than in Britain and France, where sectoral regulators and regulation are more prevalent. Also, partly in response to EU reform, the German law against restraints of competition is to undergo a 7th amendment which will involve a narrowing of the scope of exemptions from competition law (BKA 2003).

Sources

BKA (Bundeskartellamt) (2000), 'Information leaflet relating to German control of concentrations', <www.bundeskartellamt.de/competition_act.html> [7 August 2002].

BKA (Bundeskartellamt) (2002), 'The tasks of the Bundeskartellamt – an overview', <www.bundeskartellamt.de/tasks.html> [7 August 2002].

BKA (Bundeskartellamt) (2003), 'Competition experts discuss exemption areas under competition law', <www.bundeskartellamt.de/30_09_2003englisch.html> [19 November 2003].

M. Cini and L. McGowan, *Competition Policy in the European Union* (Basingstoke: Macmillan – now Palgrave Macmillan, 1998).

CdelaC (Conseil de la Concurrence) (2002), 'Missions', <www.finances.gouv.fr/minefi/entreprise/index.htm> [7 August 2002].

Commission (2003) 'Competition rules applying to undertakings' <www.europa.eu.int/comm/competition/antitrust/legislation/> [19 November 2003].

DTI (Department of Trade and Industry) (2002a), 'Competition Act 1998. What does the Act do?', <www.dti.gov.uk/cp/ca98what.htm> [7 August 2002].

DTI (Department of Trade and Industry) (2002b), 'Reform of UK Competition Policy', <www.dti.gov.uk/cp/ukcompref.htm> [7 August 2002].

DTI (Department of Trade and Industry) (2002c), 'Procedural Guidance: Guidance on DTI procedures for handling merger references and reports' <www.dti.gov.uk/cp/ukmergerguide.htm> [7 August 2002].

DTI (Department of Trade and Industry) (2002d), 'UK Mergers', <www.dti.gov.uk/cp/ukmergers.htm> [7 August 2002].

DTI (Department of Trade and Industry) (2002e), 'Competition Authorities', <www.dti.gov.uk/cp/authorities.htm> [7 August 2002].

H. Dumez and A. Jeunemaitre, 'The convergence of competition policies in Europe: internal dynamics and external imposition', in *National Diversity and Global Capitalism*, eds S. Berger and R. Dore (Ithaca: Cornell University Press, 1996): 216–38.

Financial Times, 'German cartel office rated best regulator in the world', 11 April 2000: 14.

N. Gardner, *A Guide to United Kingdom and European Union Competition Policy*, 3rd edn (Basingstoke: Macmillan – now Palgrave Macmillan, 2000).

GCR (Global Competition Review) (2000), 'Rating the Regulators', <www.global-competition.com/rating/rating.htm> [21 July 2000].

J. Maitland-Walker (ed.), *Competition Laws of Europe* (London: Butterworth, 1995).

L. McGowan and S. Wilks, 'The first supranational policy in the European Union: Competition policy', *European Journal of Political Research*, 28 (1995): 141–69.

Ministry of the Economy, Finance and Industry (2002a), 'Entente', <www.finances.gouv.fr/minefi/entreprise/concurrence/index.htm> [7 August 2002].

Ministry of the Economy, Finance and Industry (2002b), 'Exploitation abusive de position dominante' <www.finances.gouv.fr/minefi/entreprise/index.htm> [7 August 2002].

Ministry of the Economy, Finance and Industry (2002c), 'Le contrôle des concentrations', <www.finances.gouv.fr/minefi/entreprise/index.htm> [7 August 2002].

OFT (Office of Fair Trading) (1998a), 'Competition Act 1998: The Chapter 1 Prohibition', <www.oft.gov.uk/Business/Legal + Powers/ca98 + publications.htm#guide> [7 August 2002].

OFT (Office of Fair Trading) (1998b), 'Competition Act 1998: The Chapter 2 Prohibition', <www.oft.gov.uk/Business/Legal + Powers/ca98 + publications.htm#guide> [7 August 2002].

OFT (Office of Fair Trading) (2003), 'Overview of the Enterprise Act. The competition and consumer provisions', <www.oft.gov.uk/News/Publications/Leaflet + Ordering.htm>[19 November 2003].

S. Souam, 'French competition policy', in S. Martin (ed.), *Competition Policies in Europe* (Amsterdam: Elsevier, 1998).

R. Sturm, 'The German Cartel Office in a hostile environment', in *Comparative Competition Policy: National Institutions in a Global Market*, eds G. B. Doern and S. Wilks (Oxford: Clarendon Press, 1996).

S. Wilks, *In the Public Interest: Competition Policy and the Monopolies and Mergers Commission* (Manchester: Manchester University Press, 1999).

S. Wilks with I. Bartle, 'The unintended consequences of creating independent competition agencies', *West European Politics*, 25:1 (2002): 148–72.

10
Employment

Jeremy Leaman and Anne Daguerre

Introduction

The involvement of modern European states in the ordering and regulation of employment relations and in the maintenance of high levels of employment is both a commonplace and, in more recent years, an issue of considerable contention. As employment is the core precondition for the material welfare of individuals and households in societies with an advanced division of labour, and the stability of employment is threatened by changes in economic conditions – be they cyclical or structural – the modern state has found itself obliged to develop systems of protection for individual welfare, including the regulation of employment relations between employers and employees.

The nature of employment policy

Employment policy encompasses both the regulation of employment relations between employer and employee and the promotion of employment opportunities for the working population. It thus comprises:

- the establishment and policing of framework rules for the operation of wage negotiations, trade union rights, working conditions, working hours, holiday entitlement, employment protection and dismissal, minimum wages, conflict avoidance and conflict resolution, and the formal institutions of workers' participation;
- the regulation and coordination of career training in conjunction with employers, trade unions and colleges of further education;
- expenditure measures designed to influence demand in the labour market, either indirectly through the tax system or directly through financial support for schemes of job-creation, for example through public procurement programmes.

Legislative competence is primarily at the level of central government in all three countries, but includes an increasing role for the European Commission, in particular for the Directorate General for Employment and Social Affairs. The 1998 Employment Guidelines oblige all EU Member States and their national employment policy authorities to produce an annual National Action Plan on employment, which is then subject to a periodic audit to check both compliance and success rates. The Employment Guidelines involve a series of commitments to equal opportunities, the employment of the disabled and basic employment rights as well as the obligation to involve the national 'social partners' in each National Action Plan. The work of the Directorate is aimed at preventing the more blatant forms of location competition that may occur as a consequence of weak employment regulation and removing barriers to mobility. It is too early to assess the overall impact of EU employment policy on national policy-making structures; Germany, with its established architecture of regulated labour relations, was a key mover in pushing the recent guidelines through, while Britain has manifested a degree of opposition to EU employment policy initiatives, notably in relation to the Working-Time Directive.

The delivery of employment policy varies according to both the specific political structures of the individual countries and the given policy priorities of individual administrations (Table 10.1). Thus in federal Germany each of the 16 *Land* (regional) governments has a ministry which includes labour/employment as one of its main briefs. Those regions with higher levels of unemployment are eligible for funds both from Germany's refined system of vertical and horizontal financial equalization and from EU Structural Funds. Local authorities also conduct job-creation schemes. Apart from the territorial authorities, however, the main deliverer of both unemployment benefit and of large-scale job-creation initiatives is the Federal Labour Agency (BfA). The Federal Ministry of Economics and Employment is responsible for primary labour legislation and the monitoring of compliance, but deploys far fewer resources than regions, municipalities and the BfA.

In France the role of both the 26 regions and the *communes* (local authorities) in devising and delivering targeted programmes of job-creation is predominantly funded from central government grants or EU structural funds. The *communes* in particular have gained from the increase in targeted funding: long limited to granting aid for job creation and helping families in need, their role has now been broadened to encompass specific local problems of unemployment and social exclusion as well as issues of economic restructuring. Legislative and monitoring functions rest with the central Ministry of Social Affairs, Labour and Solidarity.

In Britain delivery is coordinated by the central Department for Work and Pensions and channeled through locally based Job Centres. However considerable

Table 10.1 Administration of employment policy

	Britain	France	Germany
Legislative Competence	EU	EU	EU
	Department for Work and Pensions, Department for Education and Skills	Ministry of Social Affairs, Labour and Solidarity	Federal Ministry of Economics and Labour
Employers	Confederation of British Industry Institute of Directors	MEDEF (Movement of French Enterprises) CGPME (General Confederation of Small and Medium Enterprises) UPA (Federation of Artisans)	BDA (Federal Association of Employers' Federations) BDI (Federation of German Industry) DIHT (German Association of Chambers of Trade and Commerce)
Labour	TUC (Trades Union Congress) and its constituent unions	CGT (General Confederation of Labour) CFDT (French Democratic Confederation of Labour) CGT-FO (General Confederation of Labour – *Force ouvrière*) CFTC (French Christian Workers' Confederation) CFE–CGC (French Confederation of Professional and Managerial Staff)	DGB (German Federation of Trade Unions) DAG (German Union of White-Collar Workers) DBB (German Federation of Civil Servants) CGB (Christian Federation of Trade Unions)

responsibility also falls to the Training and Enterprise Councils (TECs) and their regional networks, which incorporate local authorities, employers, local educational authorities and individual Further Education (FE) colleges. Local authorities are less important in the funding and delivery of locally relevant policies of job-creation. There is no discrete Department dealing in whole or in part with employment within either the Scottish Executive or the Welsh

Assembly, but rather an implied subsumption of employment under education and training. The Northern Ireland Office (under direct control from London at the time of writing) contains a double 'ministry' under one minister, namely the Department for Education and the Department for Employment and Learning.

Specific comparisons

Over the past quarter century there has been a sea-change in the orthodoxy of both economic thinking and state economic policies whereby the primacy of full employment has given way to the primacy of price stability and growth. Within this sea-change the German, French and Anglo-Saxon 'models' of employment relations have been subject above all to the influence of liberalized global markets for production and distribution, the concomitant new mobility of capital, the comparatively low mobility of labour and the emergence of competitive deregulation between national locations for investment. This influence has been compounded by the opening-up of the highly skilled labour markets of central Europe. Britain has shed the image of a conflictual economy with high unemployment (and failed employment policies), while France and Germany now have worse records of structural unemployment (see Table 10.2). The current and continuing shifts in both the secular development of European labour markets and the orientation of employment policy nevertheless reflect the persistent historical features of individual national politico-economic cultures.

Until the onset of mass unemployment in the 1970s, Germany's labour market and, by implication, the state's employment policies were seen as successful, if highly juridified; the depth and extent of state regulation in the labour market were seen as having influenced economic progress favourably (Koch 1992: 235), and employers by and large acknowledged the advantages a tight regulatory culture brought with it. The subsequent weakening of Germany's political economy before and after unification, leading to mass structural unemployment and sluggish growth, has generated a fierce debate about the institutions and processes of employment policy, produced significant changes to many features of the labour market and raised questions about the viability of Germany's consensual, juridified model of employment relations. In Britain, industrial relations were traditionally driven not by a strong regulatory

Table 10.2 Unemployment in Britain, France and Germany, 1988–2002 (%)

	Britain		France		Germany	
	1988	2002	1988	2002	1988	2002
Unemployment (all)	8.3	5.2	10.0	8.8	7.6	8.3
Unemployment (under-25)	13.8	13.6	17.5	20.1	7.4	10.5

Source: Eurostat.

framework but by decentralized competitive struggles between individual enterprises and a variety of larger and smaller trade unions; there were no participation rights, as in Germany, but strongly entrenched obligations for employers to accept union representation. Accommodation via conflict during the strong years of growth allowed the toleration of a wide range of restrictive practices designed to protect craft trades from job insecurity. This accommodation became increasingly unviable with the onset of mass unemployment. The shallowness of workers' rights allowed both the rapid removal of both restrictive practices and union protection, and the 'liberalization' of labour markets.

In the following sections five specific areas of employment policy are compared: training policy, labour law, regulation of collective bargaining, participation and consultation, and employment agencies.

Training policy

In contrast to France and Germany, where the state chose to spend more on active labour market policies (see Table 10.3), British governments have tended to rely on market forces to effect a reduction in overall and long-term unemployment. Youth unemployment in Britain is worse than in Germany (Table 10.2), underscoring the differences in the training cultures of the two countries; with less than 150,000 apprenticeships, Britain lags way behind Germany which has around 1,800,000. France, with the worst record of youth unemployment in this comparison, also has a much less extensive system of apprenticeship training than Germany, with little more than 200,000 apprenticeships. The dual system of training in Germany, involving both enterprise-based training and state day-release education, skews private and state employment policy towards the integration of young people into the labour market. The negative corollary of this strong apprenticeship-orientation is a higher proportion of long-term unemployed in Germany (52 per cent of total unemployed in 2000) than in Britain (28 per cent) or France (41 per cent). In turn, the active encouragement of early retirement as a means of combating structural unemployment

Table 10.3 Employment policy expenditure, 1985–95

	Britain		France		Germany	
	1985	1995	1985	1995	1985	1995
Total expenditure on labour market policies (% GDP)	2.76	1.95	3.10	3.09	2.23	3.48
Expenditure on active labour market policies (% GDP)	0.73	0.54	0.66	1.30	0.82	1.34
Unemployment (% working population)	11.5	8.7	10.2	11.7	8.0	8.2

Source: Bogai 1998.

in France and Germany has produced a lower participation ratio in the age-group 55–64 (28 per cent and 38 per cent respectively in 1999) than in Britain (49 per cent) (European Commission 2001: 83).

Labour law

The politico-economic framework for employment policy in Germany is that of ordo-liberalism, commonly known as the 'social market economy', which contrasts with the welfarist Keynesian approach traditionally pursued in both Britain and France. Ordo-liberalism eschews 'process policy' (interventionism/*planification*) and favours 'order policy' by a state which sets framework rules (for example in monetary policy) but does not intervene in market processes.

'Labour law' in Germany (*Arbeitsrecht*) is strongly rule-based and covered by a discrete branch of jurisprudence, with specialist Labour Judges presiding over Labour Courts in conflicts between individual employers and (groups of) employees; significantly, conflicts are commonly resolved in such courts through consensus, that is, without recourse to judgement (and punishment). In France there is also a separate system of Labour Law overseen by Labour Courts (*conseils des prud'hommes*), while in Britain employment relations are subsumed under the jurisdiction of ordinary civil courts and subject to the vagaries of cumulative case law (Table 10.4).

Regulation of collective bargaining

Free collective bargaining is the primary vehicle of wage setting in all three countries. In Germany wage settlements are still predominantly based on national agreements between the major employers' organizations and the eight mass unions. This highly centralized system operates on the basis of a high employer membership of branch associations and relatively high union density (32 per cent of the workforce in 1998), and the wage agreements, supplemented at company and plant level, are still acknowledged as cost-efficient processes. Arbitration, when invoked, is conducted at regional level by special Arbitration Committees appointed by the *Land* Ministries of Labour. In France there is a mixture of centralized branch-based bargaining and enter-prise-based negotiations. Branch membership is correspondingly lower; the French trade union movement is also highly fragmented with five union federations

Table 10.4 Legal framework

Britain	France	Germany
Civil Law	Labour Law overseen by Labour Courts (*conseils des prud'hommes*)	Labour Law overseen by Labour Courts
		Federal Labour Court
	Constitutional Council	Federal Constitutional Court

and low union density (1995: 9.1 per cent). British wage negotiations in the private sector are predominantly enterprise-based where trade union representation is secure; since reforms to trade union law in the 1980s there has been an increasing tendency towards individualized wage contracts. Although there has been considerable consolidation of British trade union organizations, and the Trades Union Congress functions as a unitary umbrella for the labour movement, the movement is still relatively fragmented compared to Germany, although union density in Britain was still 29.6 per cent in 1998.

There is no clear correlation between levels of union membership and the level of 'extension' of negotiated wage deals, that is, the degree to which employer–union agreements are extended to the workforce that is not unionized. In both France and Germany the 'extension' is either obligatory by law (France) or agreed practice (Germany). In Britain the situation is less clear-cut, particularly with the advent of individualized wage contracts. The general picture is altered by specific differences between individual sectors, with higher levels of unionization in the public sector and in manufacturing and heavy industry than in the service sector. Wage-setting practices are summarised in Table 10.5.

Participation and consultation

Participation and consultation in labour relations are strongest in Germany with its long-established system of Codetermination (*Mitbestimmung*), which allows varying degrees of worker participation in company decision-making, depending on the size of the enterprise, its legal form and the specific branch of the economy. In Germany's heavy industry an extensive system of Parity Codetermination covers all companies with over 1000 employees; workers in other branches of industry were granted similar, though less generous, powers in the 1976 Codetermination Law covering enterprises with more than 2000 employees. In both cases, employee representatives sit on the company's supervisory board with ostensibly parity status. In all small enterprises with at least 5 employees, the Works Constitution Act (BVG 1952) grants collective

Table 10.5   Wage-setting

Britain	France	Germany
Decentralized free collective bargaining at company and plant level	Mixture of sectoral bargaining and company-level bargaining	Centralized free collective bargaining, plus plant level bargaining
Low Sectoral Bargaining ratio: 47% (1990)	(no data on bargaining ratio)	High Sectoral Bargaining ratio: 90% (1990)

Note: Sectoral Bargaining Ratio is the ratio of nationally agreed wage bargaining agreements (as measured by workers affected) to total wage agreements within a sector.

and individual rights of consultation to employees via an elected Works Council; the consultation covers working conditions, working time, holidays, piece-work rates and other social issues. State employees enjoy similar rights via the Staff Representation Act. Codetermination conflicts are subject to the jurisdiction of the Labour Courts.

Such levels of participation are uncommon in British and French enterprises, despite the adoption of the 1998 EU Directive on consultation in companies with more than 50 employees. Concertation is absent in France for a variety of reasons, involving both employer and union hostility: 'there is a striking consensus that rejects concertation as a style of policy-making' in France (Parsons 2002: 120). While the first Blair Administration incorporated the 1998 EU Directive on European Works Councils, rejected by the Conservatives under Major, there is no sign of any desire to introduce formalized co-determination along German lines despite a strong rhetoric of 'inclusion' in the programmes of New Labour (Dorey 2002: 67).

Employment agencies

Until recently the German state was the sole provider of employment agencies under the auspices of the Federal Institute of Labour (*Bundesanstalt für Arbeit*); in contrast to Britain and France private agencies were illegal. The BfA monopoly has now been weakened by the creation of agencies covering short-term contracts, following the Hartz-Commission Report of 2002. In Britain there are countless general and specialized recruitment agencies operating parallel to the Jobcentres run by the Department for Work and Pensions, which is also the sole agency for the mediation of state unemployment and associated benefits. In France, the state's *Agence Nationale pour L'Emploi* (ANPE) has been the main channel for job seekers but, in contrast to Britain and Germany, is separate from the main benefits agency. The ANPE has a comprehensive network of local offices. A Task Force is currently re-examining the ANPE 'monopoly' with particular reference to Germany's reforms; the probable outcome is a closer coordination between ANPE and benefits agencies and a wider role for private employment agencies.

The full set of administrative agencies involved in this area is set out in Table 10.6.

Recent developments

Fiscal limitations and supply-sidism

With the reversal of the cyclical improvement of European unemployment, particularly in France and Germany, there are signs of a reappraisal of employment policy strategies. If anything, these are tending to reinforce the preference for supply-side (neo-liberal) solutions to the crisis of employment, given the apparent

Table 10.6   Administrative agencies of employment policy

Britain	France	Germany
Jobcentres Private employment agencies	*Agence nationale pour l'Emploi (ANPE)* (National Agency for Employment) *Agence pour l'emploi des Cadres (APEC)* (Executive Employment Agency) *Office des Migrations Internationales (OMI)*	*Arbeitsämter* (Employment Offices) *Sozialämter* (Social Offices) *Personal Service Agenturen (PSA)* Private temping agencies

success of supply-side policies in Britain and the Netherlands. This preference is expressed in the policy recommendations of the OECD, the IMF and many nationally based research institutes, and also by the major national organizations of employers. The failure of active/interventionist employment policies is seen to be reflected in the development of expenditure levels in the three countries: falling levels of expenditure as a proportion of GDP in Britain are seen to be accompanied by significant falls in the rate of unemployment, while the opposite is seen to apply in France and Germany (see Table 10.3). The conclusion involves a crude syllogism, considering the huge exogenous shock of unification on the German economy (see Box 10.1), but this does not deter policy-makers from employing it. Negative perceptions of the value of expensive job creation measures are further reinforced by the fiscal constraints imposed by the EU's Stability and Growth Pact, which obliges Member States of the eurozone to reduce their Public Sector Borrowing Requirement (PSBR) and overall debt ratios.

Box 10.1   Special circumstances relating to Germany

Employment policy in Germany has been fundamentally affected by the absorption of the former GDR into the Federal Republic. With a primary focus on the privatization of state enterprises, employment was virtually halved in the East from some 9 million to under 5 million between 1990 and 1991. The German state, setting aside its cultural preference for non-intervention, enacted various emergency measures such that in 1993 639,000 east Germans were receiving 'retirement transition benefit', 260,000 were in job-creation and 383,000 were in retraining schemes. Before unification in 1990, unemployment in the West was already over 2 million. Unification and sluggish growth helped raise national levels to 4.1 million in October 2003.

Co-determination rules were waived in the East in the early stages of unification, so that large companies were not obliged to establish worker participation arrangements in line with the 1976 Law; secondly, the membership intensity of employers' associations is considerably lower in the East than in the West, since national collective bargaining agreements incur costs which many east German enterprises cannot afford. Quite apart from this, in many instances voluntary plant agreements have allowed normally mandatory collective agreements to be set aside in order to assure company solvency and protect jobs.

Work and pensions

The collapse of global equity markets in 2002 brought the relationship of employment and pensions into much sharper focus. Pressure from employers in France and Germany, where statutory pension schemes and their associated social contributions entail high indirect wage costs, combined with the demographic crisis of low birthrate and increasing longevity, have altered perceptions about the viability of pension schemes, retirement ages and the need for top-up pensions. In Britain, conversely, the policy of top-up pensions supplementing minimal statutory pensions is in disarray. In all three countries, special commissions have been established to assess the future of the employment-pensions nexus.

Gender and employment

Despite differing participation ratios for women in employment in the three countries, the trend is upwards. However the integration of women into the labour market is characterized by a high level of part-time work, particularly in Britain, raising issues of pension entitlement and general social security for working mothers.

Working-time

The trend towards shorter working weeks has been accelerated by the implementation of the EU's 1993 Working Time Directive, which limits average weekly working-time to a maximum of 48 hours per week. In line with moves towards greater flexibility in relation to overall working-life, working parents and retirement, increasing consideration is being given to annual or lifetime working accounts.

Sectoral employment shifts

The inability of the tertiary sector to absorb the large numbers of workers shed by European manufacturing enterprises, and the concomitant rise in structural unemployment, has forced all European countries, including the three in this

Table 10.7   Sectoral employment % of total employed, 1997

Sector	Britain	France	Germany
Primary (agriculture etc)	1.8	4.6	3.2
Secondary (industry)	26.9	25.9	36.5
Tertiary (services)	71.3	69.5	60.2

Source: OECD.

study, to pay greater attention to the sectoral balance of employment, where only Germany retains a relatively high ratio of manufacturing employment to total civilian employment (Table 10.7). The precariousness of service sector employment has also been more apparent since the end of the dot.com boom.

Policy harmonization

The revivified interest of the EU in employment policy, notably in the wake of the Single Market Act, is becoming an increased focus for national policy-makers, as the dangers of competition between national locations, in particular in relation to welfare systems, become more apparent. The trend towards increased harmonization is likely to be accelerated by the expansion of the EU eastwards.

Sources

Dieter Bogai, 'Arbeitsmarktpolitik in der Europäischen Union', *WSI-Mitteilungen* 12 (1998).

Bundesanzeiger, *Betriebsverfassungsgesetz (BUG)* (Bonn, 1952).

Peter Dorey, 'Britain in the 1990s', in *Policy Concertation and Social Partnership in Western Europe*, eds S. Berger and H. Compston (New York/Oxford: Berghahn, 2002).

European Commission, *The Social Situation in the European Union 2001*, (Luxembourg, 2001).

European Industrial Relations Observatory Online, <www.eiro.eurofound.eu.int/> Eurostat, <europa.eu.int/comm/eurostat>[November 2003].

Frank Frick, *Arbeitsverwaltung im Wandel – Erfahrungen aus 15 Ländern im Vergleich* (Gütersloh, 2002).

Mutual Information System on Social Protection in the EU Member States and the EEA, <europa.eu.int/comm/employment_social/missoc/2002> [November 2003].

Jacqueline O'Reilly and Colette Fagan, *Part-time Prospects: International Comparisons of Part-time Work in Europe, North America and the Pacific Rim* (London: Routledge, 1998).

Karl Koch, 'Regulatory reform and German industrial relations', in *The Politics of German Regulation*, ed. K. Dyson (Aldershot: Dartmouth, 1992).

N. Parsons, 'France in the 1990s', in *Policy Concertation and Social Partnership in Western Europe*, eds S. Berger and H. Compston (New York/Oxford: Berghahn, 2002).

OECD (Organization for Economic Cooperation and Development), *Managing Decentralisation: A New Role for Labour Market Policy* (Paris: OECD, 2003).

Alain Supiot, *Beyond Employment: Changes in Work and the Future of Labour Law in Europe* (Oxford: Oxford University Press, 2001).

11
Investment

Philip Raines

Introduction

'Investment policy' can be defined as all policy actions deliberately intended to influence the location of direct corporate investments. In this context, investments are generally taken to mean the setting up, restructuring or expansion of place-specific sites which carry out significant corporate activities whether production, distribution, research and development (R&D), administration or marketing. The policy is largely associated with the attraction of foreign direct investment (FDI), though in practice it also covers the retention of investment and often applies to domestic investment decisions. As a policy area, it should be distinguished from policies affecting portfolio investments (such as share ownership regulations) as well as those influencing the general propensity of businesses to make investments (such as tax incentives for R&D expenditure).

Britain, France and Germany are characterized by distinctive approaches to FDI promotion. While all three employ similar sets of policy instruments, they differ in the importance placed on FDI attraction, the scale of activities undertaken and the structure of policy delivery. In summary, Britain has historically had the most active and sophisticated approach to attracting FDI, as reflected in its receipt of the lion's share of all foreign investment coming into Europe. At the other end of the spectrum, Germany has only recently recognized the attraction of FDI as an important policy objective. France's attitude to FDI promotion lies between both countries, but it contrasts with Britain and Germany in having a far more centralized approach to attracting FDI.

The nature of investment policy

While the attraction of investment is explicitly recognized as a policy goal by governments, investment policy is not a clearly bounded area of policy but overlaps with other policy fields covered in the book, notably regional policy (through the use of financial incentives to attract investments to the less-developed areas of a country) and taxation policy (through fiscal incentives). It also arguably encompasses government policies which have little overtly to do with investment priorities. For example, the level and distribution of tax burdens will greatly influence corporate attitudes to investing in a country, but tax policy is generally set by other factors (though there are examples where investor perception has been a key determinant, as in the case of the low rate of corporation tax in Ireland). For the most part, these marginal policy areas will not be considered here.

In discussing what might be called 'active' investment policy, there are three categories of policy activities which deserve attention:

1. *dedicated investment policy*: those measures which are explicitly designed and delivered with a view to FDI attraction (such as place marketing);
2. *targeted investment policy*: activities which are part of other policy areas but which are systematically applied to the attraction of investment (such as financial incentives);
3. *regulatory investment policy*: regulations affecting the ownership and operation of foreign investments (such as the level of labour market regulation), which can influence investor perceptions of a location.

First, with respect to *dedicated* policy activities, the active marketing of locations is the most important policy action taken by governments in investment policy. Specialized inward investment agencies have been set up in all three countries with the specific remit of attracting investment projects. Agencies operate at both national and sub-national levels, and their central functions include collecting and analysing information on the locational attractiveness of their territory, marketing the territory to potential investors, assisting interested investors in their location appraisal, offering incentive packages, liaising with other relevant public authorities, and providing after-care services to existing investors (Young and Hood 1994).

Targeted investment policy comprises the range of financial and fiscal incentives employed by governments to attract investors. In the cases of Britain, France and Germany these incentives have not been designed with the explicit purpose of attracting foreign investment. However they have become important tools of investment policy, to such an extent that whatever the original intention, some are primarily used in FDI promotion (Raines and Brown 1999). Bound by EU regulations on the levels of state aid to industry, two types of incentives are common in all three countries: financial incentives and fiscal incentives. Financial incentives take the form of one-off grants and cheap loans made to investors for assistance in acquisition and adaptation of the site and its infrastructure, construction and equipment costs and, in many cases, initial recruitment and wage costs. Fiscal incentives are usually time-limited tax 'holidays' for investors. The most important incentives used by Britain, France and Germany are variations on grant schemes for large-scale capital investments, which are only available in designated areas of a country, as determined by their relatively low levels of economic development and as subject to EU controls of state aids (Yuill *et al.* 1999).

Lastly, *regulatory* investment policy forms another important plank of government activities in investment policy. Business regulations can influence FDI promotion both explicitly (through 'discriminatory' regulations) and implicitly ('general' regulations). Discriminatory regulations refer to that set of government prohibitions which regulate foreign involvement in particular sectors of the economy. They can cover ownership (such as the requirement for government authorization of foreign acquisitions of a particular size or restrictions on foreign participation in 'sensitive' sectors) as well as operational issues (such as limits on foreign-controlled enterprises entering certain domestic markets or the imposition of additional administrative and reporting requirements on foreign businesses).

More general regulations are not specifically aimed at foreign enterprises but can often be considered by investors in their location appraisal on an international scale. For the most part, these are bound up in views of the 'business climate' of a country as defined by perceived levels of 'red tape' and bureaucracy. For example, regulations governing national labour markets can influence investor attitudes with respect to the ease with which workers can be recruited and dismissed, restrictions on temporary and part-time working, and trade union strength as permitted by legislation. However the role of these perceptions in investment decision-making has been notoriously difficult to assess.

Specific comparisons

Of the three countries, Britain has traditionally had the most systematic approach to targeting and attracting foreign investment projects. The attraction of FDI has been an explicit objective of regional and industrial policies for nearly two decades, and this has contributed to Britain having the largest share of all direct investment in Western Europe.

Over the past decade, France has experienced a 'sea change' in its approach to foreign investment, in large part in response to the persistence of unemployment. As will be seen below, this has been reflected in a significant easing of French regulations on investor entry into the country and a consequent surge in inward investment into France, which has overtaken Britain in terms of annual flows for some recent years.

Finally, Germany as a whole has not had an active investment policy. Promotional activities have been relatively limited, and overall Germany has one of the lowest European FDI:GDP ratios in terms of inward flows. In recent years, though, attitudes have begun to change, prompted by fears of investment re-locations to neighbouring Central and Eastern European countries and an awareness of the role that FDI can play in regenerating the eastern *Länder*.

Dedicated investment policy

In all three countries, FDI promotion entails similar sets of activities. What distinguishes Britain, France and Germany is the scale of action and the way in which these activities are organized. The differences are summarized in Table 11.1 and discussed in more detail in the subsequent sections.

In *Britain*, investment promotion is coordinated at national level through Invest UK, a government body responsible to both the Department of Trade and Industry (DTI) and the Foreign and Commonwealth Office. On behalf of the English regions, it provides a network of overseas offices and undertakes national marketing campaigns. Within the English regions, each of the Regional Development Agencies (RDAs) are responsible for FDI marketing of their region in cooperation with Invest UK. However Northern Ireland, Scotland and Wales have separate agencies which are better resourced, more independently represented abroad and more active in promotion than their English counterparts. Promotional responsibilities are divided territorially. In Northern

Table 11.1 Investment promotion

	Britain	France	Germany
Attitude towards FDI promotion	Historically very positive	Historically suspicious, but increasingly positive in recent years	Historically indifferent, but signs of becoming more positive recently
Structure of FDI promotion	Coordinated system with a central national agency (Invest UK) and strong territorial agencies in Northern Ireland, Scotland and Wales	Centralized system based on the Invest in France national network Some regions have their own promotional bodies	Decentralized system with a national body – the Office of the Federal Commissioner for Foreign Investment in Germany – acting as a gateway for the individual *Land* bodies
Responsibilities	Divided territorially, with central coordination provided by Invest UK	Largely centralized within the Invest in France network	Largely undertaken by the individual *Länder*

Source: Raines and Brown 1999; individual inward investment agency websites.

Ireland, Scotland and Wales the respective inward investment agencies look after all promotional tasks, investor liaison and financial incentive package offers. In England these tasks are divided between Invest UK – which is responsible for most aspects of marketing – and the English Regional Development Agencies, which oversee investor relations and (some) incentive offers.

As part of its recent more favourable attitude to FDI, *France* has also developed a more structured approach to investment promotion, though its system is more centralized than the British network. Invest in France is the official national body for marketing France, but, unlike Invest UK, it has a network of directly subsidiary offices throughout France (as well as international satellite offices). While there are no equivalents of the powerful British territorial agencies, several French regions do operate their own agencies with specific marketing remits. The Invest in France network is responsible for the bulk of marketing and investor relations activities, while incentive offers are the responsibility of DATAR, the national economic development agency, which has close organizational links with Invest in France.

In 1998 the first dedicated, national body was established to promote FDI in *Germany*: the Office of the Federal Commissioner for Foreign Investment in Germany (part of the Economics Ministry). This office acts as a gateway service, directing potential investors to the individual *Länder*. The latter are principally responsible for FDI promotion – as indeed they are for most matters relating to economic development – and their activities are typically carried out through specialized units within regional economic ministries. Their levels of activity vary greatly on a *Land*-by-*Land* basis, but for the most part the *Land* agencies are responsible for investor relations, incentive offers and nearly all promotional tasks, although the Office of the Federal Commissioner undertakes some national marketing.

Targeted investment policy

Financial incentives have long been regarded as key policy instruments for the attraction of mobile, foreign investment projects. All three countries operate very similar incentive schemes on a nationwide basis: discretionary, project-related assistance, normally taking the form of a capital grant linked to employment creation (Yuill *et al.* 1999). The incentives are only given for investments in regions designated as less-developed areas requiring additional assistance within EU state aid regulations. They are not specifically aimed at foreign investors – they are available to indigenous businesses as well – but given their focus on large-scale, investment projects, the majority of which tend to be linked to FDI, it is not surprising that they are closely associated with government efforts to attract foreign investors. Awards are not automatic and are only made if the project can demonstrate proof of need, does not entail displacement

Table 11.2   Investment incentives, 2002

	Britain	France	Germany
Main incentives	Regional Selective Assistance[1]	Regional Policy Grant	Investment Grant
Eligible area share of national population	29%	34%	35%
Decision-making authority	England: for grants of up to £2 m (€2.7 m, $3 m), the RDAs; for grants over £2 m (€2.7 m, $3 m), DTI; for grants over £5 m (€6.8 m, $7.6 m), the Treasury Welsh Assembly Scottish Executive	The national body DATAR (under delegation from the minister responsible for regional policy)	Individual *Land* ministries responsible for economic affairs
Award rates (as share of eligible costs)	Up to 35%, depending on location	Up to 23%, depending on location and project sector	Up to 50%, depending on location and size of firm
Expenditure 1999	€464m (£341.5 m, $522 m)	€88 m (£64.8 m, $99 m)	€2808 m (£2067 m, $3159 m)

Note [1] The grant is not available in Northern Ireland, where an alternative scheme is applied.
Source: Yuill *et al.* 1999.

of existing local activities or a simple transfer of activities from elsewhere in the country, and will bring regional/national economic benefits, normally measured in terms of jobs and income.

The main differences between the incentive schemes lie in the decision-making structures and expenditure, as Table 11.2 suggests. In Britain, Regional Selective Assistance awards can be made at different levels: within England, responsibility shifts between the RDAs and central government ministries depending on the award size, while Scotland and Wales have their own award authorities. France has a more centralized decision-making structure through DATAR, the national body responsible for regional economic development policy. Germany has the most regionalized decision-making system, as the individual *Länder* make decisions on investment grant offers, although the scheme itself is national.

In terms of expenditure, there are significant variations between the three countries, only part of which are explained by the size of their eligible areas. Overall, Germany has the highest incentive spending of the three countries, largely reflecting the different objective of the grant in policy terms. Whereas France and Britain tend to use financial incentives selectively in influencing

Table 11.3 Fiscal incentives, 2002

	Britain	France	Germany
Main incentives	Enterprise Zones	Local business tax concessions	No major incentives
Eligible areas	At present, seven local areas (all will have expired by the end of November 2005)	Areas covered by the Regional Policy Grant as well as a number of 'priority rural development areas' and certain urban areas	
Award rates	100% allowances on capital expenditure for corporation and income tax purposes Exemptions from non-domestic rates on industrial and commercial property	Up to 100% exemption from local business taxation	

Source: Yuill *et al.* 1999.

mobile investment decisions, grants are awarded more widely in Germany and are given not just to inward investors but often to locally based firms as well.

Grants are frequently only one element of an incentive package offered to investors. These packages can include tailored mixes of other subsidies such as grants for worker training, discounted property, and subsidized infrastructure improvements. In all three countries these other incentives are provided by a range of other public sources, including local authorities and regional development bodies.

As Table 11.3 indicates, some fiscal incentives are operated, though they are of less significance than the grant schemes. France operates a national scheme involving local business tax concessions in a number of designated areas. Britain has a highly limited scheme of tax relief for particular local areas ('Enterprise Zones'), though this applies to all enterprises locating to these areas. Germany has no major scheme in operation.

Regulatory investment policy

The regulatory environments in Britain, France and Germany affecting investment policy have been converging in recent years, as Table 11.4 suggests, not least through the operation of Investment Promotion and Protection Agreements and double taxation treaties.

In terms of discriminatory regulations, all three countries currently operate relatively few restrictions on the activities of foreign enterprises (Brown and

Table 11.4 Investment regulations, 2002

	Britain	*France*	*Germany*
Ownership restrictions	No specific restrictions on foreign investors, apart from entry into a very few sectors, such as the media	Some restrictions on entry into several sectors, notably banking, insurance, defence, and air and maritime transport Prior authorization procedures necessary for investments that pose a 'threat to law and order and public safety'	No specific restrictions on foreign investors, though the Government may opt to intervene in mergers and acquisitions of 'strategic' interest
Operational restrictions		No specific restrictions on foreign investors	

Source: Individual inward investment agency websites.

Raines 2000). Of the three, *Britain* has been the most liberalized. It has long had the most active market for corporate take-overs in Europe with its minimal sectoral restrictions and absence of pre-authorization procedures. As a result, a large share of the country's investment flows is accounted for by mergers and acquisitions. This has been further encouraged by Britain's sustained privatization programmes over the past two decades, especially in public utilities such as telecommunications, electricity and water, where foreign enterprises have assumed a significant presence.

In the past, more stringent regulations on foreign ownership have been applied in *France*, but many of these have been removed in recent years. Nevertheless, a degree of wariness remains about allowing large domestic companies to pass into foreign ownership, though France is gradually amending its corporate laws to allow greater scope for foreign companies to acquire domestic concerns. Moreover, with respect to business activity and employment law, France continues to be seen as relatively regulated, although these regulations do not specifically target the operation of foreign investors.

Lastly, in terms of ownership and operational restrictions, *Germany* applies few discriminatory regulations, although the German government has intervened in decisions of particular strategic concern, as in the case of Vodafone's acquisition of Mannesmann in 2000. Nevertheless, as with France, its wider business and employment environment is perceived as being heavily regulated. Moreover, there is a continuing lack of mergers and acquisition activity in

Germany, mainly due to the country's industrial structure, which is dominated by SMEs and firms whose controlling ownership remains relatively stable as a result of bank or family ownership.

Recent developments

In recent years, governments have placed an increasing emphasis on the attraction of FDI as a policy goal. FDI can bring numerous benefits to an economy, both quantitatively (jobs, income growth) as well as qualitatively (impact on R&D and skills levels). As a result, it has become not only an important national activity, but also a key element in sub-national approaches to economic development.

With a long-standing policy commitment to attracting FDI, Britain has in many ways been an exemplar of how foreign investment can contribute to economic development. In part inspired by the British approach, France and Germany have followed its lead – though at very different rates – by increasing the sophistication of their promotional activities, liberalizing the business environment for investors, and using regional policy instruments to attract investment projects. Their differing levels of commitment and activity mirror their differing levels of foreign investment flows: over the last few years, Britain has continued to attract the main share of European investment, France has increased its inflows significantly, and Germany continues to under-perform apart from occasional mega-deals causing statistical 'blips', such as the Vodafone–Mannesmann deal.

In recent years, though, the investment promotion climate in Western Europe has become considerably more difficult (UNCTAD 2001). Britain, France and Germany all face the same pressures: a downturn in global foreign investment flows, which are estimated to have declined by 40 per cent in 2001, the largest single fall in three decades, and greater competition from new rivals such as the countries of Central and Eastern Europe. Paradoxically, while this has forced the governments of Britain, France and Germany to refine their investment policy and promotional activities, it has also led to policy questions over the priority placed on foreign investment in economic development.

Sources

Invest UK website, <www.invest.uk.com> [8 August 2002].
Invest in France website, <www.investinfrance.org> [8 August 2002].
Invest in Germany website, <www.invest-in-germany/de> [8 August 2002].
R. Brown and P. Raines, 'The changing nature of foreign investment policy in Europe: from promotion to management', in *Regions, Globalization and the Knowledge-Based Economy*, ed. J. Dunning (Oxford: Oxford University Press, 2000): 435–8.

P. Raines and R. Brown, 'FDI policy approaches in Western Europe', in *Policy Competition and Foreign Direct Investment in Western Europe,* eds. P. Raines and R. Brown (Aldershot: Ashgate, 1999): 7–38.

UNCTAD, *World Investment Report 2001* (Geneva: UN Conference on Trade and Development, 2001).

S. Young and N. Hood, 'Designing developmental after-care programmes for foreign direct investors in the European Union', *Transnational Corporations*, 3/2 (1994): 45–72.

D. Yuill, J. Bachtler and F. Wishlade (eds), *European Regional Incentives 1999*, 18th ed (London: Bowker Saur, 1999).

12
Business Regulation

C.H. Flockton, L. Garside and P.A. Grout

Introduction

In addition to defining what a business is and how it should operate, business regulation also addresses the operation of companies by placing restrictions on who can sell and buy what, where and when. With the exception of illustrative examples, this chapter does not deal with any sector-specific regulation, only regulation that applies to most if not all sectors.

While Britain, France and Germany are similarly affected by the prevalent EC legislation, national policies vary in relation to the extent to which they expect and allow policy recipients to take an active role in shaping legislation and practice. British policies empower businesses and their consumers by encouraging self-regulation, circulating information and protecting those at an unfair disadvantage. Despite current reforms, the maze of detailed French regulations caters for most situations at the expense of policy recipients faced with a system lacking in transparency, simplicity and scope for pro-active behaviour. Germany combines both detailed and sometimes restrictive legal regulation with areas of self-regulation, displaying both its federal structure and its consensual/corporatist character.

The nature of business regulation

The structure that governs the life and death of businesses is achieved through a wide range of legal and regulated procedures. The legal framework controls incorporation; financing through contributions and issuing of shares, securities and bonds; and takeover, sale, insolvency and liquidation. Voluntary codes of corporate governance specify the rules of interaction between owners and managers in order to reduce agency problems in controlling a company. Building on this regulatory canvass, governments also intervene in many forms of transactions that arise as part of normal activity. A wealth of regulatory concerns arise, among which by far the three most prominent ones are protecting consumers' economic interests, overseeing the spending of public money, and preserving national cultural values and principles. Others include competition, employment, financial, environmental, trade, sectoral, regional and cultural policies, which are covered elsewhere in this volume. The cross-country comparisons in this chapter address:

- *company law* (including corporate governance): rules to facilitate the creation, operation, transmission, and reorganization or dissolution of businesses;
- *consumer protection policy*: means to determine which products are safe for sale to consumers;
- *public procurement regimes*: mechanisms for selling works, supplies or services to public purchasers;
- *retailing regulations*: conditions under which a business can sell its output to the general public.

Three important aspects of national *company law* can be distinguished: company formation procedures, insolvency proceedings, and practices to delegate authority and take decisions. The choice of a business form reflects the company's object and the structure of ownership and control. It is useful to contrast partnerships, with unlimited personal liability of their members and no separate legal personality, and corporations combining separate personality, limited liability, shareholder delegation of managerial control and, in the case of public listed companies, free transferability of shares. National insolvency laws govern the way in which the wealth of a failing company is distributed among its creditors. In particular, reorganization procedures determine whether a company is kept as a going concern or liquidated. Insolvency proceedings sometimes provide for the prohibition of creditor execution or enforcement actions, thereby ruling out forfeiture, distress levies, winding up petitions, repossession of goods, security enforcements and new court proceedings. In all three countries corporate governance is driven by national, voluntary codes of conduct rather than by explicit legislation.

Consumer protection policy encompasses national consumer complaint mechanisms, product safety policy (including liability rules for defective products) and product safety norms and standards. National policies are contained within a tight European framework that suffers from lack of transparency and simplicity, and the absence of regulation in several critical areas such as regulation of payments and protection of children (for example from marketing practices and against unsought content) (European Commission 2001). Product liability rules abide by the principle of liability without fault, that is, the producer can be held liable without proof of his negligence or fault. Products developed according to European Standards are presumed to conform with the essential requirements of EC directives. Furthermore, pre-market clearance is required for 23 groups of products (for example household refrigerators and freezers, and toys) and the 'CE marking' is granted following the manufacturer's declaration of conformity. At national level, new technical regulations on products and information society services must be notified to the European Commission.

Public procurement rules define criteria for the award and review of public contracts. These impact on suppliers in the areas of works (building and civil engineering works), supplies (purchase, lease, rent or hire-purchase) and services in return for remuneration. Further regulatory constraints are imposed in the particular case of public utilities contracts. For all three types of public contracts, EC procurement Directives apply above a specified minimum value that depends on the nature of the contract and on the type of contracting authority. At 1 January 2002, the threshold was set at 130,000 Special Drawing Rights (SDR) (£100,410 or €162,293) and 200,000 SDR (£154,477 or €249,681) for purchases of supplies and services by central government and sub-central government respectively, and is raised to five million SDR (£3,861,932 or €6,242,028) for public works contracts (European Commission 2002a; exchange rates as set by *OJEC* 332, 27 November 2001). Contracts above the relevant threshold must be awarded following one of three procedures: the 'open procedure' without pre-selection of contractors, the 'restricted procedure' with shortlist of bidders or, in limited circumstances, the full 'negotiated procedure'. Given that these procurement rules are set by the EU, the role of central government in each of the three countries is essentially one of information, support and guidance. However, there is scope for national governments to develop their own rules for contracts the value of which does not exceed EC thresholds.

Retailing regulations vary with respect to business authorisations (if any) and retail opening hours, with striking differences in specific retail fields such as the sale of alcoholic drinks.

Specific comparisons

In some areas, notably public procurement and consumer protection, business regulation is heavily driven by EC legislation. National differences reflect separate traditions of company regulation and arise in policy areas that are excluded from EC legislation, notably within company law and retailing regulations.

Company law in the three countries varies in transparency and flexibility. Its spirit and attitude towards employee representation are retained in corporate governance codes. Retailing conditions are distinguished by restrictions on opening and closing times which vary from the stringent German and British rules to the sole compliance with employment legislation in France. Consumer policies vary in terms of effort to transpose EC rules and willingness to rely on and issue national codes. Similarly, even though public procurement policies are principally determined by EC legislation, differences arise in national compliance above EC thresholds, and in national regulations below the thresholds.

Company law

Incorporation procedures differ in the variety of corporate forms available and the simplicity of administrative procedures. Table 12.1 compares the main characteristics of public and private companies in the three countries.

The administrative burden placed on the members of newly-created firms is summarized in Table 12.2. British incorporation procedures are flexible and transparent: the same unique point of contact attends to all corporate business forms adapted from a format menu. This applies also in the German case, except that entrepreneurs register with their local court, the *Amtsgericht*. Despite high-level similarities, incorporation procedures in France are idiosyncratic of the selected business form: the point of contact varies with the nature of the company's object.

Reluctance to freeze creditor rights makes the British corporate rescue regime prone to premature liquidations. This is mitigated by recent measures to protect businesses from their creditors while attempting reconstruction. In contrast, the reform of the debtor-orientated French system improved creditor protection and reduced vulnerability to deferred liquidations. The German system relies on a single procedure that offers administrative simplicity to businesses in difficulty, as shown in the second part of Table 12.2, although a key purpose of recent changes was also to strengthen the claims of creditors.

Table 12.1   Company law: public and private companies, 2002

	Britain	*France*	*Germany*
Private company			
Nomenclature	Ltd	SARL	GmbH
Maximum no. of shareholders	None	50	None
Minimum capital	None	€7,500 (£5,520, $8,438)	€25,000 (£18,400, $28,125)
Public company			
Nomenclature	Plc	SA	AG
Minimum no. of shareholders	2	7	1
Minimum capital	£50,000 (€67,950, $76,450)	€37,000 (£27,232, $41,625)	€50,000 (£36,800, $56,250)
Minimum par value of a share	None	None	€1 (£0.74, $1.13)

Sources: NetPME 2002, CLB 1999, Aktiengesetz (law governing shares), GmbHgesetz (limited liability company law).

Table 12.2 Company law: incorporation and insolvency, 2002

	Britain	*France*	*Germany*
Incorporation			
Single contact body for all companies	Yes (Companies House)	No (company's object dictates the relevant body)	Yes (local court)
Centralized model for company statutes	Yes	No	Yes
Insolvency			
Single corporate rescue procedure	No (four types available)	No (two types available)	Yes
Are creditors alone able to force reconstruction?	No (court ruling)	No (ruling by Commercial Court)	Yes (simple majority vote by creditors)
Is Court obliged to appoint observer in corporate rescue procedures?	No (only when company is, or is likely to become, unable to pay its debts)	No (only when company has ceased paying its debts)	Yes
Single liquidation procedure	No (two types available)	Yes	Yes

Sources: Companies House 2002, Insolvency Service 2002, Service Public 2000, NetPME 2002, Couwenberg 2001, Aktiengesetz, GmbHgesetz, Bundesministerium für Justiz 2002.

The use of corporate governance codes is common in all three countries, although introduced earlier and more extensively in Britain. These are voluntary codes established by special working groups appointed by central government. The national codes make similar recommendations that supervisory and managerial functions be divorced and that independent non-executive directors control dedicated board committees in areas of potential conflict (audit, remuneration, nomination).

There are marked differences in the codes reflecting the fact that, ultimately, national company law traditions retain a strong hold on corporate governance. The main differences relate to board structure, employee representation, mandatory disclosure requirements and shareholder rights and participation. Table 12.3 summarizes some of these. In particular, unlike France and Germany, the British regime is devoid of provisions for employee representation. In France, there is scope for employee representation in the supervisory body, stemming from three directions: the advisory role of works councils, nomination of directors when employees hold more than 3 per cent of shares, and election of members of the supervisory body when company articles allow it. German provisions include election of a third of the supervisory board when there are more than

Table 12.3   Company law: corporate governance, 2002

	Britain	*France*	*Germany*
Board structure	Single-tier	Single-tier (two-tier available but uncommon)	Two-tier for all but companies with fewer than 2 000 employees
Minimum size of board	No legal constraint	3 for single-tier public companies	No restriction
Maximum size of board	No legal constraint	18 for single-tier public companies	No maximum
Term of office	No upper bound but recommend re-election at least every three years	Six years legal maximum for single-tier public companies	No restriction
Disclosure of compliance	Mandatory if listed on London Stock Exchange	Not mandatory	Recommended
Worker representation	No	Yes	Yes

Sources: WGM 2002, Miles 2002, Aktiengesetz, GmbHgesetz.

2000 employees, rising to a half in listed public companies, together with an additional member of staff assigned to labour matters in the management board and works councils when there are more than 200 employees.

Consumer protection

In all three countries, national rules on consumer protection are driven by European regulations and enforcement mechanisms, and the major national differences reflect the speed of transposition into domestic legislation and the extent to which codes are used, Britain being especially strong on these two points. France and Germany are slower to transpose EC regulations and more reluctant to use codes instead of formal regulations. Whilst Britain does not hesitate to issue good practice guides on topics such as product recall, France and Germany (Bundesministerium für Verbraucherschutz 2002) rely instead on making detailed information available to consumers. National product safety regulations are used in all three countries to complement EC directives. They generally apply to narrow aspects, such as the British safety regulations on toys (CACP 2002), and the French decree on domestic refrigerators, thermometers and other temperature-measuring devices (DGCCRF 2001). In Germany, the DIN committee ensures product conformity to national legislation (DIN 2002). As a general rule, policy-making suffers from lack of data on consumer complaints. Britain is ahead of other countries in having reformed its monitoring system to ensure consistent record-keeping (OFT 1998), albeit even then with long publication delays.

Public procurement

Procurement procedures for large projects are principally determined by EC legislation. Above EC thresholds, the countries differ with regard to compliance with EC public procurement rules. However, it is below EC thresholds, where the absence of specific national regulations is not uncommon, that variations are greatest between the three countries.

National interpretation and implementation frequently transgress EC rules. National infringements are challenged by the EC, which sends informal and formal requests and makes references to the European Court of Justice (ECJ). Three typical infringements are unjustified use of negotiated procedures, irregular preparation of calls to tender, and award of contract without invitation to tender. Judging by the number of infringements between 1996 and 2002, summarized in Table 12.4, Britain complies more readily with EC rules than do France and Germany.

Below EC thresholds, Britain relies entirely on guidance and codes of best practice, whilst France and Germany prefer to use formal regulation. Further details are provided in the second part of Table 12.4.

Table 12.4 Public procurement, 1996–2002

	Britain	France	Germany
Above EC thresholds EC regulations apply in all three countries			
EC action on infringement cases:			
Information request	0	2	0
Reasoned opinion	6	11	14
Referred to European Court of Justice	3	8	4
Below EC thresholds only national provisions apply			
National regulations	Guidance on best practice	New Public Procurement Code	National procurement regulations apply
Award procedures	None	Above €90,000 (£66,240, $101,250) before tax: simplified competitive tender; otherwise purchase on invoice	Above €25,000 (£18,400, $28,125) competitive tender by advertisement, below this by negotiation or invoice

Sources: European Commission 2002, OGC 2002, DAJ 2002, Bundesbeschaffungsamt 2002.

Retailing regulations

In all three countries, business premises only need comply with local planning permissions, except in France where further controls are exerted. Additional approval must be obtained from a special 'police' of commercial establishments (CDU 1997). The creation or extension of retail businesses the floor area of which is greater than 300 m^2 is subject to local or, following appeal, national authorisation. Furthermore, new retail businesses greater than 6000 m^2 require a full public inquiry. Sanctions include daily fines.

Business licences and conditions of exploitation vary widely in specific retail areas such as sale of alcoholic drinks, with notable differences in restrictions on trading hours and days. For most products, Sunday trading hours are subject to restrictions. In Britain, dedicated 'Sunday Trading' legislation applies to businesses above a minimum size (Table 12.5). Save for various exemptions, French employment laws forbid paid labour on Sunday to protect the private

Table 12.5   Sunday trading, 2002

	Britain	*France*	*Germany*
Business regulations	Sunday Trading Act 1994	Prefectorial orders to set closing day	Shop Opening Law 1996
Other regulations	None	Employment legislation	None
Businesses regulated	Those with floor area over 280 m^2	Those employing paid labour	All
Sunday trading	Six-hour period between 10 am and 6 pm	24-hour weekly rest on Sunday, in addition to 11-hour daily rest	Closed (see exemptions)
Sanctions for non-compliance	Fines up to £50,000 (€67,950, $76,450)	Civil sanctions; fines up to €1500 (£1104, $1687) (double for repeat infringements) for *each* employee and *each* Sunday worked	Fines up to €100,000 (£73,600, $112,500) per infringement
Examples of exemptions	Pharmacies, petrol stations, alcohol retailers, shops in railway stations and designated airports	Pharmacies, hotels, alcohol retailers, newsagents, food retailers, museums, exhibitions, thermal and tourist resorts	Pharmacies, shops meeting needs of travellers, bakeries, newsagents, health resorts, markets

Sources: Sunday Trading Act 1994; CCIP 2002; HBV 2000; LadschlG (shop closing law) 1996.

Table 12.6 Sale of alcohol, 2002

	Britain	France	Germany
Controls on			
Opening hours	Yes	No	Yes
Type of alcoholic drink (e.g. fermented, distilled)	No	Yes	Yes
Mode of consumption (e.g. on or off the premises, ancillary to a main meal)	Yes	Yes	Yes
Permitted hours			
Sunday	Noon to 10.30pm; off-licences open earlier at 10am; restaurants close an hour later	No restrictions	Sale permitted in restaurants, bars; shops closed
Weekdays	11am to 11pm; off-licences open earlier at 8am; restaurants close an hour later	No restrictions	Shop retail hours: 6am to 8pm except Thursdays (8.30pm) and Saturdays (4pm)

Sources: Home Office 2000, Douanes 2002, Ladenschluszgesetz 1996, JöSchG (Protection of Youth Law) Para 4.

and domestic life of employees and retailers. In Germany, retail opening hours are tightly regulated through the week and closure on Sundays is the norm.

Conditions on the sale of alcohol differ mainly in relation to opening hours (Table 12.6). Despite slow movement towards liberalization, opening hours remain heavily restricted in Germany, including for the sale of alcohol, and, to a lesser extent, in Britain. By contrast, opening hours in France are only subject to employment legislation.

Recent developments

All three countries aim to reduce the administrative burden placed on businesses and have recently engaged in state modernization efforts. In Britain, the 'Modernizing Government' programme has been running since March 1999, and the 2001 Regulatory Reform Act expanded Ministerial powers to issue orders reforming primary legislation (RIU 2002). Further legislative reforms of company law are planned in Britain (DTI 2002). In France, a widespread reform of the State was facilitated by a 1995 decree, modified in 1998 (Fonction Publique 2002). Modernization of the German Federal Government was launched in December 1999 with 15 guiding projects and 23 additional projects, with ambitious targets for full use of interactive electronic media (Bundesregierung 2002).

In Britain, the debate on trading hours for the sale of alcohol is still ongoing, with a draft reform of the alcohol and entertainment licensing regime. In Germany, there is continuing debate over the reform of retail opening and seasonal sales laws.

European legislation resulting from current preparatory work would further affect national regulations. Sensitive policy areas include the regulation of European company law, safety of services for consumers, and combined rules for public contract awards.

More importantly, growing concern for the quality of regulation and its impact on governance is apparent not only at EC level, with the 'better regulation package', but also at national level in all three countries. In Britain, the Better Regulation Task Force established in September 1997 as an independent advisory body has since produced two dozen reports addressing issues such as consumer affairs, licensing legislation, self-regulation and alternatives to state regulation (BRTF 2002). In France, EC and OECD initiatives prompted close investigation of the 'better regulation' route in a 22-point proposal for reform (Mandelkern 2002). In Germany, the Economics Ministry continues to press for regulatory reform over the full breadth of business activity (Bundesministerium für Wirtschaft 2001).

Sources

BRTF (2002) (Better Regulation Task Force), <www.brtf.gov.uk> [30 September 2002].

Bundesbeschaffungsamt (2002), 'Beschaffungsordnung', <www.bescha.bund.de> [9 October 2002].

Bundesministerium für Justiz (2002), 'Insolvenzordnung', <jurcom5.juris.de/bundesrecht/inso> [9 October 2002].

Bundesministerium für Verbraucherschutz (2002), 'Ernährung und Landwirtschaft, Verbraucherinformation', <www.verbraucherschutzministerium.de> [9 October 2002].

Bundesministerium für Wirtschaft (2001), 'Bericht über Strukturreformen in Deutschland Dokumenten 498', <www.bundesregierung.de> [9 October 2002].

Bundesregierung (2002), 'Modern State – Modern Administration', <www.staat-modern.de> [30 September 2002].

CACP (Consumer and Competition Policy Directorate) (2002), <www.dti.gov.uk/cacp> [30 September 2002].

CCIP (Chambre de commerce et d'industrie de Paris) (2002), <www.ccip.fr/etudes/arch/pdf02/bla0205.pdf> [30 September 2002].

CDU (Centre de documentation de l'urbanisme, Ministère de l'Équipement, des Transports, du Logement, du Tourisme et de la Mer) (1997), <www.urbanisme.equipement.gouv.fr> [30 September 2002].

CLB (Centre for Law and Business: Company Law in Europe) (1999), <www.dti.gov.uk/cld> [30 September 2002].

Companies House (2002), <www.companies-house.gov.uk> [30 September 2002].

O. Couwenberg, 'Survival rates in bankruptcy systems: Overlooking the evidence', *European Journal of Law and Economics*, vol. 12 (2001) 253–73.

DAJ (Direction des affaires juridiques) (2002), <www.finances.gouv.fr/daj> [30 September 2002].

DGCCRF (Direction Générale de la Concurrence, de la Consommation et de la Répression des fraudes) (2001), 'Rapport d'activités: Qualité et sécurité', <www.minefi. gouv. fr/dgccrf> [30 September 2002].

DIN (Deutsches Institut für Normung) (2002), 'Geschäftsbericht 2001', <www.din.de> [9 October 2002].

Douanes (2002), 'Commerce des alcools et des boissons', <www.douane.minefi.gouv.fr> [30 September 2002].

DTI (Department of Trade and Industry) (2002), 'Company Law Review', <www.dti.gov. uk/cld> [30 September 2002].

European Commission (2002), 'Public procurement infringements', <europa.eu.int/ comm/internal_market> [30 September 2002].

European Commission (2001) 'Green Paper on European Union Consumer Protection', COM(2001)531final), <europa.eu.int/eur-lex/en/com/gpr/2001/com2001_0531en01.pdf> [30 September 2002].

European Commission (2002a), 'e-procurement Europe', <simap.eu.int/EN/pub/docs/ thres2002/thres2002-en.doc> [30 September 2002].

Fonction Publique (Ministère de la Fonction Publique, de la Réforme de l'Ètat et de l'Aménagement du Territoire) (2002), 'Cadre de la réforme', <www.fonction-publique. gouv.fr> [30 September 2002].

HBV (Gewerkschaft Handel Banken und Versicherungen: Commerce, Banking and Insurance Union) (2000), <www.hbv-berlin.de/fachgrupp/einzelha/shopclos.htm> [8 October 2002].

Home Office (2000) *Time for Reform: Proposals for the Modernisation of our Licensing Laws*, White Paper Cm 4696, <www.dcms.gov.uk> [30 September 2002].

Insolvency Service (2002), <www.insolvency.gov.uk> [30 September 2002].

Mandelkern (2002), 'Qualité de la Réglementation', <www.ladocumentationfrancaise.fr/ brp_pages> [30 September 2002].

L. Miles, 'The German Corporate Governance Codes: What Implications?' *Business Law Review* 23/6 (2002): 140–145.

NetPME (2002), <www.netpme.fr> [30 September 2002].

OFT (Office of Fair Trading), 'Cause for Complaint', *FairTrading*, 21 (1998): 10–13.

OGC (Office of Government Commerce) (2002), <www.ogc.gov.uk> [30 September 2002].

OJEC (Official Journal of the European Communities) 332, 27 November 2001.

RIU (Regulatory Impact Unit) (2002), <www.cabinet-office.gov.uk/regulation> [30 September 2002].

Service Public (2000), 'Où immatriculer une société nouvellement créée?' <vosquestions. service-public.fr> [30 September 2002].

WGM (Weil, Gotshal & Mange LLP) (2002), *Comparative Study of Corporate Governance Codes*, <europa.eu.int/comm/internal_market/en/company> [30 September 2002].

13
Financial Regulation

C.H. Flockton, P.A. Grout and M.J. Yong

Introduction

This chapter is concerned with the authorization, regulation and supervision of financial activities as they pertain to both financial and non-financial institutions. Regulation involves the development and implementation of rules while supervision is concerned with the monitoring and enforcement of those rules. Unless expressly specified, the phrase 'financial regulation' will refer to all aspects of authorization, regulation and supervision. Associated areas of regulation that are not intrinsically financial in nature, such as competition policy and business regulation, are described elsewhere in this volume.

Britain, France and Germany maintain comparable standards of prudential regulation based on internationally accepted codes, but conduct of financial regulation and degree of enforcement vary substantially. Overall, French policies and rules are probably the most lenient and least in line with international standards, although recent harmonization efforts have resulted in a state of flux. In contrast, British standards are the most stringent and conform most closely with international benchmarks, but monitoring policies tend to remain passive. Germany lies between the two. In addition, the decentralized institutional mode of policy delivery employed by France distinguishes it from Britain and Germany. However, in all three countries financial regulation is increasingly driven by EC Directives and is thus becoming progressively more homogeneous.

The nature of financial regulation and supervision

The rapid globalization of finance has both prompted and been prompted by tighter financial regulation and greater international harmonization over the last few decades. The primary objectives of financial regulation are to advance macroeconomic and microeconomic stability, protect investors, and encourage efficiency and competition. Broadly speaking, the regulation of financial activities can be classified under four principal headings, namely banking, securities, insurance and accounting regulation:

- *banking regulation* delineates the existence, organization and operation of banks and credit institutions;
- *securities regulation* outlines the management of stock exchanges, supporting infrastructure, market participants and financial products;
- *insurance regulation* defines the existence, organization and operation of insurers of life and pensions, general business (motor, household and commercial), and health and protection;
- *accounting regulation* stipulates the preparation and disclosure of financial statements according to a specified set of principles, and their verification through the audit process.

With regard to *banking* regulation, compliance with recent EC Directives and Basel principles has led to substantial harmonization of prudential regulation and a comprehensive EU-wide body of 'banking law'. However differences between Britain, Germany and France do arise in terms of entry and disclosure requirements, and conduct of banking supervision. In addition, only Britain and Germany have delegated overall responsibility for banking regulation to a single authority.

Similarly, implementation of EC Directives and compliance with the International Organisation of Securities Commission's (IOSCO) guidelines has resulted in partial convergence of prudential regulation of *securities* markets. These rules concern listing and trading practices, new issues of securities, insider trading, disclosure, takeover proposals, investor protection and investment products. In addition, comparability of disclosed information has been enhanced by the move to International Accounting Standards (IAS). However divergences in national interpretation and in the extent and speed of transposition of the directives result in significant cross-country differences. Britain boasts the most sophisticated regime and Germany the least. Further, notable disparities exist in the institutional structure of regulation and the capacity of national regulators to influence markets.

EC Directives on *insurance* set out rudimentary rules on minimum adequacy and disclosure requirements pertaining to assets and liabilities, capital and solvency, accounting treatment and reinsurance. However these directives only specify minimum prudential requirements and allow national authorities a great deal of flexibility in setting stricter regulations. Consequently Germany has managed to maintain a much tighter regulatory environment than Britain and France.

With respect to *accounting* regulation, the development of International Accounting Standards by the International Accounting Standards Board and

IOSCO has resulted in fairly consistent treatment of financial transactions and figures in the three countries. However the standard-setting processes in Britain, France and Germany differ in that they place emphasis on different parties so that the authority, scope and application of standards diverge.

Specific comparisons

In general, financial institutions in Britain are confronted with few limits in terms of allowable business but face comprehensive and strict regulations with respect to the conduct of business. Having said that, Britain has historically taken a non-interventionist approach to supervision based on a model of self-regulation and trust. Numerous financial scandals over the last two decades have questioned the effectiveness of this system and led to the creation of a universal regulator for banking, securities and insurance in the form of the Financial Services Authority (FSA). In April 2002 Germany adopted the model of universal regulation with the establishment of the *Bundesanstalt für Finanzdienstleistungsaufsicht* (BAFin). In contrast, authority over financial regulation in France remains divided between a myriad of specialized organizations that collaborate to ensure systemic soundness of financial policy (IMF 2001), and it is far from clear that France intends to follow Britain and Germany down the same route in creating a universal regulator. In fact, at least with respect to banking, France has explicitly stated that the setting of rules and the sanctioning of their non-observance should belong to distinct authorities (BdeF 2001).

The sections below compare each country's overall policy approach to financial regulation in the four categories by highlighting prominent areas of disparity through the use of illustrative examples.

Banking regulation

The Second Banking Directive laid the foundation for banking regulation in the EU in establishing the concept of a single banking licence and the principles of home country control (whereby prudential regulation is assigned to the issuing country) and mutual recognition. Thus similar minimum capital adequacy, large exposure, and deposit guarantee restrictions apply in each of the three countries. Further, the ability of banks to engage in securities underwriting, brokering and dealing, and in real estate investment, development and management, is unrestricted in all three countries, although Britain and France impose some limits on insurance activities (Barth *et al.* 2001). The British FSA is generally the most powerful of the three regulators in terms of the disciplinary sanctions available, followed by the German BAFin, as is illustrated in Table 13.1. It also appears to be the strictest in terms of entry requirements.

In Britain the transfer of authority over banking regulation from the Bank of England to the FSA in 1998 has rendered central banking independent. Likewise,

Table 13.1 Banking regulation

	Britain	France	Germany
Structure	Centralized system	Decentralized: authority is divided between six organizations	Centralized system
Legal liability	Not unless acted in bad faith	Yes	No
Number of banks	452	359	3,220
Firm entry into the market:			
• Is information on source of funds for capital required?	Yes	Yes	No
• Are law enforcement authorities consulted in each case?	Yes	No	No
Minimum liquidity requirement	Set on an individual basis; risk adjusted	Short-term liabilities + own funds ≤ liquid assets and cash	Weighted short-term assets/ short term liabilities ≥ 1
Minimum capital–asset ratio requirement	8%	8%	8% (12.5% for new banks for first two years)
Minimum reserve requirement	0.15% of eligible liabilities > £400 m (€544m, $6.2m)	2% of liabilities in the reserve base	2% of eligible liabilities in the reserve base
Must banks disclose risk management procedures to public?	Some disclosure	No	No
Can the supervisory agency suspend director's decision to distribute:			
• Dividends	Yes	Yes	Yes
• Bonuses	Yes	No	No
• Management fees	Yes	No	No
Regarding bank restructuring and reorganization, can supervisory agency or any other government agency:			
• supersede shareholder rights	Yes	No	Yes
• remove and replace management	Yes	No	No
• insure liabilities beyond any explicit deposit insurance scheme	Yes	No	No

Source: World Bank Survey 2001; IMF 2001.

monetary policy formulation was divorced from banking regulation in Germany when the *Bundesaufsichtsamt für Kreditwesen* (BAK), now part of the BAFin, assumed responsibility for banking regulations from the *Bundesbank* in 1961. However the *Bundesbank* and *Landesbanks* (*Land* central banks) retain some reporting and overview functions, especially over the smaller private banks. In France, however, the Ministry of Finance and *Banque de France* are directly involved in regulation and indirectly involved in prudential supervision and authorisation which, in contrast to Britain and Germany, are assigned to separate bodies.

Securities regulation

A clear distinction can be made between the structure of securities markets in Britain compared to those of the two continental countries. Britain is characterized by large, liquid capital markets in which ownership is highly dispersed and control rights traded frequently, and where funding is determined by price and availability. In France and Germany the converse is the case: funding tends to be long-term and connected to implicit or relational contracts based on trust and faith.

In Britain the importance of equity funding and lack of a natural corporate governance mechanism warranted the development of explicit, prescriptive and detailed regulations over and above those ordained by EC directives. Thus it possesses the most advanced system of the three countries and affords the highest level of investor protection. This is evidenced by the strict and extensive admission criteria to the London Stock Exchange (LSE) as indicated by Table 13.2. Additional disclosure requirements on directors' and key shareholder dealings, and on major transactions, ensure higher levels of transparency than in Germany and France, which merely comply with the minimum requirements specified by EC directives. There are, however, plans to increase directors' dealing requirements for companies listed on Germany's *Neuer Markt* (PwC 2002).

By and large, Britain and France take a more proactive and interventionist approach to regulation than Germany, where regulation of the primary market is the least exacting (PwC 2002).

However French and German growth markets are subject to tighter regulation than their primary counterparts, whereas in Britain secondary growth markets are self-regulated. In addition, Britain imposes fewer restrictions on specialist debt securities than it does on equity, whereas a common standard is applied to both debt and equity in France and Germany. Further, while verification and approval of all prospectuses is required in the latter two countries, exemptions are made in Britain (PwC 2002).

A final distinction lies in the distribution of power: the FSA has powers over both authorization and regulation in Britain, but the admission of securities to the official list is the responsibility of the stock exchanges in France and Germany (PwC 2002).

Table 13.2 Securities regulation

	Britain	France	Germany
Structure	Centralized system based on the FSA with support from the LSE	Decentralized system: authority is divided between five organizations	Centralized system based on *BAFin* with support from *Deutsche Börse AG*
Stock market capitalization (% of GDP)	130%	67%	27%
Number of domestic/foreign companies listed on main or parallel exchange	2450/469	1162/214 (Euronext)	750/235
Percentage of shares held in block ownership*	9.9%	20%	57%
Listing requirements on:			
• Minimum period of existence and/or operating history	Significant	Some	Some
• Shares publicly held	Significant	Significant	Some
• Financial statements and audits	Significant	Some	Some
• Ability of directors and management	Significant	Minimal	Minimal
• Minimum float of equity capital	≥£700 000 (€951,300, $1,070,300) for shares; ≥£200 000 (€271 800, $305 800) for debt securities	The Official List (25%), The Second Market (10%), The New Market (0%)	€50,000 (£36,800, $56,250) for shares
Disclosure requirements on:			
• Directors' dealings	Significant and prompt	Delayed, annual disclosure	Minimal, except for new or further share issuance
• Major transactions	Extensive: threshold at 5% and 25%	Minimal, except for share issuance	Minimal
• Related party transactions	Extensive: threshold at 5%	Minimal	Minimal
Working capital requirement	Yes	No	No

Note * 'Block ownership' means not freely traded, that is, the shares are concentrated in the hands of institutions, members of the founder's family or in corporate cross-shareholdings.
Sources: PwC 2002; IMF 2001; UKLA 2002; Haller and Kepler 2002; OEC 2002; Barca and Becht 2002; German Brief 2002, Art. 7 Aktiengesetz.

Insurance regulation

Historically the German insurance industry has been very closely regulated and exempt from wider competition and cartel laws. The insurance arm of the BAFin, the *Bundesaufsichtsamt für Versicherungswesen* (BAV), operates within a highly specified legal framework, and tight regulation ensured that little foreign penetration of this high premium market occurred. The 'special characteristics' of the insurance market were used to justify anti-competitive features such as the local *Land* building insurance monopolies, the system of tied insurance agents, and the exemption from cartel law of the private health insurers. However re-insurers face a much lighter regulatory regime and are highly internationalized.

In contrast, British and French markets have historically been subject to very light regulation in terms of solvency requirements, ease of entry into the market, contract conditions, premiums, profit and service quality, and portfolio restrictions. The only aspect that was subject to more stringent regulation was that of product distribution, for which there were high disclosure requirements (Rees and Kessner 1999). Supervision is also less rigorous in these two countries. On-site inspections do not constitute a component of the day-to-day prudential supervision in Britain (IMF 1999) and, in line with its custom of self-regulation, the FSA has recently recommended the self-identification of solvency margins by insurers based on their individual risk (ABI 2002). Mutual insurance companies in France are subject to a less explicit framework of regulation and supervision than their commercial counterparts, resulting in further erosion of transparency (IMF 2001).

The EC position appears to support the latter approach of minimal regulation, as evidenced by the string of directives concluded in the mid-1990s that forced deregulation of the more closed markets such as that of Germany. As with the banking sector, these directives established the concepts of a single EU-wide licence and of home country control. In addition, solvency regulation and financial reporting rules were harmonized (Rees and Kessner 1999). However the directives only specify minimum prudential requirements and allow national authorities a great deal of flexibility in setting stricter regulations, provided they do not contravene the above principles (EC 2002).

The consequence has been a significant easing of regulation in Germany, especially with respect to premiums and contracts such that subsequent reductions in premiums have been observed. However the exemption of the insurance industry from EC antitrust legislation, differences in legal systems and the scarcity of independent brokers in Germany have permitted it to maintain a much tighter regulatory regime than exists in Britain and France, especially with respect to portfolio restrictions, as demonstrated in Table 13.3, and there remains a distinct lack of foreign entry into the profitable German market (Rees and Kessner 1999).

Table 13.3   Insurance regulation

	Britain	France	Germany
Structure	Co-ordinated system based on the FSA in conjunction with HM Treasury and two specialized bodies	Decentralized system: authority is divided between six organizations	Centralized system based on BAFin
Degree of government involvement	Moderate	High	Low
Attitude towards regulation	Historically very light	Historically very light	Historically very restrictive
Portfolio restrictions on pension funds:			
• Quantitative restrictions on domestic assets (maxima)	No limits except that employer-related loans are forbidden; broad asset-liability matching and diversification	Quoted equities (65%), unquoted equities (0.5%), loans (10%).	Quoted equities (30%), unquoted equities (10%), real estate (25%), corporate bonds (50%), investment funds (30%), loans (50%), bank deposits (50%)
• Self-investment	≤5%	≤33%	≤2%
• Foreign asset restrictions	None	≥50% in EU government bonds	≤30% in EU equity, 25% in EU property; 6% in non-EU equity, 5% in non-EU bonds
Percentage of a liability that must be protected by assets in the same currency	80% if ≥5% of total liabilities	80%	80%

Sources: FSA 2002; IMF 2001; Rees and Kessner 1999; OECD 2002a, b.

Accounting regulation

British standards correspond most closely with International Accounting Standards (IASs) and are regarded as being even stricter in the treatment of off-balance sheet finance, joint ventures, and acquisition accounting (IMF 1999). In contrast, in Germany the degree of conformity of the commercial code with

IASs is lower and accounting transparency weaker. Similarly, discrepancies exist between IASs and the French code, which emphasizes the bookkeeping rather than the financial reporting aspect of accounting. It has been argued that greater transparency is required with respect to segment classification, financial instruments and stock options, and that this should be facilitated by a reduction in the choice of accounting treatments in France (OEC 2002). The implication is that in setting standards, primary consideration is given to informing shareholders of listed companies in Britain, defending the creditor in Germany, and protecting the interests of accounting firms in France (OEC 2002).

Britain has arguably the most advanced enforcement system in Europe by virtue of the Financial Reporting Review Panel, whereas Germany has no institutional enforcement system to speak of (Haller and Kepler 2002). However the British regime, being based on the principle of self-regulation, is less exacting than the stringent French regulatory system, which places arduous legal and State-imposed requirements on its audit firms (Mikol and Standish 1998). There is heavy reliance in all three countries on using external audits to verify compliance with accounting standards (Haller and Kepler 2002). In Britain and France regional institutes undertake audit regulation with co-ordination at the national level, whereas the national-level BAFin is responsible for auditors in Germany (see Table 13.4).

Table 13.4   Accounting regulation

	Britain	*France*	*Germany*
Structure	Co-ordinated system based on the Financial Reporting Council	Co-ordinated system based on the *Conseil National de la Comptabilité* in conjunction with the *Comité de la Réglementation Comptable*	Centralized system based on the *Deutsches Rechnungslegungs Standards Committee*
Are standards binding?	Yes, standards are underpinned by statute	Yes, standards form part of legislation	No
Degree of government involvement	Low	High	Low
Degree of compliance with IAS	High	Low; considerable differences exist at both conceptual and technical levels	Low; based on prudential principle rather than the 'true and fair view'

Sources: OEC 2002; Haller and Kepler 2002; FRC 2002; DRSC 2002.

All EU companies listed on a regulated market will be required to prepare their consolidated accounts in accordance with IASs from 2005 onwards (EC 2001). However the majority of small- and medium-sized limited companies in Germany are facing considerable problems of transition and have therefore been granted a changeover period to 2007.

Recent developments

Recent developments in all four fields of financial regulation predominantly revolve around the EC's Financial Services Action Plan (FSAP). This seeks to establish the legislative and supervisory architecture that will foster the completion of the Single Market for financial services, promote transparent and secure retail markets, and advance prudential regulation. Key elements of this reform package are revised directives on prospectuses, investment services and capital adequacy; legislation to implement an EU accounting strategy; and new directives on market abuse, takeovers, mergers, supplementary pensions, distance selling, insurance intermediaries, financial conglomerates and tax coordination (EC 1999).

Innovations such as these will finally establish a single framework and set of rules for the European financial area. In eliminating discrepancies in regulatory structures and policies that were, for example, a significant contributory cause of the failure of the proposed iX stock exchange merger, this single framework can be expected to accelerate cross-border supply of services and further concentration through mergers and acquisitions.

Sources

ABI (Association of British Insurers) (2002), <www.abi.org.uk/Display/default.asp?Menu_ID = 726&Menu_All = 1,714,726> [14 October 2002].

F. Barca and M. Becht, *The Control of Corporate Europe* (Oxford: Oxford University Press, 2002).

J.R. Barth, G. Caprio and R. Levine, 'The Regulation and Supervision of Banks around the World: A New Database', May 2001, <www.worldbank.org/research/projects/bank_regulation.htm> [6 March 2003].

BdeF (Banque de France), 'Eurosystème, Note d'Information no. 126, Le Comité de la réglementation bancaire et financière', June 2001, <www.banque-france.fr/fr/telechar/note126.pdf> [6 March 2003].

DRSC (Deutsches Rechnungslegungs Standards Committee) (2002), <www.drsc.de/> [17 October 2002].

EC (European Communities), 'Study into the methodologies to assess the overall financial position of an insurance undertaking from the perspective of prudential supervision', May 2002, <www.kpmg.co.uk/kpmg/uk/image/eus2_report.pdf> [6 March 2003].

EC (European Communities), 'Financial reporting: Commission proposes requirement for listed companies to use International Accounting Standards by 2005',

February 2001, <europa.eu.int/comm/internal_market/en/company/account/news/ias.htm> [6 March 2003].

EC (European Communities), 'Financial services: Commission outlines Action Plan for single financial market', May 1999, <europa.eu.int/comm/internal_market/en/ finances/general/action.htm> [6 March 2003].

FRC (Financial Reporting Council) (2002), <www.frc.org.uk/ [17 October 2002].

FSA (Financial Services Authority) (2002), <www.fsa.gov.uk> [17 October 2002].

German Brief, 'Unravelling Cross-shareholdings', pp6–7, 8 February 2002, FAZ.

A. Haller and J. Kepler, 'Financial accounting developments in the European Union: past events and future prospects', *The European Accounting Review*, 11/1 (2002): 153–90.

IMF (International Monetary Fund), 'Report on the Observance of Standards and Codes (ROSC) France. Transparency in monetary and financial policies', February 2001; 'Experimental report on transparency practices: United Kingdom', March 1999; <www.imf.org/external/np/rosc/rosc.asp#U> [6 March 2003].

A. Mikol and P. Standish, 'Audit independence and nonaudit services: a comparative study in differing British and French perspectives', *The European Accounting Review*, 7/3 (1998): 541–69.

OEC (l'Ordre des Experts-Comptables), P. Standish, 'Developments in French Accounting and Auditing 2000', <www.experts-comptables.fr/ [17 October 2002].

OECD (Organisation for Economic Cooperation and Development) (2002a), 'Survey of investment regulation of pension funds', <www.inprs.org/data/policies/files/survey-invregulation.pdf> [6 March 2003].

OECD (Organisation for Economic Cooperation and Development) (2002b), 'Insurance regulation and supervision in OECD countries, Asian economies and CEEC and NIS countries', <www.oecd.org/pdf/M00003000/M00003881.pdf> [6 March 2003].

PwC (PricewaterhouseCoopers), 'Primary market comparative regulation study – Key themes', April 2002, <www.fsa.gov.uk/pubs/discussion/dp14.pdf> [6 March 2003].

R. Rees and E. Kessner, 'Regulation and efficiency in European insurance markets', *Economic policy*, 29 (1999): 365–97.

UKLA (UK Listing Authority) (2002), <www.fsa.gov.uk/pubs/ukla/lr chapters4/ [17 October 2002].

World Bank Survey of Bank Regulation and Supervision, March 2001, <www.worldbank. org/research/interest/prr_stuff/bank_regulation_database.htm> [6 March 2003].

14
Research and Development

Cecile Deer, Hubert Ertl, Martin Rhisiart and Stephanie Wilde

Introduction

Research and development (R&D) as part of public policy in Britain, France and Germany has developed in parallel with nation-building, industrialization, colonization and wars. However there are important differences in the way this sector has been organized and managed in the three countries in relation to the role played by public authorities, the degree of autonomy of R&D institutions, and the qualifications and organization of the research profession.

The nature of R&D policy

Public policy in R&D is concerned with the role of public authorities in the formal organization, provision and financing of R&D activities. Broadly defined, it covers any part of the R&D process which is either directly or indirectly influenced by public decisions at national, regional and/or international level. Of these, the national level is the most important, and is concerned with:

- public funding (level, distribution, selectivity);
- legislation and regulation (scientific and professional ethics and safety);
- planning and implementation (priority areas, action plans and budgeting, government bodies employing researchers);
- evaluation;
- recruitment and training of researchers.

In all three countries, R&D operates within a European agenda, as exemplified by European Union Framework Programmes, and an international agenda that includes initiatives such as the International Thermonuclear Experimental Reactor.

In Britain and France, public R&D is funded by central government and takes place across departments. Allocation of resources is determined by periodic budgetary review processes, in particular the Comprehensive Spending Review in Britain and the *Budget Civil de Recherche et de Développement* (BCRD) in France. In Germany, public R&D has constitutional status (Article 91 of the Basic Law) and is a responsibility of both the federal state and the 16 federal *Länder* via a joint commission for educational planning and research funding (*BLK – Bund-Länder-Kommission für Bildungsplanung und Forschungsförderung*), which handles medium term planning, co-operation between the federal state and the *Länder*, and suggestions concerning future participating institutions (BMBF 2002). Details of public funding bodies are given in Table 14.1.

Historically, most public R&D in Britain and Germany has been carried out in higher education institutions. Both countries also have a number of public research institutes that work closely with universities. In Britain there is a historical dual funding structure for research based in universities whereby universities receive mainstream funding through the Higher Education Funding Councils while the Research Councils award grants on a competitive basis.

In France, public research is funded essentially at central government level, mainly by the Ministry of Education, Research and Technology, although other government departments also finance research projects. The central government also subsidizes private R&D in areas such as aeronautics, electronics and chemistry. In contrast to Britain, universities in France have traditionally been minor players in public R&D. Instead, France has a separate public and multidisciplinary research organization, the *Centre National de la Recherche Scientifique* (CNRS), which works in collaboration with higher education institutions, plus a number of other non-university public research institutes.

In Britain, the devolved administrations in Scotland, Wales and (when not being ruled from London) Northern Ireland exercise a degree of administrative control over elements such as funding councils for higher education. The devolved administrations also have a prominent role in exploiting the knowledge base through programmes that broker R&D links between knowledge providers in the university sector and companies that can exploit the know-how. In France, recent decentralizing laws have meant that the regional authorities have become more active in supporting R&D activities.

In Germany, the tendency in recent years has been towards a separation between higher education institutions and institutions which focus entirely on research. Thus the second most important actor after the institutions of higher education is the *Max-Planck-Gesellschaft* (MPG), the umbrella institution for 80 research institutes, laboratories and working groups. The focus of MPG-institutes is basic research outside universities in the fields of bio-medical research, chemical-physical-technical research, and research in the humanities. Thirdly, the *Fraunhofer-Gesellschaft* (FhG) co-ordinates the work of 56 research units

Table 14.1 Main departments and agencies concerned with R&D

Britain	France	Germany
Higher Education Funding Councils (HEFC)	*Ministère de l'Education de la Recherche et de la Technologie* (Ministry of Education, Research and Technology)	*Bundesministerium für Bildung und Forschung (BMBF)* (Federal Ministry for Education and Research)
Department of Trade and Industry (DTI)	Other ministries	*Land* Research and Education ministries
Research Councils:	*Conseils régionaux* (Regional Councils)	*Bund-Länder-Kommission für Bildungsplanung und Forschungsförderung (BLK)* (Federal-State Commission for Educational Planning and Research Support)
BBSRC (Bio-technology and Biological Science Research Council)	*Centre National de la Recherche Scientifique (CNRS)* (National Centre for Scientific Research)	
EPSRC (Engineering and Physical Science Research Council)	*Etablissements Publics à Caractère Industriel et Commercial (EPIC)* (Public Establishments relating to Industry and Commerce) such as the *CEA* (Atomic Energy Commission)	Higher education institutions
ESRC (Economic and Social Research Council)		*Max-Planck-Gesellschaft (MPG)* (Max Planck Society)
MRC (Medical Research Council)		*Fraunhofer-Gesellschaft (FhG)* (Fraunhofer Society)
NERC (Natural Environment Research Council)	*Etablissements Publics Scientifiques et Technologiques* (Public Scientific and Technological Establishments) such as the *INRA* (National Institute of Agronomic Research)	Other large, multidisciplinary research centres such as the *Helmoltz-Gemeinschaft Deutscher Forschungszentren* (Helmoltz Association of German Research Centres)
PPARC (Particle Physics and Astronomy Research Council)		
AHRB (Arts and Humanities Research Board)	Higher education institutions	
Other government departments		

that undertake commissioned work for industry, service enterprises and public institutions. Other actors include a variety of large, multidisciplinary research centres such as the Helmoltz Association of German Research Centres; 79 research centres jointly funded by the federal state and the *Länder (Blaue Liste-Einrichtungen)*; and a number of institutions funded either by the federal state or by one of the 16 *Länder*. The German Research Council *(Deutsche Forschungs-gemeinschaft – DFG)* allocates research funds to universities using peer-review procedures, and is their largest source of external funding. Half of the funds allocated by the DFG come from federal sources and the other half from *Länder* sources. In 2002 the DFG allocated funds amounting to €1.2 billion (£883 million, $1.35 billion) (DFG 2004).

Specific comparisons

Figures for R&D funding and employment of researchers indicate that in general the French and German governments are more active in R&D than the British government.

Government spending

A standard classification system is used by policy-makers and experts internationally to record – and compare – R&D activities. Gross domestic expenditure on R&D (GERD) is the most reliable indication of national R&D expenditure, as it includes the activities of both the public and private sectors. The components that are drawn together to produce GERD are government R&D (GOVERD), which includes departments, research councils and research establishments; business enterprise R&D (BERD), which includes companies and industrial research associations; higher education R&D (HERD), consisting of universities; and private non-profit institutions (PNP), consisting of charities and learned societies.

Table 14.2 shows that although overall spending on R&D in relation to GDP in 2001 was highest in Germany, government funding of R&D was marginally higher in France than in Germany. Britain was lowest on both counts.

Table 14.2   R&D funding as a % of GDP, 2001

	Britain	*France*	*Germany*
Gross Domestic Expenditure on R&D (GERD)	1.89	2.23	2.51
Government R&D (GOVERD)	0.18	0.37	0.34*
Higher Education Expenditure on R&D (HERD)	0.41	0.42	0.41

Note * Includes other classes.
Source: OECD 2003.

However funding of higher education institutions was very similar across the three countries.

Not surprisingly given these patterns, government spending on its own R&D as a proportion of total R&D spending is also highest in France and lowest in Britain (Table 14.3). R&D spending by higher education institutions, by contrast, is highest in Britain and lowest in Germany.

Table 14.4 shows that while overall budget appropriations for R&D are higher in Germany and France than in Britain, the share spent on defence R&D is much higher in Britain and France than in Germany. In fact the two countries are among the OECD countries which spend the largest proportion of their R&D public budget on defence, which explains important transfers of public funding to private corporations. In Germany, for recent historical reasons, this has been less the case. The Office of Science and Technology, using a slightly different measure, reports that in Britain in 2000/01 the defence sector received the largest share of government funded R&D (34 per cent), followed by the Research Councils (21 per cent, mainly going to biotechnology and biological sciences, medical research, and engineering and physical sciences), non-defence government departments (also 21 per cent), the Higher Education Funding Councils (18 per cent) and European Union R&D activities (6 per cent) (OST 2003).

Figures for non-defence budget appropriations for R&D reflect this pattern of higher spending in France and Germany than in Britain, with France distinctive in its emphasis on space research and Germany spending significantly more on

Table 14.3 Who performs R&D? (% total R&D Domestic Expenditure, 2001)

	Britain	*France*	*Germany*
Government	9.7	16.5	13.7
Higher Education	21.4	18.9	16.4
Industry	67.4	63.2	69.9

Source: OECD 2003.

Table 14.4 Government budget appropriations or outlays for R&D (GBAORD), 2001

	Britain	*France*	*Germany*
Total	$10.6 bn (£6.9 bn, €9.4 bn)	$16.2 bn (£10.5 bn, €14.4 bn)	$17.2 bn (£11.2 bn, €15.3 bn)
Defence budget (% total)	30.5	22.8	7.4
Civil budget (% total)	69.5	77.2	92.6

Source: OECD 2003.

Table 14.5   Civil budget outlays for R&D by socioeconomic objectives

	Britain 2001	France 2002	Germany 2003
Economic development	$997.3 (£648.2, €887.6)	$2076.1 (£1349.5, €1847.7)	$3387.4 (£2201.8, €3014.8)
Health & environment	$2372.0 (£1541.8, €2111.1)	$1722.9 (£1119.9, €1533.4)	$2427.6 (£1577.9, €2160.6)
Space programmes	$218.1 (£141.8, €194.1)	$1510.3 (£981.7, €1344.2)	$865.9 (£562.8, €770.7)
Non-oriented research	$1432.5 (£931.1, €1274.9)	$3333.2 (£2166.6, €2966.5)	$2944.5 (£1913.9, €2620.6)
General university funds	$2298.8 (£1494.2, €2045.9)	$3887.8 (£2527.1, €3460.1)	$6988.6 (£4542.6, €6219.9)

Source: OECD 2003. Figures for France and Germany are provisional.

economic development (Table 14.5). Budget spending in Britain was the lowest in all spending categories apart from health and environment, where British spending matched Germany and significantly exceeded France.

Britain, France and Germany also have strong industrial, corporate R&D sectors (see Table 14.3) whose share of the national R&D effort has increased over the last two decades (OECD 2003). This is due to the combination of stagnating and at times decreasing public expenditure on R&D, and growing R&D expenses on the part of the corporate sector. This has been particularly the case in Germany.

R&D is also partly financed by foreign interests and/or international organizations. Conversely, British, French and German public authorities contribute to the financing of R&D activities abroad via their direct contributions to European research projects such as the European Space Agency, Airbus, European Union programmes and the European Centre for Nuclear Research (CERN), as well as to other international research projects. Together Britain, France and Germany represent 65 per cent of the EU R&D effort, but this overall lead has decreased in recent years.

Employment of researchers

The most recent available figures show that while the number of researchers overall is highest in Germany, France has the highest number of researchers as a proportion of the labour force and the highest proportion of researchers in higher education institutions (Table 14.6). The figures also suggest that the number of government researchers as a proportion of all researchers is higher in Germany than in France (with Britain again trailing), although this conclusion may not be warranted in view of the fact that the French figure excludes

Table 14.6 Employment of researchers

	Britain 1998	France 2001	Germany 2001
Total researchers (Full Time Equivalent)	157,662	177,372	264,384
Total researchers per 1000 labour force	5.5	7.2	6.8
Government researchers as a percentage of total researchers	9.1	12.9*	14.6**
Higher education researchers as a percentage of total researchers	31.1	35.2	25.7

Notes
* Defence excluded (all or mostly)
** Includes other classes.
Source: OECD 2003.

defence researchers (and we have seen that spending on defence research is high in France) while the German figure includes other classes of researchers as well.

The total number of researchers grew steadily in Britain, France and Germany during the 1990s, but this was not true for government researchers, the number of which remained fairly steady during this period. The number of researchers in higher education institutions, on the other hand, grew in all three countries. This was especially true of Britain, where the number of researchers in higher education institutions increased by over 50 per cent between 1991 and 1998 (OECD 2003).

Recent developments

In all three countries, R&D policy has been guided by the claimed necessity to make R&D more relevant to the outside world through more applied research, as opposed to 'blue sky' research. Public guidelines are placing renewed emphasis on R&D public-private partnership, and public researchers have been encouraged to collaborate with the private sector, particularly in Britain.

This has coincided in Britain with increasing legal and administrative constraints from the central government, which has reinforced its role in the steering of R&D activities. In France during the same period, by contrast, R&D policy has been characterized by decentralizing measures at regional and institutional level. The development of contractual agreements between the State and R&D institutions has formed part of a significant general evolution in French public policy. However the cost of public R&D, in particular the pay and careers of public researchers, remains the responsibility of central government.

Evaluation, quality standards, and publication rates and indexes have been increasingly used by the public authorities in all three countries to manage public research activities. This is particularly true in Britain, where public funding for research in universities has been distributed per subject area according to the results of four-yearly Research Assessment Exercises since the mid-1980s. In France the 1984 Savary Law set up a national committee of evaluation (CNE) for higher education institutions. This was followed in 1988 by the creation of the *Comité National d'Evaluation de la Recherche* (CNER) for the evaluation of research. However the evaluation of public research activities in France follows a consultative, cybernetic and informational pattern: decisions concerning research funding allocations may depend on the result of this evaluation, but this is not statutory as it is in Britain. A comparable procedure does not yet exist in Germany, but the German Research Council (DFG – *Deutsche Forschungsgemeinschaft*) is a body which decides upon the major research projects to be funded in various fields of academic research. In addition, the Federal Ministry for Education and Research has developed new programme monitoring and audit structures to supervise the progress of projects funded by public sources. Large-scale evaluations of the *Max-Planck-Gesellschaft* and the *Fraunhofer-Gesellschaft* took place in 1999, and *Blaue-Liste-Einrichtungen* (joint federal-*Land* research centres) and other state research institutions were evaluated in 2001.

Another recent development is that R&D activities in fields such as biotechnology and medicine have been increasingly scrutinized from an ethical standpoint. What used to be directly the remit of the State is now increasingly that of wider civil society with the public authorities trying to answer this new demand not only via *ad hoc* ethical committees and debates but also via legislation.

Economic developments have also been important for R&D policy in all three countries. At the international level there has been a rapid increase in economic integration, mergers and acquisitions, trade in technology-intensive goods, and inward and outward research-related foreign direct investment (FDI). Public authorities have been concerned by this trend, as it means a privately-initiated rationalization of R&D activities on an international basis. In addition, the traditional knowledge generating and knowledge diffusion role of public R&D has been increasingly constrained by commercial practice, patents and copyrights.

In Britain one of the key challenges identified has been to increase R&D activity in small and medium-sized enterprises (SMEs). As a result, there has been a series of Government measures to provide tax credits for R&D in SMEs, and to bridge the gap between companies and universities. One of the significant current developments in the area of R&D is increased expenditure on science and technology by the British Government, which in 2000 announced a 10 per cent increase in real terms per year for three years (DTI 2002). The Government has been eager to promote biotechnology R&D in particular, and has invested heavily in genomic research.

In France, as in Britain, public authorities have sought to define priority areas for public R&D spending, but the recent period has been characterized by the central government's decision to step back and freeze public funding for R&D.

In Germany it is becoming increasingly difficult to distinguish between publicly and privately funded research, since research in state-run institutions such as universities is attracting more and more money from industry, and research in companies and private research centres is in many cases being partly subsidized by public funds (BMBF 2002: 206).

Sources

BMBF (Bundesministerium für Bildung und Forschung) *Faktenbericht Forschung* (Bonn: BMBF, 2002).

Bureau des Etudes sur la Recherche, <cisad.adc.education.fr/reperes/> [15 June 2003].

Comité National d'Evaluation de la Recherche, <www.cner.gouv.fr> [22 January 2004].

DFG (Deutsche Forschungsgemeinschaft) *Deutsche Forschungsgemeinschaft. Aufbau und Aufgaben* (Bonn: DFG, 2004).

DTI (Department of Trade and Industry), *The Forward Look 2003: Government Funded Science, Engineering and Technology* (London: Department of Trade and Industry/Office of Science and Technology, 2003).

DTI (Department of Trade and Industry), *Investing in Innovation: A Strategy for Science, Engineering and Technology* (London: Department of Trade and Industry/Office of Science and Technology, 2002).

V. Duclert and A. Chatriot, *Quel avenir pour la recherche?: Cinquante savants s'engagent* (Paris: Flammarion, 2003).

Fraunhofer Gesellschaft, <fraunhofer.de>

German Federal Ministry of Education, <www.bmbf.de>

German Research Council, <www.dgfe.de>

Max Planck Gesellschaft, <www.mpg.de>

Ministère délégué à la Recherche et aux Nouvelles Technologies, <www.recherche.gouv.fr/ > [15 June 2003].

OECD (Organization for Economic Cooperation and Development), *Main Science and Technology Indicators, 2003*, 2 (Paris: OECD, 2003).

ONS (Office of National Statistics), *Labour Force Survey 2000* (London: Office of National Statistics, 2000).

ONS (Office of National Statistics), *First Release Gross Domestic Expenditure on Research and Development 2000* (London: Office of National Statistics, 2002a).

ONS (Office of National Statistics), 'Research and Experimental Development Statistics 2000', *Economic Trends* 585 (London: Office of National Statistics, 2002b).

Observatoire des Sciences et des Techniques, *Rapport de l'observatoire des sciences et des techniques: Indicateurs 2000* (Paris: Economica, 2000).

OST (Office of Science and Technology) (2003), <www.ost.gov.uk> [28 January 2004].

A. Staropoli (1987), 'The Comité National d'Evaluation: Preliminary results of a French experiment', *European Journal of Education* 22(2): 123–31.

15

Regional Policy

Thomas D. Lancaster and Carolyn Forestiere

Introduction

Most political systems, including Britain, France and Germany, possess several layers or tiers of government. The central state has historically been the most powerful of these (although the European Union increasingly challenges this traditional notion). The next lower tier of government varies considerably. Some countries have a regional or meso level (Sharpe 1993), which is then further subdivided into several tiers of local authorities such as counties and municipalities. Other countries operate only with central and local government. These relationships greatly depend upon whether a country operates as a federal or unitary system.

Such variation in structures of governance readily complicates a clear and straightforward use of 'regional.' The term 'region' is frequently utilized in Europe in a fluid yet inconsistent manner, often meaning specific areas of the European Union, component parts of federal systems, or general and unspecified territories of some states. In this chapter, 'region' denotes governmental units of European nation-states below the national level, including what is generally referred to as meso (regional) and local government.

The relationship between national and regional governments varies considerably between Britain, France and Germany. As a constitutional federation, Germany's 16 states (*Länder*) are quite powerful and enjoy extensive autonomy. *Land* governments determine their own regional constitutions and are responsible for most regional activities. Each *Land* government has its own executive, legislature and judiciary. The powers of Germany's federal and *Länder* governments are constitutionally set out in Germany's Basic Law. Explicit *Länder* powers include education and the mass media, with defence, foreign affairs, regulation of international trade, and macroeconomic policy residing at the federal level. Within the large number of concurrent policy areas, federal law takes precedence over *Land* legislation. While powers not explicitly mentioned by the Basic Law are granted to the *Länder*, many Constitutional Court decisions dealing with Germany's EU integration have significantly eroded these powers.

In contrast, Britain and France possess long histories as strong unitary states. Nonetheless, they too have regional authorities but of a newer and much weaker variety. Britain's four 'countries' (England, Scotland, Wales and Northern Ireland) have recently added fascinating chapters to its history of regional policy. Westminster devolved power to the Scottish Parliament and Welsh Assembly in 1999. Devolution to Northern Ireland has fluctuated over a long period as a result of the complex religious, social and political questions there. While periodically discussed, regional devolution does not yet include England itself. Britain's regional autonomy is thus quite asymmetrical. Scotland's powers include economic development, transport, education, health, the environment, agriculture, and sports. The Welsh Assembly controls only a few functions, such as language policy and culture. Despite such changes, regional policy remains constitutionally embedded in Britain's unitary nature: Westminster can remove these devolved powers at any time, as has periodically occurred with Northern Ireland and with local government in London.

Unitary France created 22 regions in 1972, and the reforms of 1982–85 provided for the election of regional assemblies. Despite several compulsory and some optional powers, France's regional assemblies remain relatively powerless. Instead, 96 *départements* have served since Napoleon's rule as the central state's administrative units, each directed by a prefect appointed from the civil service by the Ministry of the Interior. Prefects wielded considerable power until the 1982–85 reforms, when some of their power passed to the democratically elected presidents of the *département* and regional councils. The prefects still oversee regional finances and can veto projects. More importantly, they serve as a power broker and mediator between the central state and these lower tiers. This means that France's *départements* and communes (municipalities), and not the regions, remain the country's most important regional policy components, given the highly centralized administrative style of the French state.

Despite functional similarities, local government in Britain, France and Germany varies considerably in size, structure, financial resources and policy responsibilities. In Britain, local government exists entirely at the central government's discretion apart from Scotland, where it is controlled by the Scottish Parliament. Britain's approximately 540 councils and local government units are currently divided into counties, boroughs and unitary authorities (IMF 2001: 482, 505). In contrast, France's nearly 36,000 communes serve as the basic unit of local government. Communes range from large cities to small villages, with policy functions depending upon size. Unlike British local government, France's *département* and communal councils are protected in the Constitution of 1958. (The newer regional councils have no such constitutional basis, deriving their authority from statute law.) In Germany, the *Länder*, not the federal government, grant authority to the approximately 15,000 municipalities (*Gemeinden*) and 439 counties (*Kreise*) (IMF 2001: 482, 505). While they perform many of the same services as British and French local government, German counties and municipalities are involved in policy not controlled by the *Länder* or the federal government.

The nature of regional policy

Regional authorities are potentially involved in a very wide range of policy areas. For some, the central government allocates funding to cover specific projects. However lower-tier authorities may retain autonomy for other issue areas. Regional policy also involves questions about which policy areas are distributed to sub-national governments. Consequently, regional policy might be understood as covering language utilization, tourism and the territorial consequences of investment policy. Local governments tend to implement specific policies on behalf of central and regional governments. They administer many of the state's regulatory activities and facilitate the application of policy close to the user. Generally, local governments are involved with land use and planning, fire and police protection, refuse collection, public utilities such as water and gas, the promotion of tourism, and many forms of environmental protection (Gallagher *et al.* 2001: 157–8). They also tend to be responsible for local public transportation, local road construction and maintenance as well as the provision of important welfare state components such as education, health care, other social services and public housing.

As a specific national-level policy area, however, regional policy consists of the financing and regulation of meso and local government spending insofar as this is done by central government.

Central state institutions involved in regional policy thus defined vary considerably in these three countries. France's tradition of strong administrative centralism and traditionally weak local government means that, despite greater autonomy since the 1982–85 reforms, the country's strong central state and large bureaucracy continue to intrude deep into regional and local affairs. Hierarchically organized government ministries possess a number of *Directions générales* and *Directions* with large offices in Paris as well as many in the regions, *départements*, and even some communes.

Despite its equally long history of political centralism, Britain traditionally granted special institution recognition to Scotland, and British governments included a cabinet-level Secretary of State for Scotland who formulated and executed a wide range of region-specific policies. A Secretary of State for Wales and one for Northern Ireland has also existed in many British governments to represent these regions' interests in matters reserved for the British parliament. Since regional devolution, however, the Scottish parliament, and to a lesser extent the Welsh Assembly, have administered such policies. The Northern Ireland Office fulfils the functions of that troubled region's assembly whenever it is suspended. Other new regional policy institutions include Regional Development Agencies for England, a standing committee on regional affairs in the House of Commons, and a joint ministerial committee on devolution.

In Germany, as in France and Britain, the work of government ministers in areas such as finance, economics, and economic cooperation and development directly affects regional policy. As a federal system, however, Germany institutionally locates regional policy in the *Bundesrat*, the national parliament's upper chamber composed of *Land* delegations each of which votes as a unit. The *Bundesrat*'s consent is required for all national legislation affecting the *Länder*. It thus serves to protect the *Länder*'s central role in policy-making, implementation and administration and, consequently, their financial and territorial interests.

Specific comparisons

Despite many similarities, there are also significant differences in the way that subnational governments in Britain, France and Germany are funded, and their spending regulated.

Funding

Table 15.1 presents the percentages of each country's revenue collected by the different levels of government. While the issue of how to count social security funds always remains problematic, these data show that central government accounts for only 30.4 per cent of all taxes in Germany but 44.1 per cent in France and 78.5 per cent in Britain. Equally suggestive, but not reported in this table, the German *Länder*'s revenues as a percentage of GDP is 8.4 per cent, with 2.9 per cent for German local government, while the revenue of subnational levels of government amounts to only 4.6 per cent of GDP for France and 1.5 per cent of GDP for Britain (OECD 2001: 203, 205). Expenditure patterns generally follow revenue (IMF 2001).

Table 15.1 Tax revenues as a % of total tax revenue, 1999

	Britain	*France*	*Germany*
Central	78.5	44.1	30.4
Regional	–	–	22.1
Local	4.1	10.2	7.9
Social security	17.4	45.7	39.5
Total	100.0	100.0	100.0

Source: OECD 2001.

Despite recent reforms in regional devolution, fiscal centralism dominates meso-level financing in Britain and, to a lesser extent, France. For the most part, British regional governments remain centrally funded. In fact most funding for England, Scotland, Wales and Northern Ireland arrives in lump sum annual grants from the central government. These grants are distributed according to the Barnett formula, which provides for each region to be allocated financial assistance according to a specific ratio based on population (with changes following each census). This currently means that for every £85 granted to England, Scotland receives £10, Wales £5, and Northern Ireland £2.75. Given that each region's allocation is linked to the amount England receives, this formula remains a hotly contested core of regional policy.

With few exceptions, the relatively weak French regions rely completely on nationally and locally collected revenues and central state allocations of funds.

German federalism and the Basic Law's commitment to a 'unity of living standards' make financial relations between the central government and the *Länder* quite complex. These financial relations include the sharing of tax revenue, vertical equalization through federal payments to the poorer *Länder*, horizontal equalization through richer-to-poorer *Länder* transfers, and special grants, subsidies and payments (Conradt 2001: 254). Most of the *Länder's* funding comes from sharing common tax revenues with the federal government, primarily individual and corporate income taxes and the value-added tax. In addition, the federal government collects more than it spends, and its financial distributions to the *Länder* remain a vital source of regional funding, a fact generally justified given *Länder* responsibility for the administration of federal law.

Variation in regional policy can also be seen in how local governments are financed. Local governments in Britain, France and Germany have three basic sources of revenue: local taxes, charges for local government services, and transfers and grants from the central or meso governments. Table 15.2 shows

Table 15.2   Local sources of revenue as a % of total revenue excluding grants, 1998

	Britain	France	Germany (Länder)	Germany (local)
Taxes on income/profits/ capital gains	–	11.4	43.2	51.9
Property taxes	51.2	26.5	4.7	9.9
Domestic taxes on goods and services	–	8.0	39.1	3.7
Other taxes	0.3	25.6	–	0.1
Non-tax revenues (fees, sales, fines)	48.5	28.5	12.9	34.3
Total	100.0	100.0	100.0	100.0

Source: Calculated from IMF 2001. French figures refer to 1997.

the variation in these revenue sources. In Britain, local government depends almost exclusively on property taxes and non-tax revenues while the German *Länder* and their local governments rely more heavily on their share of the national income and value-added taxes. For its part, France pursues a more diversified approach to revenue-generation, utilizing a variety of local taxes.

Such variation indicates the degree of regional and local autonomy. Britain's financing of local government is clearly a highly centralized process. The council tax is the primary local tax. As a property tax, councils set the tax rate after subtracting funds from other sources such as grants from the central government. Given that Westminster controls most taxation rates and spending levels for all tiers of government, local governments remain heavily dependent on the central government for additional economic support. With Britain's 1999 regional devolution, Scotland but not Wales obtained some autonomy in local finance and taxation.

France pursues a more mixed approach to local government revenue generation. Compared to Britain, a greater percentage of local government revenue comes from local taxes, particularly property taxes and income and commercial taxes. These taxes, however, must be based, often unrealistically, on the central state's evaluation of each community's economic situation (Safran 1995: 256). Despite the many sources of local taxes and efforts at regional reform, the central government maintains a strong role in fiscal policy: it still bears responsibility for collecting most taxes and, once collected, revenues are redistributed to the local authorities.

In Germany each *Land* is largely responsible for funding local government. Localities receive a fixed amount of the national income and value added taxes raised in that area, currently 15 per cent. German municipalities also receive money from motor vehicle taxes and real estate purchase taxes and determine the rate for property taxes and local consumer and expenditure taxes. Subject to approval by a federal supervisory agency, local authorities may also introduce new taxes not already collected by the federal government.

Central government grants also provide direct financial assistance to regional and local governments. In fact, such grants account for 70.4 per cent of British local governments' total revenue, compared to 34.2 per cent for France, 34.6 per cent for local government in Germany, and 18.7 per cent for its *Länder* (IMF 2001). Britain affords two types of grants to local authorities: general, unconditional grants that finance locally selected programmes, and special grants used for specific purposes. France also makes available two types of subsidies. First, global operating grants (DGF) provide significant funds to the communes and *départements*. Special need grants to the communes include core city, tourist, and urban solidarity grants. Secondly, investment funds are distributed as value added tax compensation to communes, *départements* and regions and as global equipment grants (DGE) to the communes and *départements*.

Germany also has several types of grants but, unlike unitary Britain and France, they are generally channelled through the *Länder*. First, Germany's general grants may be spent according to local needs, and have traditionally been used for public school transportation, road maintenance and social assistance. Secondly, Germany's investment grants may be used for local programs, road construction, or earmarked for the construction of schools, fire *departments*, hospitals, waste disposal centres, and water supply and treatment plants. Thirdly, grants on demand are intended to assist local budgets during times of financial hardship. Fourthly, grants for specific programmes often take the form of matching funds: the *Land* and local governments both contribute to the programme's cost. The amount of many of these grants depends upon the recipient's general economic situation.

Grants, as normal procedures for financial transfers, permit all three central states to maintain some type of scheme for regional financial equalization. Central to regional policy, such measures are designed to reduce financial inequalities and promote a higher standard of living in disadvantaged areas. In Britain, the central government annually calculates each local council's Standard Spending Assessment (SSA) based on demographic, physical, economic and social factors plus the relative costs of providing comparable services (Office of the Deputy Prime Minister 2003). A local government's SSA is its share of the country's Total Standard Spending (TSS). In France, operating grants are distributed according to each commune's operating costs based on factors such as general population size, number of schoolchildren, and number of social dwellings. In addition, grants are allocated by equalization measures designed to ensure that commune income is generally standard throughout France (Council of Europe 1998). In Germany, Article 106 of the Basic Law, corresponding articles in the *Land* constitutions, and *Land* legislation provide guidelines for financial equalization to compensate for municipalities' financial variations. Procedures vary widely across the *Länder* (Council of Europe 1999).

Each country also pursues unique programs for intergovernmental transfers and regional equalization. For example, Paris and the communes of the Île-de-France receive aid designed to address special needs and reduce inequalities of wealth. Corsica also receives special attention in French regional policy-making. Germany's most visible programme for regional development since reunification has involved the five eastern *Länder*. With massive amounts of funds having already been transferred, the German government continues a special 'solidarity' tax on income for redistribution to the eastern states.

Loans provide additional financial assistance to regional and local governments. The British central government limits the precise amount local authorities can borrow. The Public Works Loan Board (PWLB) grants most long-term loans. Projects often include land purchases and the building or renovating of schools and roads. Similarly, German municipalities must obtain approval from a supervisory agency to borrow money. Approval can be tied to a munici-pality's long-term financial situation and to conditions involving limits to total debt payment and appropriate market-oriented loan terms. Loans come primarily from savings banks and other domestic credit institutions, with a few being made directly by the federal government. In contrast, French local authorities have a much freer hand. They can borrow money to finance projects without national government authorization. The only limit is that new loans may not cover past ones. Local authorities are free to choose any credit institution, and are permitted to take out foreign currency loans. In contrast to some countries, such loans are given no special guarantees. French local authorities may also issue bonds on the financial market (Council of Europe 1998).

Regulation

Britain, France and Germany vary considerably in how they monitor local government expenditures. In Britain, local authorities are expected to ensure that revenue is sufficient to fund local programs. The central government guards against excessive council spending for England, Northern Ireland and Wales while the Scottish Executive carries this responsibility in Scotland (Council of Europe 2000). In France, the prefects continue to play a monitor-ing role in budgetary control. Each local budget must be balanced before it can be passed. If problems arise, the prefect refers the budget to the regional audit office (Council of Europe 1998). German municipalities' budgets are based on five-year planning schemes and are linked to the entire public sector's economic planning. Because of this interdependence, municipal budgets are subject to *Land* supervision to ensure municipal spending does not endanger long-term financial planning (Council of Europe 1999).

Recent developments

Over the last two decades or so, Europe has experienced an ethos of decentrali-zation (Gallagher *et al.* 2001: 166). Britain and France have mirrored federa-tions such as Germany and established a meso level of governance. Regional policy in these three countries has a highly dynamic flavour. Beyond the normal vicissitudes of political dialogue to create, maintain and finance such multiple layers of government, two other developments have greatly impacted regional policy in Britain, France and Germany: neo-liberal economic tendencies and the European Union.

Regional and local governments in all three countries have strongly felt the neo-liberal, free market approach to government financing that began in the 1980s. Central governments have increasingly privatized public services that traditionally provided revenue for local councils. Additionally, they have opened up the provision of some public services to increased competition. Of the three countries, Britain has witnessed this trend the most: the Local Government, Planning and Land Act of 1980 mandated that private companies could compete for contracts to provide local services, such as road construction and building repair; the Local Government Act of 1988 added more services to contract-out, such as refuse collection and janitorial service; and the Local Government Act of 1992 extended the range to high skill services such as information technology and research. Britain has also permitted 'quangos' (quasi-governmental agencies) to compete for many of the same services. While not as extensive in France and Germany, such neo-liberal trends have similarly usurped the traditional tasks of regional and local authorities. Privatization has also undercut their control of many economic-oriented policies.

Developments in the integration of the European Union continue to impact significantly on regional policy in Britain, France and Germany. Trends toward a Europe 'pulling in two directions' (greater political and economic integration while simultaneously developing a 'Europe of regions') directly affect these three countries' regional policies. The movement toward greater integration has meant, for example, economic restrictions set by the Maastricht Treaty on yearly deficits, public debt and inflation. Not all governments' regional policy, however, implemented these in the same manner. Britain and France did not strongly enforce restrictions on local governments, while German authorities took active measures to limit local government spending. The pull toward greater EU regionalization has also meant regional policy has become embedded in an enlarged matrix of economic relations. Regional policy increasingly includes EU-sponsored programmes for regional development; structural, cohesion and development funds; and other instruments to financially assist regional and local authorities. All signs suggest that the European Union has added an additional tier of governance to regional policy in Britain, France and Germany.

Sources

British Cabinet's List of Ministerial Responsibilities, <www.cabinet-office.gov.uk> [17 June 2003].

D.P. Conradt, *The German Polity*, 7th edn. (New York: Longman, 2001).

Council of Europe, *Structure and Operation of Local and Regional Democracy: France* (Strasbourg: Council of Europe Publishing, 1998).

Council of Europe, *Structure and Operation of Local and Regional Democracy: Germany* (Strasbourg: Council of Europe Publishing, 1999).

Council of Europe, *Structure and Operation of Local and Regional Democracy: United Kingdom* (Strasbourg: Council of Europe Publishing, 2000).

Environment Department's guide to local government finance, <www.local.detr.gov.uk> [17 June 2003].

European Union's Committee of Regions, <www.cor.eu.int> [17 June 2003].

French *départements*, <www.fotw.ca/flags/fr-depts.html> [17 June 2003].

French local government, <www.oultwood.com/localgov/france> [17 June 2003].

French Ministry of the Interior, <www.interieur.gouv.fr> [17 June 2003].

M. Gallagher, M. Laver and P. Mair, *Representative Government in Modern Europe*, 3rd edn (Boston: McGraw-Hall, 2001).

M.C. Hunt and J.A. Chandler, 'France', in *Local Government in Liberal Democracies*, ed. J.A. Chandler (London: Routledge, 1993).

IMF (International Monetary Fund), *Government Finance Statistics Yearbook* (Washington, DC: IMF, 2001).

J. Kingdom, 'England and Wales', in *Local Government in Liberal Democracies*, ed. J.A. Chandler (London: Routledge, 1993).

Northern Ireland Office, <www.nio.gov.uk> [17 June 2003].

A. Norton, *The International Handbook of Local and Regional Government Status: Structure and Resources in Advanced Democracies* (Cheltenham: Edward Elgar, 1991).

Office of the Deputy Prime Minister (2003), *Local Government Finance Information for Local Authorities*, <www.local.dtlr.gov.uk> [17 June 2003].

OECD (Organization for Economic Cooperation and Development), *Revenue Statistics 1965–2000* (Paris: OECD, 2001).

W. Safran, *The French Polity*, 4th edn (New York: Longman, 1995).

Scotland Office, <www.scottishsecretary.gov.uk> [17 June 2003].

Scottish Politics, <www.alba.org.uk> [17 June 2003].

Scottish Government, <www.scotland.gov.uk> [17 June 2003].

L.J. Sharpe (ed.), *The Rise of Meso Government in Europe* (Newbury Park, CA: Sage, 1993).

Wales Government, <www.wales.gov.uk> [17 June 2003].

Wales Office, <www.walesoffice.gov.uk> [17 June 2003].

Part IV
Sectoral Policies

16
Agriculture, Forestry and Fisheries

Berkeley Hill, Alan Greer, Thomas Heckelei and Peter Witze

Introduction

Agriculture and fishing are the primary source of almost all our food, as well as of many other products, so remain vital activities even though their share in the economy is small and in continuous decline. Partly for this reason public policy in these areas is almost entirely integrated at European level in the Common Agricultural Policy (CAP) and Common Fisheries Policy (CFP). Forestry policies are also heavily affected by EU-level decision-making. As agriculture dominates in terms of direct contribution to GDP and numbers of people engaged in it, as well as accounting for the largest amount of public support expenditure, it is agriculture that will receive the greatest attention here.

The nature of agriculture, forestry and fisheries policies

We look first at agricultural policy, then at fisheries and forestry policies.

Agricultural policy

Policy towards agriculture in all three countries is dominated by the CAP, which has its origins in the 1957 Treaty of Rome. Support for agriculture still accounts for half of all spending from the EU budget (48 per cent in 2002) and, though its share has been declining as other common policies have developed, the CAP continues to have great symbolic significance.

The dominant role of the CAP means that national governments are restricted to:

- inflecting the application of some aspects of the CAP by exercising discretion in those areas of policy in which they play an explicit part in implementation, especially in relation to rural development and the environment;

175

- acting in policy areas that are not covered by EU-level legislation, such as land tenure and taxation.

To understand what this means in practice, it is necessary to set out the aims and provisions of the CAP in more detail, before describing the role of national governments in this area.

The Common Agricultural Policy (CAP)

Differences between the structures of the agricultures of Britain, France and Germany, and in national value sets and priorities, mean that the CAP is viewed from overlapping but distinctly varying perspectives. France is the largest agricultural producer and a net exporter of food and agricultural products, whereas Britain and Germany are net importers (see Table 16.1). National governments exert their individual interests in helping shape the CAP but, once a common framework has been adopted by the Council (of agricultural ministers) at EU level, room to pursue national policies is constrained.

A characteristic of agricultural policy is its mix of aims, though these are often poorly defined. Within this heterogeneity the dominant thread appears to be the wish to ensure a 'fair standard of living for the agricultural community', although the intended meaning of this phrase has never been clearly set out. Improving the productivity and competitiveness of farms is seen as a contributing factor to achieving this broad aim, which is often referred to as the 'income objective'. In reality, most of the aid to agriculture is given in ways that are linked to the amount produced by being geared to output or factor use, which means that the bulk of the support goes to large farmers (directly) or large landowners (mostly indirectly) who, in general, are not those suffering from particularly low standards of living.

A fast rising policy aim concerns the provision of environmental services for the rest of society, for example by conserving biodiversity, protecting landscapes and reducing pollution. Other aims include food security and safety, promoting regional development and protecting the cultural heritage.

Table 16.1   Agricultural production and trade, 2001

	Britain	France	Germany
Agricultural production	€23 bn (£17 bn, $26 bn)	€64 bn (£47 bn, $72 bn)	€44 bn (£32 bn, $50 bn)
Net exports of food and agricultural products (EU external trade balance)	– €3.9 bn (– £2.9 bn, – $4.4 bn)	€4.9 bn (£3.6 bn, $5.5 bn)	– €3.2 bn (– £2.4 bn, – $3.6 bn)

Finally, it should be remembered that farm operators are affected by many policies that are not specifically directed at this sector, such as those relating to taxation, interest rates, poverty and deprivation, planning control, trade and currency exchange rates.

The CAP has two 'pillars': support linked to production, and support for rural development. The first of these is by far the stronger pillar in terms of expenditure, accounting for over four fifths of total spending from the EU budget on agriculture (84 per cent in 2002).

Support linked to production is provided through the CAP's Common Market Organizations (CMOs). These are product-specific regimes for each of the main commodities (cereals, wine, beef and veal, dairy products, sugar, tobacco etc.), the details of which are often highly complex and frequently adjusted. CMOs apply to the whole of the single market, covering all Member States. Individual governments are responsible for the implementation of CMOs at national level, acting as agents for the European Commission, and this can lead to some differences of interpretation and ways of operation.

Two main mechanisms are used within CMOs. First, there is intervention in commodity markets to enhance the prices received by producers, achieved by an array of instruments including import taxes and support buying, the resulting stocks mainly being disposed of on the world market using subsidies given to exporters. Quotas on domestic production apply to a few commodities, notably milk and sugar, again with national governments organizing their allocation. Regulation varies in its 'heaviness': some CMOs (such as cereals and beef) use both domestic support and import taxes while others only have import restrictions, some quite minor, with market intervention triggered only in exceptional circumstances (pigmeat, sheepmeat, eggs, fresh fruit and vegetables). Table 16.2 gives an outline of support arrangements for some of the main CMOs that apply to all three countries.

Second, there are direct payments to producers of some commodities; these have increased over the last decade and are now the major mechanism of CMO support. For cereals, oilseeds and protein (COP) crops, payments are based on the number of hectares of land each farm occupies and are conditional on a proportion being set-aside (land not used for production but for which payments are received). Area payments are based on regional yields and limited to a 'base area', both of which depend on historic data. Consequently, payments per hectare differ between Member States and regions. For beef and sheep there is a complex system of 'premium' payments paid per animal with, in Less Favoured Areas (mainly hills and mountains), extra subsidies per hectare.

From 2005 a single direct payment per farm will be introduced, based on what had been paid in a recent reference period (2000–02). Some flexibility is to be given to Member States over precisely how the sums at farm level

Table 16.2 Mechanisms used by Common Market organizations for major agricultural products, autumn 2003

Commodity	Intervention in market	Import/export	Farm level direct payments/ limits on production	Other
Cereals, oilseeds, protein plants	Support buying into intervention during specific periods (winter and spring).	Import duty. Export subsidy ('refund') to enable intervention stocks to be sold on world market.	'Compensatory' payments per hectare to producers to accompany lowering of support prices. Payments are related to historic yields and areas.	A proportion of arable area compulsorily to be set-aside for producers deemed to produce more than 92 tonne.
Sugar	'Minimum' prices set for highly supported 'A' and moderately supported 'B' quota beet.	Threshold price for sugar, import duties, export refunds.	Domestic 'A' and 'B' quotas allocated to individual producers by Member States.	Cost of market support met from a small levy on A and B quota sugar and larger additional levy on B quota sugar.
Fresh fruit and vegetables	Withdrawal of produce from the market for destruction or diversion by producer organizations, compensated by fixed payments.	Customs tariff on each of 15 products, calculated on the 'entry price'.	Aid for grubbing up of apple, pear, peach and nectarine trees. Premiums paid to processors to use Community citrus fruit.	Financial aid to set up producer organizations, and assist quality and marketing of specific fruits, nuts, etc.

Milk and dairy products	Support buying into public intervention of butter and skimmed milk powder, with quantity and time limits. Financial aid for seasonal private storage of several milk products.	Fixed import duties on certain products. Additional duties payable if import prices fall below 'trigger' price and quantities exceed 'trigger' quantities. Export refunds on most products.	Farm-level quotas on milk deliveries, based on national quotas. Scheme for voluntary cessation of milk production and for compensation for cut in quotas.	Aid for users of skimmed milk in animal feed and for processing into casein. Special measures to dispose of butter. Financial support to promote milk and milk products.
Beef and veal	Private storage aids when market price falls below a certain percentage of a set 'basic' price. Buying into public intervention when market price levels extremely low.	Fixed customs duty according to product. Export refunds.	'Premiums' per animal payable on beef animals and suckler cows subject to stocking density limits and individual farm limits. Slaughter premiums, and additional premium for extensive production etc. Rights to premiums transferable between producers.	Special payments related to BSE crisis (Over Thirty Month Scheme) and related controls. Additional payments (per ha) to producers in hill and mountain areas.
Sheepmeat (and goatmeat)	'Safety net' provided by buying into private storage if market price falls to given levels.	Fixed duties applied to imports, with special concessions for some countries (especially New Zealand).	'Premiums' paid per ewe (or she-goat) up to an individual limit per producer (1000 in Less Favoured Areas, 500 elsewhere), with a 50% reduction above these limits. Rights to premiums are transferable between producers.	Additional payments (per ha) for producers in hill and mountain areas.

Table 16.2 (Continued)

Commodity	Intervention in market	Import/export	Farm level direct payments/ limits on production	Other
Pigmeat	Financial aid to private storage offered in advance when market prices low.	Import duties and export subsidies applied moderately.		Some emergency intervention powers.
Wine	Financial aid to private storage, applied flexibly. Provision for purchase and for distillation in 'crisis' situations.	Single import duty applies dependent on alcoholic content. Some preferential tariff treatments for some countries. Export refunds, but only on a limited volume.	Grubbing premiums linked to general ban on new planting, but with some new planting rights limited in total area for where demand is rising, favouring new producers. Control of vine varieties used. Special production rules for 'quality' wines.	Aid to distillers to dispose of alcohol, and alcohol can be delivered to intervention agency. Aid for the use of grape must.

Note: CMOs also exist for rice, olive oil, hops, fibre plants and silkworms, tobacco, eggs and poultry.
Sources: The New Regulation of the Agricultural Markets: Vademecum. Green Europe 1/93, *CAP Working Notes* (Commission 1996 and 1997), CAP Monitor (AgraEurope) 2003.

should be calculated. Market price support is to be further cut back for the main commodities.

While major decisions on CMOs are taken by the Council (of agricultural ministers), operational matters are devolved to management committees chaired by the European Commission and on which Member States are represented or, for certain details, to the Commission acting within frameworks established by the Council. The prices built into support mechanisms, for example the prices at which intervention takes place, and payments to be made to farmers, are designated in euros (€), which means that prices and payments in Britain, which is outside the eurozone, are influenced by changes in exchange rates.

Support for rural development – the 'second pillar' of the CAP – consists of payments to farmers from the EU's agricultural budget, the European Agricultural Guidance and Guarantee Fund – EAGGF, or FEOGA in its French acronym. These payments are designed to improve the structure of the agricultural industry by financing diversification, vocational training to provide new skills and afforestation on farm land; achieve environmental benefits from occupiers of agricultural land, including sustaining farming in hill and mountainous areas for environmental and social reasons; and stimulate the rural economy. Legislation governing the items in the 'Second Pillar' was gathered together in the *Rural Development Regulation 1257* of 1999 (RDR), including the environmental and forestry assistances that started out as 'accompanying measures' to the 1992 reforms of the CAP. However these items are expected to account for only some 16 per cent of all spending on agriculture from the EAGGF (to 2006).

Some of the payments assist the costs of single projects, such as grants for planting trees, but many relate to contracts with farmers for taking some particular actions, such as conserving species-rich grassland by adopting suitable management practices over a five to ten year period, or refraining from doing something that might endanger these environmental features.

In areas of the EU that qualify for special general assistance because they are lagging behind, some forms of assistance (for example, for better marketing, and investments to encourage diversification that are not 'accompanying measures') are organized not under the RDR but under regional development programmes and are financed differently, although this complication is due to be phased out after 2006.

Article 41 of the RDR states that plans must be drawn up at the most appropriate geographical level. France has adopted a single national Rural Development Plan (RDP), whereas Britain has separate RDPs for England, Scotland, Wales and Northern Ireland. There are also a number of plans in Germany, reflecting the country's federal structure.

RDR programmes and the other forms of regional support benefiting agriculture are in part financed by national budgets ('co-financed'). Both France and Britain have exploited the provision in Agenda 2000 that allows some CAP funding (up to 20 per cent) to be redirected from direct payments under the 'First Pillar' to the 'accompanying measures' elements in rural development under the 'Second Pillar' (the 'modulation' option). Modulation increased total rural development expenditure in England by almost half and the EU contribution by 62 per cent, by 16 per cent in Wales (EU contribution by 41 per cent) and by 20 per cent in Scotland and Northern Ireland (EU contribution by 36 per cent). In contrast, the contribution of modulation receipts in France represents only 2 per cent.

National-level agricultural policy

In EU Member States there is a remnant of national agricultural policy covering commodities for which there is no CMO, such as potatoes, and a range of activities on which the CAP does not attempt to be comprehensive, including public research, agricultural education and the provision of technical advice to farmers. State aids are also allowed that overlap with the CAP or 'top up' its payments providing that these impact to an insignificant extent on the ability of producers to compete, thereby preserving the CAP principle of the single EU market. Under the RDR, schemes that are solely nationally financed are permitted subject to Commission approval according to state-aid rules designed to ensure consistency and fairness. This opens up the potential for considerable discretionary action on the part of national governments, provided that additional assistance can be justified. For example, additional investments relating to traditional landscapes, protection and improvement of the environment, improvement of the hygiene conditions of livestock enterprises and the welfare of animals do not count against the limits on total investment assistance. In England a further 18 per cent of funding is provided through such national state aids.

Summing up, benefits for farmers from agricultural support programmes include not only direct payments but also increased sales and higher prices made possible by measures such as export subsidies and import restrictions. Although it is difficult to quantify the total cost of agricultural support, the OECD has estimated that in 1999–2001 the Producer Support Estimates (PSEs) for the entire EU totalled 42 per cent, which implies that the transfers from taxpayers and consumers were adding almost the same amount of benefit to agriculture as was market income; the equivalent figure for the USA was 23 per cent. Furthermore, in addition to the €103.1 billion (£75.9 billion, $116 billion) of production support captured in the PSE, another €9.9 billion (£7.3 billion, $11.1 billion) of general services support was provided (8 per cent of total support).

Fisheries policy

The three countries that are the focus of this book account together for less than a quarter of the EU's fishing industry: Germany has a relatively small fishing fleet (3.7 per cent of EU tonnage in 1998) with France (8.7 per cent) and Britain (11.6 per cent) providing similar shares. In 1995 there were only some 20,000 fishermen in Britain, 27,000 in France and 5,000 in Germany, being greatly outnumbered by workers in agriculture and forestry (of the order of 20 to 1 in Britain, 40 to 1 in France and 200 to 1 in Germany).

The Common Fisheries Policy (CFP) heavily influences this activity in the EU. The CFP is largely concerned with the management of fish stocks in the Community fishing zone (waters under the sovereignty or jurisdiction of Member States) by limiting the capacity of the EU fishing industry to land catches (seasonal or permanent limitations or prohibitions on fishing activities in certain areas) and other technical measures. The CFP operates through the multi-annual guidance programmes (MAGPs) that set targets for capacity and fishing effort of the fleets of each Member State. The role of national authorities is to implement, enforce and supplement the provisions of the CFP, for example by licensing fishing vessels; monitoring fisheries using aerial, surface and port surveillance; and establishing and enforcing standards for the landing, processing and marketing of fish.

The CFP's legal base can be traced to the 1957 Treaty of Rome, though the first Regulation did not emerge until 1970 (2141/70). This introduced two key principles: fish are a common resource, and there should be open access to the waters of the Member States. The notion that fish are a common resource stemmed from the rational argument that fish spawned in the waters of one Member State could then migrate and be caught elsewhere, so that no single country could lay claim to the ownership of fish. The open access principle was based on the Community's general commitment to a single market covering the EU.

The 1983 revision of the CFP added a commitment to 'Relative Stability', according to which the EU Council of Ministers agrees a Total Allowable Catch (TAC) for the different species of fish, which varies from year to year depending on fish stocks. However this failed to acknowledge that, with technological advances, the capacity to catch fish increased year on year, with the result that fish stocks could not be sustained unless there was a drastic cut in fishing effort.

In 1992 a genuine structural policy for the fisheries sector was introduced to arrange the decommissioning of excess fishing capacity, financed by a new special structural fund (Financial Instrument for Fisheries Guidance – FIFG), but by then there was growing alarm from conservationists that fish stocks were nearing the point of collapse. In the years that followed the sector has remained in crisis, the scientific evidence pointing to the need for a complete ban but the political reality permitting quotas that are inadequate to satisfy the fishing industry yet too large to permit fish stock recovery. The next reform of the CFP is due to enter into force from 2003.

Forestry policy

Forestry is a major land user in the three countries under consideration, occupying 10 per cent of the total land area in Britain and almost three times this level in France and Germany (see Table 16.3). It is thus important to the European environment, to recreation and to rural development. However forestry is not the subject of a separate Common Policy. Rather, action is carried out as part of other policies for which such bases exist, mainly the CAP and regional policy. The Rural Development Regulation (1257) of 1999 allows for grant aid for the creation of new woodland by planting and natural regeneration, with sums also available to farmers to compensate them for loss of income when they establish trees on previously farmed land, the level of payment depending on the type of land used. Payments are also available to assist with the management of woodland.

In Britain there are also national grants for activities such as the provision of tourist access, and the long-term nature of timber as a crop has caused it to be given special tax status, at times forming a major incentive for ownership and forestry development.

In Germany the major share of public financial support for the forestry sector – about 62 per cent of €62 million (£45.6 million, $69.8 million) according to the German government in 1999 – is dedicated to rebuilding natural or 'close to'

Table 16.3   Basic characteristics of the agriculture, forestry and fisheries sector

	Britain	*France*	*Germany*
Agriculture (% GDP, 2001)	0.6	2.2	0.9
Persons employed in agriculture, forestry, hunting and fishing, 2001 (000s)	390	964	956
Number of fishermen, 1995 (000s)	19.9	26.9	5.0
Employment in agriculture, forestry, hunting and fishing as a percentage of total employment, 2001	1.4	4.1	2.6
% of total land area used by agriculture, 2000–01	66	52	49
% of total area used by forestry, 2000	10	31	31
Utilized Agricultural Area (UUA) per holding, 2000 (ha)	67.7	42.0	36.3
% of holdings below 5 ha, 1997	14.6	26.7	31.0
% of holdings above 50 ha, 1997	33.6	29.7	14.2
% of UAA in holdings of 50 ha and over, 1997	83.8	74.4	64.0
% of male holders with some other gainful employment, 1997	37	42	51

Sources: Commission *Agricultural Situation in the European Union.*

natural forests and to afforestation programmes. It is also worth mentioning that the public sector operates about 55 per cent of all forests in Germany.

In France, forestry is seen as a major way of utilizing rural areas and of helping to achieve economic, social and environmental sustainability. For example, an economically competitive and sustainable forestry sector has to play its part in the creation of new rural employment possibilities, and forests provide a major natural space that can be exploited for leisure and enjoyment. This approach is underpinned by various state measures, including the provision of investment aids and assistance to help restore forests damaged by storms or fires, and training in forest management practices. 'Developing forestry resources' is also one of the five key priorities of the French Rural Development Plan, which provides for the promotion of timber and other production as well as the sustainable management of forests and the protection of the forest environment.

Specific comparisons

Given that the CAP is intended to apply uniformly across all Member States, for the purpose of making specific comparisons attention has to fall on three areas where potential differences can arise: (a) the way that national governments inflect common CMO instruments in the 'first pillar' of the CAP, such as the way they use 'modulation' to divert a small proportion of commodity support expenditure to environmental uses, or how quantitative restrictions on output are organized; (b) the way in which the national discretion built in to the EU framework legislation on the 'second pillar' of the CAP is applied; and (c) residual national policies.

Though the CAP is a common policy, differences between the structures of agriculture in Britain, France and Germany mean that it has uncommon results. Table 16.3 shows that in each country agriculture with forestry occupies about four-fifths of the total area, the balance being more towards forestry in France and Germany than in Britain. Among the small fractions of the population that engage in these activities (with fisheries) and whose living standards are affected directly, differences in average farm size and distribution of farm size (and type) are important in determining the pattern of beneficiaries from this support. The relative impact of support also reflects the extent to which holders have other gainful employment (especially high in Germany), and there are regional differences within each country.

Three policy areas have been selected to demonstrate differences between Britain, France and Germany in agricultural policy: the administration of quotas on domestic production of milk, socio-professional assistance, and preferential taxation provisions for agriculture and forestry. All are rather minor in terms of the total cost of support, but they have disproportionate importance to the face of the agricultural industry in these countries.

Administration of milk quotas

The administration by national governments of CAP quotas on milk is more market-oriented in Britain and Germany than in France.

In Britain the milk quota at the farm level is now, in effect, a freely and privately traded commodity operating within a fixed national quota quantity, although they may not be traded across national boundaries. The original link by which quota was attached to the land of the holding (so that transfer of quota necessitated transfer of land) has been broken. In addition, the administration of quota does not make any special provision for farmers who wish to set up in milk production.

Since April 2000 milk quota rights in Germany have been exclusively transferred by auctions administered by public clearing houses except where whole farms with quota rights change owners. There are provisions meant to dampen quota prices, such as declaring bids and offers above a certain threshold ineligible, but so far all attempts to steer quota prices have been rather unsuccessful. New entrants may buy quota rights, but have to prove their intention to use it for production rather than speculation. Quota rights not used or transferred within the milk marketing year are taken away and become part of the quota reserve. As in Britain, quota rights are no longer attached to land.

France does not permit an internal market, and quotas may be transferred only through the inheritance, sale or lease of the farm to which they are attached unless milk production is halted permanently or if there is spontaneous cessation of production for more than two milk years. A 'levy' on reference quantities applies when farms are amalgamated or broken up, and this is used to constitute a national quota reserve that is then redistributed at *département* level according to criteria based on objectives such as supporting 'young' farmers and marginal areas. There is also a system of quota loans. Depending on the availability of production quotas, a provisional allocation in the form of a loan (subject to a national maximum) may be made to producers who exceed their quantities. A fund generated by excess production penalties is used to finance voluntary cessation of production, and to reduce the penalties of small producers.

Details of how milk quotas are administered are set out in Table 16.4.

Socio-professional assistance – investing in people

Socio-professional assistance within EU policy for agriculture and forestry takes the form of facilitating entry and exit and improving the skills of farmers and workers to cope with their changing economic environment. All Member States have some flexibility to adapt the provisions of the RDR to reflect their own particular circumstances. While Britain, France and Germany all provide skills training in various forms, however, governments in France and Germany are much more active than in Britain in facilitating entry and exit of farmers.

Table 16.4 Administration of milk production quotas

	Britain	France	Germany
Transfer between producers	Temporary transfers by short-term leasing – reverts to original owner at start of next quota year (1 April). Permanent transfers by (i) leasing for minimum of 10 months (England and Wales), after which the lessee owns the quota; (ii) sale or inheritance of land to which quota is attached; (iii) sale of quota (without land) for reasons of restructuring.	System of quota loans (subject to a national maximum) to producers who exceed their quantities. Internal market not permitted. Quotas may be transferred only through the inheritance, sale or lease of the farm to which they are attached.	No leasing or renting of quota rights allowed. Permanent transfers by (i) sale or inheritance of whole farm with quota rights; (ii) sale or transfer to direct relatives; (iii) all other sales only through auctions administered by clearing houses three times a year.
New entrants to milk production	Must purchase or lease quota.	Allocation from quota reserves at *département* and national levels.	Must purchase quota.

Britain adopts a non-interventionist attitude to the issue of who enters and leaves farming. However there is public provision of courses with agriculturally relevant subjects in institutions of further and higher education, and Welsh farmers aged under 40 are provided with enhanced rates of grants given for some environmental and business development purposes. In addition, taxation concessions (for example on capital gains) that apply to business operators in general on retirement are available to farmers. Where assistance for training is used, it typically involves providing grants to organizations that set up training programmes for workers in agriculture (including self-employed farmers) and forestry. Payments do not normally go to the workers themselves.

The situations in France and Germany contrast strongly with that in Britain. In France, both assisted entry and early retirement (including aid for transferring holdings) are central to the implementation of France's national rural development plan. The setting up of young farmers takes 12.2 per cent of the RDP budget, and early retirement receives just 2.5 per cent. Assistance for new entrants is provided to help them set up holdings on the basis of a single premium and favourable interest rates for loans up to a ceiling of €25,000 (£18,400, $28,125). To qualify, the individual must be entering the industry for the first time, be established as the head of the holding, be aged between 21 and 40, and have acquired occupational skills and competence. The agricultural holding must be economically viable over time and adhere to minimum requirements in terms of the environment, hygiene and animal welfare. Aid for new entrants is set between approximately €8,000 (£5900, $9000) and €36,000 (£26,500, $40,500), is weighted in favour of farmers in marginal and mountain areas, and reflects local conditions and priorities. Sums higher than the EU maximum are available for farmers in the mountain zone through the application of state aid.

The EU permits Member States to pay up to a maximum of €15,000 (£11,000, $16,875) per year, or up to €150,000 (£110,000, $168,750) in total, to farmers over 55 years of age but not yet of normal retirement age who decide to give up commercial farming having been active in the industry for at least ten years. In France support for early retirement is set at a flat rate of €5488 (£4039, $6174) per annum for farmers aged between 55 and 60. Support is also available for farm workers (family helpers or paid farm workers), up to a maximum of €3500 (£2576, $3938) per year. Pensions provided under the scheme may be paid for a maximum of fifteen years (ten in the case of a farm worker). There are also specific schemes for overseas departments, and for transfer of land to new entrants and family members.

The French Ministry of Agriculture places much emphasis on promoting rural employment, for example through its practical grass roots training programmes administered by regional training committees. Support is provided under the RDR for vocational training, and in the RDP for the period 2000–06, €116 million (£85 million, $131 million) is devoted to training schemes in France, co-financed at a level of 50 per cent and weighted heavily to increasing competence in environmental sustainability. Assistance covers training costs and expenses up to a maximum level of €12.20 (£8.80, $13.73) per hour per trainee.

Assistance for entries of young farmers and exits of older farmers has been provided in various forms in the past in Germany. Currently there are preferential conditions for young farmers in investment support programmes (as noted above for Wales in Britain). Support for vocational training takes various forms. First of all there is a general system of publicly operated and funded schools also providing agricultural education. Second, there are agencies offering training on specific topics which are reimbursed for the largest part of their expenses and have to collect fees for the smaller part. Finally there is support for the participants in these courses, mainly for the fees but partly also for lodging and travel. The forms and amount of support vary among the *Länder*, which are mainly responsible for education in the German federal system.

Preferential taxation

Taxation is an area in which national governments are protective of their autonomy, and agriculture and forestry have a history of special treatment in the way they are taxed. This special treatment is most pronounced in France and least pronounced in Britain, with Germany somewhere in between.

In Britain, for the purpose of current taxation farmers are treated very largely in the same way as other self-employed businessmen. Their profits (from unincorporated businesses) are subject to the normal rates of income tax, though with a provision for averaging over two successive years. They are also, in practice, subject to the regular Value Added Tax regime but with output zero-rated, which means that they can claim back tax paid on inputs. However there are special low rates of excise duty on fuel for agricultural use and concessions on farm vehicle annual taxes. More importantly, agricultural land and associated buildings used for production are exempt from the annual local property tax levied on other business assets (business rates). Land also receives special treatment when inheritance tax is calculated, the taxable value being reduced by 100 per cent (that is, not taxed) if owner-occupied, or by 50 per cent if tenanted. In effect, current income from forestry (both the costs and revenues sides) is now outside the tax system, a decision taken to end what had become an abuse by high-earning individuals to take advantage of the rules then in place to reduce their tax bills.

Historically, French agriculture has been subject to an extremely complex taxation system that is distinct from, and more generous than, that applying to other sectors. Variations within agriculture result, for example, from differential treatment of product sectors, whether the farmer is engaged in related activities such as processing, retailing or pluriactivity; and whether the farmer is, legally speaking, an individual entrepreneur or a member of a collective group or society.

The agricultural income tax system is composed of four core tax regimes (*forfait collectif, transitoire, réel simplifié*, and *reél normal*) and over 40 options, differentiated according to farming income and structure (there is a separate regime for forestry). The applicable regime is determined primarily on the basis of turnover, including subsidies and allowances, calculated over two years. Farmers and farm businesses with an average turnover of more than €275,000 (£202,400, $309,375) (and those below this level who opt voluntarily for the scheme) are assessed under a *réel normal* regime. This operates according to the same general principles that apply to business and industry, but there are some tax breaks relating to interest on loans, capital gains, and the installation of young farmers. In 1998 nearly 130,000 farmers were assessed for income tax under this regime, less than a fifth of the total number of farmer tax cases. At the other end of the scale, under the *régime du forfait collectif*, the profits of small farms are taxed on a collective standard basis rather than on actual income. This is an option for farmers and farm businesses with an average turnover of less than about €76,000 (£56,000, $86,000). It also applies to new entrants in their first two years. Payment is a combination of two elements: a collective reference figure calculated at *département* level (taking account of the liabilities of different types of production and farm structures), and the individual circumstances of producers in terms of their amount of land, number of animals, etc. Nearly half a million farmers – about two out of three tax cases – remain under the *forfait* regime. Between these extremes, the *transitoire* (transitional) regime applies to individual farmers with an income between about €76,000 (£56,000, $86,000) and €114,000 (£83,900, $128,250), and is designed to smooth passage between the *forfait* and *réel normal* regimes. Lastly, the *réel simplifié* (simplified regime) is available to farmers who opt out of the *régime du forfait* and have turnovers of between about €76,000 (£56,000, $86,000) and €274,000 (£202,000, $308,000). Benefits include simplified administrative arrangements and a less onerous accounting regime. Taken together, the *transitoire* and *réel simplifié* regimes applied to approximately 130,000 farmers in 1998.

Whilst most countries have special VAT arrangements for farmers, France has a separate agricultural VAT regime, again differentiated according to turnover. For example the *remboursement forfaitaire* (RFA, accounting for 25 per cent of farmers liable for VAT in 1998) applies to farm businesses with an average income of less than about €45,700 (£33,600, $51,400) in two consecutive years. The *régime simplifié agricole* (RSA) is compulsory for farm businesses with an average income over this amount.

Preferential taxation provisions also exist in Germany. Although income tax rates for farmers are the same as for other (unincorporated) businessmen, there is a simplifying and beneficial standardized profit estimation procedure for farms below an area ceiling of 20 ha and other ceilings for animal production, vineyards and other highly profitable activities. Because the benefiting farms (about 50 per cent of all farms) are quite small, the current total subsidy value of this procedure is estimated to be about €20 million (£15 million, $23 million) per year. Farms beyond certain ceilings for profit (€25,000, or £18,400, $28,100), turnover or an imputed 'economic value' are obliged to use standard bookkeeping rules; this applies to about 35 per cent of farms. In addition there is an intermediate, cash based procedure to estimate profit for those farms falling in between the above ceilings to limit the administrative burden on rather small farms. An overt subsidy element is a tax allowance for agricultural income of €1340 (£986, $1507) for married farmers. The VAT regime is also simplified for more than 90 per cent of all farms, but the subsidy element of these simplified rules appears to be quite low. In this regard it is more important that fuel for agricultural use is taxed at a lower rate and that agricultural vehicles are exempt from automobile taxes. Land and buildings are generally subject to a lower inheritance tax rate. Finally, it should be pointed out that preferential taxation weighs far less in terms of support in Germany (and France) than the subsidies for the social security system specific for the farm sector (Andersen *et al.* 2002).

Recent developments

The European Commission's mid-term review of the way in which the CAP has operated under the reforms agreed as part of *Agenda 2000*, published in July 2002, concluded that it must yield more in terms of food quality, preservation of the environment and animal welfare, landscapes, cultural heritage, and enhancing social balance and equity. An agreement reached in June 2003 on changes to the way that policy is operated includes a number of significant reforms.

First, in 2005 a Single Farm Payment (SFP) will be introduced independent from production ('decoupling') that will replace the separate direct payments received under the various main CMOs. This will be based on payments received in a three-year reference period (2000–02). How the payment is worked out for individual farms is a matter for each country to choose. For example, it could be according to what the farm was actually paid in the reference period, or based on a regional average per hectare; the latter if applied in a simple way would have some major redistributive effects, especially benefiting farmers who formerly produced crops that were not subsidized (such as horticulture) and those operating extensive farming systems at the expense of the more heavily supported arable sector. To receive the SFP there is no requirement to maintain stocking levels or intensity of land use, or crop patterns, though all farmland will need to be kept in good agricultural and environmental conditions, so cannot be abandoned. The payment rights are transferable by sale separate from the land, but for actual payments to be made the buyer must have eligible land.

These payments will be linked to the achievement of certain environmental, food safety, animal welfare, health and occupational safety standards, plus the maintenance of land in good condition ('cross-compliance'). This is to be reflected in changes to the way that individual farms keep records on material flows and balances, for example in relation to environmental, food safety and other issues.

Secondly, rural development policy (including forestry) will be strengthened with more funds and new measures, including for the environment, food quality and animal welfare.

Thirdly, there will be a compulsory and progressive reduction in direct payments ('dynamic modulation') rising from 3 per cent in 2005 to 5 per cent from 2007 onwards – but with €5000 (£3680, $5625) being returned to each farmer – to generate additional funds for environmental and rural development objectives and to finance further reforms.

Finally, the market policy of the CAP will be revised so that it provides more of a safety net than a support. Changes include differently phased price cuts for butter and skim milk powder compensated by the introduction of a direct payment 'Dairy Premium' from 2005 based on the farm's milk quota in a reference period, plus maintaining the milk quota system until 2014–15. Other changes include reform in the rice, rye, durum wheat, nuts, starch potatoes and dried fodder sectors.

Farmers will continue to receive subsidies as direct payments, now in the form of the consolidated Single Farm Payment. Though these were originally intended to compensate for cuts in market price support, the reforms do not contain any provision for the direct payment to be scaled down over time.

The lower returns coming from the market are expected to make farm operators turn increasingly to diversifying their activities. Some further downsizing of the labour force in agriculture is highly likely, and the social and environmental consequences are of particular concern in the more remote rural areas of all three countries. Policy instruments are already in place to assist farmers and their families to widen their activities as a way of enabling them to stay living on their farms. The development of alternative job and income opportunities in rural areas, together with public payments for the provision of environmental services, are seen as key to this aim.

It is inevitable that households living on farms will increase the amount that they earn from non-agricultural activity as a way of earning their living. Given that support for the living standards of the agricultural community remains central to the aims of the EU's agricultural policy, the lack of reliable information on living standards – or even rudimentary statistics on the overall incomes of agricultural households – remains an alarming gap in the evidence base available to policymakers. Their unwillingness to probe the validity of the central rationale for the CAP and to demand statistics on it reflects the political nature of this area of policy.

Though in line with what independent policy analysts have argued for years, the changes agreed in 2003 are by no means a final solution to the problems of policy as it affects agriculture and forestry. The triggers to further change are more likely to be the need to revise the CAP to a form that enables enlargement of the EU to occur from 2004 onwards at an acceptable budgetary cost, and the desirability of improving the EU's negotiating position in the next round of WTO trade talks.

In the fishing industry, there is continuing considerable divergence between the political reality and scientific realism. At the time of writing, ministers have just broken a deadlock over the future architecture of the CFP under the 2002 review by reducing the quota of landed cod to about half the previous level. This was in the face of calls by marine scientists for a complete moratorium on the fishing of cod for 2003–04 and conceivably for some years after that. As cod is relatively large, a moratorium would mean that the mesh size of the nets would need to be so wide that other species could no longer be caught either. Consequently not just fish stocks but the entire fishing industry faces a very uncertain future.

Sources

Policies for agriculture, fisheries and forestry are subject to constant change, so hard copy references quickly become out of date. For this reason it is preferable to turn to official websites. For EU policies (CAP, CFP, forestry), reference should be made to the sites of the institutions of the EU, especially the Commission and the Parliament. The portal is <europa.eu.int>. This leads to descriptions at various levels of detail as well as to statistics and the legal text of legislation behind policy. National government departments dealing with agriculture, forestry and fishing should also be consulted for alternative insights into problems, policies and statistics:

Britain: <www.defra.gov.uk>

Germany: <www.verbraucherministerium.de>

France: <www.agriculture.gouv.fr>

For an overview on taxation, see:

F.G. Andersen, L.J. Asheim, K. Mittenzwei and F. Veggeland, *Taxation of Agriculture in Selected Countries – Study of the United States, Canada, Australia, Germany, United Kingdom, Ireland, France, Switzerland, and Italy with Relevance to the WTO*, NILF-report 2002–8 (Oslo: Norwegian Agricultural Economics Institute, 2002), <www.nilf.no/Publikasjoner/Rapporter/En/2002/R200208Hele.pdf>

17
Energy
Ian Bartle

Introduction

Energy policy is concerned with the strategies for the production, supply and distribution of primary energy and, where necessary, its conversion to a form suitable for final consumption. Primary energy includes fossil fuels such as coal, oil and gas as well as nuclear fuels, and renewable energy sources such as wind, wave and solar power. The final consumption of energy is normally in the form of coal, gas, refined oils and electricity.

Energy is an essential factor in modern industrial production and transport, so effective energy policies are required to achieve objectives such as industrial competitiveness, security of supply and low prices. Energy production and consumption also have a big impact on the environment, and environmental policy plays an important role in energy policy. There are also significant geographic variations in energy resources which can lead to cross-national differences in energy policies.

The nature of energy policy

The most general aspect of energy policy consists of setting the overall policy objectives and orientation. Five key objectives are security of supply, protection of the environment, economic efficiency, social welfare, and support for economic and industrial policy. Policy orientation depends on the priority governments attach to these objectives as well as on natural energy resources, the support given to certain kinds of energy technologies and fuels, the propensity to favour competition or intervention based approaches, and national norms and traditions in industrial policy.

The specific policies used to achieve the objectives and realize the policy orientations are as follows:

- The determination of ownership and of rights and privileges in the market. Government policy on monopoly or market liberalization may be used for a variety of purposes including encouragement of economic efficiency (by planning, economies of scale or competition) and support for national industry and employment. For similar purposes policy may dictate that companies are privately owned, or partially or fully state owned;
- The provision of state aids and subsidies, which may be used for social welfare purposes to support declining industries or to promote new technologies;
- Taxation: specific energy taxes or exemptions may be imposed on production and/or consumption for purposes such as environmental protection and social welfare;
- Regulation of operations. Policy instruments here include price controls, promotion of competition, licensing and authorisations, setting environmental standards and the imposition of public service obligations (generally aimed at achieving social and regional equity). Regulatory policy is often set by governments and implemented by independent regulatory agencies;
- Research and development, and the promotion of new technologies, energy efficiency and conservation. Activities here include financial support, coordination, information provision, studies, seminars and the establishment of priorities.

In each country there is a government ministry which has overall responsibility for energy policy, and in some countries and sectors the regulation of the energy industry has been delegated to independent regulatory agencies (Table 17.1).

Table 17.1 Energy policy institutions

	Britain	*France*	*Germany*
Ministry	Department of Trade and Industry.	*Direction Générale de l'Energie et des Matières Premières* (General Directorate for Energy and Raw Materials) in the *Ministère de l'Économie, des Finances et de l'Industrie* (Ministry of the Economy, Finance and Industry).	*Bundesministerium für Wirtschaft und Arbeit* (Federal Ministry of Economics and Labour). Economics Ministries at *Land* level.
Regulatory agencies	Office of Gas and Electricity Markets (OFGEM).	*Commission de Régulation de l'Énergie.*	No sector-specific regulatory agencies, but general competition law applies.

Specific comparisons

A closer view of energy policy in Britain, France and Germany can be obtained by looking at their general policy orientations; their policies on oil, coal, electricity and gas; and their policies relating to the environmental impact of energy production and use.

General policy orientation

There is a degree of similarity in broad energy policy orientations, with all three countries pursuing market liberalization, higher environmental standards and security of supply. Britain has the greatest propensity to favour market orientated policies, while in France the emphasis is on the achievement of security of supply by interventionist means and Germany is particularly focused on achieving high environmental protection.

In Britain experiments in competition have been aided by a favourable energy resource position, as Britain is one of the few major industrial countries to have a net self sufficiency in energy (PIU 2002). The three key energy policy objectives of security of supply, environmental protection and low prices are achieved primarily by competition and various market mechanisms (Matláry 1997: 31). Private ownership very often complements competition – the energy industry is almost completely privatized – and indigenous British industries are not specially favoured. There are nevertheless some important social and environmental policies which do not rely on market mechanisms, such as the provision of help for poorer households, obligations on suppliers to increase renewable electricity generation, and schemes to encourage energy efficiency.

One reason for the French focus on security of supply is its low energy resources and high level of dependency on energy imports. High priorities are security of supply, environmental protection, low-cost supply and public service obligations (IEA 2000a). A strong state led nuclear power policy (France has a higher share of nuclear power in its energy generation than any other country) is the most significant way in which supply security and reduction of climate change gases is achieved. Energy policy objectives have traditionally been achieved by state led programmes but are gradually being replaced by privatization and liberalization, starting with oil in the 1980s and moving on in the late 1990s and early 2000s to include electricity and gas. Indigenous industry has often been given special privileges for social welfare purposes or to assist in the achievement of efficiency by the use of long term planning and economies of scale.

Germany is increasingly dependent on energy imports as indigenous coal is replaced by gas imports and nuclear power is phased out (BMWi 2002). The key energy policy objectives here are also security of supply, environmental protection and low prices. The energy law of 1998 marked a shift from a balanced mix of state intervention (for coal and nuclear power) and the market towards increasing competition and dependence on the market (Matláry 1997; BMWi 2002). Germany nevertheless retains its high level of environmental protection with, for example, schemes to promote renewable energy, conservation and efficiency via market and non-market mechanisms. Although state aids are declining, policies remain to support domestic gas and coal production and to safeguard Germany's competitiveness in oil refining.

Oil policy

In all three countries the general trend in oil policy is liberalization and very limited state aid, and in compliance with the European single market there are no restrictions on exporting and importing or on the transportation, storage and distribution of oil (Roggenkamp *et al.* 2002: 459). Britain has extensive oil resources in the North Sea and a complex licensing regime whereas oil resources in France and Germany are very small and licensing regimes are relatively limited.

In Britain the oil industry is liberalized and completely privatized. Ownership of all fossil fuel resources (in land and sea) is nevertheless vested in licences and ministerial approval is required for work programmes for the exploration and extraction of oil (Roggenkamp *et al.* 2002: 910). Licence holders established before 1982 are required to make payments to the government for royalties on the extracted fuel, although this is to be phased out, and a petroleum revenue tax is charged on oil companies. Oil exploration, extraction and refining, both onshore and offshore, is subject to extensive environmental legislation. There are no state aids to companies in the oil sector.

In France the oil industry is liberalized and almost completely privatized: the government only holds a golden share in Elf, part of the merged group TotalFinaElf, which gives it certain special rights over company policy (IEA 2000a). Landowners own energy resources but the government can grant licences to other parties to prospect and extract, with the land owner being able to claim damages (Roggenkamp *et al.* 2002: 453). Exporting, importing, storage and distribution only requires registration and notification. The government requires that 5.5 per cent of oil must be transported by French oil tankers and 25 per cent of the previous year's flow must be stored (Roggenkamp *et al.* 2002: 458). State aids are very limited – there are none to the major producers and suppliers – but the government uses the proceeds of a specific tax to subsidize small retailers of automotive fuels to maintain petrol supply in remote areas (IEA 2000a: 65).

In Germany the oil industry is fully liberalized and the industry is privately owned (BMWi 2002: 35; IEA 1998). The ownership of energy resources is vested in the *Land* governments, with whom the extraction, import, export and refining of oil must be registered. *Land* governments do not charge royalties on the extraction of oil except in Schleswig Holstein, where there is a royalty of

8 per cent. Importers are under an obligation to store 80 days of oil consumption and domestic producers 15 days (Roggenkamp *et al.* 2002: 565). There are no state aids to companies in the oil sector.

Coal policy

Coal production is loss making in all three countries and the industry requires substantial state aids. State aids are higher in Germany and France than in Britain and are used to support production and employment and to mitigate the effects of declining production by providing social security, restructuring and retraining (see Table 17.2).

In Britain the coal industry is fully liberalized and privatized. Ownership of coal resources is vested in the state owned Coal Authority which issues licences for exploration and production (Roggenkamp *et al.* 2002). State aids are available from a budget of up to £60 million (€81.5 million, $91.7 million) to help finance the continued operation of viable coal mines and to mitigate the effects of the decline in the industry, for example by helping to fund site regeneration, social security and retraining (DTI 2003a, IEA 2000b: 174). The development of cleaner coal technology is also encouraged, a key aspect of which is the removal of carbon dioxide (PIU 2002: 12). There is also aid for research and development and for the promotion of expertise in cleaner coal technology.

In France the production of coal is undertaken almost exclusively by the state owned company *Charbonnages de France* (CDF). Coal is produced at a substantial loss and government policy is to reduce production progressively with the aim of ceasing altogether in 2005 (IEA 2000a: 63). The principal aim of government policy during this period is to support the industry and employees during the phasing out of production and industry restructuring. State aids to the industry are substantial and are used firstly to support the industry and secondly to finance social security costs associated with industry restructuring (Commission 2002a; IEA 2000a: 66–7). The 2000 French electricity law allows the government to require up to 10 per cent of electricity to be generated from coal, although this figure will fall as production falls.

Table 17.2   State aids to the coal industry, 2000

	Britain	*France*	*Germany*
Aid to producers	€213.1 m (£156.8 m, $239.7 m)	€385.9 m (£284 m, $434.1 m)	€3621.6 m (£2665.5 m, $4074.30 m)
Aid for social security, restructuring and retraining, etc.	zero	€617.7 m (£454.6 m, $694.9 m)	€1090.2 m (£802.4 m, $1226.5 m)

Source: Commission 2002a.

In Germany coal markets and production are liberalized. Coal is generally produced at a substantial loss and state aids to the industry are significant. Government policy is to safeguard domestic coal production, partly for reasons of security of supply but also in order to protect employment and the industry. The government has nevertheless agreed capacity reductions, and the scale of these reductions will increase after 2005. Between 1998 and 2005 state aids will fall from €4.73 billion (£3.48 billion, $5.32 billion) to €2.71 billion (£1.99 billion, $3.05 billion) (BMWi 2002: 35).

Electricity and gas policy

Competition is becoming a dominant theme in the electricity and gas sectors in all three countries and there are no substantial state aids, although a significant part of the industry is state owned in France and small aids are available for the promotion of renewable generation. Markets are more open to competition in Britain and Germany than in France (see Table 17.3) and price regulation to achieve public service obligations is a key feature in France and, to a lesser extent, Germany.

In Britain, competition in both electricity and gas is achieved by centralized regulation. In electricity the 'New Electricity Trading Arrangements' (NETA) introduced in 2001 enable wholesale trading of electricity in England and Wales (OFGEM 2002), and will be extended to the whole of Britain with the 'British Electricity Transmission and Trading Arrangements'. In gas the 'New Gas Trading Arrangements' permit wholesale trading in gas and enable new suppliers to gain access to the national gas pipeline system. In gas and electricity the competitive aspects of the sector (supply) are required to be completely separate from the natural monopoly aspects (transmission and distribution through the electricity grid and gas pipelines), which are managed by a separate company, National Grid Transco, and regional electricity distribution companies. Price regulation of the supply of electricity and gas has been discontinued (OFGEM 2002) but charges for network use are regulated.

The gas and electricity sectors in France are partially open to competition. Both the main companies, *Gaz de France* (GdF) and *Electricité de France* (EdF), are state owned but 20 per cent of the gas market and 30 per cent of the electricity market (the larger users) are open to competition. Government policy is to

Table 17.3 Competition in gas and electricity

	Britain	*France*	*Germany*
Electricity	100%	All users above 9 GWh (about 1/3 of the market)	100%
Gas	100%	28%	100%

Source: Commission 2002b; CRE 2003.

progressively increase market opening in gas and electricity in order to comply with the EU requirement to increase this to 28 per cent by 2003 and 33 per cent by 2008. GdF is the main owner of the transmission (90 per cent) and distribution (95 per cent) systems, the remainder being owned by a small number of national and local companies (IEA 2000a: 74–5). Under the government policy of supply security the French gas system is well endowed with storage facilities and is one of the most secure in the world. As part of liberalization a separation of EdF's accounts between generation, transmission, distribution and supply is required by the Electricity Act 2000, and an independent grid system operator (the *gestionnaire du réseau de transport d'electricité*) has been specified. Public service obligations (PSOs) play an important role in the French gas and electricity sectors. All suppliers of gas from the pipeline system must sell gas according to non-discriminatory tariffs, that is, similar customers must be charged the same, though there are regional differences depending on transmission costs. Gas distributors are under an obligation to supply consumers in their supply area. PSOs will apply to all suppliers as the sector becomes increasingly open to competition. Charges for access to the electricity network are regulated, as is electricity supply. An important PSO is the geographic uniformity of tariffs in the whole of France (IEA 2000a: 102). For environmental reasons, and to support the domestic coal industry, purchasing requirements have been imposed on EdF and the non-nationalized distributors of electricity. If producers request it, EdF is required to buy power from certain kinds of environmentally friendly generators, and the minister for energy can request that up to 10 per cent of electricity is generated from domestic coal.

The German gas and electricity industries are highly fragmented, with the larger companies privately owned and many of the smaller suppliers and distributors owned by the regional and local governments. All consumers can choose their supplier, and competition is achieved by a system of negotiated network access based on an inter-association agreement designed to enable new suppliers to gain access to the grid. A public service obligation exists in both gas and electricity: the local supply companies are required, if requested by the consumer, to supply energy at a tariff set by the *Land* governments. Since 1998 Federal policy has been to phase out nuclear power by 2020 (BMWi 2002). For environmental reasons there is an 'electricity feed' law which gives renewable generators the right to supply electricity to the grid and receive a guaranteed price.

Energy policy and the environment

The energy sector is one of the major producers of pollution and each country has a target for greenhouse gas emission reduction agreed under the Kyoto protocol and within the EU burden sharing agreement. There are numerous taxes on energy and fuel consumption which are designed principally for environmental protection (OECD 2001: 55–61). All three countries have high taxes on automotive fuels as well as a variety of other energy taxes, although coal consumption is not taxed. Each country also has a large number of exemptions from these taxes, mainly in order to promote competitiveness and environmentally friendly electricity generation and consumption. Details are set out in Table 17.4.

The British government's target for greenhouse gas reduction is to be achieved by a variety of measures including a Climate Change Levy, voluntary agreements with energy intensive industries, an obligation on electricity suppliers to generate 10 per cent from renewable sources by 2010, and funding for energy efficiency programmes. The Climate Change Levy on business energy use was introduced in April 2001 and does not apply to electricity generated from renewable sources.

The French government's target under the Kyoto and EU agreements is to stabilize greenhouse gas emissions at 1990 levels by 2008–12. With its high level of nuclear power France already has a relatively low level of greenhouse gas emissions but other measures are necessary as the nuclear power share may decline. A national programme to combat climate change agreed in 2000 includes a variety of energy efficiency measures, support for renewables, and

Table 17.4 Energy policy and the environment

	Britain	*France*	*Germany*
Greenhouse gas reduction:			
– Kyoto/EU agreement	12.5% below 1990 level by 2008–12	1990 level by 2008–12	21% below 1990 level by 2008–12
– Domestic target	20% below 1990 level by 2008–12	1990 level by 2008–12	25% below 1990 level by 2005
Environmentally related energy taxes	Climate Change Levy on coal, electricity, gas and heating oil (not charged on households and several business exemptions). Non Fossil Fuel Obligation Levy charged on electricity generators (some exemptions, such as renewables). Various duties on hydrocarbon oils.	Various taxes on petroleum products	Electricity consumption tax (lower rate for manufacturing and railways). Various duties on mineral oil consumption.

Sources: OECD 2001, 2003; IEA 2000b; BMWi 2002: 18.

energy efficient policies for the transport sector. The government is also to bring in a carbon tax.

The German government's measures to reduce greenhouse gases include voluntary agreements with industry to reduce emissions and policies to increase the use of cogeneration (in which waste heat from electricity generation is used for heating or other purposes). Policies to promote the use of renewable energy include a law on the use of renewables for electricity generation, state aids amounting to €445 million (£328 million, $501 million) in the period 1999–2002 (BMWi 2002: 18) and low interest loans for the development of solar power. Energy conservation and efficiency measures are also undertaken, for example measures to reduce energy consumption in buildings.

Recent developments

In Britain a major energy review was instigated in 2001 with a White Paper published in 2003 (DTI 2003b). The energy policy context is expected to become less benign with a greater dependency on energy imports and more demanding environmental imperatives. The government wishes to encourage substantial long term investment in renewable generation while leaving the nuclear power option open. It is recognized that environmental objectives are also paramount and that it may not be possible to achieve these by market mechanisms alone. In the electricity industry several companies are struggling with falls in wholesale prices of 40 per cent. The 'New Electricity Trading Arrangements' (NETA) have not provided the right incentives for intermittent renewable electricity generators, and ensuring that it does provide these for future investment in economic and environmentally friendly electricity supply is a key aspect of the review.

One of the central developments within the French energy industry is adjustment to liberalization and to increasing competition in the electricity and gas industries within Europe. One of EdF's responses to this is to increase investment in other EU countries. Partial privatization of EdF is on the French government's agenda, partly to fund its new investments and partly in response to criticism from other EU countries of unfair competition from EdF. Public service obligations in the electricity and gas industries remain important despite increasing liberalization, and non discriminatory tariffs and obligations to supply have been restated and reaffirmed. Nuclear power generation is expected to fall as it is seen to be above an economically efficient level. As a result the government is encouraging alternatives such as renewables and other sources for both energy security and environmental protection. A new law in 2003 included an extension of the powers of the electricity regulator to include gas regulation, hence becoming the Commission for the Regulation of Energy (CRE 2003).

In Germany the Ministry of Economics published an energy report in 2002 (BMWi 2002) on long term energy policy up to 2020. The government recognizes that it will be increasingly dependent on energy imports, demand for which will be met partly from the EU internal energy market that the German government has strongly supported. Nuclear power will be phased out and the government aims to step up its already active programme of conservation and renewable energy. The government has been a strong supporter of energy liberalization but it explicitly recognizes that environmental protection and liberalization can be in conflict and, if they are, that government intervention in favour of the environment will be necessary (BMWi 2002: 4, 9). Germany has implemented liberalization in gas and electricity by the use of normal competition law and the encouragement of inter industry agreements on network access, but there is no sector specific regulator. While most government policy makers and the industry argue that this will avert the threat of over regulation, it is controversial as many market entrants argue it favours the established market players.

Sources

BMWi (Bundesministerium für Wirtschaft und Technologie), 'Sustainable energy policy to meet the needs of the future. Energy Report', *Dokumentation* no. 508, (Berlin: BMWi, 2002).

Commission (2002a), 'Competition – state aid – scoreboard – state aid by sector', Competition Commission, Brussels, <www.europa.eu.int/comm/competition/state_aid/scoreboard/> [11 December 2002].

Commission (2002b), 'Second benchmarking report on the implementation of the internal electricity and gas market', SEC (2002)1038, 1 October 2002, Brussels, <www.europa.eu.int/comm/energy/en/elec_single_market/index_en.html> [11 December 2002].

CRE (Commission de régulation de l'énergie) (2003), 'Presentation', <www.cre.fr>, [21 November 2003].

DTI (Department of Trade and Industry) (2003a), 'Energy, coal', <www.dti.gov.uk/energy/coal/index.shtml> [21 November 2003].

DTI (Department of Trade and Industry) (2003b), 'Energy White Paper. Our energy future – creating a low carbon economy', (London: February 2003).

IEA (International Energy Agency), *Energy Policies of IEA Countries: France 2000 Review* (Paris: IEA, 2000a).

IEA (International Energy Agency), *Energy Policies of IEA Countries: 2000 Review* (Paris: IEA, 2000b).

J.H. Matláry, *Energy Policy in the European Union* (London: Macmillan – now Palgrave Macmillan, 1997).

OECD (Organisation for Economic Cooperation and Development), *Environmentally Related Taxes in OECD Countries: Issues and strategies* (Paris: OECD, 2001).

OECD (Organisation for Economic Cooperation and Development) (2003), 'Environmentally related taxes database', <www.oecd.org/document/29/0,2340,en_2649_201185_1894685_1_1_1_1,00.html> [21 November 2003].

OFGEM (Office of Gas and Electricity Markets) (2002), 'Review of competition in gas and electricity connections: Survey document', 20 February 2002 <www.ofgem.gov.uk/public/pub2002q1.htm> [11 December 2002].

PIU (Performance and Innovation Unit), *The Energy Review* (London: The Cabinet Office, 2002).

M.M. Roggenkamp, A. Rønne, C. Redewell and I. del Guayo, *Energy Law in Europe: National, EU and International Law and Institutions* (Oxford: Oxford University Press, 2002).

18
Transport

John Preston, Graeme Hayes and Dirk Lehmkuhl

Introduction

The aim of this chapter is to describe the role of national governments in the transport sector in Britain, France and Germany. Despite differences in the structure of sub-national governance, the level of national government intervention in policy, unlike operations, is broadly similar in all three countries. However the level of national government intervention in the direct provision of transport operations and infrastructure is lower in Britain than in France or Germany.

The nature of transport policy

The role of national government in the transport sector covers two main areas. The first is the setting of the broad policy parameters. These involve:

- transport operations and planning, which includes investment procedures and levels, vehicle and driver licensing, and safety standards (for example vehicle maintenance standards);
- fiscal measures such as fuel tax and road tax;
- environmental standards such as exhaust controls;
- planning standards, such as the prohibition of certain land-uses because of adverse transport impacts, and the encouragement of certain transport investments because of beneficial land-use impacts;
- regulatory standards, including those related to competition policy.

The relevant governmental bodies involved in these activities in the three countries are shown in Table 18.1.

The second way in which national governments are involved in the transport sector is via the direct provision of transport operations and infrastructure in relation to air, rail, road, water and urban transport.

Table 18.1 Transport policy: areas of government activity

	Britain	*France*	*Germany*
Transport operations and planning (e.g. licensing, investment)	Department for Transport Strategic Rail Authority	*Ministère de l'équipement, des Transports, du Logement, du Tourisme, et de la Mer* (Ministry of Equipment, Transport, Housing, Tourism and the Sea)	*Bundesministerium für Verkehr, Bau- und Wohnungswesen (BMVBW)* (Federal Ministry of Transportation and Construction)
Fiscal measures (fuel tax, etc.)	Her Majesty's Treasury	*Ministère des Finances* (Ministry of Finance)	*Bundesministerium für Finanzen* (Federal Ministry of Finance)
Environmental standards	Department of the Environment, Food and Rural Affairs	*Ministère de l'Environnement et du Développement Durable* (Ministry of the Environment and Sustainable Development)	*Bundesministerium für Umwelt, Naturschutz und Reaktorsicherheit* (Federal Ministry for the Environment, Nature Conservation and Nuclear Security)
Planning standards	Office of the Deputy Prime Minister	*Directions départementales de l'équipement* (regional offices of the transport ministry)	*BMVBW: Abteilung S Straßenbau/ Straßenverkehr, Abteilung EW Eisenbahnen/ Wasserstraßen* (divisions of Ministry of Transportation and Construction) *Deutsche Einheit Fernstraßenplanungs- und -bau GmbH*
General regulation	Competition Commission	*Cour des Comptes* (Court of Accounts)	*Bundeskartellamt* (Federal Cartel Office)

A cursory examination of Table 18.1 would superficially suggest that the role of central government in transport policy is similar. Certainly, there are dedicated government departments in all three countries. However there are also a number of important differences. These include the longer tradition of central planning in France and Germany than in Britain, where there was no national transport plan until the launch of the Ten Year Plan for Transport in 2000. In France, the state has an important gatekeeping role in local transport budgets through its negotiation of six-year planning contracts with regional authorities (CPER). Another policy area that distinguishes France is the co-ordination of central government activities and the promotion of transport as a key lead factor in regional policy objectives, which is undertaken by DATAR (*Délégation à l'aménagement du territoire et à l'action régionale*, or Regional Development and Action Authority).

Similarly there is a longer tradition of transport intervention at the local and regional levels in France and Germany than in Britain. For example, in France in 2000 local authority spending on transport stood at €22.3 billion (£16.4 billion, $25 billion), almost double the €11.6 billion (£8.5 billion, $13 billion) spent by central government in 2001 (CCTN 2002: 72). In addition, in Britain there has not been a recent tradition of hypothecating tax income for transport expenditure, in contrast to the use of federal petrol taxes in Germany and local employer taxes (*versement de transports*) in France. However the 2000 Transport Act in England and Wales has provided for the hypothecation of Road User Charging and Workplace Parking Levies to local government transport expenditure, although to date this has only been taken up in two areas (Durham and London).

Specific comparisons

The most striking feature of central government activity in the transport sector in France is the public ownership of transport infrastructure and service providers. By contrast, a feature of transport policy in Britain is the limited role of government in a number of sectors: national government sold its stakes in airports, seaports, road freight operations, road passenger operations, air operations and sea operations in the 1980s. Germany is positioned somewhere between these two extremes, with a greater emphasis on corporatization.

Air transport

The role of government in air transport is greater in France than in Britain or Germany. Table 18.2 sets out the public and private bodies involved in this area.

The French state intervenes in air transport through its ownership of *Aéroports de Paris* (ADP), its current 54 per cent shareholding in national

Table 18.2 Air transport operations

	Britain	*France*	*Germany*
Operations	Privately owned airlines	Air France Privately owned airlines	Privately owned airlines
Infrastructure	Privately and municipally owned airports National Air Traffic Services (mixed ownership)	*Direction Générale de l'Aviation Civile* (DGAC) *Aéroports de Paris* Chambers of Commerce and Industry (CCIs)	Privately and municipally owned airports
Regulation	Civil Aviation Authority	Direction Générale de l'Aviation Civile (DGAC)	*Deutsche Flugsicherung GmbH Luftfahrt-Bundesamt* (Federal Aviation Office)

flag-carrier Air France, and as regulatory authority for civil aviation through the *Direction Générale de l'Aviation Civile* (DGAC), whose responsibilities include airline safety and air traffic control. A new round of decentralization initiatives may include the transfer of management of France's regional airports, currently run by Chambers of Commerce and Industry (CCIs), to regional councils.

In both Britain and Germany the central state no longer operates air services or airports, although local authorities remain active in the airport sector. Air traffic control was partially privatized in Britain in 2001. The creation of this new body, National Air Traffic Services (NATS), was highly controversial. By contrast, in Germany the delegation in 1993 of integrated civil and regional military air traffic control to the *Deutsche Flugsicherung GmbH*, a state-owned company under private law, was relatively unproblematic.

Rail transport

As in the case of air transport, it is in France that the role of the state in rail transport is most important. Details of the organizations involved in this area are set out in Table 18.3.

The French state retains the responsibility for objective setting and long-term planning for the national rail network through its ownership of the national rail company SNCF (*Société nationale des chemins de fer français*). The 1997 reform of SNCF created RFF (*Réseau Ferré de France*) to manage infrastructure maintenance and development. The absence of a formal regulatory authority for rail transport

Table 18.3 Rail transport operations

	Britain	*France*	*Germany*
Operations	Privately owned train operating companies Strategic Rail Authority	*Société Nationale des Chemins de Fer Français* (SNCF)	*Deutsche Bahn AG* (German Railways)
Infrastructure	Network Rail	*Réseau Ferré de France* (RFF, French Railway Network)	*Deutsche Bahn AG*
Regulation	Office of the Rail Regulator	RFF Regional authorities	*Eisenbahn-Bundesamt* (Federal Railway Office)

in France, added to the demise of contractual plans between the state and SNCF, means that RFF has consequently become the *de facto* regulator for rail transport.

In Britain, rail infrastructure and operations were privatized in the 1990s. Responsibility for rail infrastructure was transferred to Railtrack plc in 1996 which in 2002 was replaced by Network Rail, a not-for-dividend private company limited by guarantee. However the state retains an important presence through the Strategic Rail Authority and the Office of the Rail Regulator.

In Germany the privatization of the *Deutsche Bahn AG* (DB AG), itself a unification of the *Deutsche Bundesbahn* and the *Deutsche Reichsbahn*, has turned out to be an arduous and long-lasting process (Lehmkuhl 1996). Initiated in 1994, what has been achieved so far is a split of duties between public authorities and the organizationally privatized DB AG. The *Eisenbahn-Bundesamt* (Federal Railway Office) assumed the role of sovereign planning and licensing body. The DB AG has been established as a joint-stock company under private law, but ownership has remained unchanged.

Road transport

In the road transport sector, the contrast between statist France and the other two countries is not consistent. Table 18.4 lists the organizations involved in this area.

The maintenance and development of the French road network is shared between levels of government as a function of road classification. Communal councils are thus responsible for France's urban streets and rural C roads, *département* councils for the D roads, and the central state for the *routes nationales* (RN). However the central state retains a strong directive hand through the transport ministry's *Direction des routes* (DR). All major highway projects over 25 km long, and all road projects costing in excess of 545 million francs (€83 million, £61 million, $93 million), must be compatible with the DR network blueprint. The ministry's deconcentrated 'field services', the *Directions départementales de l'équipement* (DDE), combine the functions of project identification, evaluation

Table 18.4   Road transport operations

	Britain	France	Germany
Passenger operations	Privately owned bus and coach operators Some municipal operators	RATP (*Régie autonome des transports parisiens*) Privately owned bus and coach operators Some municipal operators	Privately owned bus and coach operators Some municipal operators Regional administrative unions
Freight operations	Privately owned freight companies	Small private companies	Privately owned freight companies *Bundesamt für Güterverkehr* (Federal Office for Goods Transport)
Infrastructure	Highways Agency Some Public–Private Partnerships (PPPs)	*Directions départementales de l'équipement* (field services of the transport ministry) Communal and *département* authorities	Federal and *Land* Ministries for Transport *Bundesanstalt für Straßenwesen* (Federal Highway Research Institute)
Regulation	Traffic Commissioners	*Directions regionales de l'équipement* (regional field services of the transport ministry)	Federal and *Land* Ministries for Transport *Regierungspräsidien* (district administrations) *Kraftfahrt-Bundesamt* (Federal Motor Transport Authority)

and implementation, and are some of the most visibly pro-active agents of state power in the provinces.

In Britain, Public Private Partnerships (PPPs) have been encouraged for the development of the road system. Between 1991/2 and 2000/1 around 7 per cent of investment in the strategic roads network in Britain came from the private sector. Over the period 2001/2 to 2010/11 this is forecast to rise to 16 per cent of total investment. PPPs and PFIs (Private Finance Initiatives) have also been used extensively for the development of urban rail systems. Similar experimentation has been undertaken in Germany where the 1992 Federal Transport Infrastructure Plan (including the *Verkehrsprojekte Deutsche Einheit*) delegated implementation to a company under private law (*Deutsche Einheit Fernstraßen-planungs- und -bau GmbH*). In addition, some 27 infrastructure projects have been initiated and partly realized since 1994 on the basis of a privately pre-financed model. Other models of privately financed and/or operated infrastructure projects have been discussed more recently by a government commission, the *Kommission Verkehrsinfrastrukturfinanzierung 2000*.

One important difference between the three countries is with respect to inter-urban road policy where, paradoxically, the market currently has its greatest role in France. Around 20 per cent of the French motorway network is toll-free and managed directly by the state, which also continues to whole- or part-fund the upgrading of existing, and the construction of new, non-toll highways. However the majority of the motorway network is operated on a *péage* (tollgate) user tolls basis by six regional public-private partnerships (SEMCA, *Sociétés d'économie mixte de concessionnaires d'autoroutes*) granted concessions by the state for each specific motorway link. Since the early 1960s the vast majority of motorway construction has been achieved by SEMCA through debt-financing. The massive acceleration of motorway-building in France in the 1990s – 2016 km of new toll motorways were opened between 1992 and 2000 – was made possible by state-authorized increases in the debt envelope available to the SEMCA. The state raises a tax of €0.35 (£0.26, $0.39) per kilometre on all motorway toll charges, absorbed since 2001 into general taxation revenues, and in spring 2002 central government privatized ASF, which operates motorways through-out the south of France, in order to raise funds to cover the company's massive debt. By contrast the motorway networks in Britain and Germany are publicly owned and toll free, although in Britain they are managed by a separate governmental body, the Highways Agency. In Germany, a distance related toll system for heavy vehicles was due to be implemented at the end of 2003. The revenues of this toll system will be used to finance infrastructure-related costs of all modes of transport. By contrast, the revenues of the so-called eco-tax on fossil fuels in Germany will not be hypothecated to the infrastructure fund but will go to the general budget.

Water transport

As in other areas, the role of the state in water transport is more significant in France than in Britain or Germany. Table 18.5 sets out the organizations involved in this area.

The French state heavily subsidizes maritime transport through the extension and development of France's ports. In conjunction with local authorities, the state manages France's six major seaports plus the two major riverports, all of which are technically classified as financially autonomous public bodies. A further sixteen commercial and industrial 'ports of national interest' are jointly administered by the state with Chambers of Commerce and Industry (CCIs). VNF (Waterways in France) is a relatively rare example of agencification in France. Accountable to the transport ministry, the agency is responsible for the management, upkeep

Table 18.5 Water transport operations

	Britain	France	Germany
Operations	Private companies	Private companies Regional companies	Private companies
Infrastructure	Privately owned, municipally owned and Trust Ports British Waterways Board	*Ports Autonomes* Chambers of Commerce and Industry (CCIs) VNF (*Voies navigables de France*, Waterways in France)	*Bundesanstalt für Wasserbau* (Federal Waterways Engineering and Research Institute) *Land Häfen- und Schiff-fahrtsverwaltungen* (*Land* port and navigation authorities)
Regulation	Maritime and Coastguard Agency	*Directions départementales des affaires maritimes* (maritime field services of the transport ministry)	*Regionale Häfen- und Schifffahrtsverwaltungen* (regional port and navigation authorities) *Regionale Wasser- und Schifffahrts-direktionen* (regional water and navigation management) *Zentralkommission für die Rheinschifffahrt* (Central Commission for Navigation on the Rhine)

and development of 80 per cent of France's public navigable waterway system. The remaining waterways are directly managed by the state or by regional authorities. In Britain and Germany the central state has some responsibilities for inland waterways, but seaports are mainly the responsibility of *Land* governments in Germany whilst in Britain the main ports are predominantly privately owned.

Urban public transport

The French state owns RATP, which operates the Paris metro, RER (*Réseau Express Régional*) and bus services, though PPPs have been trailed on some RER lines (Orlyval). In Britain, local government continues to have a role in urban rail passenger operations in certain cities (London, Newcastle, Glasgow) and in bus operations in a few areas, such as Edinburgh and Nottingham. Public ownership remains the norm in Germany. Urban public transport is one area where detailed comparisons between the three countries have been made (see, for example, Huang *et al.* 2002 and European Commission 1997). Urban public transport in Britain outside of London is characterized by privatized and deregulated markets. In France, area franchises are the norm, while in Germany, at least until the

Table 18.6   Infrastructure provision (metres per capita)

	Britain	*France*	*Germany*
Railways	0.29	0.54	0.45
Motorways	0.06	0.16	0.14
Highways, main or national roads	0.81	0.45	0.50
Inland waterways	0.02	0.09	0.09
Cars per person	0.42	0.46	0.52

Source: European Commission/Eurostat 2002.

recent Altmark court case, the classic regulated monopoly model has been commonplace, albeit with some recent experiments with tendering.

Statistical comparisons

Statistical comparisons within the transport sector are notoriously difficult due to factors such as differences in definitions and data collection methods. Nonetheless, data collected by the Directorate-General for Energy and Transport of the European Commission (see, for example, European Commission/Eurostat 2002) illustrate the impact of the different transport polices adopted in the three countries.

Table 18.6 indicates that Britain (or more accurately the UK) has substantially less railway, motorway and commercially used inland waterways per capita than France or Germany, but this is compensated for by a more extensive network of highways, main and national roads. Over four per cent of the French rail network is classified as high speed (capable of over 250 km/hour), while only a little over one per cent of the German network is so classified. Currently there are no high speed rail lines in Britain, but this will change with the completion of the Channel Tunnel Rail Link.

Table 18.6 also shows that while car ownership per capita in France and Britain is broadly similar, ownership levels in Germany are significantly higher. These differences are largely explained by variations in GDP per capita.

Table 18.7 indicates that car ownership taxes in the three countries are broadly comparable. Petrol and diesel prices are broadly similar in France and Germany but significantly higher in Britain, due largely to higher taxation.

Work for the UK Commission for Integrated Transport has produced further comparisons of taxes on car ownership (purchase tax and road tax) and car use (fuel tax and tolls) (Burnham 2001). For a standard 1600 cc family saloon, for example, the tax levels in Britain and France are remarkably similar, while those for Germany appear substantially lower (see Table 18.8).

The UK Commission for Integrated Transport has also published work that compares transport investment levels and public transport prices in the three

Table 18.7   Fiscal measures

	Britain	France	Germany
% of tax added to new car price	17.5	19.6	16.0
Automotive diesel fuel price per litre, 2001	€1.29 (£0.95, $1.45)	€0.81 (£0.60, $0.91)	€0.82 (£0.60, $0.92)
– tax as a share of the price	74%	62%	61%
Unleaded petrol price per litre, 2001	€1.21 (£0.89, $1.36)	€1.00 (£0.74, $1.13)	€0.97 (£0.71, $1.09)
– tax as a share of the price	76%	71%	68%

Source: European Commission/Eurostat 2002.

Table 18.8   Taxation on a standard 1600cc family saloon car, 2000

	Britain	France	Germany
Tax on owning (purchase tax and road tax)	€386 (£284, $434)	€359 (£264, $404)	€246 (£181, $277)
Tax on use (fuel tax and tolls)	€950 (£699, $1069)	€949 (£698, $1068)	€776 (£571, $873)
Total	€1336 (£983, $1503)	€1308 (£963, $1472)	€1022 (£752, $1150)

Source: Burnham 2001.

countries (Atkins 2001). This indicated that between 1990 and 1995 transport investment levels in Britain were only at 67 per cent of the levels in France and 59 per cent of the levels in Germany. Similarly, in 1995 public transport fares were only 63 per cent of British levels in France and 87 per cent of British levels in Germany. Detailed comparisons between Britain and France suggest that in 1998 transport infrastructure spend per capita was almost 50 per cent higher in France than in Britain, while revenue support per capita was almost 80 per cent higher in France than in Britain. Calculations of revenue support in Germany are difficult because of the practice of cross-subsidizing local public transport with the profits from local electricity generation and transmission, although deregulation of electricity markets means that this practice is no longer feasible.

Recent developments

The transport sector has traditionally been characterized by a large degree of government intervention, but this has been reducing recently. As we have seen, this is particularly marked in Britain but has also been occurring in France and Germany (Preston 1999). In Britain this reduction was largely driven by national policies originating in the 1980s. For France and Germany, European initiatives in the 1990s have been more important, with the completion of reforms that liberalized air markets in 1997 and implemented cabotage in the road freight market in 1998, thus enabling permits foreign hauliers to operate in domestic markets.

Transport policy continues to be a test case for the principle of subsidiarity, with national government involvement pressured in two directions. From above, the European Commission is increasingly becoming involved in transport, as evidenced by the 2001 White Paper (European Commission 2001). Emphasis is placed on infrastructure provision at a European level (the Trans-European Networks), 'fair and efficient' pricing for the use of that infrastructure and the concept of sustainable mobility. The rail sector remains particularly problematic, with deterioration in performance and rising debts (Filleul 2002, SRA 2003, Teutsch 2001). From below, regional and local authorities continue to play an important role. In Britain this has been given impetus by the creation of devolved regional bodies in Scotland, Wales, Northern Ireland and Greater London. An example of different levels of governance coming together to effect a policy shift is the introduction of road user charging in central London in February 2003. This is being implemented by the Greater London Authority but is consistent with European Commission and national policy. The London experiment will be monitored closely throughout Europe and, if successful, there may well be other such schemes in Britain, France and Germany.

Sources

For further details of transport policy in Britain see Glaister (2002), Docherty and Shaw (2003) and Hine and Preston (2003); for France see Merlin (1994) and Carrère (1997); and for Germany see Teutsch (2001) and von Suntum (1986). Useful comparative studies include Simpson (1987) and Nakagawa and Matsunaka (1997).

W.S. Atkins, *Study of European Best Practice in the Delivery of Integrated Transport: Summary Report* (London: CfIT, 2001), <www.cfit.gov.uk/research/ebp/exec/pdf/exec.pdf> [19 March 2003].

BMVBW (Bundesministerium für Verkehr, Bau- und Wohnungswesen), *Investitionsprogramm für den Ausbau der Bundesschienenwege, Bundesfernstraßen und Bundeswasserstraßen in den Jahre 1999–2002* (Bonn, 1999), <http://www.bmvbw.de/Anlage1773/Inhalt-und-Erlaeuterung-der-Projektlisten.pdf> [13 April 2003].

J. Burnham, *European Comparison of Taxes on Car Ownership and Use: Review Produced for the Commission for Integrated Transport* (London: CfIT, 2001), <www.cfit.gov.uk/research/scoto122/pdf/scot0122.pdf> [12 February 2003].

G. Carrère, *Le Transport en France* (Paris: Presses Universitaires de France, 1997).

CCTN (Commission des Comptes des Transports de la Nation), *39ème Rapport de la Commission des Comptes des Transports de la Nation, 2001* (Paris: La Documentation Française, 2002).

I. Docherty and J. Shaw (eds), *A New Deal for Transport: The UK's Struggle with the Sustainable Transport Agenda* (Oxford: Blackwell, 2003).

European Commission, *Improved Structure and Organization for Urban Transport Operations of Passengers in Europe* (Luxembourg: Office for Official Publications of the European Communities, 1997).

European Commission, *European Transport Policy for 2010: Time to Decide. White Paper* (Luxembourg: Office of the Official Publications of the European Union, 2001).

European Commission/Eurostat, *European Union Energy and Transport in Figures 2002* (Luxembourg: Office of the Official Publications of the European Union, 2002), <www.europa.eu.int/comm/energy_transport/etif/index.html> [12 February 2003].

J.-J. Filleul, *Evaluation de la Réforme du Secteur du Transport Ferroviaire* (Paris: La Documentation Française, 2002).

S. Glaister, 'UK transport policy 1997–2001', *Oxford Review of Economic Policy*, 18 (2002): 154–5.

J. Hine and J. Preston (eds), *Integrated Futures and Transport Choices: UK Transport Policy Beyond the 1998 White Paper* (Aldershot: Ashgate, 2003).

B. Huang, T. Holvad and J. Preston, 'On the assessment of public transport regulatory reforms in Europe', in *Proceedings from the European Transport Conference* (London: Association of European Transport, 2002).

Kommission Verkehrsinfrastrukturfinanzierung, *Sachverständigenkommission zur Entwicklung neuer Modelle der Verkehrswege-Finanzierung Abschlussbericht* (Bonn, 5 September 2000).

D. Lehmkuhl, 'Privatizing to keep it public? The reorganization of the German railways', in Arthur Benz and Klaus H. Goetz (eds), *A New German Public Sector? Reform, Adaptation and Stability* (Aldershot: Dartmouth, 1996): 71–92.

D. Lehmkuhl, *The Importance of Small Differences: The Impact of European Integration on Road Haulage Associations in Germany and the Netherlands* (The Hague: Thela Thesis, 1999).

P. Merlin, *Les Transports en France* (Paris: La Documentation Française 1994).

D. Nakagawa and R. Matsunaka, *Funding Transport Systems: A Comparison Among Developed Countries* (Oxford: Pergamon, 1997).

OECD (2003), *National Accounts*, <www.oecd.org/pdf/M00009000/M00009294.pdf> [19 March 2003].

J. Preston, 'On the ground, over ground and all at sea: a review of organisational reforms of the European transport sector', in H. Meersman, E. Van de Voorde and W. Winkelmans (eds), *World Transport Research. Proceedings of the 8th World Conference on Transport Research. Volume 4: Transport Policy* (Oxford: Pergamon, 1999): 541–54. (See also the SORT-IT project web site: <www.its.leeds.ac.uk/projects/sort-it> [12 February 2003].)

B.J. Simpson, *Planning and Public Transport in Great Britain, France and West Germany* (Harlow: Longman, 1987).

SRA (Strategic Rail Authority) (2003), *Strategic Plan 2003*, <www.sra.gov.uk/sra/publications/strategic_plan_2003/SRA_Plan1.pdf> [18 March 2003].

M. Teutsch, 'Regulatory reforms in the German transport sector: how to overcome multiple veto points', in Adrienne Héritier (ed.), *Differential Europe. The European Union Impact on National Policymaking* (Boulder, CO: Rowman and Littlefield, 2001): 133–72.

19
Communications

Ian Bartle

Introduction

Communications consists of the transfer of information and data from one point (a person or a machine) to a second and occurs in one or both directions. Communications policy normally relates to communication at a distance, that is, beyond normal spoken and other communication between people close together, and is directed towards networks, services and content. Traditional types of two way communications systems consist of post, telegraph and telephone services. Traditional one way communications systems are mainly radio and television.

Advances in information technology (IT) (electronics and digital technology which involves the storage, transmission and processing of information) have led to a convergence of communications services as well as to rapid changes in the nature of the services. The first manifestation of convergence was between telecommunications, consisting of the transmission and storage of information, and computers, which consist of the processing and storage of information. This resulted in the development of a wide range of advanced communications services such as online database services, electronic funds transfer, electronic banking services, videotex, and audio and video conferencing. In recent years convergence has taken place between telecommunications and media technologies. The internet, interactive TV and mobile phone services are examples of services arising from this convergence.

There has also been significant cross national convergence of telecommunications policy in Europe. In part this is due to trends in the globalization of telecommunications but it is also due to the increasingly central role of the EU in telecommunications policy (Natalicchi 2001; Schneider 2001). Some aspects of communications policy, such as industry ownership, are clearly the responsibility of the member states but the majority of policy is determined, at least in framework form, at the EU level. In policy detail there are limits to convergence as

217

most EU policies are in the form of directives which leave substantial scope for interpretation and implementation (Commission 2001a). Despite the increasing convergence of telecommunications and media the two areas retain some distinctive policy features. Network and services policy applies to both areas but content policy is focused more on media. This chapter focuses on network and services policy.

The nature of communications policy

The main instruments of communications policy are:

- the determination of the basic organization of the telecommunications and postal industries, such as ownership, competition, and provision of services by governmental bodies;
- direct provision of postal services;
- regulatory policy and regulation. Regulatory policy is often set by government departments and implemented by specific rules and regulations set by independent regulatory bodies. Regulatory policy is wide ranging and outlined in Box 19.1;
- research and development, and the promotion of new technologies (such as the internet and broadband), national industry and competitiveness. Activities include financial support, coordination, information provision, studies, seminars and the establishment of priorities.

Box 19.1   Telecommunications and post regulatory policy

Licensing and authorisation of service and network providers, to ensure that operators comply with technical requirements and public interest objectives.

Economic regulation of services and systems, the main elements of which are price controls, normally on the dominant operator, and the regulation of network access and interconnection, to facilitate market entry and competition.

Social equity regulation, normally manifested through universal service obligations which define a minimum set of services available to all users at an affordable price and irrespective of geographic location or rate of use.

Regulation of the radio spectrum. Radio frequencies are a scarce resource and policy is required on their allocation and availability. This has an increasingly important impact on telecommunications policy with the rise of mobile and satellite communications systems.

Regulation of satellite communications, in particular the provision of, and access to, space communications capacity, and the provision of earth and space based satellite services and equipment.

The representation and protection of the interests of domestic consumers and business users.

Regulation of numbering conventions, access to number resources, numbers for the selection of carriers, and internet naming and addresses.

Environmental regulation, in particular in relation to the location of infrastructure such as transmitters/receivers and poles, and overhead and underground lines.

Regulation of rights of way and of rights telecommunications operators have to install equipment and transmission lines on public and private land, and their rights to share the facilities of other operators, particularly dominant operators.

Ensuring the security of information transmitted over public networks, the protection of personal data and privacy, and confidentiality in personal communications.

Source: Commission 1999.

In each country there is a government ministry which has overall responsibility for post and telecommunications policy, plus independent regulatory authorities for telecommunications, as required by the EU (see Table 19.1). There is a separate regulator for postal services in Britain, while in Germany telecommunications and post are regulated by the same institution and in France there is currently

Table 19.1   Communications policy institutions

	Britain	France	Germany
Ministry	Department of Trade and Industry	*Ministère de l'Économie, des Finances et de l'Industrie* (Ministry of the Economy, Finance and Industry) *Direction Générale de l'industrie, des technologies de l'information et des postes* (General Directorate for Industry, Technology, Information and Postal Services)	*Bundesministerium für Wirtschaft und Arbeit* (Federal Ministry of Economics and Labour)
Regulatory agencies	Office of Communications (OFCOM) Postal Services Commission (Postcomm)	*l'Autorité de régulation des télécommunications (ART),* (Telecommunications Regulatory Authority), (will include post regulation)	*Regulierungsbehörde für Telekommunikation und Post* (Regulatory Authority for Telecommunications and Post)

no post regulator, although it is intended that the telecommunications regulator will take over post regulation.

Specific comparisons

This section compares public policy on ownership and competition, then examines three key areas of telecommunications policy: licensing, regulation of networks and dominant operators, and universal service.

Competition and ownership

Under EU directives all telecommunications services and networks are fully liberalized, and parts of the postal services are open to competition in all three countries. In telecommunications, competition depends in practice on the regulation of network access and the former monopolies, and on the systems of licensing and universal service. The former nationalized telecommunications monopolies have been fully or partly privatized. Postal services in all three countries are partially liberalized. Some areas such as parcel and express services are fully liberalized. The main restriction on competition relates to the 'reserved areas' of domestic mail service, provision of which is restricted to the national postal service provider.

Table 19.2 gives details of competition and ownership policy in Britain, France and Germany.

Licensing of telecommunications operators

Under the new EU telecommunications regulatory package which came in force in July 2003, member states can only use 'general authorisations' and not 'individual licences' for all telecommunications services and networks (Commission 2003). 'General authorisations' cover all or certain groups of providers and are less onerous than 'individual licences' applying to individual companies, and mean that an explicit administrative decision is not required for an undertaking to start up a business, although undertakings can be individually regulated when there are issues of rights of way, rights to use the radio spectrum, rights to use of telephone or similar numbers, significant market power, and universal service obligations. These general principles apply in Britain (enacted in the 2003 Communications Act) and, after the enactment of the necessary legislation (expected in 2004), will apply in France and Germany as well. However until the legislation is enacted in France and Germany there will remain some notable variations in the categorisation of licences, that is, in the number of different categories of class licences and the extent of use of individual licences (ETO 1999).

A key aspect of recent licensing policy has been the issue of third generation (3G) or UMTS (Universal Mobile Telephone System) licences. 3G combines

Table 19.2 Competition and state ownership

	Britain	*France*	*Germany*
Telecommunications services and infrastructure subject to competition	100%	100%	100%
State ownership of telecommunications	British Telecom: 0%	*France Telecom*: 55.5%	*Deutsche Telekom*: 43% (17% of DT is held by the state construction bank *Kreditanstalt für Wiederaufbau*)
Reserved areas in post	In packages of less than 4000: 0–100g or up to 3 times basic tariff	0–350g or up to 5 times basic tariff	0–100 g or up to 3 times basic tariff
State ownership of post	Royal Mail: 100%	*La Poste*: 100%	*Deutsche Post*: 69% (19% of DP is held by the state construction bank *Kreditanstalt für Wiederaufbau*)

Sources: BT 2002; Postcomm 2002; FT 2002; DT 2002; RegTP 2002; DP 2002; Commission 2002a.

high speed internet access with mobile phone technology (the first generation was analogue while the second was based on digital technology with higher quality and expanded services). Allocation of these licenses was subject to the basic EU licensing framework but a new way of issuing licences was introduced in some member states, including Britain and Germany, namely auctions, which resulted in very high licence fees (Commission 2001b). The French government rejected the auction procedure due to concerns about the burden of high licence fees on operators and instead adopted a system of comparative bidding (so called 'beauty contests') for four 15 year licences (ART 2001a).

Table 19.3 gives details of the recent 3G licensing procedures and outcomes.

Network regulation and dominant operators

A basic policy in all three countries is asymmetrical regulation of telecommunications. Operators with 'significant market power', often the former national monopolies, can be regulated more stringently than others. The main reasons for this are to control the market power of dominant operators and to enable network access and interconnection. Two of the central aspects of economic regulation of telecommunications are price control, which is aimed at achieving acceptable tariff regimes and imposing efficiency incentives on dominant

Table 19.3 3G licensing

	Britain	France	Germany
Procedure	Auction	Comparative bid	Auction
Awards and total charges	5 licences of 21 years issued in 2000 – TIW, Vodafone, BT, One2One and Orange – for € 38.475 bn (£28.32 bn, $43.28 bn)	3 licences issued in 2001 – SFR, Orange and Bouygues Telecom – for € 9.8 bn (£7.21 bn, $11.03 bn)	6 licences issued in 2000 – Mannesmann Mobilfunk, Group 3G, E-Plus 3G, MobilCom Multimedia, VIAG, T-Mobil – for € 50.8 bn (£37.4 bn, $57.2 bn)

Sources: ART 2001a, 2002a; RegTP 2000; Commission 2001b.

operators before full competition is established; and network regulation, namely the establishment and enforcement of procedures for network inter-connection, leased lines (lines leased normally from the dominant operator to providers of public or private services) and 'unbundling of the local loop' (see below for details). Sometimes operators with significant market power are more strongly regulated to ensure the provision of universal service.

In Britain and Germany the 'RPI-X' formula, a price cap of inflation (Retail Price Index) minus an efficiency factor 'X', is used for price control and imposed mainly on the dominant operators British Telecom (BT) and *Deutsche Telekom*. In France price control is achieved by the imposition of specific tariffs and price reductions (see Table 19.4).

The objectives of interconnection policy are specified in an EU directive and are to ensure that all network operators can interconnect their networks with others to achieve 'any-to-any' communication. Interconnection arrangements are supposed to be transparent and non-discriminatory and priority is to be given to commercial negotiations. The framework for negotiation is set by the national regulatory authority and must include an effective system for dispute resolution: if an acceptable agreement is not reached within a reasonable period, the regulator will intervene and issue a determination. Interconnection is another aspect of asymmetrical regulation: operators with 'significant market power' are required to publish a 'reference interconnection offer' which is cost orientated and approved by the regulator and available to all other operators. In Britain, France and Germany the incumbent operators – British Telecom, *France Telecom* and *Deutsche Telekom* – are deemed to have significant market power and the regulators approve negotiated interconnection tariff agreements or impose a revised tariff.

The 'unbundling of the local loop' is an important aspect of asymmetrical network regulation and is designed to increase consumer choice by allowing

Table 19.4   Price controls*

	Britain	*France*	*Germany*
Main public services	RPI – 4.5% on connection, line rental, operator assistance and call fees of British Telecom	Prices are set within the tariff regime required by the universal service obligation	RPI – 5% for city calls, RPI – 2% for national calls and RPI – 1% for international calls
Mobile operators	RPI – 12% on call termination charges of Vodafone, British Telecom, Cellnet, One2One and Orange	In 2002: 15% (on average) price reduction on call termination charges imposed on SFR and Orange France	Not controlled
Network and leased lines	Various network price caps. X varies between 0 and 13 per cent	In 2002: 10–20% decrease of France Telecom's leased lines	RPI + 1% for leased lines

Note
* RPI-X formula means that price rises are capped at the rate of inflation (as measured by changes in the Retail Price Index) less an efficiency factor X.

Sources: OFTEL 2001a,b, 2002; ART 2002b,c; RegTP 2001, Commission 2001a.

market entrants access to the lines from the local termination centre to the consumer's premises. 'Unbundling' in general refers to the separation of the component parts of a system, and in networks enables operators to interconnect to a particular part of the network. The 'local loop' is the physical circuit in the public telephone network, normally belonging to the operator with 'significant market power', that connects the network termination point at the subscriber's premises to the main distribution point. An EU regulation specifies the requirements for local loop unbundling (Commission 2000). Negotiation is the preferred method of achieving satisfactory access to the local loop but it is recognized that an imbalance of market power means that regulatory intervention is also likely to be necessary. Local loop access agreements are required to be cost orientated and transparent.

In Britain local loop unbundling has been implemented by a modification made to BT's licence in 2000 by the regulator, OFTEL. It has proved difficult to achieve unbundling in practice and the regulator has issued several directions and determinations, for instance on colocation and connection charges. In France the government issued a decree on unbundling in 2001 and the regulator, the ART, became more committed to achieving it, for example by forcing *France Telecom* to release information on the local network termination points in a timely manner and revise its reference charges. In Germany the liberalisation law in force in 1998 provided for network access to the local loop but *Deutsche Telekom* only offered basic copper lines. The EU regulation requires access to all lines (higher capacity lines) and in 2001 the regulator determined that DT must submit a tariff for the offer of higher capacity lines to market entrants (RegTP 2001).

Universal service

The principles and scope of the provision of Universal Service for telecommunications in Britain, France and Germany are set out in EU directives and are based on user affordability and the sharing of costs by operators. Universal service is defined as a minimum set of services at a specified quality available to all users at an affordable price and independent of users' geographic location. It includes the right to connection to a public telecommunications network to support voice telephony and low speed data and fax transmission, the provision of public pay phones, directory services, free emergency services, and special measures to help disabled users and others with special social needs. Affordability includes geographic averaging of tariffs and provision of a basic service to low income users.

There is some latitude in the EU rules for members states to specify aspects of universal service requirements. These include the scope of universal service, tariff systems such as geographic averaging and low user schemes, and the funding mechanism such as a universal service fund, although the funding mechanism must be transparent and based on cost.

In Britain there is a universal service obligation on British Telecom and, in the Hull area, on Kingston Communications (OFTEL 2001c). The universal service obligation is not separately funded as it is considered that the market benefits of providing universal service are at least equal to the burden. In France the universal service obligation falls on *France Telecom*. There is also a universal service fund to which contributions are made by the market players who are not subject to the universal service obligation (Commission 2001a). In Germany the universal service obligation falls on *Deutsche Telekom*. As in Britain this obligation is not separately funded (Commission 2001a).

Recent developments

A significant recent development affecting all three countries is a new communications package at EU level adopted in 2002 consisting of the Framework Directive, the Access and Interconnection Directive, the Universal Service Directive, the Authorisations Directive, and the Radio Spectrum Decision (Taylor 2002), to be implemented in the member states by mid-2003. The package covers all types of electronic services and networks, including broadcasting systems as well as telecommunications. The package seeks to establish a clearer, more focused and harmonized framework, and is a response to the perceived barriers to a full single market in communications identified in the Commission's review of communications in 1999 and its reports on implementation (Commission 1999, 2001a). One key provision in the new package is the shift to a competition law based test for the definition of significant market power from existing sector and country specific ad hoc methods. Another important change is the replacement of individual licence regimes with general authorisations except where scarce resources of radio frequencies and numbers are concerned, and the establishment of clearer limits on the constraints that national regulators can impose on operators. A new EU postal directive was adopted in late 2002 which specified a steady reduction in the maximum level of the reserved service (services not subject to competition) that member states can apply to mail weighing 0–100 g and less than three times basic tariff on 1 January 2003, and to mail weighing 0–50 g and less than 2.5 times basic tariff in January 2006. Reserved services may be completely abolished in 2009 (Commission 2002a).

In Britain the 2003 Communications Act includes provisions for implementing the new EU framework (DTI 2002). The Act is a response to the vast change in the modern communications environment, including media and the internet, and their importance to society and the economy (DTI 2001). The key proposals include the establishment in late 2003 of the Office of Communications (OFCOM) to replace the five existing telecommunications, radio and TV regulators (OFTEL, the Broadcasting Standards Commission, the Independent Television Commission, the Radio Communications Agency and the Radio Authority). There are also new rules on media ownership, individual licences are abolished, and a system of radio spectrum trading is introduced. In 2002 the Postcomm, the postal services regulator, announced a staged programme of further market opening ahead of EU requirements, starting in 2003 and moving to full market opening in 2007 (Postcomm 2002).

In France a consultation process on a new communications law for the implementation of the new EU framework was initiated by the Minister of Industry and the Minister of Culture and Communications in August 2002 (ART 2002d). Despite the requirement to implement the EU framework in mid 2003, by late 2003 the new law had not been enacted (Commission 2003 but is expected in 2004). Despite the desire to move closer to ordinary competition law, the regulator seeks to retain the flexibility of sector specific regulation to enhance competition in the sector. The regulator also continues to defend the achievement of universal service by imposition of price controls and a fund. Competition in the local loop, mobile phones and high speed access to the internet are priority areas for the regulator (ART 2002e). The new law will also include provisions for the telecommunications regulator to take on the regulation of postal services and the reduction of reserved postal services (MEFI 2003).

The German government aimed to amend the 1996 law on telecommunications by mid 2003 to comply with the new EU framework (BMWi 2002) but by late 2003 the new law had not been enacted (Commission 2003 but is expected in 2004). Policy priorities include broadband access to the internet, the continuing promotion of working competition in telecommunications access to the local loop, and adequate provision of leased lines (BMWi 2002). The postal services act amendment in 2002 included the reduction of reserved postal services, in line with EU requirements (RegTP 2002).

In 2001 and 2002 there has been general concern in all three countries and in the European Commission about the rollout of third generation mobile phone services. One aspect of significant concern is the extremely high price of licences and the debt burden that the large telecommunications companies are having to shoulder. While not pressing for change, the European Commission has stated that high fees and long periods for licences cannot be justified on the basis of effective spectrum use. The French government and regulator rejected the auction system and substantially reduced the licence fees on the basis of concern about the ability of companies to invest in third generation technology (ART 2001a). Another policy proposal to overcome the problems of 3G rollout is to promote the sharing of networks, and this has been considered by the British, French and German regulators (OFTEL 2001d; ART 2001b; RegTP 2001) and by the European Commission (Commission 2002b).

Sources

ART (l'Autorité de régulation des télécommunications) (2001a), 'UMTS: Results of the allocation procedure for 3rd generation mobile metropolitan licences in France', 31 May 2001, <www.art-telecom.fr> [8 November 2002].

ART (l'Autorité de régulation des télécommunications) (2001b), 'Position of the *Autorité de régulation des télécommunications* on infrastructure sharing on third generation mobile networks', 10 December 2001, <www.art-telecom.fr> [8 November 2002].

ART (l'Autorité de régulation des télécommunications) (2002a), 'UMTS: ART approves Bouygues Telecom's application', 27 September 2002, <www.art-telecom.fr> [8 November 2002].

ART (2002b) 'Decrease of the price of fixed to mobile calls', 6 November 2002, <www.art-telecom.fr> [8 November 2002].

ART (l'Autorité de régulation des télécommunications) (2002c) 'Leased lines: ART imposes a price decrease on France Telecom leased lines for other operators', 15 February 2002, <www.art-telecom.fr> [8 November 2002].

ART (l'Autorité de régulation des télécommunications) (2002d), 'Transposition of the new European regulatory framework: ART publishes its response to the Government's public consultation', 9 October 2002, <www.art-telecom.fr> [8 November 2002].

ART (l'Autorité de régulation des télécommunications) (2002e), 'Introducing ART', <www.art-telecom.fr> [8 November 2002].

BMWi (Bundesministerium für Wirtschaft) (2002), 'Politik Felder: Telekommunikation und Post', <www.bmwi.de> [8 November 2002].

BT (British Telecommunications) (2002), 'British Telecom Annual Report 2001', <www.btplc.com> [6 November 2002].

Commission of the European Communities (1999) 'Status Report on European Union Electronic Communications Policy', INFOSO/A/1, Brussels, 22 December 1999.

Commission (Commission of the European Communities) (2000), 'Regulation of the European Parliament and of the Council on unbundled access to the local loop', 2000/0185 (COD), Brussels, 5 December 2000.

Commission (Commission of the European Communities) (2001a), 'Communication from the Commission to the Council, the European Parliament, the Economic and Social Committee and the Committee of Regions. Seventh Report on the Implementation of the Telecommunications Regulatory Package', COM (2001) 706, Brussels.

Commission (Commission of the European Communities) (2001b), 'Communication from the Commission to the Council, the European Parliament, the Economic and Social Committee and the Committee of the Regions. The Introduction of Third Generation Mobile Communications in the European Union: State of Play and the Way Forward' Brussels, COM(2001)141, Brussels, 20 March 2001.

Commission (Commission of the European Communities) (2002a), 'Directive 2002/39/EC of the European Parliament and of the Council amending Directive 97/67/EC with regard to the further opening to competition of Community postal services', Brussels, 10 June 2002.

Commission (Commission of the European Communities) (2002b), 'Communication from the Commission to the Council, the European Parliament, the Economic and Social Committee and the Committee of the Regions. Towards the full roll-out of third generation mobile communications', COM/2002/0301, Brussels, 11 June 2002.

Commission (Commission of the European Communities) (2003), 'Communication from the Commission to the Council, the European Parliament, the European Economic and Social Committee and the Committee of the Regions. Ninth report on the implementation of the EU electronic communications regulatory package', COM(2003) 715, Brussels, 19 November 2003.

DP (Deutsche Post) (2002), 'Annual Report 2001', <www.deutschepost.de> [28 January 2003].

DT (Deutsche Telekom) (2002), 'Annual Financial Report 2001', <www.telekom.de> [6 November 2002].

DTI (Department of Trade and Industry and Department of Culture, Media and Sport) (2001), 'Communications White Paper. A New Future for Communications', <www.dti.gov.uk> [6 February 2001].

DTI (Department of Trade and Industry) (2002), 'Communications Bill', <www.dti.gov. uk> [4 November 2002].

ETO (European Telecommunications Office) (1999), 'Final report on categories of authorisations', <www.eto.dk> [6 November 2002].

FT (France Telecom) (2002), 'France Telecom Annual Report 2001: Investor Fact Sheet 2001 results', <www.francetelecom.com> [6 November 2002].

MEFI (Ministère de l'Économie, des Finances et de l'Industrie), 'Secteur Postal', <www.industrie.gouv.fr> [20 November 2003].

G. Natalicchi, *Wiring Europe: Reshaping the European Telecommunications Regime* (Lanham, Maryland: Rowman and Littlefield, 2001).

OFTEL (Office of Telecommunications) (2001a), 'Review of charge controls on calls to mobiles', 26 September 2001, <www.oftel.gov.uk> [4 November 2002].

OFTEL (Office of Telecommunications) (2001b), 'Guidelines on the operation of the network charge controls from October 2001', 5 December 2001, <www.oftel.gov.uk> [4 November 2002].

OFTEL (Office of Telecommunications) (2001c), 'Universal service obligation. Statement', 30 August 2001, <www.oftel.gov.uk> [4 November 2002].

OFTEL (Office of Telecommunications) (2001d), '3G mobile infrastructure sharing in the UK – note for information', May 2001, <www.oftel.gov.uk> [4 November 2002].

OFTEL (Office of Telecommunications) (2002), 'Draft determination: rollover of general price controls', 27 June 2002, <www.oftel.gov.uk> [4 November 2002].

Postcomm (2002), 'Postcomm's market opening decision announced', 29 May 2002, <www.psc.gov.uk/Index2.html> [20 November 2003].

RegTP (Regulatory Authority for Telecommunications and Post) (2000), 'Universal Mobile Telecommunications System: Allotment of the UMTS/IMT-2000 frequency blocks bought at auction', <www.regtp.de> [8 November 2002].

RegTP (Regulatory Authority for Telecommunications and Post) (2001), 'Annual Report 2001', <www.regtp.de> [8 November 2002].

RegTP (Regulatory Authority for Telecommunications and Post) (2002), 'Annual Report 2002', <www.regtp.de> [20 November 2003].

V. Schneider, 'Institutional Reform in Telecommunications: The European Union in Transnational Policy Diffusion', in *Transforming Europe. Europeanisation and Domestic Change*, ed. Maria Green Cowles, James Caporaso and Thomas Risse (Ithaca and London: Cornell University Press, 2001): 60–78.

S. Taylor, 'The EU electronic communications package – competition based regulation for the digital age', *Utilities Law Review*, 12:4 (2002).

20
Information Society

Martin Ferguson

Introduction

A fundamental change from an industrial to an information-based society is taking place in countries such as Britain, France and Germany. Underpinned by the emergence of new information and communication technologies, this information revolution affects the way people live, learn and work. It affects how governments interact with civil society through the provision of services, the governance of communities and the selection and formulation of policies. Information also acts as a powerful tool for economic and social development.

In 1994 the Bangemann Report for the European Commission awakened governments throughout Europe to the opportunities presented by the information society. Ten years on, the governments of Britain, France and Germany have pursued varying approaches to the development of information society policy and action. Each has attempted to set out information society policy following a strong political lead from the Prime Minister in Britain, the

Box 20.1   Definition of information society

> The information society is a term used to describe a society and an economy that makes the best possible use of new information and communication technologies (ICTs). In an Information Society people will get the full benefits of new technology in all aspects of their lives: at work, at home and at play. Examples of ICT's are: ATM's for cash withdrawal and other banking services, mobile phones, teletext television, faxes and information services such as the internet and e-mail.
>
> *Source*: Information Society Commission, Department of the Taoiseach, 1999.

President in France and the Chancellor in Germany. At one extreme, Britain has approached implementation following a centralized model driven by the government's e-Envoy. On the other end of the spectrum lies France with a fragmented approach to implementation by government and regional departments. Germany lies between these extremes, with co-ordinated action at various levels of its federated governmental structure.

All three governments have developed programmes to expand access and skills to participate in the information society. For Britain, legislative and regulatory action has focused on deregulation of telecommunications to stimulate broadband provision. In France, action has addressed simplification of citizen access to government. Meanwhile Germany has majored on creating the legal frameworks required for citizen authentication as the key to establishing e-business and e-government.

The nature of information society policy

Information society policy, with its very focus on 'society', impinges on almost every area of government activity. It is no surprise, therefore, that we find both holistic and fragmented approaches being taken to policy-making and implementation in Britain, France and Germany, with their different governmental structures and as disparate government stakeholders attempt to address information society issues.

As information society policy is a new area of public policy, its content is not yet fully defined. However, the key government activities in this area at present are:

- Measures to improve access to electronic information and to overcome the so-called 'digital divide' between those who have the means and the skills to participate in the information society and those who do not, by means of providing public Internet access points and ensuring that IT skills are integral to education and training in schools and elsewhere;
- Legislative and regulatory action to create the conditions in which citizens, businesses and government enjoy 'trusted' relationships with one another, by providing service providers and citizens with secure means for electronic identification (such as e-signatures) and adapting existing regulation to take account of e-business;
- Provision of national and local government services online where appropriate, including services relating to health, social security, education, employment, police, business activities, permits, personal documents such as passports, and libraries;
- Measures to improve citizen participation in decision-making by means such as online consultation, online participation in meetings, and electronic voting (e-democracy).

Table 20.1   Information society policy actors and strategies

	Britain	*France*	*Germany*
Government minister(s) responsible	Secretary of State for Trade and Industry (also known as 'e-Minister')	Minister of Public Affairs, Government Reform and Regional Planning Secretary of State for Reform of the State, including electronic administration	Secretary of State, Federal Ministry of Economics and Technology Secretary of State, Federal Ministry for Internal Affairs
Organization	Office of the e-Envoy (attached to the Cabinet Office)	The Interministerial Committee for the Information Society (CISI)	Federal Ministry of the Interior Federal Ministry of Economics
Stakeholder engagement	Information Age Partnership	Strategic Advisory Board on Information Technologies (CSTI), chaired by the Prime Minister	'Initiative D1' group including over 200 leading companies and chaired by the Chancellor
National strategy	UK online Local Government Online	*Le plan pour une Republique numérique dans la Société de l'information*	Jobs in the Information Society of the 21st Century *Bundonline 2005 Media@Komm*

Source: After Booz Allen Hamilton 2002: 50–2.

Table 20.1 summarizes the main national government bodies that deal with information society policy.

At European level, information society policy is coordinated via eEurope Action Plans, the latest of which, *eEurope 2005*, has as its particular objectives connecting public administrations, schools and health care to broadband; introducing interactive public services accessible to all and offered on multiple platforms; providing online health services; removing obstacles to the deployment of broadband networks; reviewing legislation affecting e-business; and creating a Cyber Security Task Force (CEC 2002).

In all three countries, national ministries have been given responsibility for information society policy and action. The British organizational model is the most highly centralized and is unique in having a senior civil servant armed with responsibility for implementing the Government's policy. Here, within the Prime Minister's Cabinet Office, the Office of the e-Envoy (OeE) sets information society policy, leads the *UK online* strategy, ensures co-ordination across government, tracks progress, and manages selected projects that are of cross-departmental benefit, for example a government intranet, *Knowledge Network*, and a secure gateway for communicating with the public: *Government Gateway*. The OeE also has an advisory input into the central government Treasury's financing decisions.

Germany shares responsibility for information society policy across different government departments and levels of government. The Ministry of the Interior is responsible for the delivery of e-government, the Ministry of Economics is responsible for delivery of e-economy initiatives, and other Ministries are involved for other elements. In collaboration with the *Länder*, which have their own e-government programmes and are responsible for the provision of the majority of core government services, the Federal Government seeks to accelerate the creation of a regulatory and legal environment for e-commerce and e-government and to promote associated initiatives at all levels of government. One of the key initiatives is to modernize the State through e-government initiatives under the *BundOnline 2005* programme, which aims to have online by 2005 all those administrative services that lend themselves to electronic service delivery.

In France, no single authority takes control of the e-agenda. An Interministerial Committee for the Information Society (CISI) sets the e-agenda in accordance with a national plan, *Le plan pour une Republique numérique dans la Société de l'information*, which envisages building an information society faithful to the French constitutional principles of liberty, equality and fraternity. Implementation of the plan is co-ordinated through a loose network of contacts across government and regional departments in France.

Specific comparisons

Four of the most important areas of information society policy are access, regulation, delivery of government services (e-government), and e-democracy.

Access

All three countries address the issue of access as a priority area for government policy, particularly to deal with the prospect of a 'digital divide' between those who have the means and the skills to participate in the information society and those who do not.

For the German Federal Government, access is addressed in the context of a 5-year €1.5 billion (£1.1 billion, $1.7 billion) action programme, *Innovation and Jobs in the Information Society of the 21st Century*, which aims to modernize government, promote the use of ICT in all areas of society to combat unemployment, and make Germany one of the IT sector leaders in Europe. Targeted to conclude in 2005, the programme's first strategic line of action is 'ensuring broad access to the new channels and providing IT skills' for citizens, businesses and government organizations. *Germany 21 – Entering the Information Age* is a cross-sector initiative (Federal, *Land* and private sector) to promote and accelerate the use of IT in Germany. As part of this initiative, the *Internet for All* project includes a focus on Internet skills becoming part of general education, public libraries being equipped with Internet access, and an Internet 'driving licence' for the unemployed.

For Britain and France, a broadly similar policy line has been taken to access issues. One of the core objectives of the British Government's *UK online* programme is 'to ensure that everyone who wants it has access to the Internet by 2005' (OeE 2003: 5). In Britain, one in two homes now has access to the Internet, the price of Internet access is amongst the lowest in the world, and some 96 per cent of Britain's population are aware of a place where they can access the Internet (OxIS 2003). There is now a network of 6000 UK online centres, many located in local libraries and community centres, and some 10 per cent of all Internet users (equivalent to 3 million people) report that they have recently accessed the Internet in a library (ONS 2003). Similarly, in France, the focus has been on an initiative targeted at bridging the digital divide by providing 7000 public access points with free Internet services in key locations throughout the country. In addition to physical access, training to give people the skills to access the new services and to teach them to use them effectively has been a focus of government activity in France and Britain. France, for example, is using its youth employment scheme to create 4000 jobs for multimedia instructors, to provide back-up at the Internet access points.

Britain leads Europe in low-cost availability of broadband (OeE 2003), yet this position has sprung from fragmented policy initiatives and funding arrangements for broadband in a number of functional service areas, such as health, education and libraries, and in local government, and from deregulated supply of telecommunications. Only now is the focus is shifting to the development of national policy and its implementation through nationally created Regional Aggregation Boards to address issues of supply, development of content and stimulation of demand. A particular focus is on rural areas, with the launching of a *Community Broadband Network* in 2004 to support community broadband initiatives.

The *LGOL* programme in England and the *MEDIA@Komm* programme in Germany both seek to address access issues for local communities. These programmes include a series of projects that aim to establish practical experience of implementing 'access channel strategy' and deploying contact centres, websites, text messaging and smart cards.

Legislative and regulatory action

For Britain, France and Germany, e-business has been a driving force in their attempts to address the regulatory environment to facilitate the emergence of an information society. However priorities and approaches have differed.

In France, legislative and regulatory action has focused on enabling access through development of an Information Society Law to govern public access to essential government data as well as to regulate e-commerce (including e-advertising and e-contracts), wide area networking, fighting cybercrime, the use of secure data exchanges including electronic signatures, and practical rules for implementation.

Similar concerns have been addressed in Germany. Here the emphasis has been on legislation to provide service providers and citizens with the means for electronic identification and authentication, and on promoting e-commerce development by continuing to modernize the regulatory framework. As part of this process, a new electronic signature law was passed in March 2001 to provide the necessary security infrastructure for e-signatures, which are recognized as equal to hand-written signatures for private and public sector activity.

In contrast, Britain's emphasis has been on deregulation of particular technology sectors in order to make the country 'the best environment in the world for e-commerce by 2002' (Booz Allen Hamilton 2002: 3). According to a recent assessment by the Office of the e-Envoy (OeE 2003), Britain has a world-leading regulatory framework, bringing the regulation of broadcasting and telecommunications under a single regulator, the Office of Communications (OFCOM), from December 2003. On the other hand, Britain has made much more limited progress with citizen identity and authentication due to the cultural and political reluctance generated by fears of invasion of privacy, which is hampering attempts to join up public services in ways that make sense to the citizen.

Delivery of government services

Britain's strategy for e-government has focused particularly on the development of the *UK online* portal and *Government Gateway* platforms to support a growing number of government services online. Britain also was one of the first nations to publish an interoperability framework (*e-GIF*), which other countries have since followed, including Germany with its *SAGA* framework. In Germany, *BundOnline* sets out a wholesale reform of federal administrative processes. Although France has an overall information society plan, there is no evidence of a specific e-government strategy, with the result that the approach is relatively fragmented.

All three countries have set targets for introducing electronic services delivery. For Britain the target was for all government services to be available electronically 'in ways that citizens and businesses will use' by 2005. A similar target has been adopted in Germany: all administrative services that lend themselves to electronic services delivery are to be made available by 2005. For Britain and Germany, these targets are translated into specific programmes, UK Online and BundOnline 2005. France, on the other hand, has only recently set a target for electronic service delivery, having relied upon a general policy of providing public access to government services and information. The emphasis here has been on simplifying citizens' and businesses' dealings with government, with a specific focus on renewing public sector information systems and training civil servants.

Comparative progress in implementing online government services has been measured for a specific basket of 20 services according to their stage of 'online sophistication' (ranging from information only to full electronic case handling, including decision and delivery) and whether they were 'fully available online' (CAP Gemini Ernst & Young 2004). The results for all government services, set out in Table 20.2, show that while France (at 73 per cent) leads marginally over Britain in terms of online sophistication, Britain has the highest percentage (at 50 per cent) of government services fully available online. This compares with the highest scoring countries of Sweden (87 per cent online sophistication) and Denmark (72 per cent of services fully available online).

Table 20.3, which sets out the state of online sophistication for all 20 government services surveyed, reveals a mixed picture. All three countries have achieved high levels of online sophistication for a number of operations relating to taxation and social security contributions as well as for job search. Britain leads on obtaining social security benefits, passports and drivers licences, as well as on declaring cases of theft to the police and enrolling in higher education. France is ahead on changes of address, car registration and applying for building permission. Germany's strength lies in procurement, with well-developed online facilities for tender announcement and the receipt of tender responses. Germany and France together lead on the submission of data to national statistical offices and customs declaration, while France and Britain lead online facilities for new company registration. Weak areas across the board are public libraries, access to hospital services information, environment-related permits, and registration of births, marriages and deaths.

Table 20.2   Online government services, 2003 (%)

	Britain	*France*	*Germany*
Online sophistication	71	73	52
Fully available online	50	45	40

Source: CAP Gemini Ernst & Young 2004: 17. The measure for 'online sophistication' ranges from information only to full electronic case handling, including decision and delivery.

Table 20.3   Online sophistication of individual services, 2003 (%)

	Britain	France	Germany
Income taxes: declaration and notification of assessment	100	100	100
Corporate tax: declaration and notification	100	100	100
Job search by government-run labour offices	100	100	100
Declaration of social security contribution for employees	100	100	100
Value Added Tax: declaration and notification	100	100	100
Obtaining social security benefits	100	90	40
Obtaining personal documents: passport and driver's licence	100	70	10
Declaration to the police: in cases of theft	100	65	35
Enrolment in higher education	100	35	45
Announcement of personal change of address	35	100	20
Car registration	50	100	5
Application for building permission	50	100	5
Public procurement: tender announcement and responses	50	50	100
Submission of data to national statistical offices	No data	100	100
Customs declaration by corporations	50	100	100
Registration of a new company	75	75	15
Obtaining environment-related permits	50	50	5
Public libraries: availability of catalogues and research tools	30	5	25
Obtaining birth and marriage certificates	15	40	10
Health-related services: advice on service availability in different hospitals	No data	5	20

Source: CAP Gemini Ernst & Young 2004: 46–52. The measure for 'online sophistication' ranges from information only to full electronic case handling, including decision and delivery. Figures are rounded to nearest 5%.

A common feature of interaction between citizens and government, and between businesses and government, is that the great majority of these transactions take place between citizens and local government. In Britain, some four billion out of five billion annual interactions with government are local rather than central (Booz Allen Hamilton 2002: 141). It follows that the delivery of information society and e-government policy depends heavily on the active participation of local governments. England is unique in being the only country to have developed a national strategy for the delivery and implementation of local e-government (ODPM 2002). This sets out a model of the 'e-organization' based on a series of e-government building blocks, and plans for spending £750 million (€1.0 billion, $1.1 billion) between 2000/01 and 2005/06 to transform services, renew local democracy and promote economic vitality through the delivery of local e-government. A key instrument used to embed local implementation of e-government into the wider strategies of different levels of English government has been the preparation, annually, of 'Implementing e-Government (IEG) Statements' by all 388 local councils. A recent shift in thinking has been to focus action on a series of priority services with specific outcomes in order to demonstrate public value from the investment that has been made (ODPM 2003b).

Both Germany and England have national organizations that provide additional capacity and support to local governments in implementing e-government. The Improvement and Development Agency (IdeA) has been instrumental in creating a network of local government e-champions, comprising both officers and politicians from 100 per cent of English councils, to undertake research on progress being made, share best practice, and provide strategic and implementation support for the national strategy for local e-government and its building blocks. In Germany, the *Deutsches Institut für Urbanistik* (DIFU) has been tasked with supporting evaluation and dissemination of practice from the *MEDIA@Komm* projects. France has no equivalent programme for implementing local e-government.

E-democracy

E-democracy has attracted varying degrees of attention at national and local levels of government in the three countries. According to Drücke (2002), e-democracy has been a secondary interest in Germany, limited to information provision, handling citizens' enquiries, and participation in urban planning. However both France and Britain have experimented with online consultations and mediated forums (CoE 2002). The French Senate has organized a number of forums enabling the public to discuss legislation, such as the Information Society Law, with experts before and after its adoption. In Britain, the House of Lords collected public evidence on-line on the issue of stem cell research, and an online consultation carried out in March 2000 by the e-democracy programme of the Hansard Society enabled female victims of domestic violence to give evidence confidentially and on-line to the All-Party Domestic Violence Group. In just one month almost 1000 contributions were collected, and 94 per cent of the participants reported that the consultation was a worthwhile exercise.

In France and Britain there have been various local initiatives. Issy-les-Moulineaux, for example, has a simple effective procedure which allows local residents to participate, on-line, in certain local council meetings: they enter questions or suggestions during the discussion, and the councillors then break to inspect them, discussing them when the meeting resumes. Similar schemes exist in Amiens and Parthenay, which also provide free Internet access. In addition, Britain has undertaken a number of pilots of electronic voting in local elections.

Recent developments

Information society policy is a new area of public policy, so almost all the measures described in this chapter can be classed as recent developments. However there are a number of areas in which developments are currently in train.

In particular, authentication, privacy and data sharing, interoperability and take-up by citizens remain unresolved issues. Whether in Britain with its cultural and political aversion to identification cards or Germany with electronic signature and smart card initiatives, authentication for e-business and e-government has yet to gain widespread acceptance. France has made strides to share data for simplified service delivery. Yet the tensions between privacy and data sharing in addressing citizens' needs for simplified access to services still have to be addressed in Britain, despite recognition of these as blockages to e-business and e-government (Performance and Innovation Unit 2002). While Britain has led the establishment of interoperability standards, uncertainties over data protection are hindering attempts to join up government services delivery. Meanwhile, increasing concerns are being voiced about low levels of citizen take-up and a requirement to demonstrate 'public value' outcomes (Kelly and Muers 2002) for citizens from the information society initiatives and investments that have been undertaken.

Sources

A growing body of evidence is becoming available about comparative levels of progress in implementing information society policies and associated e-government programmes. Britain's Office of the e-Envoy has produced three international benchmarking reports (OeE 2000, 2001; Booz Allen Hamilton 2002), while several major consultancies and think-tanks have produced a range of models and frameworks for assessing e-government progress (see, for example, Accenture 2003 and Bertelsmann Foundation 2002). A recent report ranks online delivery of a basket of 20 government services (CAP Gemini Ernst and Young 2004). In Britain, the Improvement and Development Agency (IDeA), with the Society of IT Management (Socitm) and the Local Government Association (LGA), has produced a series of reports on local implementation of e-government, including a worldwide study (IDeA *et al.* 2001, 2002, 2003), and the Office of the Deputy Prime Minister has published a review of progress in implementing England's national strategy for local e-government (ODPM 2003a). In Germany, the *Deutsches Institut für Urbanistik* (DIFU) has reported extensively on the *MEDIA@Komm* smart card and authentication programme. There is no equivalent reporting available for France.

Accenture, *eGovernment Leadership: Engaging the Customer* (Accenture, April 2003).

Bangemann Report (1994), *Europe and the Global Information Society*, <europa.eu.int/ISPO/infosoc/backg/bangeman.html> [7 February 2004].

Bertelsmann Foundation (2002), *Balanced e-Government* (Berlin: Bertelsmann Stiftung), <www.begix.de> [7 February 2004].

Booz Allen Hamilton (2002), *The World's Most Effective Policies for the e-Economy*, <www. oee.gov.uk> [7 February 2004].

BundOnline 2005, <www.bund.de> [7 February 2004].

Cabinet Office, *In the Service of Democracy* (London: Cabinet Office consultation paper, 2002), <www.e-democracy.gov.uk> [7 February 2004].

CEC (Commission of the European Communities) (2002), *eEurope 2005: an Information Society for All* (Brussels: COM(2002) 263 final), <europa.eu.int/information_society/ eeurope/2002/news_library/documents/eeurope2005/eeurope2005_en.pdf> [7 February 2004].

Community Broadband Network, <www.broadband-uk.coop> [7 February 2004].

CoE (Council of Europe), *Replies to the Questionnaire on the Democratic Potential of the New Communication and Information Services* (Strasbourg: CoE, 2001), <www.coe.int/t/e/ integrated_projects/democracy/02_activities/01_e_governance/82_AMMSOD17. asp# TopOfPage> [7 February 2004].

Deutsches Institut für Urbanistik (DIFU), <www.difu.de> [7 February 2004].

H. Drücke, *Local e-government German Style – the MEDIA@Komm Projects* (Presentation to the Society of IT Management Annual Conference in Newport, October 2002), <www. mediakomm.net/en/index.php?mode=publications> [7 February 2004].

C. Handy, *The Future of Work* (Oxford: Blackwell, 1985).

IDeA Knowledge, <www.idea-knowledge.gov.uk> [7 February 2004].

Improvement and Development Agency (IDeA), <www.idea.gov.uk/egovernment>

Improvement and Development Agency and Society of IT Management, *Local e-government Now* (London: IDeA and Socitm Insight, 2001, 2002, 2003).

Improvement and Development Agency and Society of IT Management, *Local e-government Now: a Worldwide View* (London: IDeA and Socitm Insight, 2002).

Improvement and Development Agency, Local Government Association and Society of IT Management, *Casting the Net Wider: Local e-democracy 2003* (London: IDeA and Socitm Insight, 2003).

Information Society Commission, *What Is the Information Society?* (Dublin: Department of the Taoiseach, 1999), <www.isc.ie> [7 February 2004].

Institute of Public Policy Research (IPPR), *E-participation in Local Government* (London: IPPR digital society programme, 2002), <www.ippr.org.uk/topical/index.php?current=48&table=project&id=80> [7 February 2004].

G. Kelly and S. Muers, *Creating Public Value: An Analytical Framework for Public Service Reform* (London: Cabinet Office Strategy Unit, 2002), <www.strategy.gov.uk> [7 February 2004].

L'action de l'Etat pour le developpement de la société de l'information (2002), *Le plan RE/SO 2007 Le plan pour une Republique numérique dans la Société de l'information*, <www.internet.gouv.fr> [7 February 2004].

MEDIA@Komm, <www.mediakomm.net> [7 February 2004].

ODPM (Office of the Deputy Prime Minister), <www.odpm.gov.uk> [7 February 2004].

ODPM (Office of the Deputy Prime Minister), *The National Strategy for Local e-government* (London: ODPM, 2002), <www.localegov.gov.uk> [7 February 2004].

ODPM (Office of the Deputy Prime Minister), *One Year On: The National Strategy for Local e-government* (London: ODPM, 2003a), <www.localegov.gov.uk> [7 February 2004].

ODPM (Office of the Deputy Prime Minister), *Defining e-government Priority Services and Transformation Outcomes in 2005 for Local Authorities in England* (London: ODPM Consultation Paper, 2003b), <www.localegov.gov.uk> [7 February 2004].

OeE (Office of the e-Envoy), *e-Government Interoperability Framework Version 5* (London: OeE e-GIF), <www.e-envoy.org.uk/resources/frameworksandpolicy/fs/en> [7 February 2004].

OeE (Office of the e-Envoy), *E-Democracy – 'A Connection Waiting to Happen'* (London: OeE e-democracy team discussion paper, September 2003).

OeE (Office of the e-Envoy), *International Benchmarking* (London: OeE, 2000, 2001), <www.oee.gov.uk> [7 February 2004].

OeE (Office of the e-Envoy), *UK Online Annual Report* (London: OeE, 2003), <www. e-envoy.gov.uk> [7 February 2004].

ONS (Office for National Statistics) (2003), *Internet Access Survey*, <www.statistics.gov.uk/cci/hugget.asp?id=8> [7 February 2004].

OxIS (Oxford Internet Institute) (2003), *New Internet Survey*, <users.ox.ac.uk/-axis> [7 February 2004].

Performance and Innovation Unit, *Privacy and Data Sharing: the Way Forward for Public Services* (London: Cabinet Office PIU, April 2002).

Society of IT Management (Socitm), <www.socitm.gov.uk> [7 February 2004].

21
Water

Graeme Hayes, Jeremy Leaman and William A. Maloney

Introduction

The management and provision of water resources has become increasingly important in western European societies, with concerns over social equity, public control and private profit providing a focus for consumer action groups and citizens' protest movements. However in Britain, France and Germany, central government plays only a limited role in supply and regulation; rather, the sector is characterized by decentralization, privatization, and international-ization.

The nature of water policy

Public water policy is concerned with the management of the water cycle (abstraction, purification, distribution, sewerage, waste water treatment), focusing primarily on provision and regulation. Central government activities in this sector embrace:

- economic and environmental regulation (typically, states have separate institutional arrangements for dealing with supply and waste water issues on the one hand and resource management on the other);
- setting and collecting taxes and charges;
- re-distributing monies raised through grants, loans and other financial incentives;
- inspecting and monitoring water quality;
- running information and education programmes.

Though influenced by policy-makers in numerous sectors (including agriculture, defence, energy, health, industry, regional development, transport and urban planning), water policy is coordinated and managed by environment ministries, which also directly fund key resource improvement and protection schemes, such as the aid and development packages launched in France and Germany following serious flooding in 2002. However in none of the countries under discussion is central government directly responsible for treating or supplying water to users; rather, it essentially fulfils a strategic framework-setting role.

European directives, the latest of which (2000/60/EC, 23 October 2000) establishes a framework for EU action in water policy and promotes sustainable resource use (notably through water pricing), have significantly influenced the form, development and basic tenets of the water industries in all three countries over the last thirty years, but important cross-national differences do remain, and these have significant consequences at the point of consumption.

Specific comparisons

A better understanding of national water policy in Britain, France and Germany can be obtained by looking at the structure of the water industry in the three countries and the role of different levels of government in its ownership, management and regulation; the resulting patterns of consumption by agriculture and industry, and by households; and the management of water resources.

Institutional water supply arrangements

In all three countries, central government plays at best a secondary role in the provision of water, restricted to the definition of norms and the construction of the juridical infrastructure within which subnational authorities and/or private concerns deliver services. The institutional arrangements for these functions, which take different forms in each country, are set out in Table 21.1.

In France and Germany, water networks are geographically highly fragmented and subject to varying management regimes. In France, municipal authorities (*communes*) can either manage water supply and waste treatment themselves (individually or within inter-municipal syndicates), or elect to delegate one or both of these functions to private companies through a variety of pluri-annual contractual programmes. France's 36,763 *communes* are serviced by 11,992 wastewater and 15,244 water supply networks, approximately 2000 of which are intercommunal syndicates. Wastewater is publicly managed in 62 per cent of *communes* (47 per cent of the total population), whilst water supply is publicly managed in 48 per cent of communes. However, though such major cities as Strasbourg, Nantes and – after a brief flirtation with private management – Grenoble all operate important municipally-controlled supply networks, *communes* that do this are mainly small and rural, and account for only 21 per cent of the total population. Two private companies, Vivendi and Ondeo, control

Table 21.1   Institutional water supply arrangements

	England and Wales	Scotland	France	Germany
Public supply	Regional	Single public utility	Inter-municipal/ municipal	Inter-municipal/ municipal/ regional
Ownership	Private	Public	Public	Public and private
Management	Private	Public	Public and private	Public and private
Economic regulator	Independent (Office of Water Services, OFWAT)	Independent (Water Industry Commissioner for Scotland)	Municipal	Municipal/ regional
Environmental regulator	Independent (Environment Agency)	Independent (Scottish Environment Protection Agency)	Central government (Direction de l'eau)	Regional (Länder)

Source: adapted and updated from OECD 1999a: 37.

85 per cent of private water supply networks, and a third, part of the Bouygues group, controls a further 13 per cent.

In Germany, some 6700 waterworks supply water to 99 per cent of the population. While other utilities (electricity, gas, coal) are and traditionally were privately organized, water utilities (supply, sewerage and wastewater treatment) remain largely in the public sector. Despite some rationalization of local government in Germany, there are still some 13,000 elected local authorities (municipal, district and local councils) operating as separate representative and administrative entities. In consequence, water management is very frequently organized on a cooperative basis between individual local authorities. The water treatment companies are thus owned and secured in partnership between public bodies and, in the wake of new public management reforms, have frequently been given either joint stock or limited liability status. Individual local authorities or their utility departments (*Stadtwerke*) hold blocks of equity in the joint enterprises. These limited companies often operate integrated utility supply involving not just water but also gas, electricity and combined heat and power stations.

Only in Scotland is water provided by a single national public sector utility. Accountable to the Scottish Parliament, Scottish Water is nonetheless structured and managed like a private sector company and aims to match its performance to its counterparts in England and Wales, where supply is by contrast wholly undertaken by 24 private sector service providers organized as private regional monopolies combining asset ownership and management. Of these, 10 combine supply and sewerage and 14 are 'water-only' companies. As in France, these private supply companies are typically part of cross-national multi-utility organizations.

Agricultural and industrial consumption

Water is supplied to three principal user groups: agriculture, industry, and domestic consumers. In each of the countries there is considerable variation in water consumption patterns, as shown in Table 21.2.

Perhaps the most striking difference between the countries is in the agricultural sector. In 1993, land covered by irrigation networks in Britain totalled only some 108,000 ha, which is low in comparison to Germany (475,000 ha) and especially France (1,485,000 ha) (OECD 1999a: 17). As a consequence, the supply and treatment of water for agricultural use occupies differing levels of importance and institutional sophistication in each polity. In Germany and Britain, where irrigated land is relatively inextensive, there are few specific sectoral arrangements for provision and regulation. In England and Wales, a charge taking environmental and seasonal factors as well as volume into account is levied on abstraction for spray irrigation, while in Scotland water is abstracted at source for agricultural purposes without charge. In Germany, a number of *Länder* operate a water tax, which can be used for an agricultural rebate and compensation scheme. In France, where irrigation represents 42 per cent of net water consumption, abstraction charges are levied by private regional development bodies known as *Sociétés d'Aménagement Régional*, according to volume abstracted (catchment) and recycled (consumption).

Pricing structures for industrial users – chiefly the chemical, iron, steel, metallurgy, oil, petroleum, pulp and paper, and food and drink industries – include tariffs for water supply, separate sewerage charges, and charges for direct water abstraction, and are determined by different methods. In England and Wales, industrial users are metered, with standard discounted tariffs available to designated 'large users'. In Germany, industrial users can negotiate special

Table 21.2   Sectoral division of water abstractions (%)

	England and Wales	France	Germany
Public supply	31	14.5	11
Industry	14	9.7	29
Power stations	46	63.5	56
Agriculture	6	12.3	2
Other	3		2

Source: OECD 1999b: 14. The quasi-totality of water abstractions for power production, used in cooling for reactors, is recycled.

contractual agreements, with lower rates available for water consumption outside peak times. In France, the principle of 'non-discrimination' excludes preferential tariffs for individual users: reductions are only available to entire user categories *en bloc*. Municipal authorities may nonetheless offer seasonal tariffs (though this is not the norm), and industrial users are eligible for water basin agency grants to finance water and wastewater treatment plants (see below) (OECD 1999b).

Domestic consumption

Price tariffs for domestic consumers are calculated according to different methods in each country. In Britain, domestic water bills are calculated on the basis of a fixed or 'flat-fee' charge predominantly based on average property prices. Anglian Water, which services England's lowest rainfall areas, has been at the forefront of initiatives to extend metering, introducing innovative tariff systems designed to palliate social inequities in consumption charging. However although all new homes in Britain are required to be fitted with water meters, domestic volumetric metering remains low in England and Wales, and it is negligible in Scotland (see Table 21.3).

In France and Germany, metering for all individual households is in practice considerably lower than 100 per cent (in fact, 88 per cent for France and between 55 and 60 per cent for Germany) given the number of people in each country who live in apartment blocks, where water is collectively metered and included in rent charges. Nonetheless, metering enables both France and Germany to apply volumetric charging systems. In France, which like Britain falls into the 'middle-range' category for domestic water consumption, charges have been legally obliged since 1996 to be calculated as a two-part tariff (*tarification binôme*): a fixed charge covering 'ongoing' customer costs (such as maintenance and billing), and a volumetric rate on all consumption. In Germany, where domestic consumption patterns display stable 'low-use', a similar two-part tariff structure operates, with the addition that water charges are calculated on the basis of 'full-cost recovery', meaning that water prices should not simply

Table 21.3 Estimated per capita domestic water consumption

	England and Wales	Scotland	France	Germany
Metering penetration in single-family houses connected to the public water supply system	22% (2002)	negligible (1997)	100% (1995)	100% (1997)
Domestic water consumption (litres per head per day, 1997)	153	148 (1991)	137	116

Source: OECD 1999a: 19, 46.

cover the direct economic costs of supply and waste service but also related or indirect costs such as negative environmental externalities.

The combination of geographical, cultural and institutional factors produces significant disparities between countries in the price paid by domestic consumers for water, as shown in Table 21.4.

Such mean national tariffs mask significant disparities within each country. In France, the cost of water supply and sanitation varies between €0.79 (£0.58, $0.89) and €3.16 (£2.33, $3.56) per cubic metre in 90 per cent of *communes* (the price disparity exceeds a factor of seven if all *communes* are included). Two factors predominate in such disparities. First, water rates tend to be higher in rural areas than in urban areas. Secondly, private water networks are on average more expensive than publicly-managed networks; a recent sample produced mean differences of 27 per cent for water supply and 20.5 per cent for wastewater treatment (IFEN 2001). In England and Wales, unit costs to customers (per property in 2001–02) vary from £97 (€132, $148) to £175 (€238, $268) for water supply, and from £116 (€158, $177) to £237 (€322, $362) for sewerage (OFWAT 2002a). In Germany, meterage rates for drinking water vary from one authority to another; the newer east German local authorities typically charge considerably more than west German water companies, chiefly as a result of the particular problems of local government finances in the east and the cost of upgrading water quality in the five new *Länder*. Wastewater treatment prices, which can consist either of a blanket charge based on the quantity of freshwater consumed and thus requiring reprocessing (40 per cent of households) or on a split scale differentiating between rainwater and freshwater consumed, vary more significantly: in 1998, average annual per capita wastewater costs in Bremen were €137.54 (£101.23, $154.73) compared to only €74.14 (£54.57, $83.41) in Saxony.

National governments impose VAT charges at different rates, but central government has only a secondary role in price regulation. In England and Wales, where the private utilities are responsible for setting charges for all user groups, the independent regulator, OFWAT (Office of Water Services) is empowered to monitor the specified levels of service they provide and, through the periodic review, can cap annual price increases. Current price limits came into force on 1 April 2000; on average, regulation will see prices reduced by 2.1 per cent each year for the five years 2000–05. Scottish Water is similarly accountable to the Water Industry Commissioner for Scotland for customer and economic issues.

In France, the great variation in tariffs is matched by a lack of transparency. Price regulation is undertaken by municipal authorities, with rates calculated according to the management system in operation. Where the municipality retains control through direct management, prices are set annually by the council; but where water is supplied privately through one of various types of

Table 21.4 Average annual household water tariffs

	England and Wales (May 2002)		France (1998)[a]	Germany (1998)	
	Flat fee; some metering		Basic charge plus volumetric charge	Basic charge plus volumetric charge	
				west	east
Formula	Metered	Un-metered	Metered	Metered	
Total	£198 (€269, $303)	£236 (€321, $361)	€302.92 (£223, $341) plus €2.52 (£1.85, $2.84)/m^3	€193.78 (£143, $218)	
Basic charge			€47.56 (£35, $53.50)	€34 (£25, $38)	
Combined volumetric charge			€201.54 (£148, $227)	€80.27 (£59, $90.30)	
Water supply	£91 (€124, $139)	£112 (€152, $171)	€1.30 (£0.96, $1.46)/m^3	€1.34 (£0.99, $1.51)/m^3	€1.49 (£1.09, $1.68)/m^3
Sewerage[b]	£106 (€144, $162)	£125 (€170, $191)	€1.32 (£0.97, $1.49)/m^3	€113.51 (£83.54, $127.70)	
Additional charges			€53.81 (£39.60, $60.54)		
VAT	0%	0%	5.5%	7% on supply 0% on wastewater removal	

Notes [a] Based on annual average household consumption of 120 cubic metres.
[b] Approximately 15,000 French communes are not connected to sewerage networks, and therefore pay no sewerage charges. The mean cost of water supply in these communes is €1.35 (£0.99, $1.51) per cubic metre. The mean cost of water in communes with both sewerage and supply is €2.60 (£1.91, $2.93) per cubic metre.

Sources: OFWAT 2002a; IFEN 2001; Bundesministerium für Umwelt, Naturschutz und Reaktorsicherheit and Umweltbundesamt 2001.

delegated management contract, the private operator and municipal council agree a price regime for the duration of the concession.

In Germany, where supply and waste water treatment costs are required to be covered by the prices charged, there is no formal monitoring of prices; local democratic accountability is held to be sufficient to control charging by publicly owned utilities.

Water resource management

Central government occupies a more prominent position in water resource management in all three countries, though environmental regulation is highly regionalized in France and Germany in particular. In Germany, water has been traditionally excluded from the ownership provisions of private law: surface and ground water is considered a public good, where ownership rests with either the Federation (for major water courses and lakes) or the *Länder*. Resource management and protection is the preserve of the 16 *Länder*, which have their own legislative competence within Federal law and supervise the implementation and operation of water bylaws at intermediate (district) and local level. Water quality is monitored most regularly by local water authorities, and intermittently by individual *Land* ministries, the Working Group of the Federal States on Water Problems (LAWA), the Federal Institute of Hydrology (BfG), and other public authorities.

In France, *la police des eaux* is carried out by the departmental agents of various central government ministries, coordinated by the water directorate within the environment ministry (*direction de l'eau*). Six river basin agencies (*agences de l'eau*) are responsible for resource management, setting economic incentives to control pollution and funding water quality improvement and infrastructural programmes. Basin committees (*comités de bassin*) define five-year action programmes and raise money for re-distribution by levying taxes (*redevances*) covering pollution and abstraction; the *redevance pollution* is the more important, providing agencies with 80 per cent of their budgets. Domestic consumers pay 84 per cent of the *redevance pollution*, effectively cross-subsidising agriculture, which causes a third of organic pollution and nearly three-quarters of nitrate pollution but pays less than one per cent of the *redevance* and receives 15 per cent of agency subsidies.

Environmental regulation is undertaken in England and Wales by the Environment Agency (EA), and in Scotland by the Scottish Environment Protection Agency. Both are independent agencies part-funded by central government: the EA raises 35 per cent of its income from charging schemes (such as abstraction charges) and 37 per cent from flood defence levies raised on local authorities. 28 per cent comes from a grant from the Department of the Environment, Food and Rural Affairs (DEFRA) and the National Assembly of Wales. The EA's duties include the conservation and augmentation of water resources, as well as flood defence (which alone accounts for over half the EA's annual budget), maintenance of water quality, waste minimization, and regulation of fisheries and navigation. It monitors compliance, records pollution incidents and takes enforcement action. Drinking water quality is monitored by the Drinking Water Inspectorate in England and Wales, and the Drinking Water Quality Regulator in Scotland. In 2000, 2.7 million tests were carried out in England and Wales. In 99.83 per cent of cases the water tested met set quality standards.

Recent developments

Concerns over the transparency and equity of domestic water pricing, allied to a number of high-profile corruption scandals over the municipal delegation of water supply to private companies (one of which resulted in a prison sentence for government minister and mayor of Grenoble Alain Carignon), have dominated the national water agenda in France over the last ten years and led to a succession of legislative measures regulating water supply contracts, budgets and tarification. In terms of resource management, the principal recent development in France concerns the strengthening of central government control through the promotion of eco-system protection and sustainable development in the 1992 water law. Basin agencies must now establish fifteen-year integrated basin-wide plans, mirrored by localized catchment plans drawn up in consultation with local water commissions composed of representatives of local authorities, water users and the state. Attempts by the 2002 *loi Cochet* to strengthen central coordination of price regulation, further reduce delegated management concession periods and extend the polluter-pays mechanism to agriculture (by setting its contribution at 5 per cent of the basin *redevance*) fell with the Jospin government in the 2002 legislative elections. New conservative environment minister Roselyne Bachelot has promised a revised water bill in 2004, to be drawn up in close consultation with agricultural interest groups: it is likely that the polluter-pays principle will be shelved in favour of an incentive system rewarding de-pollution initiatives, at least for agriculture.

In Germany, there has hitherto been little political appetite for the privatization of water supply despite very heavy pressure on local government finances, the lobbying of international utility companies and interest groups, and EU liberalization initiatives. In its 2002 Report, the Federal Government's Environmental Council (*Umweltrat*) raised serious doubts about the efficacy of privatization, underscoring its potential negative effects on water quality and prices. The report was applauded by the Association of German Municipalities (*Deutscher Städtetag*) and by LAWA. There are nevertheless indicators of other policy preferences, such as the public–private partnership established in Berlin for water management (owned 50.1 per cent by the municipal authority, 49.9 per cent by a consortium headed by Vivendi and Allianz), and the increasing support emanating from the Federal Ministry for Economic Cooperation for proposals for the privatization of water management in developing countries. Given the fiscal priorities of German unification, the imperatives of the eurozone's Stability and Growth Pact and the cost of reconstruction in flood-damaged eastern regions, resistance to privatization may be severely weakened. Damage to over 80 waterworks in east Germany will, in the absence of equalization measures, put further upward pressure on water and sewerage charges.

In Scotland the most recent development concerns the amalgamation under the 2002 Water Industry (Scotland) Act of East of Scotland Water, North of Scotland Water and West of Scotland Water to form Scottish Water. In England and Wales, numerous 'live' issues are currently affecting the water industry, of which two concern the structure of the industry. First, proposals to replace the economic regulator by a corporate regulatory body have been tabled, though there is no intention to alter regulatory powers. Second, the industry is to be opened up to more competition. To date competition has been comparative, and involves OFWAT comparing each undertaker and setting prices on the basis of the most efficient performance. The proposal is to permit new entrants to the water industry to be licensed to access water undertakers' distribution networks under the terms of the 1998 Competition Act, thus enabling them to supply water to eligible customers. A number of applications for common carriage are in the process of being made by some undertakers who wish to operate in other regions, and by a small number of new entrants; the Government's proposed competition framework will remove any remaining uncertainties in the case of access to distribution networks. New entrants will be licensed by OFWAT (or more likely its successor organization). Other important developments include the consultation process launched by the Government on the implementation of the amended EC Directive on environmental impact assessment and diffuse water pollution from agriculture in England, and the increase in the number of nitrate vulnerable zones in England, extending the total land area coverage from 47 to 55 per cent.

Sources

Bundesministerium für Umwelt, Naturschutz und Reaktorsicherheit and Umweltbundesamt (eds), *Water Resources Management in Germany* (Bonn: Federal Ministry for the Environment, Nature Conservation and Nuclear Safety, Public Relations Division, 2001).

IFEN (l'Institut français de l'environnement), 'Eau potable: diversité des services ... grand écart des prix', *Les Données de l'environnement*, 65 (2001).

IFEN (l'Institut français de l'environnement), *L'Environnement en France* (Paris: La Découverte, 2002).

W.A. Maloney and J. J. Richardson, *Managing Policy Change: The Politics of Water* (Edinburgh: Edinburgh UP, 1995).

OECD (Organization for Economic Cooperation and Development), *The Price of Water: Trends in OECD Countries* (Paris: OECD,1999a).

OECD (Organization for Economic Cooperation and Development), *Industrial Water Pricing in OECD Countries* (Working paper ENV/EPOC/GEEI(98)10/FINAL, 1999b).

Office International de L'Eau, <www.oieau.fr/gest_eau/france/index.htm> [14 August 2002].

OFWAT (Office of Water Services), *Water and Regulation: Facts and Figures May 2002* (Birmingham: OFWAT, 2002).

OFWAT (Office of Water Services) (2002a), 'Water and Sewerage Bills 2001–02', <www.ofwat.gov.uk/aptrix/ofwat/publish.nsf/Content/bills01to02> [12 January 2004].

OFWAT (Office of Water Services), <www.ofwat.gov.uk>

Y. Tavernier, *Rapport d'information no. 3081 sur le financement et la gestion de l'eau* (Paris: Assemblée Nationale, 2001).

22
Media

Ian Bartle

Introduction

The media industry, often referred to as the 'mass media', involves the mass production and communication of a wide range of messages to mass audiences (McQuail 1999) for purposes such as education, information, news, entertainment and advertising. The main areas of the media industry are the press, broadcasting – radio or television transmission for general public reception – and cinema. In recent years communication has become less mass with increasingly smaller scale and interactive communication, exemplified most notably by the internet.

The mass media have popular appeal, can exert significant political, cultural and commercial power, and are of considerable political and social importance (Hutchison 1999). They often act as arenas of public debate between the governors and the governed and can be forces for social cohesion. The role of the media in society, however, is contested. The media can be seen as a force for good via education and cultural enlightenment but are also often seen as culturally debasing and commercially exploitative. Similarly, individuals can be perceived as citizens and the media as facilitators of citizenship, or individuals can be seen simply as consumers of media products. The role of the media *vis-à-vis* society and the state also strikes at the heart of contemporary notions of liberal democracy. Freedom of expression and pluralism can be enabled by the media, but the media can also be a vehicle for the dissemination of propaganda. For all these reasons media policy is highly politicized and a special area of public policy. The regulation of media ownership is an especially important area of media policy, as safeguarding pluralism requires significant limitations on, and control of, the concentration of media ownership (Doyle 2002: 6–7).

The high level of politicization of media policy also means that one of its key features in Western Europe is enduring cross-national divergence.

Although a West European model of media policy in contrast to the US can be discerned, most notably in relation to the idea of 'public service broadcasting', the politics of media policy mean that there are also distinctively different versions of public service broadcasting in individual West European countries (Humphreys 1996: 299; Kelly *et al.* 2004). Although technological change, particularly the development of digital media and multi media, has had a profound impact on media policy in all countries, cross-national divergence in Britain, France and Germany remains an enduring feature, for instance in the development of digital TV services (Levy 1997; McQuail and Siune 1998: 223).

The nature of media policy

Media policy in Britain, France and Germany consists of five main types of government activity:

1. *The determination of ownership and industry organization.* Includes restrictions on media ownership.
2. *The provision of media.* The most prominent form of this is via state owned broadcasting companies operated independently of the government.
3. *Content regulation.* This normally consists of restrictions on certain kinds of content plus requirements to provide certain types of content. The objectives and legal framework of content policy are set by the government while regulation – the rules which apply to a specific area – is often undertaken by independent agencies.

   Content regulation covers the following categories:
   (i) *Specification of content.* Includes broadcasting quotas specifying the number and duration of domestic programmes and the number of news, educational and children's programmes, as well as requirements on cable and satellite broadcasters to carry certain public service TV channels.
   (ii) *Restrictions on content.* Includes restrictions on the amount of advertising, restrictions on target audience (for instance by certification of films), requirements for accuracy, and impartiality of public service broadcasters' news programmes.
   (iii) *Prohibition of content.* Prohibited content includes certain kinds of advertising, portrayal of sex and violence, and violation of personal privacy.
4. *Tax, subsidy and other public funding regimes.* To fund public service broadcasters, assist the press, promote selected areas of the domestic media industry, and promote the development of new technologies such as digital broadcasting.

5. *Regulation of media communications systems.* Includes frequency allocation for TV and radio broadcasters (see Communications Policy chapter for further details).

In Britain and France there is a central government ministry with overall responsibility for media policy (see Table 22.1). In Germany much of media policy is constitutionally defined as the responsibility of *Land* governments, including almost all broadcasting policy, while press policy is governed by both levels of government. Many aspects of media regulation, including the regulation of broadcasting, press and cinematic content, and carriage and frequency regulation, are delegated to independent agencies. Telecommunication regulators oversee the cable TV industry and some aspects of the regulation of media communications networks.

Table 22.1   Media policy institutions

	Britain	*France*	*Germany*
Ministries	Department of Culture, Media and Sport Department of Trade and Industry	*Ministère de la Culture et de la Communication* (Ministry of Culture and Communication) *Ministère de l'Économie, des Finances et de l'Industrie* (Ministry of the Economy, Finance and Industry)	*Bundesministerium des Innern* (Federal Ministry of the Interior) *Land* governments *Bundesministerium für Wirtschaft und Technologie* (Federal Ministry of Economics and Technology)
Regulatory agencies	Independent Television Commission Radio Communications Agency Radio Authority British Film Institute Press Complaints Commission Office of Telecommunications (OFTEL)	*Conseil Supérieur de l'Audiovisuel* *Centre national de la Cinématographie* *l'Autorité de régulation des télécommunications* (Telecommunications Regulatory Authority) No press regulator	*Landesmedien-anstalten* (Regional media authorities) *Filmförderunganstalt* (Federal Film Board) *Land* Film Boards *Deutsche Presserat* (German Press Council) *Regulierungsbehörde für Telekommunikation und Post* (Regulatory Authority for Telecommunications and Post)

Sources: Kelly *et al.* 2004; OECD 2001; European Commission 2003a.

Specific comparisons

Three especially important areas of media policy relate to media ownership and organization, state funding of media, and content regulation.

Media industry ownership and organization

The ownership and organization of the media industry in all three countries is highly regulated. Private ownership is dominant in the press (McQuail and Siune 1998: 7), but there are significant levels of public funding and ownership in the broadcasting industry (see Table 22.2). Although governments can and do intervene in the affairs of these publicly owned media providers in a variety of ways, none of them are under direct ministerial control but rather function as autonomous bodies subject to the control of a variety of regulatory arrangements (McQuail and Siune 1998: 129).

It is important to recognize the distinction between the simple concept of public ownership and the complex concept of 'public service broadcasting', as the latter does not exclude private ownership or commercial revenues. In Britain, for example, Channel 4 is publicly owned but derives much of its income from commercial advertising. Universality, close regulation of content and organization, and a degree of public finance all contribute to the notion of public service broadcasting (McQuail and Siune 1998: 25).

There is a complex range of limitations on ownership of the press and broadcasting industry in all three countries. The objective of these measures is to guard against excessive concentration in the industry in order to promote socio-political and cultural pluralism in which a diversity of political views and cultures can be represented (Doyle 2002: 13).

There are controls on single sectors of the media, cross media controls and controls on foreign ownership. Single sector controls limit concentrations

Table 22.2 Publicly funded public service broadcasters

Britain	France	Germany
BBC (British Broadcasting Corporation) Channel 4	France Télévision Radio France RFO (Radio France Outre-mer) RFI (Radio France Internationale) ARTE (Association Relative à la Télévision Européene) (a Franco-German collaboration)	ARD (Arbeitsgemeinschaft der Rundfunkanstalten Deutschlands) ZDF (Zweites Deutschlands Fernsehen) Deutschland Radio Deutsche Welle ARTE

Source: Kelly *et al*. 2004.

in a single sector of the media such as the press, TV or radio broadcasting. Cross-media controls refer to limitations on ownership across more than one sector of the media, for example the press and broadcasting. Cross-media ownership also refers to 'vertical concentration', that is, ownership of more than one part of the media supply chain, such as ownership of both programme makers and broadcasting network providers. In Britain and Germany ownership of the press is regulated by modified anti trust laws (Humphreys 1996: 93–100), while in France there are more specific and rigid rules on press ownership. Table 22.3 summarizes some of the main restrictions on media ownership.

State funding of media

In all three countries a variety of public subsidies, grants, licence fees and favourable tax regimes are used both to extend media diversity and to support public service broadcasters (Doyle 2002: 27). The main source of public funding of broadcasting in all three countries is by licence fee paid by individuals, and there are rules regarding whether public service broadcasters can gain revenue from commercial advertising. In Britain there is a single licence for TV ownership which is used to fund the BBC. Revenue from commercial advertising is not allowed for the BBC but Channel 4 receives much of its revenue from advertising in addition to some subsidies targeted at specific programming. In France the public service broadcasters receive income from a licence fee and some of the public channels are allowed to receive income from advertising. In Germany a licence fee is used to support the regional broadcasting organizations while national and regional public broadcasters are able to draw revenue from commercial advertising (Kelly *et al.* 2004). Details of public funding are given in Table 22.4.

Although almost all of the press is privately owned in all three countries and there is no press equivalent of public broadcasting, in order to guard against excessive concentration a wide variety of state subsidies have been developed (McQuail and Siune 1998: 13), including 'indirect' subsidies such as low postal and telecommunication rates, interest free loans and low VAT rates: 0 per cent in Britain, 2.1 per cent in France and 7 per cent in Germany (McQuail and Siune 1998: 13).

Content regulation

The content of the various communications media is subject to extensive regulation, particularly the press and broadcasting media. Broadcasting media are subject to regulations such as quotas for certain types of programmes (for example news and educational programmes), requirements to provide programmes deemed to be of national significance, prohibitions on certain content for reasons of taste and decency, and controls on advertising (OECD 2001: 127).

Table 22.3   Main controls on media ownership

	Britain	France	Germany
TV ownership	A single entity may not control more than 15% of the total audience for analogue TV and between 20–25% of digital programme services	No more than 49% of a national broadcaster can be owned by one entity Broadcasters licensed for an area of more than 4 million people may not hold another licence	A single broadcaster may not have more than 30% of average annual viewer share
Press ownership	Modified anti trust law	Specific and rigid rules, ministerial discretion	Modified anti trust law
Cross-media controls	Holder of a national radio licence may not own a TV licence Newspaper owners with more than 20% of national market may not hold national or regional radio or TV licence. The BBC may not provide cable TV services Terrestrial commercial TV licensees may not provide cable TV services	Terrestrial broadcasters licensed for services to 4 m people may not supply cable TV infrastructures Cable TV broadcasters licensed to provide services to 6 million people may not provide terrestrial TV services	TV broadcaster with other media activity may not reach more than equivalent of 30% of TV audience Newspaper operators dominant in a region are limited in the amount of broadcasting company shares they may own
Foreign ownership controls	Only UK and EEA nationals may hold licences to provide national and local analogue TV, radio and domestic satellite services	(No media-specific controls)	Broadcasting licence only issued if applicant represents a wide range of opinions in Germany (in practice highly restrictive)

Source: OECD 2001.

TV content regulation can be split into two categories: programme production, which relates to who produces, where they produce and in what language; and programme type, which refers to programme categories such as news, entertainment, drama and sport. All three countries are subject to the programme production requirements of the EU directive 'TV Without Frontiers' (European Commission 2003b). *Inter alia* this directive specifies that over a half of TV

Table 22.4   Public funding of broadcasting

	Britain	France	Germany
Total public funding in 1999	€3749 m (£2759 m, $4218 m)	€2011 m (£1480 m, $2262 m)	€3580 m (£2635 m, $4028 m)
Public funding as a proportion of total market revenue of TV companies	26.36%	24.32%	33.62%
Annual licence fee	2003 colour TV: €158 (£116, $177)	2001: €114 (£84, $128)	2001: €193.80 (£143, $218) Radio only: €63.84 (£47, $72)

Sources: OECD 2001; Zenith 2002.

programmes must be produced within Europe and that at least 10 per cent must be produced by independent producers (producers who are independent of the broadcasting companies). Tables 22.5 and 22.6 show that there are significant cross-national variations in both types of content regulation. Programme production in France, for example, is particularly highly regulated for reasons of cultural protection and a high proportion of programming must be in the French language, whereas there are no similar language requirements in Britain or Germany.

Table 22.5   TV content obligations: production

Britain	France	Germany
Channels 3 (ITV), 4 and 5: at least 25% of programmes in specific categories must be independently produced	*Films and audiovisual programmes*: 60% must be European, 40% must be original French language	No quantitative restrictions except as specified by EU directive
ITV regional: at least 65% of broadcasting time programmes must be independent, and at least 80% of regional programmes must originate in the region	*Terrestrial broadcasters* must invest 15% of revenue in French language programmes, 3% in European programmes and 2.5% in French language films	

Sources: OECD 2001; EIM 2002.

Table 22.6 TV content obligations: programme type (minimum quotas)

Britain (hours per year)	France	Germany

Channel 3:
News/weather 365
Current Affairs 78
Religion 104
Children's 520
Documentaries 91
Education 91
Arts 39
	France 2:
	Drama 15 times/year
	Music 2 hours/month
	European and French classical music
	  16 programmes/year
	Weekly consumer information
	  10 minutes/week prime time
		No quantitative
		specifications

Channel 4:
News 208
Current Affairs 208
Religion 52
Schools 364
Multicultural 156
	France 3:
	Foreign residents 30 minutes/week
	Drama 15 times/year
	Music 2 hours/month
	European and French classical music
	  16/year
	Weekly consumer information
	  4 minutes/week prime time
	Overseas territories 1/week prime time	

Channel 5:
News/weather 469
Current affairs 130
Religion 52
Children's 608
Documentaries 104
Education 156
Arts 26
Drama 12
	France 5:
	General obligation to broadcast
	  educational and social content
	TF1:
	News/current affairs 800 hours/year,
	  prime time
	Children and youth 1000 hours/year,
	  50/year for youth
	M6:
	Diverse range of music, invest 30%
	  annual turnover
	Majority of animation
	  to be French or European
	Promote newly released films	

Source: EIM 2002. Categories not specified are often subject to general obligations (qualitative).

In Britain, the BBC's Royal Charter and its annual reports specify its basic objectives and principles in qualitative terms such as the duty to inform, educate, entertain and more generally to provide high quality programmes, but other than the requirements of the EU's directive there are no quantitative content specifications in relation to programme type (EIM 2002: 85–6). Instead the BBC's management specifies programme type and production, and this is monitored by the Board of Governors. The content of the commercial terrestrial TV broadcasters is subject to certain general qualitative requirements but there are also some quantitative requirements.

In France, the public broadcasters France 2, France 3 and France 5 are subject to general qualitative requirements (EIM 2002). France 2 and France 3 are required to be general interest channels aiming at a wide audience and carrying a wide range of programmes. France 2 has a predominantly national orientation while France 3 is more regionally focused. The main obligations on France 5 are to promote knowledge, interest and understanding of the world and to facilitate acquisition of skills for employment. These channels and the main commercial channels, Television Francaise 1 (TF1), Metropole Television (M6) and Canal Plus, are also subject to quantitative regulations for programme type.

In Germany there are no quantitative specifications of TV content but there is an agreement between the federal states (*Rundfunkstaatsvertrag*) which specifies that broadcasters should be committed to encouraging freedom of opinion and plurality and which requires them to provide comprehensive services, including a balance of education, information, culture and promotion of German culture (EIM 2002: 51). For the national channels ARD and ZDF the Director General plays a central role in specifying content, monitored by the regulatory authorities. At *Land* level the authorities are concerned to maintain plurality and diversity, and this influences decisions about whether to grant commercial broadcasters a licence.

In all three countries advertising on the main channels is either prohibited completely or limited to a certain length of time (see Table 22.7).

In recent years cable TV has become significant, and cable TV operators are subject to regulations to ensure they provide a certain amount of public service broadcasting channels. These 'must carry' obligations on cable TV companies are summarized in Table 22.8.

Regulation of press content is less stringent but does cover rights to privacy and protection of information sources. In all three countries privacy can be protected through normal libel and defamation laws but legal costs mean

Table 22.7   TV advertising limits

Britain	*France*	*Germany*
BBC: no advertising *Channels 3, 4, 5*: maximum 7 minutes per hour *Other services*: maximum 9 minutes per hour	*France 2 and France 3*: maximum 8 minutes per hour	*ARD, ZDF*: maximum 20 minutes per day before 8pm *Sat 3*: no advertising *Other services*: maximum 20% of total broadcast time

Source: CIT 2000.

Table 22.8 'Must carry' obligations on cable TV companies

Britain	France	Germany
Cable TV operators must carry all national programmes Digital cable TV operators must carry all national and regional programmes	Cable TV operators must simultaneously transmit terrestrial programmes normally received in the area	Analogue cable TV programmes: obligations vary – set by regional governments Digital TV: an inter-regional government agreement: (i) 4 channels reserved, 3 for public service broadcasters, 1 for regional/local programmes (ii) 1/3 capacity for broadcasters must offer diverse (non specialist, non niche) programmes

Source: OECD 2001.

these give little protection to most people. In addition, in Britain the Press Complaints Commission incorporates the respect for privacy in a code of practice, but deploys no special legal sanctions. In France there is special privacy legislation and in Germany there are several criminal laws aimed at protecting privacy. In all three countries the confidentiality of journalistic sources is protected, although there is some legal variation in the very limited circumstances when sources are not protected, such as cases relating to national security (Humphreys 1996: 56–9).

Recent developments

Technological change is fundamentally reshaping the media industry. Two significant developments to which governments are responding with new policies are digital TV and radio and the internet (McQuail and Siune 1998: 60–94). Digital TV and radio has enabled a substantial increase in the number of channels and services provided by both public service and private broadcasters. Pay TV, interactive TV and specialist channels, for example, all impact on policy areas such as content regulation. The way in which the transition to digital TV is funded (particularly public service broadcasting), the question of simultaneous transmission of analogue and digital, and the eventual switching off of analogue, are all issues that have significantly affected recent developments and proposals in media policy (OECD 2001: 121). The development of the internet has led to a dramatic rise in the amount of information distributed and accessible across the globe. Policy makers are faced with dilemmas between the need to protect free expression and exchange of ideas and the obligation to ensure public order and safety. In all three countries these challenges have generally been approached not with radical new policies but by adaptation and development of existing policies (OECD 1999).

In Britain, new media technology has led to a major overhaul of media policy culminating in the Communications Act 2003 (DTI/DCMS 2003). The new policy framework seeks to create a dynamic and competitive communications industry in Britain, maintain plurality of media ownership, protect consumers, ensure all sections of society can benefit from the new communications, and address the tensions between protection of the freedom of speech and expression and the maintenance of decency, quality and public order. Controversially it is proposed to relax foreign media ownership rules, ostensibly to promote competition and diversity but also, in the view of many, to enable media mogul Rupert Murdoch to gain greater control of the British media. The new legislation also includes the establishment of a new regulatory agency, the Office of Communications (OFCOM), as the result of a merger between the Independent Television Commission, the Broadcasting Standards Commission, the Office of Telecommunications, the Radio Authority and the Radiocommunications Agency (OFCOM 2003).

In France recent reforms include provisions for the launch of terrestrial digital TV, the promotion of free to air digital TV, and the reinforcement of public service broadcasting within the new digital environment (IDATE 2000a; CIT 2000). Digital TV via cable and satellite has developed rapidly in the less regulated environment of the late 1990s, but new legislation was required for terrestrial digital TV. This determined that 36 digital terrestrial channels are to be launched in the early 2000s, to cover 85 percent of the population by 2005. Analogue services are envisaged to be switched off but not before 2010 at the earliest. To strengthen public service, the new law included a reduction of the time permitted for advertising on public service channels from twelve minutes per hour to eight.

In Germany the introduction of digital TV has also been a key issue of recent media policy. In 1997 a digital broadcasting initiative was launched with the formation of a forum including policy makers and industry actors (IDATE 2000b). In 2000 an inter-regional broadcasting agreement was reached which included the promotion and development of digital TV. A regional approach for the launch of digital TV between 2000 and 2010 was adopted involving short periods of simultaneous analogue and digital broadcasting with the aim for full digitalisation by 2010 and the termination of analogue once 95 per cent of households receive digital TV. Limits have been placed on the extent of involvement of the public broadcasters ARD and ZDF in digital TV as some disquiet has been expressed by private broadcasters about support for their competitors, the public service digital TV channels, coming from licence fees. Private satellite and cable digital TV broadcasting has developed in the

1990s without significant political initiative or policy change, but regulations had to be introduced in 2000 to provide all broadcasting companies with non-discriminatory access to the cable network, much of which is owned by *Deutsche Telekom*.

Sources

CIT, *The Media Map 2001: European Media Markets and Players* (Exeter: CIT Publications, 2000).

European Commission (2003a), 'Links to regulating, control and funding bodies in the audiovisual sector (cinema and broadcasting)', <www.europa.eu.int/comm/avpolicy/intro/links_en.htm> [8 April 2003].

European Commission (2003b) 'The New "Television Without Frontiers" Directive', <www.europa.eu.int/comm/avpolicy/regul/twf/newtwf-e.htm> [29 April 2003].

DTI/DCMS (2003) (Department of Trade and Industry and Department of Culture, Media and Sport), 'Communications Bill', <www.communicationsbill.gov.uk> [10 April 2003].

G. Doyle, *Media Ownership. The Economics and Politics of Convergence and Concentration in the UK and European Media* (London: Sage, 2002).

EIM (The European Institute for the Media) (2002), 'A comparative analysis of television programming regulation in seven European countries: a benchmark study', <www.eim.de/Library.htm> [23 April 2003].

M. Feintuck, *Media Regulation, Public Interest and the Law* (Edinburgh: Edinburgh University Press, 1999).

P. Humphreys, *Mass Media and Media Policy in Western Europe* (Manchester: Manchester University Press, 1996).

D. Hutchison, *Media Policy: an Introduction* (Oxford: Blackwell, 1999).

IDATE (Institut de l'audiovisuel et des telecommunications en europe) (2000a), 'Digital TV development in Europe. 2000 Report. France', <europa.eu.int/ISPO/infosoc/telecompolicy/en/Study-en.htm> [27 May 2003].

IDATE (Institut de l'audiovisuel et des telecommunications en europe) (2000b), 'Digital TV development in Europe. 2000 Report. Germany', <europa.eu.int/ISPO/infosoc/telecompolicy/en/Study-en.htm> [27 May 2003].

IDATE (Institut de l'audiovisuel et des telecommunications en europe) (2000c), 'Digital TV development in Europe. 2000 Report. United Kingdom', <europa.eu.int/ISPO/infosoc/telecompolicy/en/Study-en.htm> [27 May 2003].

M. Kelly, G. Mazzaleni and D. McQuail (eds), *The Media in Europe: The Euromedia Handbook* (London: Sage, 2004).

D.A.L. Levy, 'Regulating digital broadcasting in Europe: the limits of policy convergence', *West European Politics* 20 :4 (1997) 24–42.

D. McQuail (1999), 'Mass Media', in *The Social Science Encyclopedia*, eds. A. Kuper and J. Kuper (London: Routledge, 1999).

D. McQuail and K. Siune, *Media Policy: Convergence, Concentration and Commerce*, Euromedia Research Group (London: Sage, 1998).

OECD (Organization for Economic Cooperation and Development), *Approaches to Content on the Internet* (Paris: OECD, 1999).

OECD (Organization for Economic Cooperation and Development), *Communications Outlook* (Paris: OECD, 2001).

OFCOM (Office of Communications) (2003), 'OFCOM's transitional web site', <www.ofcom.org.uk> [10 April 2003].

TV Licence (2003), <www.tv-l.co.uk/tvlic/index_frameset.html> [23 April 2003]. Zenith, *Western European Market and Mediafact* (Zenith Optimedia Group, 2002).

23

Environmental Policy

Graeme Hayes, Hartmut Aden and Andrew Flynn

Introduction

Over the last three decades or so, the environment has developed into a significant area of national politics and policy-making, providing a policy focus for actual and prospective problems from acid rain and deforestation in central and northern Europe in the early 1970s to global warming and massive biodiversity loss in recent years and in prospect, and environmental policy has been highly influenced by growing popular consciousness of environmental issues and the increasing reliability and importance of scientific data and modelling. Key policies seek to reduce pollution, preserve habitats and species, and promote environmentally beneficial technologies and practices.

The nature of environmental policy

The main aims of environmental policy are (i) to preserve habitats, species and landscapes, and (ii) to reduce pollution and waste, differentiated by source (chemical, industrial, domestic) and measured by media (air, water, soil). To this end, the role of national governments in environmental policy covers:

- direct regulation;
- levying of taxes and charges;
- funding and regulation of the many parapublic agencies established for specific task management in areas such as forestry, hunting, energy conservation and national parks;
- distribution of grants;
- sponsoring of research;
- monitoring of environmental standards and quality.

Environment ministries typically suffer not only from structural and budgetary weaknesses but also reliance on interministerial bargains, due to the cross-sectoral and cross-media approaches that policy objectives increasingly demand, as policies dealing with sustainable development, climate change, genetically modified crops, renewable energies, packaging, chemical and industrial emissions, waste, conservation, land-use and planning invariably require detailed policy co-ordination with at least one, and normally several, other administrative branches. The European Union is the pre-eminent level for the formation of environmental policy, though individual states display considerable divergence in the policy repertoires favoured in the transposition of directives. Subnational authorities are important actors in the management and delivery of key policies such as recycling, waste disposal, and the granting of planning permission.

There are major differences in the structure and style of central government action on the environment in Britain, France and Germany, though there are also a number of common features, such as the increasing use of market-based instruments and the importance of agencies.

In Germany, environmental policy is mainly characterized by multi-level governance: legislation is distributed between the Federal administration and the 16 *Länder*, with different levels enjoying different key areas of responsibility. The main bodies at federal level are the Federal Ministry for the Environment, Nature Conservation and Nuclear Safety (*Bundesministerium für Umwelt, Naturschutz und Reaktorsicherheit*) and associated central agencies, in particular the Federal Environmental Agency (*Umweltbundesamt*), which coordinates scientific support, and the Federal Nature Conservation Agency (*Bundesamt für Naturschutz*), which coordinates nature protection policy. Central government activity focuses primarily on waste, air pollution and atomic energy, but only defines framework legislation for nature protection and water policy. The *Länder* are the main actors in the implementation of environmental policy and law. Policy is still very much characterized by 'command and control' approaches, including authorisations for polluting activities and limit values for emissions. Since the 1980s more flexible policy approaches and instruments, such as environmental impact assessment, access to environmental information, voluntary agreements and eco-taxes, have been introduced under the influence of European and international decision-making.

The organization of central government in Britain and its key delivery agencies has historically owed much to the dynamic between political and organizational imperatives, to which devolution has added a further layer of complexity: Scotland, and to a lesser extent Wales, enjoy responsibility for developing their own policy, though at the international level they work with the British government. The key central government body is the Department for the Environment, Food and Rural Affairs (DEFRA), whose responsibilities include sustainable development, environmental protection, rural development and energy efficiency. Land use planning, an important environmental tool, is the responsibility of the Office of the Deputy Prime Minister. Policy delivery takes place through a small number of nationally-based agencies. The Environment Agency operates in England, Scotland and Wales and has responsibility for water, waste and integrated pollution control; in England, landscape protection and nature conservation functions are currently, and perhaps uniquely in Europe, split between the Countryside Agency and English Nature, whilst in Wales and Scotland these tasks are integrated into the Countryside Council for Wales and Scottish Natural Heritage. Policy is largely top-down and, especially as it affects the business community, is characterized by a command and control approach. Rural conservation, however, relies much more on negotiation with private actors such as landowners.

In France, central government action is predominantly the responsibility of three core directorates established within the Ministry of the Environment and Sustainable Development *(Ministère de l'Ecologie et du Développement durable)* dealing respectively with nature and landscapes, the prevention of pollution and risks, and water. These functionally-differentiated directorates are complemented by two regionally organized sets of state 'field services': the DIREN *(Directions Régionales de l'Environnement)*, which is responsible for nature conservation, architecture and town planning, and the DRIRE *(Directions Régionales de l'Industrie, de la Recherche et de l'Environnement)* which enforces industrial regulations and inspects licensed industrial sites. Central government action is further augmented by six water basin agencies and the Environment and Efficiency Agency (ADEME). Policy style is characterized both by command and control, top-down regulatory measures and by more flexible market-based solutions, with an emphasis on sub-sectoral negotiation with private actors (Szarka 2003: 94–101).

For further reading on national environmental policy-making in Britain, see Carter (2001). For France, see especially Rumpala (2003) and Szarka (2002); for Germany, see Jänicke *et al.* (1999).

Specific comparisons

Three of the most prominent areas of environmental policy are concerned with atmospheric pollution, climate change and biodiversity.

Atmospheric pollution

Action to combat atmospheric pollution and climate change, two of the most pressing areas for environmental action in western Europe, illustrate both how central governments are constrained in their autonomy by international agreements and legislation, and how national regulatory frameworks and policy repertoires produce dissimilar methods of policy delivery. For example, measures to reduce atmospheric pollution, such as the 2001 agreement on national emissions ceilings which set maximum-allowable concentrate levels for volatile organic compounds, nitrogen oxides, sulphur dioxide and ammoniacs, are established by European directives negotiated within the framework of EU programmes such as Auto-Oil (1992) and Clean Air for Europe (2001). Directives are subsequently transposed into national law, but responsibility for achieving targets rests with Member States.

In France, the environment ministry is responsible for establishing the methodology of air quality monitoring and certifying the 40 separate associations which manage the procedure in the country's 55 major urban conurbations, with technical coordination carried out by the national energy conservation agency (ADEME). In Germany, federal law aimed at the reduction of atmospheric pollution is still primarily based on command-and-control and end-of-the-pipe regulatory approaches, primarily the issue of permits for industrial plants. Air quality monitoring is the responsibility of the *Länder*, with revised targets introduced by European directives transposed by central governmental decree. In Britain, air pollution monitoring is based on a national network of over 1600 sites. Air quality standards are defined by the Expert Panel on Air Quality Standards (EAPQS, a government advisory body) and are largely based upon EU directives, though the Scottish Executive has set more rigorous standards for particle objectives and the Mayor of London has to work with more generous limits than those for Britain. For many of the pollutants, local authorities prepare a Local Air Quality Management (LAQM) plan to demonstrate how they will meet national standards in a cost effective manner. Attaining objectives is non-mandatory, though central government has powers to force local authorities and the Environment Agency to act to improve air quality to comply with the absolute obligations in the Air Directives.

Individual states retain responsibility for short-term emergency public safety measures in cases where maximum-allowable ozone levels (set at $240 \, mg/m^3$ by a 2002 European directive) are exceeded. In France, where the August 2003 heatwave saw this level exceeded on thirteen consecutive days, a sliding scale of regulatory measures – from reduction of vehicle speed limits and industrial emissions to the provision of free public transport and restrictions on personal car use – are brought into operation by prefectoral decree. In Britain, by contrast, emergency measures are non-binding and the responsibility of local authorities, which must declare an Air Quality Management Area (AQMA) covering the area of the problem and then formulate measures that will help towards (but not necessarily achieve) problem resolution. In Germany, where restrictions on vehicle use were considered ineffective when introduced in the mid-1990s, short-term reactive measures are the responsibility of the *Länder*. At the federal level, strategies to reduce ozone concentration have been integrated into general efforts to reduce atmospheric pollution, including fiscal incentives such as the reduction of road tax (*Kraftfahrzeugsteuer*) for vehicles respecting European norms.

Climate change

Action on climate change is undertaken within the parameters of the 1992 United Nations Framework Convention (UNFCCC), the 1997 Kyoto Protocol, and the 2001 Bonn and Marrakech agreements, which set sanctions for non-attainment of targets for reducing carbon emissions. Reduction is measured on a regional basis, with the EU committed to cutting 1990 emission levels by 8 per cent by 2012. Targets for individual Member States were set by a 1998 EU Environmental Council agreement, according to which Germany must cut emissions by 21 per cent and Britain by 12.5 per cent, while emissions in France must not exceed the 1990 levels. Given that emissions have increased in Britain and France since 1990, these countries must cut actual current levels by much more. However this is not the case for Germany due to the reduction in industrial output in the former East Germany since re-unification. Disparities between Member States' targets are predicated on existing levels of greenhouse gas emissions (see Tables 23.1 and 23.2), with France's comparatively strong

Table 23.1 Carbon dioxide emissions per capita (tonne)

	Britain	France	Germany
1990	2.77	1.82	3.37
1996	2.68	1.80	3.03
1997	2.56	1.69	2.94

Source: Jaudet 2002: 38.

Table 23.2 Sectoral trends in emissions and removals of greenhouse gases, kilotonnes (carbon dioxide equivalent)

	Britain		France		Germany	
	1990	*2001*	*1990*	*2001*	*1990*	*2001*
Energy	228 090	199 229	67 636	57 487	412 896	345 293
Industry	108 281	101 957	105 833	101 876	224 063	156 946
Transport	116 753	123 165	119 135	140 670	162 281	178 313
Agriculture	nd	nd	nd	nd	nd	nd
Waste	1 952	1 308	2 130	1 601	nd	nd
Other	138 732	135 189	100 538	109 719	215 199	190 209
Total	593 807	560 849	395 272	411 353	1 014 439	870 762

Source: EEA 2004.
Note: nd = no data.

record (it has the third lowest per capita emissions of carbon dioxide in the EU) predominantly explained by its high levels of nuclear power generation.

The 1998 EU agreement also stipulates that each Member State is responsible for devising its own programmes to account for 50 per cent of the targeted reductions. In France, action against climate change was given the status of national priority with the launch in 2000 of the National Plan to Combat Climate Change (PNLCC), which combines fiscal measures, voluntary agreements and long-term action to promote renewables and reduce consumption. Although total environmental tax revenues are low in France in comparison with Germany and Britain, due largely to differences in energy generation and lower levels of fuel duty (see Table 23.3), market-based instruments are a standard feature of French environmental policy, with fiscal measures to combat climate change integrated into the General Tax on Polluting Activities (TGAP), itself introduced in 1999 to re-organize the formerly hypothecated taxes on atmospheric pollution raised by the ADEME. Though the tax was extended in 2000 to include some water pollutants, a further extension to include energy generation has not materialized, with the current government definitively ruling out an energy eco-tax and championing voluntary agreements with industry despite the fact that these have a relatively poor track record (Szarka 2003: 107–9).

The principal eco-taxes in Britain are the Landfill Tax and the Climate Change Levy. The former aims to change waste management practices by increasing

Table 23.3   Size and structure of environmental tax revenues, 2001

	Britain	*France*	*Germany*
Energy taxes	€36.5 bn (£26.9 bn, $41.1 bn)	€24.0 bn (£17.7 bn, $27.0 bn)	€44.9 bn (£33.0 bn, $50.5 bn)
Pollution taxes	€0.8 bn (£0.6 bn, $0.9 bn)	€0.1 bn (£0.07 bn, $0.11 bn)	–
Resource taxes	–	€1.5 bn (£1.1 bn, $1.7 bn)	–
Transport taxes	€7.9 bn (£5.8 bn, $8.9 bn)	€3.8 bn (£2.8 bn, $4.3 bn)	€8.4 bn (£6.2 bn, $9.5 bn)
Total environmental taxes	€45.2 bn (£33.3 bn, $50.9 bn)	€29.3 bn (£21.6 bn, $33.0 bn)	€53.3 bn, (£39.2 bn, $60.0 bn)
Environmental taxes % total taxes and social contributions	7.6	4.4	6.2
Environmental taxes % GDP	2.8	2.0	2.6

Source: Johansson and Schmidt-Faber 2003: 6.

the cost to local authorities and businesses of disposal in landfill sites. The tax is collected by landfill operators who can either pass the revenue directly to the government, use it to assist communities affected by landfill sites, or use it to promote sustainable waste management. The Climate Change Levy, introduced in 2001, is a revenue-neutral tax on energy used in the industrial, commercial and public sectors. Most of the income raised has been used to reduce the rate at which employers pay National Insurance contributions, shifting taxation from a 'good' (employment) to a 'bad' (pollution). Both the Landfill Tax and the Climate Change Levy have been pitched at modest levels and have promoted only minor changes in company behaviour.

In Germany, eco-taxes were introduced in 1999 and by 2003 were generating an estimated €17 billion (£12.5 billion, $19.1 billion), with the major part of the revenue raised earmarked for the public retirement insurance scheme (*Rentenversicherung*, an independent institution). Eco-taxes have been increased every year between 1999 and 2003, rising by approximately 3 (euro) cents (2.2 p, 3.3 American cents) per litre on petrol, two cents (1.5 p, 2.25 c) per litre on oil for heating, 0.25 cents (0.18 p, 0.28 c) per kilowatt hour on domestic electricity consumption and 0.16 cents (£0.12 p, 0.18 c) per kilowatt hour on gas.

There is also considerable divergence between countries over the introduction of emissions trading. Despite its tendency to adopt market solutions, France has adopted a sceptical, wait-and-see approach towards the development of national tradable permits, whilst Germany has actively lobbied in favour of them in international and European negotiations. Their introduction forms a central commitment of the current government's programme in Germany, with debate centring on the exact form of distribution for the first 'round' of allowances. In Britain, central government has promoted voluntary, market-based schemes to achieve its own target of a 20 per cent reduction in carbon dioxide emissions from 1990 levels by 2010. Measures include what is claimed to be the world's first economy-wide greenhouse gas trading scheme, the United Kingdom Emissions Trading Scheme (UKETS): the central government asked organizations what level of emission reductions they were prepared to offer for an allocated sum of money, and 34 organizations agreed annual reductions totalling 1.1 million tonne of carbon from 1998–2000 levels by the end of 2006.

Biodiversity

Action to protect biodiversity is, like climate change, predominantly structured by international conventions and European directives. Thus the 1992 EU Habitats directive provides a framework for the application of the World Convention on Biological Diversity adopted at Rio de Janeiro. This provides for a European network of special conservation areas of habitats and of wild fauna and flora under the title Natura 2000, which also comprises the sites designated under the 1979 Birds directive. Central governments define the relationships between protected spaces and are responsible for establishing the specific modalities of the process, involving site designation, the establishment of management rules to ensure conservation, local consultation with social and political actors, and the co-funding of programme costs. Table 23.4 shows that there is considerable variation in the extent of site designation among Member States.

In France the implementation of the Natura 2000 programme has included such high-profile schemes as the re-introduction of the sturgeon, the European beaver and the Pyrenean brown bear, but overall progress has been poor, attracting censure from the European Court of Justice. Progress on designation of special protection areas for birds, where by dint of its geographical position France hosts key migratory sites for Siberian and Scandinavian species en route to west Africa, is the worst in the European Union.

Among Member States only France and Britain carry out habitat management, upkeep and restoration through a voluntarist system of contractualization. In France this procedure is based around the establishment of locally-negotiated five-year management plans (documents of objectives, DOCOB) with social and political actors (land-owners, forestry commissioners, local authorities and representatives of hunting, agriculture, angling and environmental organizations), supported by national and sub-national consultation committees with representatives of similar interests. However the procedure is currently in crisis: scientific representation is chronically low, and in 2003 not one single new DOCOB was negotiated, leaving another 710 still to be agreed by 2008 if France is to meet its comparatively modest current target of 1300 DOCOBs.

In Britain, lists of sites considered to be of national or international importance are maintained by the conservation agencies, which accordingly took the lead role in Natura 2000 site selection. The conservation agencies are also responsible for preparing management plans and establishing site objectives, in keeping with

Table 23.4 Natura 2000 site designation, October 2003

	Britain	*France*	*Germany*
Habitats			
Number of sites	601	1 202	3 536
Total surface area (km^2)	24 721	41 300	32 151
Percentage of national territory (land and sea)	10.1	7.5	9.0
Birds			
No. of sites	242	155	466
Total surface area (km^2)	14 704	11 749	28 977
Percentage of national territory (land and sea)	6.0	2.1	8.1

Source: ECEDG 2003: 8–9.

private property rights, and landowners and occupiers negotiate management agreements in return for various types of financial payments ranging from compensation for land-use restrictions to incentives for achieving wildlife gain and supporting conservation.

Under the influence of European and international environmental law, Germany now has a variety of categories for the protection of sites and species, as traditional German protected areas (*Naturschutzgebiete, Landschaftsschutzgebiete*) are only partly identical with the new Natura 2000 network. The Federal polity sets the framework legislation for nature protection, transposing the legal framework for the Natura 2000 network into federal law (mainly into the *Bundesnaturschutzgesetz*) in 1998. The *Länder* are responsible for more detailed regulation and concrete measures, including site identification (though some *Länder* have encountered major difficulties in identifying sufficient Natura 2000 areas) and the prohibition of activities that might affect network objectives; all planned land-use projects are assessed in relation to Natura 2000 targets (Gellermann 2001).

Recent developments

In Britain, recent developments have concerned preparations for the development of an EU emissions trading market from January 2005, and have focused in particular on the size of the British emissions cap. The European Commission expects about 13,000–14,000 installations in the existing Member States to come under the trading scheme, and that it will be dominated by companies from Germany, France, Britain and Italy. Further organizational reforms may also be afoot as the government seeks to link conservation and development, and a review of the work of English Nature has suggested it should become more responsible for the delivery of rural policy.

In France, recent developments concern the biodiversity and climate change programmes. The October 2003 Le Grand report on biodiversity proposes the transfer of powers for the organization of local consultation from the prefect to sub-national authorities, and further proposes a greater involvement of business interests in order to resolve the breakdown in Natura 2000 site identification and management. Action on climate change, particularly concerning transport and housing, for which emissions increased by 21 per cent and 17 per cent respectively between 1990 and 2001, is to be re-launched with a new *Plan Climat* in 2004. Finally, if the measure is ratified in 2004, the preamble to the French Constitution will be amended to include environmental protection as a fundamental goal of the French nation, obliging all future legislation to respect the objectives and responsibilities enshrined in an Environmental Charter.

One of the most prominent recent developments in Germany concerns waste and recycling policy. The introduction of economic instruments in the early 1990s improved the separation of waste by private households, with the collection and recycling of packaging waste, especially plastics, delegated to a private company, *Grüner Punkt*. In 1991 the former Federal government introduced a mandatory deposit on *Einwegverpackungen*, or packaging which is only used once (such as cans and plastic bottles), to enter into force if the quota of packaging used several times (*Mehrwegverpackungen*) fell below 72 per cent, with targets based on voluntary agreements between producers and the federal environment ministry. Given the consistent failure of producers to meet this quota since 1998, the Federal government introduced a mandatory deposit on drinks cans in 2003 of 25 euro cents (£0.18, $0.28) for small cans and 50 cents (£0.37, $0.56) for large cans, to be collected at the point of sale.

Sources

ECEDG (European Commission Environment Directorate General), *Natura 2000 Newsletter*, 17 December (Brussels: EC DG ENV, 2003).

EEA (European Environment Agency) (2004), 'Trends in emissions of greenhouse gases (EEA Sector Classification)', <dataservice.eea.eu.int/dataservice/viewdata/viewpvt.asp?id=207> [27 January 2004].

N. Carter, *The Politics of the Environment: Ideas, Activism, Policy* (Cambridge: Cambridge UP, 2001).

Federal Environment Ministry (Bundesministerium für Umwelt, Naturschutz und Reaktorsicherheit, BMU), <www.bmu.bund.de>

Federal Environmental Agency (Umweltbundesamt), <www.umweltbundesamt.de>

M. Gellermann, *Natura 2000. Europäisches Habitatschutzrecht und seine Durchführung in der Bundesrepublik Deutschland*, 2nd edn (Blackwell: Berlin, 2001).

M. Jänicke, P. Kunig and M. Stitzel, *Umweltpolitik* (Bonn: Dietz, 1999).

M. Jaudet, 'Le changement climatique: un défi majeur', *Regards Sur l'Actualité*, 277 (2002): 23–41.

U. Johansson and C. Schmidt-Faber, 'Environmental taxes in the European Union 1980–2001', *Statistics in Focus: Environment and Energy, 8/9* (Brussels: Eurostat, 2003).

Y. Rumpala, *Régulation Publique et Environnement: Questions écologiques, Réponses économiques* (Paris: L'Harmattan, 2003).

J. Szarka, *The Shaping of Environmental Policy in France* (Oxford: Berghahn, 2002).

J. Szarka, 'The politics of bounded innovation: 'new' environmental policy instruments in France', *Environmenal Politics* 12/1 (2003): 93–114.

Part V
Social Policy

24
Health

Andrew Street and Clare Bambra

Introduction

The government dominates health care in Britain, France and Germany, but there are a number of significant differences between the three countries. In Britain, health care is financed by general taxation, whereas the French and German systems are both insurance-based. Spending on health is higher, and the health systems are more decentralized, in France and Germany than in Britain.

The nature of health policy

The boundaries of the 'health care system' are indistinct. A broad definition might specify all positive influences on health, which would include housing, education, income and environmental factors – anything that would advance the World Health Organization's definition of health as being 'a state of complete physical, mental and social well-being and not merely the absence of disease or infirmity' (WHO 2002). A narrower definition might be based on the *services* provided by the health care system. But there is no strict definition of a health care service. Elderly people often have underlying health problems that, along with old age, contribute to the difficulties they face in going about their daily lives. Should the assistance such people receive be considered health care or social care? Another example: is it the task of the health care system to improve sexual performance? If the answer is 'possibly', should Viagra be provided to all middle-aged men, or just those (medically diagnosed) with specific limitations to sexual functioning? The answers to such questions vary over time and across countries, and often depends on how central government defines the remit of the health care system.

For the purposes of this chapter, however, public policy in the area of health in all three countries consists of the provision, financing and regulation of:

- doctors and other health professionals such as nurses, dentists, opticians/ optometrists, midwives, physiotherapists, counsellors and psychologists;
- organizations that deliver health care, such as hospitals and nursing homes;
- pharmaceuticals and medical devices;
- preventive services such as occupational health and safety, consumer protection in areas such as food safety, and control of environmental health hazards;
- research into health and health services.

The government dominates the health care sectors of Britain, France and Germany. In each of the three countries, private sector activity is restricted to the margins of the health system, with private insurers and providers filling in any gaps in financial coverage and provision left by the public sector.

Public provision involves public ownership of health facilities such as hospitals, plus the assignation of public employee status to health sector staff. Governments also finance the health care system, via direct funding of the National Health Service in Britain and operation of health insurance systems in France and Germany. The role of central government in Britain, France and Germany has been especially important in determining the organizational structure, working practices, and size of the health system and, more fundamentally, in deciding how the system itself is defined.

In all three countries the health care system is administered at subnational level and overseen by the central government, but there are significant differences in the ways in which this is done.

Despite moves toward decentralization in recent years, central government retains substantial influence over the British health system. The responsibilities of the Department of Health cover policy development, regulation of pharmaceutical products and medical devices, management of human resources and capital, public health and health promotion, and setting and monitoring national standards for the National Health Service (NHS) and for social services provided by local health authorities (British Department of Health 2003).

The NHS is entirely publicly financed through general taxation and National Insurance contributions, with total funding negotiated between the Treasury and Department of Health. Health care is free at the point of use, although patients face co-payments for pharmaceutical prescriptions, dental care, eye tests and some other items. Even so, many are exempt from these co-payments. All citizens have the right to register with a general practitioner (GP), and require a referral from a GP for non-emergency specialist care.

Although the NHS has a highly centralized bureaucratic structure, devolution of political power has brought with it a slightly different structure to the health service in the four constituent countries of the United Kingdom (British Department of Health 1999). In general, NHS funds are allocated by central government to 'purchasers', which are responsible for purchasing services from providers on behalf of their resident population. Purchasing organizations have taken a variety of forms since their creation in the early 1990s, with the dominant model since 1998 comprising GPs and other community-based health professionals.

In France, central government dominates the health care system through the Ministries of Health and Social Affairs (French Health Ministry 2003). The Ministry of Health is concerned with the location of hospitals, training and conditions of employment for health personnel, licensing of pharmaceutical products, and public health. Financial matters, such as insurance premiums, co-payments, physician fees and pharmaceutical prices, are the responsibility of the Ministry of Social Affairs (Jacobs and Goddard 2000).

The French health care system is founded on employment-based statutory health insurance with premiums paid by employees and employers and with sickness funds organized along occupational lines. There is no choice about which sickness fund to belong to, and all members of a sickness fund pay the same premium (Jacobs and Goddard 2000). Sickness funds rarely cover the full cost of care, for which patients pay up-front and are reimbursed later. Because of the shortfall in financial coverage, 87 per cent of the French population insure against having to make a co-payment by taking out supplementary cover with private insurance companies (Lancry and Sandier 1999). Access to health care is conventionally through membership of a sickness fund, but since January 2000 French residents who are not enrolled, for example because they are not in stable employment or are on very low incomes, have been eligible for universal health insurance (Imai et al 2000). Patients enjoy freedom to choose a general practitioner (GP) and do not require a referral to see a specialist. Patients are also free to choose among public hospitals in their area, or any private hospital.

The German health care system is highly decentralized, with most decision making delegated to *Land* governments and non-governmental bodies such as sickness funds, hospitals and physician associations (Busse 1999; Kamke 1998). The Federal Ministry of Health retains responsibility for health care insurance, regulating the pharmaceutical and medical devices markets, disease prevention and control, and consumer protection. *Land* governments are responsible for hospital planning and supervision of health professionals.

As in France, the German health care system is insurance-based: employees pay an insurance premium, jointly with their employers, to sickness funds that purchase health care on their behalf. Premiums are based on current income, not the risk of illness, and provide insurance for employees and their families. High-income earners can elect to insure privately rather than through a sickness fund. Health care entitlements depend upon contributions to one of these funds rather than being a right of citizenship. Patients face co-payments for most services, with the majority of out-of-pocket spending on pharmaceuticals. Sickness funds are free to set their own premium rates, subject to central government approval, but cannot discriminate by employment status, and since 1996 employees have had the right to choose among competing funds. In order to discourage funds from seeking to attract only healthy individuals, central government has introduced a mechanism to compensate funds that enroll members with greater risks of requiring care. In 2000 there were some 420 sickness funds, the majority (80 per cent) being company-based (Busse 2002).

Specific comparisons

This section compares funding arrangements and provides details of policy with respect to the hospital sector, ambulatory care, long-term care and pharmaceuticals.

Funding

Health funding is far higher in France and Germany than in Britain (Table 24.1).

Centralization has allowed the British government to keep a tight rein on health care expenditure. In 2000, health expenditure amounted to 7.3 per cent of gross domestic product (GDP), some way below the European average. The current government has increased health spending as a proportion of GDP in recent years, and aims to take health expenditure up to 9.4 per cent of GDP by 2008 (Robinson 2002).

In contrast, France and Germany have the most expensive health systems among European Union (EU) countries, with health spending amounting to

Table 24.1   Health finances, 2000

	Britain	*France*	*Germany*
Total expenditure on health as a % of GDP	7.3	9.5	10.6
Public expenditure on health as a % of total expenditure on health	80.8	75.8	75.5
Source of public finance	General taxation	Employer–employee sickness insurance	Employer–employee sickness insurance
Percentage of total expenditure on health from:			
– general government	81.0	2.5	6.4
– social security funds	0	73.5	69.4
– private sources	19.0	24.0	24.2
Purchasers	Local Health Groups/ Primary Care Trusts	Sickness funds	Sickness funds

Source: OECD 2002.

9.5 per cent and 10.6 per cent of GDP respectively. Around 75 per cent of their funding comes from public sources, compared to 81 per cent in Britain.

Unsurprisingly, the higher level of expenditure in France and Germany translates into a greater availability of physical resources. Proportionate to the size of the population, Germany has around twice as many hospital beds, doctors and nurses as Britain (Table 24.2).

Hospitals

The hospital sector is diverse, comprising specialist (tertiary) facilities, general (secondary) hospitals, mental health units and community hospitals. These categories are not clearly defined and there is no standardization in what services hospitals provide across countries. Most general hospitals in Britain provide inpatient, day case and ambulatory (outpatient) care. German hospitals tend to provide inpatient care only, the reason being that office-based physicians have a legal monopoly on the provision of specialist ambulatory services (Busse 1999). French hospitals lie somewhere between these extremes, with specialists operating out of both hospital and office settings.

Table 24.2 Hospital care, 2000

	Britain	*France*	*Germany*
Spending on hospital sector as a % of total expenditure on health	42.2 (1998)	42.8	34.0
Specialists per 1000	1.6	1.5	2.4
Physicians per 1000	1.8	3.0	3.6
Nurses per 1000	5.3	6.0	9.3
Acute beds per 1000	3.3	4.2	6.4
Total hospital beds per 1000	4.1	8.2	9.1
Public beds (%)	95	75	54
Private for-profit beds (%)	5	21	7
Private non-profit beds (%)	0	14	39
Form of revenue payments	Local negotiation	Public: global budget Private: per diem	Casemix payment
User charges for medical services	None	25–30%	None
User charges for hospital services	None	20% of total cost of treatment (unless exempt)	Charges for hotel costs

Sources: OECD 2002; Yuen 2001.

Hospital ownership varies across countries. In Britain, most hospitals are publicly owned, although new building tends to be financed from a mix of public and private sources, with ownership residing in a limited company created specifically for the building project (Dawson 2001). Less than 5 per cent of the total bed stock in Britain is in private hospitals, compared to 35 per cent in France and 46 per cent in Germany (Table 24.2).

The autonomy enjoyed by the management of public hospitals also differs. In Britain, hospitals appoint their own Boards of Directors and have autonomy over financial, employment and clinical matters. Nevertheless, British hospitals face a number of centrally determined performance targets and, ultimately, the chief executive faces dismissal by the Secretary of State for management failures. French hospitals are restricted in their decision-making, in large part because the civil servant status of staff means that hospitals have little discretion over recruitment, redundancies, promotion or wages (Imai *et al.* 2000). German hospitals enjoy greatest discretion, being private voluntary organizations subject to private law (Busse 1999).

German hospitals receive income from two main sources. Capital is provided through the *Land* government, which is responsible for maintaining the hospital infrastructure (Busse 2002). The costs of providing care are financed by the sickness funds, with the composition of payments dependent upon the amount and type of activity undertaken. In France, public hospitals are financed according to global budgets while private hospitals are reimbursed on a *per diem* basis. In Britain the form of payment is a matter of negotiation between purchaser and hospital.

Ambulatory (primary) care

The meaning of 'ambulatory care' differs across countries. In Britain the term is usually applied to services provided by hospital outpatient departments, while 'primary care' refers to services provided by general practitioners (GPs). In Germany, where it is illegal for hospitals to provide outpatient services, ambulatory care refers to all services provided in an office setting. It is this definition that is used here.

Some of the main features of ambulatory care in Britain, France and Germany are set out in Table 24.3, which reveals among other things that there are significantly more GPs per inhabitant in Germany than in France, with their numbers being lower still in Britain.

In Britain, the GP is the main focal point for managing the provision and delivery of health care. Citizens register with a GP of their choice, who provides primary health care and acts as a 'gatekeeper' to the rest of the health system. Like dentists and pharmacists, GPs are self-employed and generally own their own premises. Their NHS income is managed by central government and consists of capitation fees based on the number of people registered with

Table 24.3 Ambulatory care, 2000

	Britain	*France*	*Germany*
Spending on physician services as a % of total expenditure on health	14.7 (1997)	12.5	17.0
GPs per 1000	0.6	1.5	1.0
Generalist–specialist mix	100% generalist	54% generalist	40% generalist
Form of payment	Mix of capitation, fee-for-service and other payments	Fee-for-service	Fee-for-service
User charges for GP services	None	22% of GP bill (unless exempt); physicians free to charge above negotiated fees	None for the majority of services
Budgetary responsibility of GPs exercised through:	Primary Care Trusts (England and Scotland); Local Health Groups (Wales)	na	Physician Assocations
Purchasing responsibility of GP organizations	All health care services	None	None

Source: OECD 2002.

them, fees for specific services, and other payments such as rental for their premises. About 10 per cent of GPs work single-handed, but most enter into partnership with other GPs. Other health professionals, such as health visitors, community midwives and district nurses, are often attached to GP practices. All GPs in a geographical area are part of larger organizations, called Primary Care Trusts in England and Scotland and Local Health Groups in Wales. These organizations are responsible for purchasing hospital services, managing pharmaceutical budgets and, in some cases, for providing community and mental health care.

In contrast to Britain, in Germany and France ambulatory physicians are a mixture of generalists and specialists, the majority operating from solo practices. In Germany, sickness funds and physician associations negotiate a predominately capitated budget for ambulatory care (Wilton and Smith 2002). The physician association manages this budget, paying individual physicians on a fee-for-service basis. Unlike their counterparts in Britain, physician associations are not responsible for purchasing hospital care.

Collective organizations similar to those in Britain and Germany do not exist in France, where ambulatory physicians are paid on a fee-for-service basis according to a fee schedule negotiated between physician unions and central government (Lancry and Sandier 1999). Physicians are able to charge above these fees, with patients (or their supplemental insurers) paying the difference.

Long-term care

Long-term care encompasses a broad range of health and social services for the elderly such as residential nursing care, day care centres and home care (Wittenberg *et al.* 2002). The sector exemplifies the blurred boundaries that surround health, with long-term care regarded as a health service in France and as a social service in Britain. In France, such care is funded via sickness fund contributions, non-medical home care is subject to user charges, and the provision of beds is comparatively low (Table 24.4). In Britain, long-term care is mainly

Table 24.4 Long-term care, 2000

	Britain	*France*	*Germany*
Cost (% GDP)	1.7	0.7	1.3
Main financing principle	Central/local taxation	Sickness insurance	Statutory long-term care insurance and social assistance
Administration-regulation	Local authorities – social services	Social insurance funds / hospitals	Sickness funds / private insurers / local authorities
Residential care beds per 1000	4.2	1.4	6.5
Provision	Home care: meals on wheels, special aids and equipment, adaptations to home, attendance at day care centres. Residential care in a nursing home	'Allowance for loss of autonomy' is awarded to pay for home and residential care	Long-term care insurance covers costs of home care up to €1918 (£1412, $2158) per month and residential care up to €1432 (£1053, $1611) per month (exact amounts vary by income). Social assistance pays benefits up to the amount needed
User charges in public sector?	Means test on all income and assets above a set capital limit for residential and home care	'Hotel' costs. Non-medical home care charges are proportional to income	Financial contribution by long-term sickness insurance recipients varies by income

Sources: Eurostat 2001; MISSOC 2002; OECD 2002; Wittenberg *et al.* 2002.

the responsibility of local social services and is funded from general taxation. In Germany, where there are more than four times as many long-term beds as in France, the sector is administered separately to both social services and health care, with funding raised through a long-term care insurance scheme and with provision dominated by the voluntary sector.

Pharmaceuticals

In all three countries the role of central government is most evident in the regulation of the pharmaceutical sector. Typically, central government intervenes in the licensing, reimbursement, prescribing and distribution of pharmaceuticals (Table 24.5).

Central government approves what drugs may be licensed for sale and whether their purchase will be reimbursed from public funds. In all three countries, pharmaceutical companies have to demonstrate that their drug is safe for it to be licensed, although there are fewer criteria in Germany than in France and Britain. France operates a positive list, stating which drugs are eligible for reimbursement, while Britain and Germany have a negative listing of those drugs that will not be reimbursed.

Further reimbursement decisions affect what patients pay and what companies receive. Patients have to pay co-payments in all three countries, although in France most are covered by supplementary insurance and in Britain and Germany many are exempt.

On the supply side, Britain, France and Germany have markedly different methods of controlling the price and volume of pharmaceuticals. In France

Table 24.5 Pharmaceuticals, 2000

	Britain	*France*	*Germany*
Spending on pharmaceuticals as a % of total expenditure on health	15.9 (1997)	20	12.7 (1998)
Public spending on pharmaceuticals as a % of total spending on pharmaceuticals	64.2 (1997)	65.1	69.2 (1998)
Licensing	Positive list	Negative list	Positive list
User charges	Flat charge per item	Co-payment rate proportionate to drug price	Three tiers of fixed charges
Supply-side regulation	Rate-of-return regulation	Volume control	Reference pricing

Source: OECD 2002.

prices are set by central government agencies, the result being that it has the lowest priced drugs in Europe (Bloor *et al.* 1996). However because there are no effective controls on consumption, per capita spending on drugs is the highest in Europe (Imai *et al.* 2000). In an effort to control consumption, since 1999 central government and the pharmaceutical industry have agreed target volumes of sales in each therapeutic class, with price reductions if the target is exceeded (Imai *et al.* 2000). In Germany, the Federal Committee of Physicians and Sickness Funds (rather than government agencies) introduced a reference price system in 1996, with reimbursement based on the cost of the most cost-effective (the 'reference') drug in each therapeutic class (Schneeweiss *et al.* 1998). If a more expensive alternative is used, the patient has to pay the difference. In Britain companies are free to set their own prices but profits are regulated according to a voluntary agreement between central government and industry under which companies are able to negotiate a profitable return on their drug sales to the NHS (Maynard and Bloor 1997).

Central government also tries to influence prescribing behaviour by doctors and pharmacists, in particular to encourage greater use of generic drugs. In Britain, generics account for almost 70 per cent of total drug sales (Imai *et al.* 2000). This has been achieved through a combination of measures, including setting prescribing budgets for GPs and disseminating information about prescribing behaviour (Bloor and Freemantle 1996). Similar measures have been applied in Germany, with successive governments putting caps on pharmaceutical expenditure by sickness funds which, in turn, have relied on the provision of comparative data to alter patterns of prescribing by doctors (Busse 1999). Physician associations manage the collective risk of financial overspends, and individual physicians face a loss of income if their prescribing is 25 per cent above average (Wilton and Smith 2002). In 1999 the French government introduced incentives for pharmacists to substitute generic for branded products, but no such incentives apply to doctors or consumers (Imai *et al.* 2000). Both France and Germany use legally binding guidelines as a means to standardize and intervene in prescribing behaviour (Bloor and Freemantle 1996).

Although there is little regulation of the pharmaceutical industry in Germany, wholesalers and pharmacies are tightly regulated by central govern-ment. For instance, pharmacists may own only a single pharmacy, with chains and online pharmacies illegal (Busse 1999). In France, legal restrictions limit the number of pharmacies so that each serves a population of 2500. Retailers are paid a mark-up on wholesale prices, but the government has imposed con-trols on the amount of mark-up allowed (Lancry and Sandier 1999). Restricted entry to the community pharmacy market in Britain means that there is just one pharmacy per 5000 people (OFT 2003).

Recent developments

The health care systems of Britain, France and Germany have undergone many changes in recent years. Three important developments relate to the influence of the EU, the ageing population, and rationing of health care.

Traditionally, health care has been managed at a national level but, with greater standardization of economic and legal conventions across Europe, sovereignty is changing. For instance, the European Court of Justice has upheld the right of EU citizens to seek non-emergency health care in other EU countries than their own and to be reimbursed the costs of that care on the same basis as if they had received care in their own country (Mountford 2001). Similarly, the European Community is working toward a single EU-wide market for pharmaceuticals, which will involve harmonization of licensing requirements (MHRA 2002).

It is predicted that by 2050 the number of Europeans over the age of 65 will increase by 42 million and the number of over 80s will triple from 14 million to 38 million (CEC 2002). If current service levels are to be maintained, it is estimated that expenditure on health will have to rise by an average of 30–40 per cent, with expenditure on long-term care 70 per cent higher than at present. In view of such predictions, the organization and funding of health services and long-term care is the subject of debate in all three countries.

Rationing is inevitable in a publicly funded health care system and, traditionally, it has occurred implicitly and in an *ad hoc* fashion. But some recent rationing decisions have been made explicitly, with Viagra being a high profile example. In Britain, Viagra can be prescribed for specific medical causes of impotency but reimbursement has been ruled out in France and Germany, where it is considered a 'lifestyle' drug. The rationing debate sets the boundaries of the health care system and must address the typical public policy questions of who should decide, for whom and according to what criteria? It is unlikely that the answers will be the same in Britain, France and Germany, suggesting that, despite greater EU harmonization, common boundaries of each country's 'health care system' will not emerge in the near future.

Sources

K. Bloor and N. Freemantle, 'Lessons from international experience in controlling pharmaceutical expenditure II: influencing doctors', *British Medical Journal*, 312 (1996): 1525–7.

K. Bloor, A. Maynard and N. Freemantle, 'Lessons from international experience in controlling pharmaceutical expenditure III: regulating industry', *British Medical Journal*, 313 (1996): 33–5.

M. Brazier, J. Lovecy, M. Moran and M. Potton, 'Falling from a tightrope: doctors and lawyers between the market and the state', *Political Studies*, XLI (1993): 197–213.

British Department of Health, *Concordat on Health and Social Care* (London: The Stationery Office, 1999).

British Department of Health, <www.doh.gov.uk/about/index.htm> [21 March 2003].

R. Busse, 'Priority-setting and rationing in German health care', *Health Policy*, 50 (1999): 71–90.

R. Busse, *Health Care Systems: Towards an Agenda for Policy Learning Between Britain and Germany* (London: Anglo-German Foundation, 2002).

CEC (Commission of the European Communities) (2002), DG Economic and Financial Affairs, <europa.eu.int/comm/economy_finance/epc/epc_aging_en.htm> [20 August 2002].

D. Dawson, 'The Private Finance Initiative: a public finance illusion?' *Health Economics*, 10 (2001): 479–86.

Eurostat, *Social Protection in the EU Member States* (Luxembourg: Eurostat, 2001).

French Health Ministry, <www.sante.gouv.fr/htm/minister/index.htm> [21 March 2003].

Y. Imai, S. Jacobzone and P. Lenain (2000), 'The changing health system in France', (Paris: OECD Economics Department Working Paper 29), <www.oecd.org/eco/eco> [21 March 2003].

R. Jacobs and M. Goddard, *Social Security Systems in European Countries* (York: University of York Centre for Health Economics, 2000).

K. Kamke, 'The German health care system and health care reform', *Health Policy*, 43 (1998): 171–94.

P-J. Lancry and S. Sandier, 'Rationing health care in France', *Health Policy*, 50 (1999): 23–38.

P-J. Lancry and S. Sandier, 'Twenty years of cures for the French health care system', in *Health Care and Cost Containment in the European Union*, eds E. Mossialos and J. Le Grand (Aldershot: Ashgate, 1999).

MHRA (Medicine and Healthcare Products Regulatory Agency) (2002), <www.mca.gov.uk/> [20 August 2002].

MISSOC (2002), *Mutual Information System on Social Protection in the EU Member States*, <www.europa.eu.int/comm/employment_social> [21 March 2003].

L. Mountford, *Health Care Without Frontiers?: The Development of a European Market in Health Services?* (London: Office of Health Economics, 2001), <www.ohe.org> [21 March 2003].

OFT (Office of Fair Trading), <www.oft.gov.uk> [17 March 2003].

OECD (Organization for Economic Co-operation and Development), *OECD Health Data 2002: A Comparative Analysis of 30 Countries* (Paris: OECD, 2002).

R. Robinson, 'Going for gold', *British Medical Journal* 324 (2002): 987–8.

S. Schneeweiss, Q. Schöffski and G.W. Selke, 'What is Germany's experience of reference based drug pricing and the etiology of adverse health outcomes or substitution?', *Health Policy* 44 (1998): 253–60.

WHO (World Health Organization), <www.who.int/about/definition/en/> [30 August 2002].

P. Wilton and R.D. Smith, 'Devolved budgetary responsibility in primary care', *European Journal of Health Economics*, 3 (2002): 17–25.

R. Wittenberg, B. Sandhu and M. Knapp, 'Funding long-term care: the public and private options', in *Funding Health Care: Options For Europe*, eds E. Mossialos, A. Dixon, J. Figueras and J. Kutzin (Buckingham: Open University Press, 2002), <www.euro.who.int/document/e74485.pdf> [21 March 2003].

P. Yuen, *OHE Compendium of Health Statistics 13th edition* (London: Office of Health Economics, 2001).

25
Social Security

Majella Kilkey

Introduction

The role of the state in the provision of social security is very comprehensive in Britain, France and Germany, although non-state schemes such as private occupational pensions exist in all three countries. In Britain, social security benefits are financed by a combination of compulsory national (or social) insurance contributions, which are levied on employers and all but the lowest paid employees, and general taxation, with taxation being the larger contributor. The Department for Work and Pensions (DWP), a ministry of central government, is responsible for delivering the benefits. In contrast, the French and German social security systems are overwhelmingly social-insurance based, and most benefits are delivered by semi-autonomous social insurance funds.

Another important difference between the systems is that in Britain most benefits are paid at a flat-rate level irrespective of previous earnings, while in France and Germany most benefits are paid at a rate proportional to previous earnings. The result of this difference is that British benefits are generally less generous than those in the other two countries.

The nature of social security policy

Social security involves the provision of benefits, usually in the form of cash but sometimes in kind, to:

- those who cannot or are not expected to work (old age benefits, disability benefits, benefits in relation to occupational injury and disease, sickness benefits, benefits for carers, maternity benefits, widows'/survivors' benefits, and unemployment benefits);

- those whose resources fall below certain levels (social assistance and other means-tested benefits);
- parents and others to compensate for the expenses of raising children (family allowances and child supplements to other benefits).

Specific comparisons

Social security systems are complex, with numerous pensions and benefits most of which vary in payment levels according to criteria such as age, income and number of dependants, but it is possible to get an idea of the main contours of provision in each country by describing the key features of old-age pensions, disability and care benefits, unemployment benefits and minimum safety-net benefits as they relate to single people without dependants (maternity, family, sickness and housing benefits are covered in other chapters).

Old-age pensions

Men retire earlier in France, at 60, than in Britain and Germany, where they retire at 65. For women, the age in France is also 60, while in Germany it has increased for those insured since 1993 from 60 to 65. Britain is following a similar route to Germany by phasing in an increase in women's retirement age from 60 to 65 between 2010 and 2020.

In all three countries the principal element of state social security provision for retirement is a contributory social insurance benefit (see Table 25.1). In France and Germany the benefit is earnings-related while in Britain it is flat-rate, although Britain also has a contributory 'Second Pension' (called the State Earnings-Related Pension Scheme until April 2002) which pays an earnings-related benefit. However membership of the Second Pension is not compulsory, as members of occupational, stakeholder or personal (private) pension schemes can opt out (DWP 2003).

Contributory-based pension schemes are most beneficial to those with a standard (life-long, full-time and continuous) employment pattern, but all three countries attempt to mediate the contributions-record of those with interrupted work histories by providing credits for certain non-contributory periods, for example during sickness, invalidity and unemployment. Of particular significance for women is the provision existing in all of these countries to provide contribution credits for periods spent out of the labour market undertaking care for children and/or adult relatives (DWP 2003; CNAV 2003; Federal Ministry of Labour and Social Affairs 2003). Despite such provisions, however, across the three countries there are workers who upon retirement do not qualify for the contributory pension or who receive only a small proportion of the full rate of the benefit. In such circumstances, in both Britain and France there may be

Table 25.1   Old-age pensions, 2003

	Britain	France	Germany
Delivery	Central government	Social Insurance Funds, Central government	Social Insurance Funds
Structure	Contributory flat-rate pension (Basic Pension); contributory earnings-related pension (Second Pension); means-tested non-contributory top-up (Pension Credit)	Contributory earnings-related basic and supplementary pensions; means-tested non-contributory old-age allowance	Contributory earnings-related pension
Indicative rates, per month	Basic – maximum of £335.62 (€456, $513) and minimum of £83.89 (€114, $128); Second – up to 20% of the average earnings over person's working lifetime; Pension Credit – £506.52 (€688, $774) maximum	Up to 50% of person's average earnings over best 17–25 years, with maximum payment of €1216 (£895, $1368); means-tested pension of up to €340.42 (£251, $383)	Pensions based on number of years spent in insured employment, amount of life-time earnings and average earnings of those currently in work, with no statutory minimum or maximum
Supplements	Spouse and child dependants, those aged 80+, Christmas bonus, Winter Fuel Payment, Cold Weather Payment	Spouse and child dependants if there are at least three children	None
Variations	Non-contributory pension for those aged 80+	Partial pensions for those above retirement age working part-time	Early and partial pensions, and separate scheme for tenured civil servants. Rates vary between Old and New *Länder*.

Sources: MISSOC 2002; DWP 2003; Sécurité Sociale 2003; CNAV 2003; Federal Ministry of Labour and Social Affairs 2003.

recourse to a means-tested non-contributory benefit, while in Germany there may be support within the general social assistance scheme (see below).

Given the various components, it is difficult to compare the pension provisions in respect of their generosity across the three countries. The contributory components are clearly potentially more generous in France and Germany than in Britain. In Germany a full pension may yield between 60 and 80 per cent of previous earnings (Federal Ministry of Labour and Social Affairs

2003), while in France the social security fund to which most private sector workers belong, CNAV, provides pensions of up to 50 per cent of one's average earnings (CNAV 2003). In Britain, meanwhile, contributions yield a low flat-rate benefit and a very small earnings-related supplement. However the means-tested minimum pension in Britain is higher than that in France.

Disability and care benefits

All three countries provide benefits to those with a permanent disability, which in the case of adults are designed to replace income from work and contribute towards the costs of care. The systems of income-replacement disability benefits in all of the countries have two tiers: relatively high payments for victims of occupational accidents and illnesses (Table 25.2), and lower payments for those disabled for other reasons (Table 25.3).

Table 25.2 Benefits for permanent disability as a result of occupational accidents and illnesses, 2003

	Britain	*France*	*Germany*
Delivery	Central government	Social Insurance Funds	Social Insurance Funds
Structure	Non-contributory flat-rate benefit determined by degree of incapacity	Contributory benefit determined by previous earnings and degree of incapacity	Contributory benefit determined by previous earnings and degree of incapacity
Minimum level of incapacity for entitlement	Generally 14%	No minimum level	20% after the 26th week following injury
Indicative rates, per month	Maximum – £506.13 (€688, $774) if over 18; £310.05 (€421, $474) if under 18; minimum – £101.23 (€137, $155) if over 18; £62.01 (€84, $95) if under 18	Maximum level of incapacity delivers 100% of previous salary up to a limit of €2529 (£1861, $2846)	Maximum level of incapacity delivers 66.7% of previous salary
Supplements	Care needs, unemployability, retirement, reduced earnings capacity	Care needs, disability arising from fault by employer	Care needs
Variations	None	If incapacity is less than 10% only a flat-rate capital payment is made	Rates vary between Old and New *Länder*

Sources: MISSOC 2002; DWP 2003; Sécurité Sociale 2003; CNAMTS 2003; Federal Ministry of Labour and Social Affairs 2003.

In Britain, a non-contributory (tax-financed) scheme pays a flat-rate benefit to victims of job-related accidents and illnesses who suffer a level of incapacity of at least 14 per cent. The benefit is determined by the degree of incapacity, with a maximum rate of £506.13 (€688, $774) per month for those over 18 years.

In France the scheme is contributory and pays earnings-related benefits to victims of job-related accidents and illnesses incurred at work or on the way to or from work (CNAMTS 2003). Unlike Britain, there is no specified minimum level of incapacity for entitlement. The benefit is potentially more generous in France than in Britain, paying a maximum of €2529 (£1861, $2846) per month depending on previous earnings and degree of incapacity.

Germany is unique among the three countries in that its scheme covers not just workers but also children and young people attending educational establishments. As in France, it covers travel to or from work as well as the workplace itself (Federal Ministry of Labour and Social Affairs 2003). The scheme is contributory, with earnings-related benefits determined by previous earnings and degree of incapacity (for children a fictitious amount of earnings dependent on age is arrived at) paid to those with a minimum level of incapacity of 20 per cent. The maximum level of incapacity can deliver two-thirds of the previous salary.

In all three countries entitlement to benefits for those disabled for reasons unconnected with work is more strictly governed, requiring both a sufficient social-insurance contributions record and a higher degree of incapacity – 100 per cent incapacity in Britain, 66.6 per cent in France and either 50 or 100 per cent in Germany (see Table 25.3 for details). Likewise, the rate of benefit tends to be less generous. In Britain, it is worth £312.65 (€425, $478) per month, and in France it pays a maximum rate of €1216 (£895, $1368) per month to those deemed incapable of work. In Germany, disability pensions are part of the old-age pension system, and 100 per cent incapacity (unable to work at least three hours per day) entitles one to the full rate of the old-age pension, while 50 per cent incapacity (able to work between three and six hours per day) gives half the old-age pension rate (Federal Ministry of Labour and Social Affairs 2003).

In addition to income-replacement benefits, disabled persons in all three countries may also be entitled to benefits to assist with the costs of their care-needs (see Table 25.4). The German scheme is by far the most comprehensive. It takes the form of a long-term care insurance, and incorporates children via their parents' contributions. The insurance can pay for residential care or can be used either in-kind and/or in the form of a cash benefit to pay for care at home. The rate of payment varies by how support is delivered and by the level of care needed. A person opting to remain at home, for example, could receive up to €665 (£489, $748) per month as a cash benefit to pay for care, or receive care directly up to the value of €1917 (£1410, $2157) per month (MISSOC 2002).

Table 25.3 Non-occupational disability benefits, 2003

	Britain	*France*	*Germany*
Delivery	Central government	Social Insurance Funds	Social Insurance Funds
Structure	Flat-rate contributory benefit conditional on having been entitled to a short-term incapacity benefit for 1 year*	Contributory pension determined by previous earnings, degree of incapacity and having a sufficient work or contributions record	Contributory pension determined by previous earnings, degree of incapacity and having a sufficient contributions record
Minimum level of incapacity for entitlement	100%	66.6%	Partial incapacity of 50%; total incapacity of 100%
Indicative rates, per month	£312.65 (€425, $478)	30% of previous earnings for persons capable of work, with maximum rate of €729.60 (£537, $821) and minimum of €233.98 (£172, $263); 50% of previous earnings for persons incapable of work, with maximum rate of €1216 (£895, $1368) and minimum of €233.98 (£172, $263)	A function of person's 'earnings points', degree of incapacity (100% or 50%) and current pension value, with no maximum or minimum limits**
Supplements	Care needs, spouse, dependent children	Care needs, inadequate resources	None
Variations	Higher rate for those disabled early in life, a benefit for severely disabled persons who have insufficient contributions		Rates vary between Old and New *Länder*

Notes

*Entitlement to this short-term incapacity benefit is dependent on having a sufficient contributions record.

**For an average earner, one earnings point corresponds to one contribution year.

Sources: MISSOC 2002; DWP 2003; Sécurité Sociale 2003; CNAMTS 2003; Federal Ministry of Labour and Social Affairs 2003.

Table 25.4   Care benefits for the disabled and their carers, 2003

	Britain	France	Germany
Delivery	Central government	Social Insurance Funds	Social Insurance Funds
The disabled:			
Structure	Range of non-contributory flat-rate benefits to cover costs of home-care	Contributory benefit paid as a supplement to disability, old-age or work-injury pension to cover costs of home-care and some forms of residential care	Contributory benefit delivered in cash and/ or in kind for home care and in kind for residential care
Indicative rates, per month	Rates vary across benefits, and within each benefit depending on level of care needed	Benefit worth 40% of pension, with a minimum amount of €916.32 (£674, $1031)	Rates vary by whether delivered in cash or in kind and whether for home or residential care, as well as by degree of care-need
Supplements	Some benefits have additions to cover cost of mobility needs	None	Aids and appliances; short-term care in a care-centre in absence of main carer
Variations	Local Authorities may fund long-term or temporary respite care in a residential home, dependent on a means-test, as well as home-care support in kind	A supplement to family benefits for disabled children requiring care; regional social assistance schemes may also provide cash benefits for care	A similar set of provisions is available through regional social assistance schemes for those without insurance
The carers:			
Structure	Non-contributory flat-rate benefit*	No provision	No provision
Indicative rates, per month	£186.98 (€254, $286), plus dependant additions		

Note

* Because of its wage-compensation nature this has previously only been available to those under 65 years, but from December 2002 it can be carried over beyond 65.

Sources: DWP 2003; Sécurité Sociale 2003; CNAMTS 2003; Federal Ministry for Health 2003.

Britain, meanwhile, has four separate benefits for care, the applicability of which is differentiated by age, the level of care needed and the cause of disability. All of these benefits are designed to assist the disabled person with the cost of the purchase of home-care. The rate at which they are paid varies across the benefits, and also within each benefit depending on the level of care required. The most common benefit for working-aged disabled persons – Disability Living Allowance – has a care component worth a maximum of £243.75 (€331, $373) per month (DWP 2003). Uniquely among these three countries, Britain also has a specific benefit for carers payable to those who have given up full-time work (defined as at least 35 hours per week) to care for a person in receipt of one of the four disability benefits (DWP 2003). Finally, in France recipients of disability benefits may receive assistance with the costs of care in the form of a 40 per cent supplement to their benefit.

Unemployment benefits

Each of the three countries has a two-tier system of unemployment benefits. In all countries the first tier is contributory, with benefits paid to those with a sufficient contributions record (see Table 25.5). Receipt of these benefits is time limited – up to six months in Britain, 32 months in Germany, and 60 months in France (DWP 2003, Service-Public 2003, Federal Ministry of Labour and Social Affairs 2003). The benefits are fully earnings-related in Germany, where they are also the most generous at 60 per cent of previous net earnings. In France, they combine an earnings-related and flat-rate component, with a fixed minimum of €23.88 (£17.58, $26.87) per day. The British benefit is the least generous, being paid at a flat-rate level of £54.65 (€74, $83) per week.

The second tier in all countries consists of a non-contributory means-tested benefit paid indefinitely to those without a sufficient contributions record or whose entitlement to the first tier contributory benefit has run out. The benefit is most generous in Germany, where it is earnings-related; in the other two countries it is flat-rate.

Minimum safety-net benefits

All three countries have a scheme designed to assist people without sufficient income from other sources – a minimum safety-net scheme often termed social assistance (see Table 25.6). The key characteristic of these schemes in all the countries is the very low level of flat-rate, severely means-tested benefits, although in most cases recipients are also eligible for other support as well, for example in respect of housing costs. Variations in the availability of such other allowances, as well as in the strictness of the means-testing, render the schemes difficult to compare, particularly in respect of generosity (Eardley *et al.* 1996). As an indication, though, the basic rate of the British scheme (Income Support) is £236.82 (€321, $360) per month, while the French *Revenue Minimum*

Table 25.5 Unemployment benefits, 2003

	Britain	France	Germany
Delivery	Central government	Local level Associations for Employment in Industry and Trade	Social Insurance Funds
Structure	Contributory flat-rate benefit conditional on sufficient contributions record; non-contributory flat-rate, means-tested benefit	Contributory partly earnings-related benefit conditional on sufficient contributions record; non-contributory flat-rate means-tested benefit	Contributory earnings-related benefit conditional on sufficient contributions record; non-contributory earnings-related (but means-tested) benefit
Indicative rates	Contributory – £54.65 (€74, \$83) per week; non-contributory – £54.65 (€74, \$83) per week	Contributory – 40.4% of daily wage plus €9.74 (£7.20, \$11) per day (or 57.4% of daily wage if higher), with a floor of €23.88 (£17.58, \$26.87) per day; non-contributory – €13.36 (£10, \$15) per day for long-term unemployed; €9.41 (£7, \$10) for special groups	Contributory – 60% of net earnings; non-contributory – 53% of net earnings
Supplements	Dependants, disabled and carers for those receiving non-contributory benefits	Higher rates in both schemes for older persons	Dependent children
Variations	Rate of both benefits is lower for 16–24 year olds	Partial unemployment scheme to compensate for reductions in working hours caused by economic problems	Partial unemployment scheme to compensate for reductions in working hours caused by economic problems or weather conditions (construction sector); scheme for older workers working part-time; rates vary between Old and New *Länder*

Sources: MISSOC 2002; DWP 2003; Service-Public 2003; Federal Ministry of Labour and Social Affairs 2003.

Table 25.6 Minimum safety-net benefits, 2003

	Britain	*France*	*Germany*
Delivery	Central government	Local Social Insurance Funds (family branch) and local government	Local authorities
General scheme:			
Age eligibility	Generally 18 years +	Generally 25 years +	All
Duration	Indefinite	3–12 months, but renewable	Indefinite
Indicative rates, per month	£236.82 (€321, $360)	€405.62 (£299, $456)	Up to €332 (£245, $373), depending on region
Supplements	Dependants, home-owners, disabled, carers, pensioners	Couples, children	Dependants, old-age, disability, illness, lone parents, pregnant women, housing and heating costs and one-off needs
Variations	Lower rate for 18–24 year olds	None	Rates vary by region
Other specific schemes for:	Old-age pensioners, invalidity, housing costs, council tax charges, one-off and/or urgent expenses	Old-age pensioners, disability, lone parents, some groups of unemployed	Blind persons, housing costs, further education

Sources: MISSOC 2002; DWP 2003; Sécurité Sociale 2003; CAF 2003; Federal Ministry of Labour and Social Affairs 2003.

d'Insertion pays up to €405.62 (£299, $456) and the German *Sozialhilfe* is worth €332 (£245, $373) in the highest-paying authority.

Recent developments

A commonly perceived problem with social security provision in Britain, France and Germany (indeed in most, if not all countries) is its cost, which increased across all three during the 1980s and 1990s. Causes of the increase common to the three include rising unemployment, an ageing population, and an increase in family breakdown, while in Germany re-unification was also a factor. Efforts to contain costs, therefore, have been a key feature of social security reform in the three countries during recent years. Germany, for example, has recently introduced a regulated private old-age pension scheme, and France has recently lengthened the contribution periods required to receive some pensions. While all of the three have been developing 'active labour market programmes' to reduce the pressures exerted on social assistance by unemployment, especially youth unemployment, recent reforms in Britain have also been concerned with improving financial incentives to take up paid work (Lødemel and Trickey 2001).

Sources

CAF (Caisse d'Allocations Familiales)(2003), <www.caf.fr> [15 December 2003].

CNAMTS (Caisse Nationale d'Assurance Maladie des Travailleurs Salariés)(2003), <www.cnamts.fr> /www.ameli.fr> [15 December 2003].

CNAV (Caisse Nationale d'Assurance Vieillesse)(2003), <www.cnav.fr> [15 December 2003].

DWP (Department of Work and Pensions)(2003), <www.dwp.gov.uk> [15 December 2003].

T. Eardley, J. Bradshaw, J. Ditch, I. Gough and P. Whiteford, *Social Assistance in OECD Countries: Synthesis Report*, DSS Research Report No. 46 (London: HMSO, 1996).

Federal Ministry of Health (2003), <www.bmgesundheit.de> [15 December 2003].

Federal Ministry of Labour and Social Affairs (2003), <www.bma.de> [15 December 2003].

I. Lødemel and H. Trickey, *'An Offer You Can't Refuse': Workfare in International Perspective* (Bristol: Policy Press, 2001).

MISSOC (Mutual Information System on Social Protection in the EU Member States and the EEA)(2002), <www.europa.eu.int/comm/employment_social/missoc2002/> [15 December 2003].

Sécurité Sociale (2003), <www.securite-sociale.fr/> [15 December 2003].

Service-Public (2003), <www.service-public.fra> [15 December 2003].

26
Social Services
Majella Kilkey

Introduction

Britain, France and Germany exhibit both similarities and differences in respect of their social services. In all three countries, the organization of social services is devolved to local government agencies: Social Services Departments in Britain, *Centres communaux d'action sociaux* in France and Offices of Social Assistance, Youth Welfare and Health in Germany. Germany is distinct from the other two in that historically it has been the not-for-profit sector or voluntary sector which has delivered the services, receiving funding from central government and being regulated by law. This sector has been dominated by about six large organizations linked to religious denominations and political parties. In contrast, in Britain and France local government retains greater responsibility but increasingly contracts out service provision to the private sector. In Britain, services are as likely to be contracted out to for-profit providers as to voluntary organizations. A further difference between these countries, especially in the area of services to older people, is that there is greater reliance on funding via individuals' social insurance in France and Germany, while general taxation is the main source of funding in Britain.

The nature of social services

The terminology used to describe this area of state activity varies across countries. In Britain it is usually referred to as 'personal social services', while elsewhere it may be called 'social welfare services' or 'social care services' (Munday 1996). What is common to all countries is the emphasis upon the provision of non-cash services, largely in the field of care. Countries vary, however, in the extent to which such in-kind support is combined with cash benefits. In both France and Germany, social services are situated within the broader framework of social assistance, and it is difficult to differentiate their social service provisions from their cash benefit systems. Even in Britain, where historically the activities of social services focused on in-kind provisions, this distinction is increasingly hard to maintain due to the emergence of payments for care within the social security system.

There is perhaps more commonality across countries in terms of which groups are the focus of social services. In all countries older people, children and families, people with disabilities and illnesses, young people, those with addictions, and the socially excluded more generally, are target client groups (for details see Table 26.1). This list indicates that the work of social services may be focused on the most vulnerable in society. Certainly in Britain the emphasis is on working with the most marginalized, but social services in France and Germany combine work with 'at risk' groups with universal provisions for the whole population. This is especially the case in the area of mother and child health. The difference exists in part because in France and Germany it is difficult to draw a line between health services and social services, while in Britain there is a clear differentiation between the two.

In all three countries responsibility for social services has been delegated to local governments. Central government, through the Department of Health in Britain, the Ministry for Social Affairs in France and the Ministry for Health and Health Insurance in Germany, defines and regulates the responsibilities of local government in the field of social services. In France and Germany, where social services may also include cash payments, central government also fix minimum and maximum levels of payments. In Britain, central government general taxation is the main source of funding for social services, although local governments can also use revenue gathered from local taxes. In France, social services are funded by a combination of general taxation and, on an individual basis, social insurance funds. German local authorities can also expect individuals to draw on their social insurance funds to pay for certain services. In addition, local taxes are used to fund services; rarely does central government provide direct funding to the local level for this purpose.

In all three countries, however, local government is not the only service provider. Social services might be described as having a 'mixed economy of welfare' in that there are a variety of actors involved in delivering provision: local government, the informal sector, the not-for-profit sector and the for-profit sector. The balance between the responsibilities of each of these actors varies across countries. While it is in Germany that service provision is most skewed towards the not-for-profit sector, a common trend in both Britain and France is for local government agencies to contract provision to the private sector while retaining a supervisory role, particularly in respect of quality.

Table 26.1 The nature of social services

	Britain	France	Germany
Older people	Residential services, community services, home-based care services	Residential services, community services, home-based care, discretionary financial assistance	Residential services, community services, home-based care, discretionary financial assistance
Families and children	Child protection services, residential care, foster care, adoption services, aftercare services, family centres	Child protection services, residential care, foster care, adoption services, home-based support services, discretionary financial assistance, mother and infant health services	Child protection services, residential care, foster care, adoption services, family education and counselling services, shelters for women, discretionary financial assistance, mother and infant health services
People with disabilities	Residential services, community services, home-based care services, sheltered housing, employment training and placement services	Residential services, community services, home-based care services, employment training and placement services, discretionary financial assistance	Residential services, community services, home-based care services, employment training and placement services, discretionary financial assistance
Young people	Some youth offending services	Sport and leisure facilities, holiday camps	Sport and leisure facilities
People with addictions	Some counselling and support services	Preventive services, counselling services, residential services	Preventive services, counselling services, self-help groups
People with physical illness	Resettlement after hospitalization	Resettlement after hospitalization	Discretionary financial assistance with medical costs
Socially excluded	Housing support for homeless families with children, sites for travellers	Housing support for the homeless, discretionary financial assistance for various groups, including long-term unemployed, supervision of ex-prisoners and servers of non-custodial sentences	Housing support for the homeless, residential accommodation for ex-prisoners, discretionary financial assistance for various groups, including long-term unemployed

Sources: Munday and Ely 1996; Pacolet *et al.* 1999; Pringle 1998.

Specific comparisons

Due in part to their delivery at the level of local government, and in part to their 'mixed economy', it is notoriously difficult to obtain comparative information on social services. The focus here is on two client groups that have had a high political and policy profile in recent years, as this high profile has resulted in the emergence of at least some comparative material. The first is older people, who because of the ageing of European populations are probably the largest category of people receiving care in Europe, and around whom there is considerable debate about the ability of welfare states to respond to their care needs. The second is families and children, upon whom the issue of child abuse has focused attention.

Social services for older people

Social services for older people in the three countries fall into three broad categories: residential services, community services and domiciliary or home-based services (see Table 26.2 for details). Local authorities take on a variety of roles across the three countries in respect of these services: they may be a direct provider of the service as in the case of public residential care homes for the elderly, or they may contract out services to the private sector either to not-for-profit voluntary organizations or to for-profit providers. In the latter case, local authorities will take on the role of inspecting and monitoring the quality of provision. In Britain, but not in the other two countries, local authorities also take the lead in assessing the care needs of individuals and, on the basis of the assessment, in designing, purchasing (either from the local authority itself or from private providers) and monitoring a package of care.

Residential services may provide permanent or temporary care in institutions such as nursing homes, old-age homes or sheltered housing. While temporary hospital services are part of social services provision for older people in France and Germany, in Britain these are the responsibility of the National Health Service. All of the countries share the view that the main objective of their overall package of services is to enable individuals to remain in their own homes for as long as possible (Hennessy 1995). The result is that over the last couple of decades there has been a shift away from residential provision towards home-based services supplemented by services provided within the community. Community-based provision in all of the countries includes day-care and social centres. The latter, in particular, are designed to counter the isolation that older people living alone may experience. In addition, community-based foyer restaurants are common in France and Germany. Home-based services in all of the countries include assistance with basic domestic tasks such as cleaning, laundry and cooking. Increasingly, however, as home-based services are targeted on the most frail and disabled older people, these also include help with personal

Table 26.2 Types of care services for older people within social services

	Britain	France	Germany
Permanent residential services	Nursing homes, old-age homes, multi-level homes, sheltered housing	Nursing homes, old-age homes, sheltered housing, service flats	Nursing homes, old-age homes, multi-level homes, sheltered housing
Temporary residential services	Short-term nursing homes, short stay in old-age homes	Short-term nursing homes, short stay in old-age homes, hospital services	Short-term nursing homes, short stay in old-age homes, hospital services
Home and community services	Day care, social centres, social work, home help services, cleaning services, meal distribution, transport services, sitting/respite services, home adaptation, aids and facilities	Day care, social centres, social work, home help services, cleaning services, odd job services, meal distribution, foyer restaurant, transport services, sitting/respite services, home adaptation, aids and facilities, district nursing services	Day care, social centres, home help services, meal distribution, foyer restaurant, district nursing services, health advisory services and health education

Source: Pacolet *et al.* 1999.

care such as bathing and dressing (Pacolet *et al.* 1999). In Britain and France this also includes respite care and sitting services to support carers. As with residential services, home-based services in France and Germany include health care such as district nursing. While Britain also has a system of district nursing, this falls under the remit of the local health authority.

It is difficult to establish reliable estimates of the prevalence of the different types of social service provision for older people, particularly on a comparative basis (Pacolet *et al.* 1999). One estimate suggests that the percentage of the population aged over 65 in residential care during the mid-1990s was very similar across the three countries at around 5 per cent (Hennessy 1995). The same source, however, demonstrates that the use of residential care by older people increases quite considerably with age. This is especially the case in Britain: more than 20 per cent of the 80–4 years population is in residential care, compared with 15 per cent in France. Other data indicate that the most common form of residential care is sheltered housing in Britain, old-age homes in France and multi-level homes in Germany (Pacolet *et al.* 1999). The use of home-care services by the over 65 population is greater than residential care in Britain and France, where 9 and 7 per cent respectively receive some form of home help, but in Germany it is less, with an estimated 1–3 per cent in receipt of home care (Hennessy 1995).

While in all of the countries very few of the social service provisions for older people are free at the point of use, the degree to which, and the mechanisms by which, older people are expected to pay for services varies between them (see Table 26.3). Germany has perhaps the most comprehensive system. Its statutory compulsory long-term care insurance scheme can be received either in kind or in cash to cover both residential and home care. Additionally, for those remaining at home, the insurance may cover the costs of aids and appliances, training for family carers and respite care. A substitute source of financial assistance is the local social assistance scheme, which is available to those with insufficient resources. This covers most of the services recognized within the insurance scheme, and can also be received in cash or in kind.

France also has a social insurance benefit, which is available to those who were assessed prior to the age of 65 as in need of the constant aid of a third party. It is paid as a supplement to the old-age pension and can be received in cash to enable an individual to purchase home- or residential- based care. Unlike the German scheme, however, it does not cover in-kind home-care provisions. The social assistance safety-net can also intervene to support those with insufficient resources to pay for their care. This takes the form of a cash benefit for those over the age of 60 who need the constant aid of a third party, which can be used for either home or residential care as well as for in-kind provisions for those remaining at home.

Finally, Britain is unique in providing a cash benefit both to older people in need of care and to their informal carers. Unlike the case in the other two

Table 26.3 Paying for care services provided for older people, 2003

	Britain	France	Germany
Cash benefits for home-care:			
Paid to the older person	Central non-contributory flat-rate benefit. Payment varies according to the impact of disability, but maximum rate is £243.75 (€331, $373) per month.	(i) Compulsory social insurance benefit worth 40% of old-age pension, minimum rate €916.32 (£674.41, $1030.86) per month; (ii) means-tested local social assistance benefit. Rate varies according to need and locality.	(i) Compulsory statutory long-term care insurance pays a benefit worth up to €665 (£489, $748) per month; (ii) means-tested local social assistance benefit may provide the same benefits as under long-term care insurance.
Paid to the carers	Central non-contributory flat-rate benefit, available to those who have given up full-time work to care, of £186.98 (€254, $286) per month, plus dependant additions.	No provision.	No provision.
In-kind benefits for home-care	Local authorities provide some services free of charge and means-test others.	The means-tested local social assistance benefit may be received in-kind.	(i) Long-term care insurance benefit can be received in kind up to the value of €1917 (£1411, $2157) per month, and additional resources may be provided; (ii) social assistance may meet needs and provide additional resources.
Paying for residential care	Whether and how much local authorities contribute to the costs depends on the resources of the individual.	Social insurance and social assistance benefits can contribute towards the costs.	(i) Long-term care insurance can cover elements of residential care costs up to €1687 (£1242, $1898) per month; (ii) social assistance may meet some costs.

Sources: MISSOC 2002; DWP 2003; Service-Public 2003; Federal Ministry of Labour and Social Affairs 2003.

countries, both of these are non-contributory benefits. There is less flexibility in the British system: the cash benefit, for example, is strictly for home care and cannot be used to pay for residential care. Residential care fees may be met by the local authority, but, in England and Wales at least, assistance with fees depends on the resources of the individual requiring care. Local authorities also means-test most in-kind provisions used to support home-care.

Social services for families and children

In respect of what is included under the umbrella of social services for families and children, Britain differs quite markedly from both France and Germany (Pringle 1998). In the first place, while the responsibilities of local social service agencies in Britain around families and children are heavily oriented towards the protection of children at risk from abuse (neglect or physical, sexual or emotional abuse), in France and Germany there is a greater emphasis on both providing universal rather than targeted services and intervening in a wider range of spheres. Thus, in France and Germany local social services include provision for the health of mothers, infants and young children in the form, for example, of health visitors, school health services and health education and promotion. Moreover, in both countries the material well-being of families and children is also a concern of local social services, and local social assistance schemes can be used to direct financial resources to families in need (Madge and Attridge 1996; Pringle 1998). Secondly, even in respect of child protection Britain differs from the other two countries in that its services are overwhelmingly reactive, while in France and Germany the emphasis is more strongly on prevention and therapy (Pringle 1998). To this end, for example, child protection services in France and Germany can include cash support for vulnerable families.

A degree of similarity between the three countries, however, is demonstrated in the provisions made for children without families and for children whom it has been necessary to remove from family care. The options in such cases in all countries are residential care (either provided directly by local social services departments or contracted to not-for-profit or, more rarely, for-profit providers), foster care and adoption. While the trend in all of the countries has been towards a decline in the use of residential care, and an increased emphasis on foster care, this has been most marked in Britain, where at any one point in time around two-thirds of all children in public care are cared for via foster placements (DoH 2003; Madge and Attridge 1996).

Recent developments

The ageing of the population is recognized as a common pressure across these three countries, but while in France and Germany the current debate is focused largely on financing pensions, in Britain the issue of meeting the long-term care needs of an increasingly older population remains high on the political agenda. This is partly because, unlike the other two countries, the social insurance system does not extend into this area of need. The question of the quality of services is also being debated in these three countries. In the case of Britain and France this has emerged in part within the context of the increasing tendency to contract service provision out to the private sector. While Germany's use of the voluntary sector to deliver services is longstanding, it is also facing concerns about quality given the almost monopoly position of several large voluntary organizations. One aspect of quality that is being debated in all countries is the extent of 'user involvement', that is, the degree to which the users of the services actually have a voice in shaping the services they receive. This issue is currently of concern in most aspects of public welfare.

Sources

J. Baldock and P. Ely, 'Social care for elderly people in Europe: The central problem of home care', in *Social Care in Europe*, eds B. Munday and P. Ely (London: Prentice Hall Harvester Wheatsheaf, 1996).

DoH (Department of Health)(2003), <www.doh.gov.uk/HPSSS/TBL> [15 December 2003].

DWP (Department of Work and Pensions)(2003), <www.dwp.gov.uk> [15 December 2003].

Federal Ministry of Labour and Social Affairs (2003), <www.bma.de> [15 December 2003].

P. Hennessy, *Social Protection for Dependent Elderly People: Perspectives from a Review of OECD Countries*, Labour Market and Social Policy Occasional Paper, No. 16 (Paris: OECD, 1995).

N. Madge and K. Attridge, 'Children and families', in *Social Care in Europe*, eds B. Munday and P. Ely (London: Prentice Hall Harvester Wheatsheaf, 1996).

MISSOC (Mutual Information System on Social Protection in the EU Member States and the EEA)(2002), <www.europa.eu.int/comm/employment_social/missoc2002/> [15 December 2003].

B. Munday, 'Introduction. Definitions and comparisons in European social care', in *Social Care in Europe*, eds. B. Munday and P. Ely (London: Prentice Hall Harvester Wheatsheaf, 1996).

J. Pacolet, R. Bouten, H. Lanoye and K. Versieck, *Social Protection for Dependency in Old Age in the 15 EU Member States and Norway* (Luxembourg: Office for Official Publications of the European Communities, 1999).

K. Pringle, *Children and Social Welfare in Europe* (Buckingham: Open University Press, 1998).

Service-Public (2003), <www.service-public.fra> [15 December 2003].

27
Education

Cecile Deer and Stephanie Wilde

Introduction

Education as part of public policy in Britain, France and Germany has developed very much in parallel and with broad similarities since the end of the 19th century, but significant differences exist between the three countries in the role played by public authorities, the degree of autonomy of educational institutions, and the organisation of qualifications and of the teaching profession.

The nature of public policy in education

Public policy in education is concerned with the role of government in the formal provision, financing and/or regulation of educational services at a range of different levels. Broadly defined, it covers any part of the formal educational process directly or indirectly influenced by public decisions at local or national level. Public policy in education is therefore concerned with issues of funding and implementation, access policy and evaluation procedures, curricula and examinations, and teacher recruitment and training. In all three countries, educational public policy operates within the comparative and harmonizing European agenda of initiatives such as the PISA project and the European Credit Transfer System in higher education.

Overall government spending on education in relation to Gross Domestic Product (GDP) is higher in France than in Britain and Germany. However while France spends significantly more per student in secondary schooling, Britain spends significantly more per student in higher education. Funding is predominantly by the central government in France and by regional government in Germany. In Britain most funding comes from local government, which in turn is predominantly funded by central government (see Table 27.1).

There are also differences in the way that the education systems are administered (see Table 27.2) In Britain, education is administered at regional level and

Table 27.1 Expenditure on education, 1998

Indicator	Britain	France	Germany
Total public expenditure on education as % GDP	4.9	6	4.6
Total public expenditure on education as % total public expenditure	11.9	11.3	9.8
Total public expenditure on educational institutions as % GDP			
– Primary, secondary, and post-secondary non-tertiary	3.4	4.1	2.8
– Tertiary	0.8	1.0	1.0
% of funding from public sources:			
– Primary, secondary, post-secondary non-tertiary	na	92.7	75.9
– Tertiary	62.7	85.5	92.1
Expenditure per student on public and private institutions			
Primary	$3329 (£2151, €3296)	$3752 (£2423, €3714)	$3531 (£2281, €3496)
Secondary	$5230 (£3379, €5178)	$6605 (£4267, €6539)	$6209 (£4011, €6147)
Tertiary (all)	$9699 (£6266, €9602)	$7226 (£4668, €7154)	$9481 (£6125, €9386)
% of funding of primary, secondary and post-secondary non-tertiary education by level of government, 1997			
– central government	21	73	5
– regional government	–	11	77
– local government	79	16	18

Note Currency conversions to pounds and euros use 1998 PPPs.
Source: OECD 2001, 2002.

organized at municipal level. In France, compulsory education is defined at central level and organized essentially through geographical administrative divisions (*académies*) headed by government-appointed civil servants (*recteurs*) directly answerable to the Minister. However political divisions (*régions*, *départements*, *municipalités*) are also important. The *départements* are both decentralized territorial authorities with an elected assembly (*Conseil Général*) and an administrative stratum of the State headed by a government-appointed civil servant (*préfet*). The *municipalités* are responsible for the building, maintenance and administrative control of elementary schools, but need the agreement of the *préfet* to open or close a school or a class. In Germany, the 1949 Basic Law (*Grundgesetz*) spells out the legal and administrative responsibilities for education. Each *Land* is responsible for its own primary, secondary, tertiary and adult/continuing

Table 27.2   Administration and funding of education

	Britain	France	Germany
Departments	Department for Education and Skills (DFES)	Ministère de l'Education Nationale (MEN)	Land Ministries of Education and Cultural Affairs and Science
Agencies	Local Education Authorities (LEAs) Teacher Training Authority (TTA) Qualifications & Curriculum Authority (QCA) Office for Standards in Education (Ofsted)	Académies Rectorats Préfectures Conseils municipaux, généraux and régionaux	Regional authorities (Bezirksregierung/ Oberschulamt) Schools' offices at local level (Schulamt) National government (higher education)

education policy. The Federal Government legislates on the overall organisation of higher education and can co-operate with the *Länder* in areas such as planning and research. The *Länder* also finance and manage the schooling part of the dual system of initial vocational training (school and work placement, involving two-thirds of all young people), while workplace activities are supervised at national level by public-law corporations. Staff inspection and supervision are carried out in each *Land* by school supervisory authorities.

All three countries have a private education sector (denominational, commercial, independent). In Britain, state schools may be denominational. The private/ independent sector is not large – approximately 7 per cent of the total school population, with strong regional disparities – but it is influential. It is subsidized by public authorities through tax allowances and grants. In France, all state schools are constitutionally non-denominational. The independent sector caters for roughly one-sixth of the schools population. Most non-state schools are Catholic schools (85 per cent) with contractual agreements with the State whereby the latter assumes considerable funding responsibility, in particular for teachers' pay, in return for a large degree of compliance with the centrally-defined national educational policies. In Germany, denominational schools may be authorized and, in some cases, subsidized by the *Länder*.

Specific comparisons

In this section the various levels of education are examined in more detail: pre-primary schooling, compulsory primary and secondary schooling, non-compulsory upper secondary education, and higher education (HE).

Pre-primary schooling

The provision and organisation of pre-primary schooling is very different in Britain, France and Germany. In Britain, the level of funding per pupil in pre-primary education is higher and the teacher-student ratio lower than in Germany and France but participation rates across age groups are higher in France than in Germany and Britain (see Table 27.3).

In France, state pre-primary schooling is free and available for 2–5 year olds on a non-compulsory basis for 26 hours per week in either *écoles maternelles* (nursery schools) or in *classes enfantines* (infant classes) attached to primary schools. Public pre-primary provision is run at local level by the *communes* but its general aims and curriculum are defined by central government, as are staff salaries and training. *Académie* inspectors decide whether to open or close classes in state pre-elementary or special schools. They also allocate teaching jobs in each *département*.

In England and Wales, central government subsidizes nursery schooling for four-year-olds through a voucher scheme. Pre-primary provision is organized

Table 27.3 Pre-primary schooling

	Britain	France	Germany
Responsibility for provision	Local Education Authorities (LEAs) Voluntary sector Private sector	*Communes* (municipalities) run nursery schools but their activities are determined at central level	Voluntary sector (70%) *Länder* (30%)
Funding	LEA Voucher scheme	State provision: free Private provision: fee paying	Fee paying (regional subsidies)
Total expenditure per pre-primary pupil (full-time equivalents, 1998)	$4910 (£3172, €4861)	$3609 (£2331, €3573)	$4648 (£3003, €4602)
Participation rates at different ages	2: – 3: 48% (1997) 4: 97% (1997) 5: –	2: 35.2% (2000) 3: 100% (2000) 4: 100% (2000) 5: 100% (2000)	3: 54.3% (1999) 4: 83.5% (1999) 5: 90.7% (1999)
Student–teacher ratio in state pre-school education (1998)	21.5	25.5	23.2

Sources: Eurydice 2001; OECD 2001; MEN 2002.

at local level on a non-compulsory basis apart from special needs. There are four types of provision: day nurseries, pre-school groups or playgroups, nursery schools or classes and reception classes at primary school (England and Wales only, from age four). The Office for Standards in Education (OFSTED) is responsible for inspecting pre-school provision in England.

In Germany, pre-school education provision varies from *Land* to *Land* as its responsibility lies with the *Land* social ministries. There are fee-paying *kindergärten* for children aged three to six, which are run by non-governmental institutions such as churches and welfare associations but largely subsidized by public money.

Compulsory schooling (primary and secondary)

In all three countries, compulsory public education is provided free of charge at the point of delivery.

Primary schools are not officially selective in any of the three countries. French and German teachers in state primary and secondary schools have civil servant status and are recruited on the basis of a competitive examination. In Britain, schoolteachers are not civil servants and are employed either by the local education authority or by the school governing body.

In Britain and France, most state secondary schools are not officially selective at entrance, with the exception of a dwindling number of grammar schools in Britain. In France, pupils enrol in state schools according to stricter catchment area rules than in Britain. No formal class streaming is allowed but pupils are divided into classes according to their choice of optional subjects. In Germany, pupils are streamed into separate secondary state schools at an early stage (see Table 27.4).

Table 27.4   Compulsory education (primary and secondary)

	Britain	*France*	*Germany*
Age range during which schooling is compulsory	5–16 (4–16 in Northern Ireland)	6–16	6–15/16, depending on *Land*
Primary school age range	5–11/Key stages 1 and 2	6–11/Cycles	6–10
Lower secondary age ranges and types of schools	(11–16) – Comprehensive – Grammar – Specialist – Independent	(12–15) *Collèges* (15–16) *Lycées*	(11–16) – *Gymnasium* – *Realschule* – *Hauptschule* – *Gesamtschule*
Teacher-student ratio in state sector primary education, 1998	22.0	22.4	21.6

Sources: Eurydice 2001; OECD 2002; MEN 2002.

Table 27.5 Lower secondary education: level of decision

Type of decision	Britain	France	Germany
Choice of textbooks	School	School	School (with *Land* approval)
Design of programmes on offer	Central	Central	*Land*
Selection of programs on offer	School (framework at central level)	Central	*Land*
Range of subjects taught	Central	Central	School (framework at *Land* level)
Teachers' salaries in public lower-secondary education after 15 years experience, 1998	$38,010 (£24,554, €37,630)	$29,615 (£19,131, €29,319)	$38,640 (£24,961, €38,254)

Note Currency conversions to pounds and euros use 1998 PPPs.
Sources: Eurydice 2001, OECD 2002.

In Britain and France the central government fixes the national curriculum guidelines and targets but does not prescribe textbooks or pedagogical practice (see Table 27.5). In Britain, pupil assessment and examinations are organized at school level through autonomous examination boards whose activities are guided by regional qualification authorities. In France, pupils' assessments and examinations follow rules that are set nationally and organized at regional level. In Germany, the *Länder* ministries determine the curriculum and approve the textbooks. Pupil assessment and examinations depend on the type of school and vary from *Land* to *Land*.

The autonomy of action of British educational institutions at all levels is greater than that of their French and German counterparts. The reverse is true for individual teachers' professional autonomy. In Britain, regional bodies such as the Office for Standards in Education (OFSTED) in England are responsible for inspection. In France, primary school teachers are inspected by national education inspectors, while teachers in secondary schools are inspected by regional inspectors. In Germany, inspection is organized on a regional basis by school supervisory authorities.

Non-compulsory upper secondary level

In all three countries this is a politically sensitive area of educational public policy as it constitutes the entrance path to higher education or the job market. In England, all non-HE post-16 education and training is the responsibility of the Learning and Skills Council for England through a network of local Learning and Skills Councils. Schools and Sixth Form Colleges (for ages 16–18) provide general teaching, Further Education Colleges (16+) provide vocational training and Tertiary Colleges (16+) provide both. Curricula depend on various regulatory bodies. Students may apply to any institution offering their choice of course.

In France, there are three types of *lycées*: general, technological and vocational. These provide preparation for various types of *baccalauréat* on a basis of compulsory and non-compulsory subjects taught in accordance with national curricula. The relative importance of the subjects studied is weighted (time and marks) according to the type of *baccalauréat* prepared (literary, scientific, vocational etc.).

In Germany, general teaching is provided at the *Gymnasiale Oberstufe* (16–19) where studies are chosen from three subject groups: Arts, Social Sciences and Sciences. Vocational training (ages 15–16 to 18–19) is available at the *Berufsfachschule* full-time and alongside more general teaching, at the *Fachoberschule*, and in the dual system of training and work placement. Admission requirements for full-time vocational education depend on the type of school chosen but the dual system is open to all secondary school leavers. The school curricula are defined by the *Länder*.

Higher education

In Britain, France and Germany higher education is funded mainly by central government. In all three countries this is increasingly a source of contention. British universities as institutions are more autonomous than German ones, which in turn are more autonomous than their French counterparts. This is particularly true concerning budgets and staffing. In Britain, publicly funded higher education institutions come essentially in the form of selective multidisciplinary universities. As in France, their teaching activities are centrally funded according to centrally defined criteria. Undergraduate fees have been undifferentiated so far, but this is changing and the government intends to allow universities to charge up to £3000 (€4077, $4587) annual tuition fees on a means-tested basis. Non-EU students pay full-cost fees. Selective funding for research activities is determined by the results of four-yearly, disciplinary-based nationwide research assessment exercises.

In France and Germany there are two separate types of higher education: the non-selective universities and the more selective higher vocational schools. In France, university study is open to anyone with a *baccalauréat* or equivalent but a number of university institutes impose selection at entrance. There is also a selective public-funded non-university sector comprising higher vocational schools (*grandes écoles*) attended by some 8 per cent of students. The universities and *grandes écoles* are mostly teaching institutions. There is an annual budget and four-year contractual agreements for university funding. Administrative fees of between €95 and €177 (£70–130, $100–200) are paid by university students and these are not differentiated for non-EU students. Universities may offer two types of degree: state degrees recognized nationally (in particular for taking competitive public service examinations) and university degrees. Publicly funded research is carried out in the various research institutes and in separately-funded research units of the *Centre National de la Recherche Scientifique* (CNRS), which are often based in the universities. University institutes and schools are created by governmental decree.

In Germany, passing the *Zeugnis der Allgemeinen Hochschulreife* entitles the holder to continue to higher education regardless of the institution and the subject chosen. The *Zeugnis der Fachgebundenen Hochschulreife* entitles the holder to study any subjects at the higher education level without selection unless a course is oversubscribed. Studies at publicly funded higher education institutions are free of charge. The universities take about 70 per cent of students, with the remainder attending the *Fachhochschulen* (higher vocational schools). The new Bachelor's and Master's Study Courses were accompanied by an accreditation procedure to guarantee minimum standards in terms of academic content and to check the vocational relevance of the degrees.

Recent trends

In all three countries, educational public policy has been guided by the claimed necessity to make formal education more relevant to the outside world through the vocationalization of existing curricula and/or the setting up of vocational tracks and courses. Recent public guidelines concerning primary schooling have placed a renewed emphasis on basic apprenticeship. In secondary schools the acquisition of non-academic skills and continuous assessment have been encouraged. In higher education, joint degrees, optional subjects, credit accumulation systems, multidisciplinary and vocational higher degrees have been encouraged.

In Britain and France, the comprehensive ethos at lower secondary school level is being questioned in the face of the growing diversity of the pupil intake.

In Britain there have been increasing legal and administrative constraints from central government, which has reinforced its role in the formal delivery of education services at all levels. The National Curriculum was introduced in 1988 and revised in September 2000 to allow for greater emphasis on perceived key areas. This trend has been partly reversed since devolution of certain powers to the Scottish Parliament and Welsh Assembly, with the administration of education being carried out at regional level. At the same time, state schools have been allowed to become increasingly autonomous in tackling the educational market. Catchment areas have been abolished and replaced by parental choice and school admissions policies determined by each school's governing body or the local authorities, with right of appeal for unsuccessful applicants.

During the same period, educational public policy in France has been characterized by decentralizing measures at regional, local and institutional level. Regional authorities have been made responsible for the building and maintenance of upper-secondary schools (*lycées*) and given considerable powers regarding vocational training. In the *départements*, the *préfets* have lost most of their executive powers to the *conseils généraux*, which have also been made responsible for school transport and the maintenance and building of lower-secondary schools (*collèges*). Catchment rules for enrolment have been applied less stringently. State schools have been encouraged to be autonomous within the limits of government imposed rules, hence the development of mission statements. In higher education, up to 50 per cent of the funding for the 'Université 2000' development plan (8 new universities, 24 *Instituts Universitaires de Technologie*) was provided by the regions. The development of contractual agreements between the State and higher education institutions has formed part of a significant general evolution in French public policy. The cost of public education, in particular teachers' pay, remains the responsibility of central government.

In all three countries the main funding issue concerns the role of public authorities in funding the non-compulsory part of education, in particular pre-primary and tertiary education. In England the government has recently set up the Sure Start programme to support pre-primary children's welfare and education, and the stated government aim is universal free nursery provision for three-year-olds by 2004. In Germany the adequate funding of pre-primary schooling provision was the focus of public debates during the 2002 general election. In Britain and Germany, direct public expenditure for tertiary education has seen a slight decrease whilst direct private expenditure has been on the increase. The reverse has been true in France (see Table 27.6).

Finally, evaluation has played an increasing part in the steering of higher education by public authorities. In Britain, research assessment exercises and

Table 27.6   Index of change in direct expenditure for educational institutions, 1998 (1995 = 100)

	Britain	France	Germany
Public – Primary and secondary	108	106	102
Private – Primary and secondary educational institutions	Missing data	102	101
Public – Tertiary educational institutions	99	107	99
Private – Tertiary educational institutions	105	97	107

Source: OECD 2001.

teaching quality assessments have been controversially implemented. In France the *Comité National d'Evaluation* was set up in 1985 in parallel with the contractual agreements with the task of evaluating higher education firstly on an institutional basis and then on a subject and regional basis. In Germany, an amendment to the Framework Act of Higher Education of 1998 provided for compulsory teaching quality assessment. So far, however, the results of these evaluation procedures have not been used for selective higher education funding in either France or Germany.

Sources

Arbeitsgruppe Bildungsbericht am Max-Planck-Institut für Bildungsforschung, *Das Bildungswesen in der Bundesrepublik Deutschland* (Reinbek: Rowohlt, 1994).

J.L. Boursin and F. Leblond, *L'administration de l'Education nationale* (Paris: Presses Universitaires de France, 1998).

P. Broadfoot, *Perceptions of Teaching: Primary School Teachers in England and France* (London: Cassell, 1993).

C. Chitty, *The Education System Transformed* (Tisbury: Baseline Book Company, 1999).

A. Corbett and B. Moon (eds), *Education Reforms in France: Change in the Mitterrand years 1981–1995* (London: Routledge, 1996).

C. Deer, *Higher Education in England and France since the 1980s* (Oxford: Symposium, 2002).

Department for Education and Skills (DFES), <www.dfes.gov.uk/index.htm> [27 April 2003].

J. Docking (ed.), *New Labour's Policy for Schools: Raising the Standards?* (London: David Fulton Publishers, 2000).

European Commission, *European Education Thesaurus* (Luxembourg: Office for Official Publications of the European Communities, 1991).

European Commission, *Structures of the Education and Initial Training Systems in the European Union* (Luxembourg: Office for Official Publications of the European Communities, 1995).

European Commission, *Key Topics in Education: Financing and Management of Resources in Compulsory Education: Trends in National Policies*, vol. 2 (Luxembourg: Office for Official Publications of the European Communities, 1999).

EURYDICE Education in Europe, <www.eurydice.org/accueil_menu/en/frameset_menu.html> [27 April 2003].

E. Friedberg and C. Musselin, *L'Etat face aux Universités en France et en Allemagne* (Paris: Anthropos, 1993).

Christoph Führ, *The German Education System Since 1945: Outlines and Problems* (Bonn: Inter Nationes, 1997).

German Federal Institute of Vocational Education, <www.bibb.de>

German Federal Ministry of Education, <www.bmbf.de>

German Federal Ministry of Education, Report on vocational education in Germany, <www.bmbf.de/pub/bbb2003.pdf>

German Federal Office of Statistics (education), <www.destatis.de/themen/d/thm_bildung.htm>

A. Green, *Education, Globalization and the Nation State* (London: Macmillan – now Palgrave Macmillan, 1997).

Her Majesty's Stationery Office (HMSO), <www.hmso.gov.uk> [27 April 2003].

A. Green, A. Wolf and T. Leney, *Convergence and Divergence in European Education and Training Systems*, Bedford Way Papers (London: Institute of Education University of London, 1999).

H.-J. Hahn, *Education and Society in Germany* (Oxford: Berg, 1998).

Higher Education Statistics Agency (HESA), <www.hesa.ac.uk> [27 April 2003].

INSEE (Institut National de la Statistique et des Etudes Economiques), *Annuaire Statistique de la France* (Paris: INSEE).

Journal Officiel, <www.journal-officiel.gouv.fr/> [27 April 2003].

Kultusministerkonferenz (Standing Committee of the Ministers of Education of the sixteen *Länder*), <www.kmk.org>

D. Lawton, *The Tory Mind on Education, 1979–94* (London: Falmer, 1994).

Gero Lenhardt and Manfred Stock, *Bildung, Bürger, Arbeitskraft: Schulentwicklung und Sozialstruktur in der BRD und der DDR* (Frankfurt am Main: Suhrkamp, 1997).

Achim Leschinsky and Karl Ulrich Mayer (eds), *The Comprehensive School Experiment Revisited: Evidence From Western Europe* (Frankfurt am Main: Lang, 1999).

D. Mackinnon, D. Newbould and D. Zeldin with M. Hales, *Education in Western Europe: Facts and Figures* (London: Hodder and Stoughton in association with the Open University, 1997).

D. Mackinnon, J. Statham and M. Hales, *Education in the UK: Facts and Figures* (London: Hodder and Stoughton in association with the Open University, 1995).

Max-Planck-Institute of Educational Research, <www.mpib-berlin.mpg.de>

MEN (Ministère de la Jeunesse, de l'Education nationale et de la Recherche), *Repères et références statistiques sur les enseignements, la formation et la recherche* (Paris: MEN, 2001 and 2002).

MEN (Ministère de la Jeunesse, de l'Education nationale et de la Recherche), <www.education.gouv.fr/index.php> [27 April 2003].

OECD (Organisation for Economic Co-operation and Development), *Vocational Training in Germany: Modernisation and Responsiveness* (Paris: OECD, 1994).

OECD (Organisation for Economic Co-operation and Development), *Secondary Education in France: A Decade of Change* (Paris: OECD, 1995).

OECD (Organisation for Economic Co-operation and Development), *Education at a Glance* (Paris: OECD, 1998, 2001, 2002).

OECD (Organisation for Economic Co-operation and Development), *OECD Education Database*, <www1.oecd.org/scripts/cde/viewbase.asp?DBNAME=edu_uoe> [27 April 2003].

D. Phillips (ed.), *The Education Systems of the United Kingdom* (Oxford: Symposium Books, 2000).

D. Phillips, 'Transitions and traditions: educational developments in the new Germany in their historical context', *Aspects of Education*, 47 (1992): 111–27.

D. Phillips, 'Educational developments in the new Germany', *Compare*, 25(1) (1995): 35–47.

D. Phillips (ed.), *Education in Germany: Tradition and Reform in Historical Context* (London: Routledge, 1995).

D. Phillips (ed.), *Education in Germany Since Unification* (Wallingford: Symposium Books, 2000).

Rosalind M.O. Pritchard, *Reconstructing Education: East German Schools and Universities After Unification* (Oxford: Berghahn, 1999).

A. Prost, *Education, Société et Politiques: une histoire de l'enseignement en France de 1945 à nos jours* (Paris: Seuil, 1992).

H.-G. Rolff, H.G. Holtappels u.a. (Hg.), *Jahrbuch der Schulentwicklung. Daten, Beispiele und Perspektiven*, Band 12 (Weinheim und München, 2002).

D. Rust and V. Rust, *The Unification of German Education* (New York: Garland Publishing Inc., 1995).

UNESCO Institute for Statistics, <portal.unesco.org/uis/ev.php?URL_ID = 5187&URL_DO = DO_TOPIC&URL_SECTION = 201> [27 April 2003].

Hans Weiler, Heinrich Mintrop and Elisabeth Fuhrmann, *Educational Change and Social Transformation: Teachers, Schools and Universities in Eastern Germany* (Lewes: Falmer, 1996).

28
Housing and Urban Affairs

Jane Ball and Thomas Knorr-Siedow

Introduction

Britain, France and Germany have a good deal in common in the development of their housing policies. This is less so in the case of eastern Germany, where policy developed differently after World War II until unification and which still has different characteristics and problems. In all three countries, housing policies began intervention on health grounds in response to epidemics and overcrowding following industrialization. The three countries also all responded to the needs of post-war reconstruction and urban renewal by large scale housing construction that was often system built and high-rise, causing long-term problems.

The nature of housing and urban affairs policy

Housing, its related infrastructure and impact on social and economic relations affects many policy areas, ranging from welfare to economic and spatial policies, but there is little European agreement on the definition of housing policy (Donner 2000). While housing policy is affected by EU policies on regional development, social exclusion, competition, compulsory competitive tendering, consumerism (for tenancies), the environment and VAT on construction, there is no coherent EU policy in this field despite strong indications that national developments in housing could lead to cross-national consequences in terms of social polarization and migration. This means that responsibility for housing policy rests primarily at the national level. The housing political agenda ranges from strong state responsibility for housing to limited framework-responsibilities for a social housing market, and housing is an important element of economic management in terms of having housing available for key workers, facilitating mobility, using housing interest rates as a tool of economic management, and using housing construction to boost investment and employment.

While most areas of housing policy action are common to all three countries – mainly regulation, provision of housing and other services, and provision of fiscal incentives – the forms of action and the levels of government at which action is taken vary.

The *health and safety of buildings* was an early area of intervention. All countries' administrations have powers of entry, repair, seizure, compulsory purchase and sometimes demolition. France, for example, intervenes in relation to *bâtiments menaçant ruine* (buildings in a serious dangerous condition), *bâtiments insalubres* (buildings threatening health), and problems such as deteriorated co-owned blocks of flats. In Britain the aims of intervention in this area include 'fitness for human habitation', a measure recently reformed to produce a rating grade rather than a simple pass or fail. There are also various powers in relation to specific physical problems such as infestations, dangerous materials such as asbestos, and problem plants such as dangerous or overhanging trees.

A related area is *regulation of newbuild and improvement and planning control*. Building standards are set centrally in Britain and France but are decentralized in Germany (with the exception of energy conservation), leading to differences from region to region. The granting of planning permissions is decentralized to the lowest level in all three countries, although this process takes place within a larger planned framework. In France a new holistic planning regime of which construction is just a part takes into account separate departmental plans for housing, transport, commercial activity and the environment.

Public interventions in housing conditions also take place in the framework of *urban development*. Government support in all three countries may be provided to special zones and may combine extra funding, special administrative and contracting arrangements and, except in Germany, extra government powers. Housing zones in Britain include 'improvement areas' and 'renewal areas', in which action may include wholesale demolition. There are also a variety of special schemes for urban renovation for different purposes, using different funding streams. Similarly, in France there are zones such as the *Zones Urbaines Sensibles*, special funded town plans such as the *Grand Plan Urbain*, and special action templates such as the Programmed Operation for Housing Improvement (OPAH). In Germany, new areas of the 'Socially Integrative City' and 'Urban Regeneration' programmes link social policy to spatial and economic policy.

Action for the environment is an important aspect of urban and housing policy. British policy has tended to protect green spaces, which has affected housing supply (Barker 2003). In Germany the regional planning and environmental laws restrict building on green space, and a recent change in public subsidies for private builders means higher levels of support for inner-urban building.

Another important area of policy is *facilitating access to housing by people on a modest income*. Financial aids in all three countries include aids to construction, housing benefit and fiscal incentives.

Aids to construction may involve increasing housing supply to promote afford-ability, creating social housing, provide schemes for access to the purchase or letting of housing for lower income groups, or assisting with repair and improve-ment. These aids generally consist of state assisted loans in France and grants in Britain, with Germany using both. The major aids are controlled centrally in France and Britain but are decentralized to the *Land* level in Germany, apart from particular federal tax schemes. Grants and loans are available to individuals for home improvement in all three counties, but in Britain eligibility tends to be confined to special groups such as the disabled and elderly.

The structure of the construction industry and the lending environment that supports it differs radically from country to country. Construction is not considered to be part of housing policy in Britain but is a major component of it in France and Germany, which may explain their greater production of houses for a similar population (Table 28.1).

Housing benefits are available in all three countries, but are most likely to cover the whole rent in Britain. France and Germany both use a 'level of effort' calculation to work out the level of housing cost relative to income (Bégassat 1997). All countries vary the payments by income, family size, housing type and locality. However it is difficult to make meaningful financial comparisons in this area due to the fact that the German system has a non discriminatory housing allowance (*Wohngeld*) for lower middle income households, while the poor are paid the full rent within the social-assistance benefit scheme.

Tax incentives for housing are complex, but home ownership has often been encouraged in all three countries. Table 28.2 shows that both home ownership and social renting are more widespread in Britain than in France or Germany, while private renting is most common in Germany and relatively insignificant in Britain. There is some tenure neutrality in French fiscal policy, a requirement for equality. Social landlords in all countries, and landlords providing housing at a reasonable rent (Germany), usually receive extra fiscal benefits or special loans in exchange for keeping within certain rent limitations.

There are many *measures to assist access to housing for the homeless or poorly housed*. One such measure is the establishment of Rights to Housing. On a more concrete level, all countries have hostels for the homeless, which are increasingly being provided by voluntary organizations under contract to the

Table 28.1 Housing construction, 2000

	Britain	*France*	*Germany (west)*
Housing starts	192,000	303,000	285,000
Social housing starts	42,000	18,000	na

Sources: Euroconstruct 1997–2001 assembled in DGUHC 2002 and Ball 2004.

Table 28.2   Housing tenure (%)

	Britain 2001	France 1996	Germany 1998
Owner occupiers	69	54	43
Social renting	22	17	7
Private renting	9	21	50
Other tenures	0	8	0
Total	100	100	100

Source: DGUHC 2002.

government rather than directly by public authorities. However in Germany the main aim is to prevent homelessness in the first place, so often the full rent of poor residents is taken over by the municipality to enable these residents to remain in their homes. In France, contracts with voluntary organizations include the payment of benefit according to the number of occupied rooms in a hostel.

Protection of occupants of housing is another major area of government activity. This type of regulation tends to be centralized in all three countries and involves regulation of tenancy agreements; property law including the law relating to squatters; regulation of mortgages and financial services; requisition of property for social homes (France); consumer law; regulation of eviction (including protection from eviction in France); regulation in relation to over-indebtedness and insolvency; laws regulating misbehaviour by landlords, neighbours and outsiders; provision and regulation of sewerage, domestic waste and utilities; provision of roads and other infrastructure; family law (for division on dispute); and inheritance law.

Finally, there are special policy considerations for the *provision of housing or adaptation for special groups* such as the aged, the disabled, travellers, asylum seekers, and women suffering from domestic violence, in line with the European Convention on Human Rights.

Housing policy in Britain and France is increasingly administered in the context of urban policies in general. Accordingly, the Ministry for Housing in Britain is now a component of the Office of the Deputy Prime Minister. In France there is no longer a Housing Minister; instead the responsibility is now part of the broader *Ministère de l'Équipement, des Transports, du Logement, du Tourisme, et de la Mer* (Ministry of Infrastructure, Transport, Housing, Tourism and the Sea), although there is a Minister for the Towns with responsibility for policy integration. In the German federal system, the constitutional principle of subsidiarity allocates housing policies to the *Land* and local level, with the federal government's activities restricted to contributing to funding in fields connected to securing equal standards of opportunities across the whole country.

Most legislative and administrative powers in housing are centralized in France, with central state representatives (prefects) in each *département* playing an important funding and co-ordinating role. However every level of subnational government has relevant powers and works in partnership with the State, while housing benefits are distributed by the national networks of various social security funds.

In Britain most housing administration, including benefit delivery, is decentralized to local housing authorities. Local authorities are unitary except in England and Northern Ireland, where there are two levels, with most housing powers at the lowest level and social services at the higher county level. The regional development agencies in England have a promotional role, which will be expanded if government proposals for regional government are accepted, while the Scottish Parliament has extensive housing regulatory powers, which it has used to improve the law for the homeless and tenants, and the Welsh Assembly has some housing powers, which it has used to change the right to buy council housing (social housing) and allocations (Northern Irish Housing is presently regulated from London due to the suspension of the Northern Ireland Assembly). However funding, regulation, control and standards are increasingly centralized. Privatization of council housing by transfer to Registered Social Landlords, which has meant a large injection of private capital into this sector, has brought with it more central regulation and funding by national government agencies: the Housing Corporation in England, Communities Scotland, Tai Cymru in Wales and the Northern Ireland Housing Executive.

Housing policy is highly decentralized in Germany: for several years after quantitative demand was met during the 1980s no national housing policy existed, and federal activities were restricted to special fields such as urban rehabilitation and urban and housing experiments. However unification in 1990 and its attendant problems led to the federal state becoming highly active in supporting the transformation of the eastern housing system from planned system to market system, using direct and indirect (tax relief) subsidies.

Specific comparisons

One of the most significant areas of housing policy relates to social housing. This is compared below, along with rights to housing in Britain, France and Germany.

Social housing

Smith and Oxley suggest that social housing can be defined as: '... subsidized rented housing which is allocated with reference to need' (1997: 49), although in France and Germany it is defined in relation to funding stream and may include homes for purchase by low and medium income groups (Amzallag and Taffin 2003), which allows homes constructed for purchase and private provision to come within the definition.

Social housing allocation in Britain and France is a joint exercise in regulation and implementation between central government, local government and the social landlords, whereas in Germany contractual arrangements between private and public housing companies have led to new forms of social housing, including owner occupied homes and municipal purchase of housing rights in the existing housing stock in exchange for rent limitations.

In Britain the majority of social housing is still provided by local authorities and known as 'council housing'. Since 1979, however, much council housing stock has been sold to tenants at a discount under the 'right to buy', or privatized by transfer to private independent Registered Social Landlords with the aid of a private loan. For the latter to occur, a majority of tenants voting must agree with the transfer, which has the advantage of enabling access to additional funds for repairs and improvements to homes (funds for building and repair by local authorities for council homes are limited). Registered Social Landlords may be Housing Associations, not-for-profit companies or 'Local Housing Companies' (also not-for-profit, but with one third tenant representation on the board).

In France social housing is provided mainly by HLM (*Habitations à Loyer Modéré*, or 'Homes at a Moderate Rent') organizations, which have recently been renamed *Organismes de l'Habitat Social* (Social Housing Organizations). The social housing movement consists of public and private HLM organizations, various forms of co-operative HLM organizations and the *Société Anonyme de Crédit Immobilier*, which specializes in providing credit for home purchase by individuals on a low income. One third of the housing constructed by the HLM movement is for purchase by people with incomes below a certain income ceiling, usually with assisted loans. HLM organizations may also participate in construction by others at different stages and assist in urban regeneration. French local authorities are generally not allowed to own social housing directly, but every level of subnational authority is allowed to own social housing companies. Public and private HLM organizations have a common regulatory framework found in the *Code de la Construction et de l'Habitation*, and local authorities may provide grants, land or exemption from local taxes to assist them. All HLM organizations have boards consisting of volunteers and are generally non-profit making. For public HLM organizations, one third of directors on the boards are from central government, one third from the local authority to which it is attached, and one third consists of tenant and other representatives. Around 10 per cent of social housing is provided by *sociétés d'économie mixte*, which are joint venture public/private companies that are similarly funded and regulated as HLM organizations. All these organizations have tenant representatives on their boards. Private landlords may be co-opted by agreement into providing housing at a reduced rent or to people on a low income for a limited period, usually 9 years, in return for capital allowances against rental income (Ball 2004).

In Germany, social housing was built on a contract basis by public and private housing companies and rented out at controlled rents to lower and lower middle income residents. The special status of social housing, which is linked to favourable loan agreements, is limited to a period of between 15 and 40 years, after which the normal regulated market rents apply. As the majority of existing social housing was built between the 1950s and 1980s, the number of directly accessible social homes is going down, and since 2000 hardly any new social homes have been added.

Rights to housing

In France there is a Right to Housing which has constitutional status following decisions of the Constitutional Council, but no such constitutional right exists in Britain or Germany.

The French Right to Housing acts as the framework for a raft of related legislation to help the disadvantaged. Among other things this has led to the establishment of a Fund, *le Fonds de Solidarité Logement*, which provides aid to those in housing difficulty, including linked support by social workers. In addition, allocation of social housing has recently been reformed to assist the disadvantaged, although an individual has little recourse for refusal. The Right is also the basis for imposing an obligation on landlords to furnish a 'decent' home.

Although Britain and Germany have no constitutional Right to Housing, there are rights provisions for the inviolability of the home. In addition, local authorities in both countries are obliged to house people who are homeless (or roofless in Germany) or classed as such due to housing difficulty, provided they fall within priority classes and are not voluntarily homeless. Local authorities also have an obligation to provide housing advice and assistance to all in their area.

Recent developments

Funds for construction and improvement in all three countries are increasingly being delivered by means of local contractualization with active parties as part of a holistic urban improvement package, rather than relating to housing in isolation. This approach is being accelerated by the application of EU aid to a limited number of deprived areas.

In all three countries there is also a continuing stress on increasing owner occupancy. In France, aid is available for home purchase for people on a low income by way of assisted loans, and the government has recently announced a home ownership initiative improving loan terms (Infrastructure Ministry 2004).

Although there are currently no aids or tax relief available generally for home purchase in Britain, there are schemes to assist key workers and to facilitate low cost part-ownership through 'shared-ownership' schemes, while owner-occupied principal homes are exempt from income tax (for notional rent) and capital gains taxes. Affordability is also promoted by making developers agree to provide cheaper homes for purchase as a condition of the grant of planning permission.

In Britain, access to funding for housing improvement for local authorities frequently depends either on their agreeing to privatize housing or on their achieving a high rating on inspection for delivering quality services. For example, only high performing authorities are permitted both to retain their housing within autonomous 'Arms-Length Management Companies' and to obtain funding for repair or improvement.

In France, urban improvement has been facilitated by the new holistic planning system introduced recently. In addition, the *communes*, which may be small and individually lack resources, may now pool their powers and related budgets within a corporate body, which makes bidding for funding within various city initiatives easier. It also provides a useful platform for taking advantage of the further decentralization planned by the current government.

Since unification and the consequent appearance of new disparities, housing policy in Germany has undergone a fundamental change of paradigm. The integration of housing policies and social policies has started with a programme for the 'Socially Integrated City'. Even more important is the change from growth to quality management in shrinking regions and towns. Currently over 1.2 million dwellings are vacant, mostly in inner-cities and peripheral estates. This will have to lead to large scale demolition, as the population is expected to decrease from the present 86 million to some 60 million over the coming 40 years. In this respect eastern Germany is apparently a testing ground for new spatial and housing policies, which will include social integration, enhanced attraction through quality and the demolition of homes on a large scale. However this European demographic problem will also be found in western Germany as well as in other European countries in the future.

Sources

M. Amzallag and C. Taffin, *Le logement social* (Paris: LGDJ, 2003).

A.J. Ball, *Housing People on a Middle to Low Income in France: Planned Bias in the Law* (Sheffield: Sheffield University Press, 2004).

K. Barker, *The Barker Review of Housing Supply*, Interim Report (London: The Treasury, 2003).

Luc Bégassat, 'Les Aides Personnelles au Logement à la Lumière des Expériences Européennes', *L'Observateur de l'Immobilier* 35 (March 1997).

J-P Brouant and Y. Jégouzo, 'La Territorialisation des Politiques du Droit de l'Habitat Social', *Les Cahiers du GRIDAUH* 2 (Paris: GRIDAUH, 1998).

DGUHC (Direction Générale de l'Urbanisme, de l'Habitat et de la Construction) (2002), *Le Logement en Europe*, <www.logement.equipement.gouv.fr/actu/logeurope/parc_logt.pdf> [26 July 2003].

Ch. Donner, *Housing Policies in the European Union: Theory and Practice* (Vienna, 2000).

French National Housing Information Agency (2004), <anil.org>

Housing and Construction Bulletins (2004), <www.batiactu.com>

Infrastructure Ministry (Ministère de l'Équipement, des Transports, du Logement, du Tourisme, et de la Mer) (2004), <www.logement.equipement.gouv.fr> [9 January 2004].

Joseph Rowntree Foundation (2004), <www.jrf.org.uk>

Office of the Deputy Prime Minister (2004), <www.odpm.gov.uk>

J. Smith and M. Oxley, 'Housing investment and social housing: European comparisons', *Housing Studies* 12(4) (1997).

M. Stephens, N. Burns *et al.*, *Social Market or Safety Net* (Bristol: The Policy Press, 2002).

29
Women
Majella Kilkey

Introduction

Gender has long been recognized as an important social division, with women occupying a disadvantaged position relative to men in a wide range of areas. Britain, France and Germany are broadly similar in their formal legislation around sex equality, but the extent to which they are able to ameliorate the position of women depends very much on the substance of these formal provisions, and in this they differ quite markedly. In respect of promoting employment, for example, French policy is firmly focused on providing affordable childcare designed to meet the needs of working mothers. By contrast, in Germany childcare provision is comparatively poor, and initiatives in the form of leave arrangements are oriented towards enabling mothers of young children to take time out of the labour market to care for children at home, and/or to combine part-time work with childrearing. Britain, meanwhile, is the laggard of the three in respect of recognising the barrier that motherhood poses to women's employment; it combines poor childcare provision with weak rights to take time off to care or to re-organize working patterns to better reconcile work and family responsibilities.

The nature of women's policy

Women's policy generally takes two forms. On the one hand, states develop discrete areas of intervention to address needs that are overwhelmingly women's needs (see Table 29.1). Key examples of aspects of women's lives where governments intervene include pregnancy and childbirth as well as domestic violence and rape. Special provisions for pregnancy and maternity, for example, exist within a wide range of public policy areas: employment legislation includes measures to protect the health and well-being of pregnant and nursing women, such as the right to maternity leave, as well as anti-discrimination

Table 29.1   Policies specifically aimed at women

Policy area	Policy instrument
Employment	Maternity leave
	Health and safety regulations specific to pregnancy and nursing mothers
	Anti-discrimination regulation
	Funding and/or direct provision of childcare
	Parental leave
	Re-organization of working time to allow flexible working (France and Germany only)
Social security	Maternity leave benefits
	Parental leave benefits (France and Germany only)
	Childcare benefits
	Financial and childcare support for women returning to the labour market
Health	Funding and/or direct provision of ante-natal and post-natal care
	Screening services for women-specific cancers
	Funding and/or direct provision of contraceptive and abortion services
Social services	Funding and/or direct provision of women's shelters and refuges
	Funding and/or direct provision of survivor support groups
	Mother and infant health services (France and Germany only)
Criminal law	Legislation on rape and domestic violence
Civil law	Legislation on the rights to abortion

measures to safe-guard the jobs of pregnant women; in the area of social security there may be benefits which replace the wages of women who are on maternity leave; and in health services there are ante-natal and post-natal provisions. Concerns around protecting women from domestic violence and rape, penalising such abuses and supporting the survivors of violence cut across many areas of government activity: criminal justice systems define and legislate against such crimes, as well as fixing penalties for those found guilty of perpetrating violence; and through social services governments provide or fund safe-havens such as women's shelters and refuges for those experiencing violence, as well as more therapeutically oriented survivor support groups.

On the other hand, governments attempt to 'mainstream' concerns around women within their generic areas of public policy. Thus, for example, account may be taken within pensions, health and housing systems of the particular needs of women stemming from women tending to live longer than men. Since women are over-represented among the poor, particular attention may be given to women within the development of national minimum wage schemes, and governments may develop mechanisms to ensure that women are not financially disadvantaged in divorce settlements. Finally, account may be taken of women's overwhelming responsibility for providing the care of children and other family members through, for example, the awarding of credits within contributory social insurance schemes for times spent caring, making carers' benefits available within social security schemes, and legislating within employment policy to protect part-time workers.

Specific comparisons

The mainstreaming of women's concerns makes the decision as to what to include under the umbrella of 'women's policy' particularly difficult, since virtually any area of public policy could be considered to have a particular relevance to women. This section focuses on policies specifically aimed at women, in particular sex equality legislation and policies to promote women's employment.

Sex equality legislation

European Community law has been a driving force in the development of Member States' national anti-sex-discrimination legislation. This has been the case since the Treaty of Rome established the principle of equal pay for men and women (European Commission 2002). Reflecting Community initiatives, Britain, France and Germany now have a fairly extensive body of sex equality legislation, particularly in the field of employment.

All three countries have laws designed to ensure equal treatment between men and women in relation to access to employment, vocational training, promotion, and terms and conditions of employment including pay rates. In the field of occupational health and safety, all the countries have introduced legislation to protect pregnant women and nursing mothers from working practices and environments that might be detrimental to their health. Legislation on protection at work has recently been extended to the area of sexual harassment in all of the countries. Also related to the area of employment and associated rights is legislation that all the countries have adopted to ensure that men and women are treated equally in statutory and occupational social security schemes, especially in respect of pensions. Finally, an evolving element of attempts to promote equality between women and men in employment matters in the three countries has been the development of legislation around reconciling work and family life, which is discussed in more depth later in the chapter. One criticism of the scope of sex equality legislation in all of these countries, however, is that it is overwhelmingly limited to the field of paid work. Exceptionally, France has also extended such legislation to the area of political representation at the local, national and supra-national parliamentary levels, in a bid to achieve a more proportionate representation of the sexes in formal political arenas (ILO 2002).

Sex equality legislation, and the promotion of gender equality more generally, is overseen by a range of legislative and administrative institutions. In Britain, the Minister for Women and the Women and Equality Unit are responsible for mainstreaming gender equality concerns across government, while responsibility for sex (along with disability and age) discrimination legislation and policy lies with the Department for Education and Skills. The Equal Opportunities Commission, a non-civil service government-funded body, monitors compliance with elements of sex discrimination legislation, issues codes of practice, assists individuals with sex discrimination claims and conducts research. In France the major responsibility for sex equality legislation and policy lies within the Ministry of Employment and Solidarity with the Secretary of State for Women's Rights and Vocational Training, who is supported by the Women's Rights Service. In addition, the Prime Minister's Office has recently established the Observatory for Parity with the aim of centralizing and mainstreaming sex equality issues across government. In Germany, the Federal Ministry for Family Affairs, Senior Citizens, Women and Youth has responsibility for gender equality issues. In 1986, when it adopted this mandate, it established the Federal Ministry for Women and the Federal Minister for Women's Affairs. This body is replicated at the *Land* level, with *Land* ministries for women's affairs (ILO 2002).

Policies to promote women's employment

Promoting women's employment is currently a concern in each of these three countries, partly as a result of the EU's Employment Strategy initiated under the Treaty of Amsterdam in 1997. Under the Strategy, a target has been set to increase the rate of women's employment to an average of more than 60 per cent across the EU by 2010, with an intermediate target of 57 per cent by 2005. To support this target, Member States are required, among other things, to give attention to measures designed to enable parents to reconcile work and family life (European Commission 2002).

The EU has issued directives on policy areas such as parental leave (1996) and the organization of working time (1993). More recently, it has required Member States to provide childcare to at least 90 per cent of children aged three to school-age, and to 33 per cent of children under three, by 2010 (European Commission 2002). Despite EU intervention, however, the characteristics of work-life balance provisions differ across the three countries.

Childcare

Public childcare is much more extensive in France than in Britain or Germany. Indicative of this is the fact that only France has a statutory guarantee of a childcare place for children under three. This is more specifically targeted at children aged two years and above and refers to an early education place in an *école maternelle*. France is also the only country to have set a target, following the EU's requirements, to increase the provision for the under threes: it aims to expand the number of places available in collective childcare by 250,000 between 2001 and 2004 (EGGE 2002b). While cross-national comparisons of enrolment rates in formal childcare are fraught with difficulty (Eurostat 2002a), estimates indicate that France currently has the highest rate of attendance for children under three among these countries (see Table 29.2 for details).

The provision of childcare for children aged three to compulsory school age is greater in all three countries (Table 29.2). In Britain the National Childcare Strategy launched in 1998 required Local Education Authorities to provide an early education place to all four year-olds by 2001, and to all three year-olds by 2004, although the Government did not specify that these places should be full-time (EGGE 2002c). German Federal Law gives all children between the age of three and six a right to a place in a *kindergarten*, but like Britain does not specify full-time provision (EGGE 2002d). Only France approximates near universal provision for this age group.

In comparing enrolment rates, though, it is vital to have regard to other characteristics of provision, including the provider and opening hours (see Table 29.3). In Britain, the state has a limited role in provision for the under threes and targets its childcare on children deemed to be 'at risk'. While its role in providing childcare for children aged three to school-age is more extensive, provision is largely part-time (about two-and-a-half hours per day) in nursery schools and classes, which follow school terms. The daily and annual opening regime of schools also creates a childcare gap for older children. Again, while provision exists in Britain in the form of breakfast clubs, after-school clubs and holiday play-schemes, the role of the state is minimal. In the absence and/or inadequacy of state provision, British parents must rely on private childcare

Table 29.2 Indicators of the provision of formal childcare places

	Britain	*France*	*Germany**
Under three year olds			
Statutory guarantee of a place	No	Yes**	No
Percentage enrolled in all formal facilities	34%	41%	10%
Comparative level of provision	Low	Medium	Low
Three to school age			
State guarantee of a place	Yes***	Yes	Yes
Percentage enrolled in all formal facilities	60%	99–100%	73%
Comparative level of provision	Medium	High	High

Notes
* Mainly refers to the system in the former West Germany.
**Applies from the age of two in an *école maternelle*.
*** Applies to four year-olds in an early education place.
Sources: EGGE 2002a; Eurostat 2002a.

Table 29.3 Characteristics of state childcare provision

	Britain	France	Germany
Under three year olds			
Scope of public provision	Minimal	Extensive	Minimal
Main type of public provision	Local Authority Nursery	*Crèche*	*Kinderkrippen*
Dominant opening-regime of public provision	Part-time	Full-time	Full-time
Three to school age			
Scope of public provision	Extensive but part-time	Extensive	Extensive but part-time
Main type of public provision	Nursery school/class	*L'école maternelle**	*Kindergarten*
Dominant opening-regime of public provision	Part-time and term time	School hours (closed Wednesdays)**	Part- or full-time and term-time
School-aged children			
Scope of public provision	Minimal	Extensive	Minimal
Main type of public provision	Breakfast club, after-school club and holiday play-scheme	*Centre de Loisirs sans Hébergement*	*Kinderhorte*
Dominant opening-regime of public provision	Before school, after school until 18.00, and full-day during school holidays	Before school, after school until 18.00/19.00, Wednesdays and full-day during school holidays	Before and after school usually during term-time only

Notes
* Children can attend this from the age of two.
** Services (*Garderie Périscolaire* and *Centre de Loisirs sans Hébergement*) exist to fill the daily, weekly and annual gaps in the opening hours of *les écoles maternelles*.
Sources: Eurostat 2002a; Clearing House 2002.

provided largely by the market in the form of day-care centres and childminders, or on informal networks of family and friends, or, in the case of older children, leave them home alone (Clearing House 2002; Kids Club Network 2002).

The German state also plays a minimal role as a provider of childcare services for the under threes, and while it is more active in provision for three to school-aged children, the facilities – *kindergarten* – are not generally open for the full length of the working day, nor the full working year. There is also very limited capacity in the state provision for school-aged children – *kinderhorte*. This is particularly problematic for working parents, since German children attend school in the mornings only. Moreover, the length of the school morning is irregular, ending sometimes at 11.30 and other times at 12.30 or 13.15. One effect is that 'more young school-age children are left alone at home or in the care of a sibling than many would consider desirable' (Eurostat 2002a: 78).

The French state is far more active than the other two in the provision of childcare for all age groups. The dominant form of state provision for the under-3s is the collective *crèche*, which is a full-time, full-year service. Approximately 50 per cent of two-year olds, however, attend an *école maternelle*. This is a public pre-school service which incorporates almost all three to six year olds. *Les écoles maternelles* are open during term-time from 8.30 to 16.30 on week- days, except Wednesday when all schools are closed. Unlike Britain and Germany, though, France has a comprehensive network of 'wrap-around' services for both pre-school and school-aged children to fill the daily, weekly and annual gaps in the school system (Clearing House 2002).

A final dimension of childcare provision is its affordability, details of which are set out in Table 29.4. While in Britain public sector provision is generally free, or charges are income-related, most working parents must rely on the private sector and research has indicated that Britain has the most expensive market-based childcare in Europe (Day Care Trust 2002). To offset some of the costs of this, there is a state subsidy paid directly to parents and delivered through the Working Tax Credit This is targeted on low-income families and can only be used against the costs of registered /formal childcare.

In France, state provision is either free (*les écoles maternelles*), or fees are related to parental income and number of children. In collective *crèches* parental fees are limited to 25 per cent of the costs, regardless of income. France also provides financial assistance with the costs of childcare directly to parents in the form of tax relief and a variety of benefits, each covering different forms of childcare. The most generous of these – *Allocation de garde d'enfant à domicile* (AGED) – is worth a maximum of €508 (£374, $573) per month.

In Germany, parents are expected to contribute to the costs of all forms of childcare but the amount they pay is dependent on income and number of children. In both *kinderkrippen* and *kindergarten* the fees are limited to between 16 and 20 per cent of the costs. Unlike Britain and France, Germany does not provide assistance directly to parents for the costs of childcare. It does, how-ever, provide a tax relief to families employing a household servant, who could arguably also be providing childcare (Kilkey 2000).

Childcare leaves and the reorganization of working times

Giving parents time off to care for children and reorganizing the working day to enable parents to achieve a 'work-life balance' are further mecha-nisms that states can adopt to promote parental, and in particular mothers', employment.

Table 29.4   Paying for childcare, 2003

	Britain	France	Germany
Fees in public provision			
Under 3 year olds	Free, or income-related reductions	Income and child-related reductions, with parental contribution fixed at 25% of costs	Income and child-related reductions, with parental contribution fixed at 16–20% of costs
3 to school age	Free	Free	Income and child-related reductions, with parental contribution fixed at 16–20% of costs
School-aged	May be free; otherwise no reductions	Income and child-related reductions	Income and child-related reductions
Other financial assistance	Childcare element of the Working Tax Credit	(1) AGED* (2) AFEAMA** (3) AFEAMA (Supplement) (4) Tax Credit	No provision
Maximum value, per month	£409.50 (€557, $626) if 1 child; £606.67 (€824, $928) if 2 or more children	(1) €508 (£374, $573) (2) Covers social security contributions for a 'nanny' (3) €200 (£147, $225)	–
Variations	Amount reduces as income increases	(4) 25% of net expenditure (1&3) Amount reduces with income and age of child	–

Notes
*AGED = *Allocation de garde d'enfant à domicile.*
**AFEAMA = *Aide à la famille pour l'emploi d'une assistante maternelle.*
Sources: Eurostat 2002a; MISSOC 2002; Day Care Trust 2003; SOCCARE 2002.

Table 29.5 Childcare leaves and the reorganization of working time, 2003

	Britain	*France*	*Germany*
Childbirth related leave			
Maximum duration	67 weeks	162 weeks	162 weeks
% of leave paid	42%	10% for first child, 100% for second and subsequent children	68%
Annual leave for family reasons:			
No. of days	In emergencies	3 days per parent or 5 days per parent if child under 1 year or 3 or more children	10 days per parent per child (20 up to a maximum if a lone parent)
Payment	No statutory right	No statutory right	70% of gross earnings
Reorganization of working time	Right to request to reorganize working time	Can combine parental leave with part-time work	Can combine parental leave with part-time work

Sources: DTI 2003; Clearing House 2002, International Reform Monitor 2002; Bradshaw and Finch 2002.

Table 29.5 reveals that Britain has the least generous provisions in this area despite the introduction in April 2003 of new legislation designed to enable parents to achieve a better work-life balance. In Britain parents may take a total of 67 weeks leave. Only 42 per cent of this, however, will be paid. This falls far short of Germany, where parents are entitled to a total of 162 weeks leave, 68 per cent of which is paid. Since April 2003 British parents have also had the right to *request* flexible working hours, but in France and Germany parents have the *right* to combine parental leave with part-time working. Overall, German leave provisions emerge as more generous than those in France. The key weakness in French provision is the very low replacement of pay available to parents taking leave for their first child, although it should be noted that for second and subsequent children France is more generous than Germany.

Recent developments

Variations in the substance of sex equality legislation, as well as childcare and 'work-life balance' provisions across these countries, may help to account for the differences observed in women's employment patterns. Thus, for example, it is in France where parenthood has the least impact on women's employment, reducing it by only 15.9 per cent compared with 26.6 and 27.1 per cent in Britain and Germany respectively. France also has the lowest rate of part-time working among women in general. This is perhaps a product of its comparatively comprehensive system of childcare, just as the greater prevalence of part-time working in Britain and Germany may be related to the paucity of state childcare provision, and particularly the overwhelming reliance on part-time educational places for pre-schoolers (Eurostat 2002b; EGGE 2002e).

Interestingly, in all three countries parenthood works to increase the rate of men's employment. Changing men's behaviour with regard to parenting has recently been recognized as an important element in the strategy to promote gender equality. This again is being led by the EU, and in recognition of the low take-up by men of parental leave times, both Britain and France have recently either instituted separate parental leave provisions or extended existing provisions (Bradshaw and Finch 2002).

Sources

J. Bradshaw and N. Finch, *A Comparison of the Child Benefit Package in 22 Countries*, DWP Report No. 174 (London: DWP, 2002), <www.dwp.gov.uk/asd/asd5/rrep174> [1 November 2002].

Clearing House (The Clearing House on International Developments in Child, Youth and Family Policies at Columbia University) (2002), <www.childpolicyintl.org> [27 September 2002].

Day Care Trust (2002) 'The price parents pay. Sharing the costs of childcare', <www.daycaretrust.org.uk> [8 October 2002].

Day Care Trust (2003) 'Tax Credits', <www.daycaretrust.org.uk> [16 December 2003].

DTI (Department of Trade and Industry) (2003), <www.dti.gov.uk> [16 December 2003].

EGGE (EC's Expert Group on Gender and Employment) (2002a), 'Gender equality in the European Employment Strategy: An evaluation of the National Action Plans for Employment 2001', <www.umist.ac.uk/management/ewerc> [26 September 2002].

EGGE (EC's Expert Group on Gender and Employment)(2002b) 'Evaluation of the French National Action Plan for Employment 2001', <www.umist.ac.uk/management/ewerc> [26 September 2002].

EGGE (EC's Expert Group on Gender and Employment)(2002c) 'Evaluation of the United Kingdom National Action Plan for Employment 2001', <www.umist.ac.uk/management/ewerc> [26 September 2002].

EGGE (EC's Expert Group on Gender and Employment)(2002d) 'Evaluation of the German National Action Plan for Employment 2001', <www.umist.ac.uk/management/ewerc> [26 September 2002].

EGGE (EC's Expert Group on Gender and Employment)(2002e) 'Indicators on Gender Equality in the European Employment Strategy 2001', <www.umist.ac.uk/management/ewerc> [25 October 2002].

European Commission (2002), 'Equality between women and men', <www.europa.eu.int/comm/employment-social/equ_opp> [25 September 2002].

Eurostat (2002a) 'Feasibility study on the availability of comparable childcare statistics in the European Union', <www.europa.eu.int/comm/eurostat> [26 September 2002].

Eurostat (2002b), 'Labour Force Survey', <www.europa.eu.int/comm/eurostat> [25 October 2002].

ILO (International Labour Office)(2002), <www.ilo.org/public/english/employment/gems/eeo/> [25 September 2002].

International Reform Monitor (2002), <www.reformmonitor.org> [27 September 2002].

Kids Club Network (2002) 'News – back to school but...where's the childcare?', <www.kidsclubs.org.uk> [8 October 2002].

M. Kilkey, *Lone Mothers Between Paid Work and Care* (Aldershot: Ashgate, 2000).

MISSOC (Mutual Information System on Social Protection in the EU Member States and the EEA)(2002), <www.europa.eu.int/comm/employment_social/missoc2002/> [16 December 2003].

SOCCARE (Social Care)(2002), <www.uta.fi/laitokset/sospol/soccare> [27 September 2002].

30
Minorities

Catherine Lloyd and Uwe Richter

Introduction

In Britain, France and Germany, as elsewhere, there are significant numbers of people who do not belong to the dominant ethnic/linguistic/religious majorities (see Table 30.1). However each country defines 'minority' differently. In Britain the term 'ethnic minority' refers mainly to post 1945 immigrants. France emphasizes the equality of citizens, while formulating policies to deal with the problems of immigrants and their descendants. Germany distinguishes between 'indigenous' minorities and immigrants. In all countries, collecting data about minorities is a sensitive matter and there are debates about the correct terminology to be used to describe them. After discussing the general nature of minorities policy and the government bodies responsible for it, we will compare the ways in which minorities are defined, before going on to look at national policies on language, education and religion as these relate to minorities.

The nature of minorities policy

Policies to support minorities focus on regulating the rights and duties of minority residents (citizens or non-citizens). They cover three main aspects:

- Political rights to equal representation and to be safeguarded against discrimination;
- Cultural rights (language, religion);
- Social and economic rights which take specific cultures into account.

To some extent minorities policy is made at supranational level, as international laws such as the Universal Declaration of Human Rights (1948), the European Framework Convention for the Protection of National Minorities

Table 30.1   Minorities statistics

	Britain	*France*	*Germany*
Population	58.8 m (2001)	59.1 m (2001)	82.5 m (2003)
Indigenous minorities	Not available	Not available	Danes: 50,000
			Sorbs: 60,000
			Saterland Frisians: 12,000
			North Frisians: 50–60,000
			East Frisians: no estimates
Non-Indigenous minorities	Not available	Not available	Sinti and Roma: 70,000
Other ethnic groups	Black: 1.3 m	Algeria 574,208	Foreigners: 7.3 m (2002)
	Indian	Portugal	Ethnic Germans from the
	subcontinent:	571,874	former Soviet Union and
	2.1 m	Morocco	east European countries:
	Chinese and	522,504	1950–2001 4.2 m
	other Asians:	Italy 378,649	
	825,000	Spain 316,232	
		Tunisia 201,561	
		Turkey 174,160	

Sources: ONS 2001; INSEE 2003; D_statis 2003a, 2003b; BAFL 2002; BMI 2002; Framework 1999 Part I.

(1998) and the European Charter for Regional or Minority Languages of the Council of Europe (1999) all supersede national and state laws. Minorities policy at national level is largely concerned with implementing the provisions of these international agreements.

Responsibility for this area of policy at national level is divided between central and local government. Recent measures empowering regional assemblies in Britain, and decentralization in France, have enabled more resources to be channelled to national and ethnic minorities.

In Britain the Commission for Racial Equality (CRE), which is responsible for dealing with matters of 'racial discrimination' at the national and local level, is a publicly funded, statutory but non-governmental body that reports to the Home Office and to committees of the House of Commons. The CRE provides information and advice to people who think they have suffered racial discrimination or harassment and liaises with public bodies, businesses and organizations from all sectors to promote policies and practices to ensure equal treatment for all regardless of their race, colour, or national or ethnic origin, with regional and local offices to support this work. It is also a campaigning body and has a statutory duty to ensure that all new laws take full account of the protection given against discrimination.

In addition, since 2001 there has been an enforceable and positive duty on all public authorities, including immigration authorities, to eliminate racial discrimination.

Since 1999 the importance of national pluralism in Britain has been recognized by devolved government in Britain for Scotland and Wales (plus Northern Ireland when not ruled directly from London). The Race Relations Act 1976 (Statutory Duties) (Scotland) Order 2000 requires all Scottish public bodies to publish a Race Equality Scheme to ensure public access to information and services. The Fair Employment and Treatment (Northern Ireland) Order 1998 makes discrimination on grounds of religious belief and/or political opinion unlawful in employment and in the provision of goods, facilities and services; the sale or management of land or property; further and higher education; and the establishment of partnerships.

French republican doctrine holds that all citizens are equal, so that there should be no distinction between them on the grounds of ethnicity, religion or country of origin. However this concept of citizenship is being affected by immigrants who are gradually asserting the principle of residential citizenship and voting rights based on residence rather than nationality. There are also a growing number of advisory Communal Councils varying in powers. The oldest is in the city of Amiens, the most recent (2002) in Paris. The Paris Communal Council is composed of 60 men and 60 women chosen on the basis of their country of origin, numbers of their community living in districts of Paris and their socio-professional backgrounds. The 'integration' of immigrant minorities has been largely implemented through urban policy, particularly the social treatment of exclusion. Four organizations manage urban policy: the Inter-ministerial Committee for Towns, the Inter-ministerial Delegation for Towns, the High Council for Integration and the National Council for Immigrant Populations. Organizations such as the High Council for Integration report to the Prime Minister regularly on key issues such as reception of newly arrived immigrants as well as social and professional training, and there is a 'mediation structure' to ensure equal treatment and non-discrimination (Prime Minister 2003).

Until the ratification of the European Framework Convention for the Protection of National Minorities, minorities in Germany were mainly subject to *Land* legislation. Schleswig-Holstein, Saxony, Brandenburg and Lower Saxony, the main settlement areas of the Frisians, Danes and Sorbs, have articles in their *Land* Constitutions implemented in laws, ordinances and statutes which define and protect the rights of minorities (Winkler *et al.* 1999), while the federal Basic Law protects the general human rights and freedoms of minorities in matters such as freedom of expression, equal treatment, and the prohibition of discrimination on the grounds of faith. At federal level the Ministry for Interior (*Bundesministerium des Innern*) is responsible for minority legislation, but enforcement, support and promotion of minority rights are mainly a matter for the *Länder*.

Specific comparisons

The following four sections compare national definitions of what a minority is for the purposes of public policy, then national policies on minority languages and on education and religion as they relate to minorities.

Definitions and terminology

The definition of minorities is one of the main differences between Britain, France and Germany, at least on a semantic level.

In Britain 'national minority' is not a legally defined term, but the Race Relations Act 1976 defines a racial group as 'a group of persons defined by colour, race, nationality (including citizenship) or ethnic or national origins.' This includes both ethnic minority communities (or visible minorities) and the Scots, Irish and Welsh, who are defined as a racial group by virtue of their national origins. Gypsies (and Travellers in Northern Ireland) are also considered a racial group under the Act (British Government 1999). The Census defines ethnicity in terms of five categories: White (British; Irish or any other White background), Mixed (White and Black Caribbean; White and Black African; White and Asian or any other Mixed background), Asian or Asian British (Indian; Pakistani; Bangladeshi; any other Asian background), Black or Black British (Caribbean; African; any other Black background), and Chinese or other ethnic group (ONS 2001).

In France the basic distinction is between foreigner and citizen. All are protected against discrimination by the amended 1972 Law against Racism, which focuses on acts of defamation, mainly in the press. With 4.3 million foreigners in France, comprising 7 per cent of the total population, France is the second largest country of immigration in Europe, just behind Germany. Although ethnic minorities are not officially recognized, the government works with representative organizations such as the Jewish *Conseil Representative des Institutions Juives de France* (CRIF 2003). In April 2003 the French Muslim Council (*Conseil français du culte musulman*) held its first indirect elections to select representatives of the different Islamic tendencies to liaise with the government (Vie Publique 2003).

Ethnicity in Germany is not defined as 'race', due to the racist policies of the Third Reich, and it is not permitted to gather statistics based on ethnic criteria. Indeed minorities in Germany have only recently been defined at a Federal and Constitutional level with the ratification of the European Framework Convention for the Protection of National Minorities in 1997. In relation to this the German government has stated that 'Germany considers national minorities to be groups of the population who meet the following five criteria: their members are German nationals; they differ from the majority population insofar as they have their own language, culture and history, in other words, they have their own identity; they wish to maintain this identity; they are traditionally resident in Germany; and they live in the traditional settlement areas' (German Government 2002).

In practice, Germany identifies four national minorities: the Danes, the Sorbian people and the German Sinti and Roma, and the Frisians. Except for the German Sinti and Roma, all minorities have their traditional settlement areas only in certain *Länder*, namely Schleswig-Holstein, Lower Saxony, Brandenburg and Saxony.

In addition to indigenous minorities there are also ethnic minority groups comprised of labour immigrants ('guest workers'), their descendants, and refugees and ethnic Germans from former Eastern Bloc countries. These include approximately 1.9 million Turks (D_statis 2003a, 2003b). The recognition of these ethnic groups may improve as a consequence of recent amendments to the naturalization law that took effect on 1 January 2000.

Minority languages

In 1992 the Council of Europe drew up the Charter for Regional or Minority Languages to encourage the preservation and promotion of indigenous languages as part of the European cultural heritage. Britain, France and Germany have all signed this charter, which obliges them to recognize regional or minority languages, respect the geographical area in which they are spoken, take resolute action to promote such languages, provide facilities for teaching and studying them, provide facilities to enable non-speakers of the languages to learn them, eliminate discrimination, promote mutual respect and understanding between linguistic groups, establish bodies to represent the interests of regional or minority languages, and apply the Charter's principles to non-territorial languages.

In Britain, the 1991 Census recorded that 1.4 per cent of the Scottish population aged three or over were able to speak, read, or write Gaelic, and that 18.7 per cent of the Welsh population were able to speak Welsh. The Welsh Language Act 1993 places a duty on the government to treat Welsh and English equally when providing public services in Wales and gives Welsh speakers an absolute right to speak Welsh in courts of law. The Welsh Language Board oversees the delivery, promotion and facilitation of Welsh language use (Welsh Language Board 2003). Among British Asians, whose languages are not covered by the Charter, the most commonly spoken languages are Punjabi (52 per cent), Urdu (31 per cent), Hindi (27 per cent) and Gujarati (25 per cent). 66 per cent of ethnic Chinese people speak Cantonese and 22 per cent of Caribbeans speak Patois. At least a quarter of school children speak a language other than English at home, and 275 languages are spoken by pupils in London's schools (CRE 1999).

In France, French is the first language of 88 per cent of the population and most minority language speakers can also speak French. The main indigenous minority languages are Occitan (12 per cent of the population, mainly in the South of France), German (3 per cent), Italian (1.7 per cent) and Breton (1.2 per cent). Other minority languages include Catalan (0.4 per cent), the Corsican language Corsu (0.3 per cent), Flemish (0.2 per cent) and Basque (0.1 per cent). The main immigrant language is Arabic, which is spoken by about 1.7 per cent of the population (INSEE 2003).

In Germany, the main regional language is Low German and the main minority languages are Danish (about 50,000 speakers), Upper (Lusatia) Sorbian and Lower (Lusatia) Sorbian (Wendish) (20,000), North Frisian (20,000), Saterland (East) Frisian (4000) and the Romany language of the Sinti and Roma (70,000) (ECRML 2000).

Education and religion

Although education policy and public policy relating to religion are both subjects of separate chapters elsewhere in this book, they are of special concern to minorities. For this reason the aspects of these policy areas of particular relevance to minorities are compared here. The two topics are considered together because, in relation to minorities, issues of education and religion are closely entwined.

Table 30.2 sets out the main religious affiliations in Britain, France and Germany.

Britain is not a secular state: the Church of England is the established church. In 2001 just over three-quarters of the British population reported having a religion. More than seven out of ten were Christian (72 per cent), but nearly 3 per cent were Muslim (1.6 m).

The major issues confronted by education policy towards minorities involve underachievement and demands for respect for religious beliefs. Recent measures implementing language and citizenship tests for people applying for British nationality have led to the provision of extra funding for the education of minorities. In 1998 the government restored what was once known as

Table 30.2 Main religious affiliations

Religion	England and Wales	France	Germany
Christian	37.3 m	35 m Catholics 800 000 Protestants	55.1 m
Buddhist	180 000	700 000	155 000
Hindu	590 000	Not available	97 000
Jewish	300 000	600 000	100 000
Muslim	1.8 m	Not available	3.2 m

Sources: ONS 2001; Winkler *et al.* 1999; REMID 2003. Figures refer to different years.

'Section 11' special funding (under the Local Government Act) of ethnic minority education, allocating £430 million (€584 million, $657 million) extra funding to help overcome the problems of low achievement among Black and Asian pupils.

The Labour government has also encouraged state funding for 'faith' or denominational schools. There are approximately 6384 primary and 589 secondary faith based schools, of which 4716 are Church of England and 2108 Roman Catholic. Only 32 are Jewish, four Muslim, two Sikh, one Greek Orthodox and one Seventh Day Adventist. The state pays 85 per cent of capital costs and also pays the teachers. All state schools must teach the national curriculum, although for the religious education component more than half of faith schools teach their own faith. The remaining 43 per cent (voluntary-controlled or foundation schools) teach the locally agreed religious education syllabus, which has a more multi-ethnic approach. Admissions policy is determined by the school governors, but in many cases the local education authority is also involved. A school can insist that children come from a particular faith background and may insist on proof of baptism and regular church attendance, although they must operate in accordance with the Race Relations Act.

Muslims argue that anti-discrimination legislation in Britain fails to protect them because it only covers discrimination against an ethnic or national group. This means that Muslims lack protection against acts that prevent them taking time off work for religious holidays, while multicultural educational policies fail to take account of their concerns and they are among the most deprived groups in the country.

In France the separation of Church and State was established in 1905 and secular education is very important. Wearing religious clothing or symbols, such as the Christian crucifix, Jewish kippa or Muslim hijab, is thought to contravene the basic principles of secular education. Since the late 1980s there has been a dispute about the right of Muslim girls to wear headscarves in state schools, accompanied by a variety of contradictory rulings by different authorities.

In Germany, faith based schools are in a small minority and are mainly either Catholic or Protestant. In order to receive recognition as a church community and to be eligible for benefits from the taxation system and religious classes in schools, a religious community has to be represented by a central committee. The Jewish communities are organized hierarchically in state associations and these in the Central Council of Jews in Germany (*Zentralrat der Juden in Deutschland*), and Jewish schools can be found in Berlin, Frankfurt, Munich and Düsseldorf, but meeting this organizational requirement has been difficult for the Muslim community, with Muslims from over 40 countries and many different, diverse branches of Islam living in Germany with different conceptions of religious authority. Of the 3.2 million Muslims living in Germany, only about 10 per cent are organized in Muslim mosque associations and organizations (Engin 2001).

Within the state school system, students of Islamic faith have a constitutional right to religious classes, but again the translation of this right into practice is hindered by Islam being divided into many diverse branches of faith and lacking a leadership recognized by all. In addition, the *Länder* have taken very different approaches in implementing this provision of the Basic Law. As a result, Islamic religious classes do not form an integral part of the school curriculum (Engin 2001). Instead there are different forms of religious teaching, such as mother tongue lessons (*Muttersprachenunterricht*), usually delivered by consulates and embassies in conjunction with the *Land* Ministry of Education; Islamic instruction (*Islamische Unterweisung*), which is run in German as a regular part of the school curriculum in Nordrhein-Westfalia; and the religious classes for all (*Religionsunterricht für alle*) in Hamburg, which are interdenominational and delivered by trained German teachers. Muslim organizations as well as embassies also offer various Islamic classes, often referred to as Koranic schools, although these have caused some concerns in educational as well as political circles as fears are growing over uncontrolled, fundamentalist Islamic teaching to Muslim children.

Legally Germany separates state affairs from religion or philosophy of life. 'The legal status of the state church system is based on the following constitutional conditions: collective freedom of faith and religion, prohibition of a state church and the obligation of the state to neutrality, and the right to self-determination of faith and religion' (Bundesministerium des Innern 2003). However there remain open questions about religious dress code and customs in public life and office. For instance, the case of a German Muslim born in Afghanistan who was refused employment as a schoolteacher by the Ministry of Education in Baden-Württemberg because she insisted on wearing her head scarf to work, claiming a constitutional right to religious freedom and expression, remains unresolved. It seems inevitable that Germany will face similar conflicts and court cases as it has neither decided to follow the British approach, which allows people of different creeds to express their religious belonging in dress code and behaviour, nor the secular French way, leaving Germany open to biased rulings which seem to permit the wearing of crucifixes, the Star of David and the kippa by people working in a public function, but not the head scarf.

Recent developments

In France the most important developments have been in the area of religion, with the election of the French Muslim Council, which has given rise to controversies between different tendencies within Islam. In addition, the government is planning to legislate to ban religious symbols in state schools to put an end to the ambiguous situation.

Recent developments in Germany involve debates about defining groups such as foreigners living in Germany as minorities, which was rejected by the German government. There is also a debate around the implementation of the European Charter for Regional or Minority Languages (Council of Europe 1992). The German government has agreed a second law which aims to improve the protection of minority languages – Danish, Sorbian, Friesian, and Romany as well as Low German as a regional language. This law would improve the daily use of these languages by introducing bilingual road signs and the use of these languages in communal affairs.

Sources

BAFL (Bundesamt für die Anerkennung ausländischer Flüchtlinge) (2002), *Zahl der zuge-zogenen Aussiedler Zeitraum: 1950–2001*, <www.bafl.de/template/index_migration.htm> [5 January 2004].

BMI (Bundesministerium des Innern) (2002), *Zahl der eingereisten Aussiedler von 1950–2001*, <www.bmi.bund.de/top/sonstige/Themen_der_Innenpolitik/Aussiedler/Statistiken/ix8616_81066.htm> [5 January 2004].

BMI (Bundesministerium des Innern) (2003), *Das System des Staatskirchenrechts in der Bundesrepublik Deutschland*, <www.bmi.bund.de/frame/liste/Themen_der_Innenpolitik/Religionsgemeinschaften/Daten_und_Fakten/ix3910_artikel.htm? categoryVariant = bmi_DF&Thema = 65&language =de&language= de&categoryVariant=bmi_DF&Thema = 65> [27 September 2003].

British Government (1999), *Report submitted by the United Kingdom pursuant to Article 25, paragraph 1 of the Framework Convention for the Protection of National Minorities*, ACFC/SR 013, 1999, <www.coe.int/T/E/human_rights/minorities/> [9 July 2003].

CRE (Commission for Racial Equality), *Ethnic Minorities in Britain*, CRE Fact Sheets (London: CRE, 1999).

CRIF (Conseil Representative des Institutions Juives de France) (2003), <www.crif.org> [11 December 2003].

Council of Europe, *European Charter for Regional or Minority Languages* (Strasbourg: Council of Europe, 1992), <www.coe.int/T/E/Legal_Affairs/Local_and_regional_Democracy/Regional_or_Minority_languages/> [9 July 2003].

D_statis (Statistisches Bundesamt Deutschland) (2003a), *Ausländische Bevölkerung 1980 bis 2002*, <www.destatis.de/basis/d/bevoe/bevoetab7.htm> [5 January 2004].

D_statis (Statistisches Bundesamt Deutschland) (2003b), *Ausländische Bevölkerung nach Geburtsland am 31.12.2002*, <www.destatis.de/basis/d/bevoe/bevoetab10.htm> [5 January 2004].

ECRML (European Charter for Regional or Minority Languages) (2000), *Initial Periodical Report by Germany Presented to the Secretary General of the Council of Europe in accordance* with Article 15 of the Charter, <www.coe.int/T/E/Legal_Affairs/Local_and_regional_ Democracy/Regional_or_Minority_languages/Documentation/> [27 September 2003].

ECRML (European Charter for Regional or Minority Languages) (2002), *Application of the Charter in Germany*, <www.coe.int/T/E/Legal_Affairs/Local_and_regional_Democracy/ Regional_or_Minority_languages/Documentation/> [27 September 2003].

Engin, H. (2001), *Wenn sechs Prozent aller Schüler Muslime sind. Islamischer Religionsunterricht an deutschen Schulen? Eine Bestandsaufnahme*, Islam in Deutschland Heft 4, Baden-Württemberg: LpB., <www.lpb.bwue.de/aktuell/bis/4_01/islamreli6.htm> [27 September 2003].

Federal Ministry of the Interior (2002) *Principles of the Policy on Foreigners*, <www.eng.bmi.bund.de/> [3 March 2003].

Framework Part I (1999), *First Report submitted by the Federal Republic of Germany under Article 25, paragraph 1 of the Council of Europe's Framework Convention for the Protection of National Minorities*, ACFC/SR,001, 2000, <www.coe.int/T/E/human_rights/minorities/> [9 July 2003].

Framework Part II (1999), *First Report submitted by the Federal Republic of Germany under Article 25, paragraph 1 of the Council of Europe's Framework Convention for the Protection of National Minorities*, ACFC/SR,001, 2000, <www.coe.int/T/E/human_rights/minorities/> [9 July 2003].

German Government (2002), *Comments by the Federal Republic of Germany on the Opinion of the Advisory Committee on the Implementation of the Framework Convention for the Protection of National Minorities in the Federal Republic of Germany*, Advisory Committee on the Framework Convention for the Protection of National Minorities, GVT/ĆOM/INF/ OP/I (2002)008, 19 July 2002, <www.coe.int/T/e/human_rights/Minorities/> [9 July 2003].

INSEE (Institut National de la Statistique et des Études Économiques) (2003), <www.insee.fr> [16 December 2003].

Northern Ireland Assembly (2003), <www.ni-assembly.gov.uk> [11 December 2003].

ONS (Office for National Statistics) (2001), *Census, April 2001*, London, ONS <www.statistics.gov.uk/> [11 September 2003].

Paris City Council (2003), <www.paris.fr> [12 December 2003].

Prime Minister (2003), <www.premier-ministre.gouv.fr/> [12 December 2003].

REMID (Religionswissenschaftlicher Medien- und Informationsdienst e. V.) (February 2003), <www.uni-leipzig.de/~religion/remid_info_zahlen.htm> [January 2004]

Vie Publique (2003), <www.vie-publique.fr/actualite/alaune/breve_cultemusulman.htm> [12 December 2003].

Welsh Language Board (2003), <www.bwrdd-yr-iaith.org.uk/en/index.php> [5 September 2003].

F. Winkler, A. Rößler and M. Jaster (1999), *Ethnische Minderheiten und ihre Rechte in Deutschland*, Comenius Project, <www.esj-lille.fr/atelier/magan2/teo/reperes/stats2.html (Prälat Diehl Schulewww.esj-lille.fr/atelier/magan2/teo/reperes/stats2.html> [5 January 2004].

31
Family Policy
Mary Daly

Introduction

Britain, France and Germany have historically taken quite different approaches to the family. They have varied not just in terms of how they envisage the relationship between the family and the state but also in regard to the generosity of support offered to families. Germany and France have been far more generous to families than Britain. Recent reforms are bringing the countries closer together, however. For example, cash benefits to families are being more closely tied to paid employment and there is a greater push for mothers to be employed. Yet there are also significant differences and, from a comparative perspective, exciting developments to be uncovered.

The nature of family policy

Family policy is usually taken to refer to policies for families with children and, more specifically, to cash payments to assist families with the costs of child rearing. That is, it is now customary to consider as family policy a range of instruments (cash payments, tax allowances and employment leaves) which the state uses to support different types of families with children. After first outlining the functions and institutional structure of family policy in the three countries, this chapter reviews in turn cash benefits for families with children, family taxation, maternity and other leaves for the purpose of caring for children, and the financial support of lone parents. Childcare is covered by Chapter 29 on women, and other services for families in Chapter 26 on social services.

Although in each of the three countries a specific unit exists for family policy, the scope, functions and significance of this unit varies. Both Germany and France have a designated unit for family-related policy making which is integrated into a ministry. In Germany the ministry (*Bundesministerium für Familie, Senioren, Frauen und Jugend*) deals with the family together with older people and youth, while in France the *Délégation Interministérielle à la Famille* (attached to the Ministry for Health, the Family and Handicapped Persons) is the unit charged with policy making on the family. In considerable contrast, no specific body exists in Britain for policy making on the family, despite the existence of an agency entitled the Family Policy Unit formerly attached to the Home Office but since June 2003 attached to the Department of Education and Skills.

Both France and Germany specify a set of aims and objectives in relation to family policy. In Germany the ministry is charged with, *inter alia*, fashioning measures to protect the family, ensuring that the interests of the family are taken account of at federal government level, improving the conditions whereby parents can assume parental responsibility and supporting family organizations. The functions specified for the *Délégation Interministérielle* in France include the reconciliation of work and family life, improving and simplifying family benefit, reinforcing parental responsibility and focusing on child poverty as well as safeguarding children's rights and the situation of young adults. The Family Policy Unit in Britain is quite different in that, being charged with encouraging greater awareness of the importance of the family and parenting issues, it looks outwards towards the public rather than inwards towards policymakers and policy making.

Specific comparisons

Further insight into family policy can be gained by looking in more detail at cash payments to families with children; family taxation; maternity, paternity and parental leave, and provisions for lone parents.

Cash payments to families with children

Historically across Europe child benefits or family allowances were the main pillar of family policy. Designed to assist families with some of the costs of raising children, they date mainly from the period around World War II. At the time of their introduction and subsequently, they represented a truly innovative form of social right since they tended to have no conditions attached (Montanari 2000: 309). They have other notable features as well in that they are usually funded from general taxation revenues (although less so in France) and are administered by a specialist agency. The universal character of the child benefit has been undermined over time, however. As Table 31.1 shows, of the three countries only in Britain are child benefits universal for all children irrespective of their family's circumstances. In France, the pronatalist roots of policy on the family are to be seen in the fact that the allowance is paid only for second and subsequent children. In Germany the family must be subject to the levying of income tax to qualify. There is in each country an upper age limit but the actual age threshold varies.

Table 31.1   Cash payments to families with children

	Britain	France	Germany
Name of allowance	Child Benefit	*Allocations Familiales*	*Kindergeld*
Financing (sources of funds)	Central government	Employers' contributions, central government	Federal government
Administration	Child Benefit Office (Department of Work and Pensions)	*Caisse Nationale des Allocations Familiales*	*Familienkassen der Arbeitsämter (Nichterwerbstätige)*
Structure	Universal benefit for persons responsible for raising a child aged under 16*	Universal benefit for residents with 2 or more children aged under 20**	Universal benefit for taxable residents with 1 or more children aged under 18***
Monthly rates 1 January 2003			
1 child	£68.25 (€92.75, $104.35)	–	€154 (£113, $173)
2 children	£113.70 (€154.52, $173.85)	€111.26 (£81.89, $125.17)	€308 (£226.69, $346.50)
3 children	£159.90 (€217.30, $244.49)	€253.81 (£186.80, $285.54)	€462 (£340, $519.75)
Supplements	Lone parents (abolished in 1998 for new claimants)	Children aged 11 + Low income families with three or more children	–

Notes
* If in full-time education, age threshold is 19; if actively seeking work it is 18.
** If they are not working or are earning less than 55% of minimum wage.
*** If unemployed age threshold is 20, and 27 if in vocational training/further education.
Sources: MISSOC 2003.

There is also considerable variation in the generosity of the payment. Germany offers the most generous support, with a monthly rate of *Kindergeld* of around €154 (£113, $173) per child for the first three children and a higher rate from the fourth child on. Compare this to Britain, where not only is the payment per child less (£68.25, €92.75, $104.35) for the first child but the amount paid per child is actually reduced as the number of children increases. Hence a three-child family in Germany receives €462 (£340, $520) a month in child benefit compared with £160 (€217, $425) for the equivalent British family. France is closer to Britain than to Germany in terms of the level of support offered through child benefit. However in France the value of the benefit increases with both the number and age of children (the latter when the child reaches the age of 11 years). In addition, a 'large family supplement' exists for families with three or more children. While this supplement is income-related, around 80 per cent of large families secure entitlement to it.

Family taxation

Britain is a major innovator in regard to income taxation. A new Child Tax Credit was introduced in 2003 as part of a robust policy drive to increase the attractiveness of paid work and integrate benefit and taxation payments. This credit is payable to families with at least one child aged under 16 years. Only one credit exists for each family, payable to the partner with the highest income. If the partner who receives the credit does not pay sufficient tax to use all the credit, he or she may transfer the unused credit to the other partner after the end of the tax year. At April 2003, the credit consisted of an income tax relief up to a set amount (£545, €741, $833) per family and a relief of £1 445 (€1 964, $2 209) per child. The introduction of the Children's Tax Credit was part of a major reform of policy, having been preceded in 2000 by the introduction of the Working Families' Tax Credit. In an effort to increase income levels among families where the parents are in employment, this precipitates the transfer of key aspects of income support from the social security system to the tax system. In the eyes of contemporary family policy in Britain, all families should have at least one worker. What are called 'workless households' – households where no adult is in employment, including those of lone mothers – are especially targeted by this reform.

France is very different to Britain in that it is the family rather than the individual that is the unit of assessment for tax liability, and while no tax allowances or credits are given for children *per se*, children are included in the formula for calculating a family's tax liability (Table 31.2). Hence the household income of married or registered cohabiting couples is divided by the number of all family members, including children (a 0.5 quotient being applied for the first and second child, except for lone parent households). The relevant tax rate is then applied and the resultant sum multiplied by the number of family members to arrive at the family's tax liability.

Germany has a different system. There the married couple is the unit for calculating taxes and while the number of children is not taken into account in the calculation of the tax liability the couple's tax is reduced if they have children. However since a series of reforms effected in the late 1990s upgrading

Table 31.2   Taxation of families

	Britain	France	Germany
Unit of assessment	Individual	Family	Spouses (optional)
Family tax allowances and credits	Children's Tax Credit Working Families Tax Credit (low income working families with children only)	None	Tax allowances for lone parents, children and owner occupiers with children
Tax deductions for family-related expenses	Childcare Tax Credit (dual earning couples and lone parents on low income only)	Tax credits for childcare expenses	Tax allowances for childcare expenses (lone parents only)

Sources: Dingeldey 2001; German Embassy in the UK 2001; Inland Revenue 2003; O'Donoghue and Sutherland 1999; Service Public 2003.

child benefit, the income threshold for tax relief for children is now so high that only families with a high income qualify.

In all three countries parents are allowed to offset some of the costs of childcare against tax. While this is unconditional in France – granted through a system of tax credits – in Britain it is dependent on the use of recognised or approved child-care services and in Germany it is limited to particular families (mainly lone parents).

Maternity, paternity and parental leave

Maternity leave is one of the oldest social security benefits since maternity has long been recognized as an income risk for female workers. Today Britain offers women paid maternity leave of 18 weeks whereas French women get 16 weeks of paid leave upon the birth of a child and their German counterparts receive 14 weeks. As Table 31.3 shows, in France and Germany women receive 100 per cent of their net income for the entire period of the leave. Compensation is considerably lower in Britain where payment is on an earnings replacement (at a 90 per cent compensation rate) basis for the first six weeks. Following this, workers receive a flat-rate weekly payment of £75 (€102, $115) for the remaining 12 weeks. Women who do not qualify for Maternity Pay and have weekly earnings of between £30 (€41, $46) and £75 (€102, $115) receive the flat-rate weekly payment (£75, €102, $115) for the entire 18 weeks. In Britain and Germany a maternity grant is paid to women on low incomes (Britain) and to those who do not qualify for the maternity benefit (Germany). France is much

Table 31.3 Maternity leave

	Britain	*France*	*Germany*
Duration	18 weeks	16 weeks	14 weeks
Rates	First 6 weeks – 90% average earnings. Next 12 weeks – £75 (€102, $114.68) per week	100% net earnings	100% net earnings
Other cash payments	Means-tested maternity grant for recipients of social assistance payments (£500, €679.50, $764.50)	Means-tested allowance paid from 4th month of pregnancy until child's third birthday (€159.76, £117.58, $179.73 per month)	Maternity grant for insured women not entitled to maternity benefit (€77, £56.67, $86.63)

Sources: Bundesministerium für Familie, Senioren, Frauen und Jugend 2003; CNAF 2003; DTI 2003; DWP 2003; Ministère des Affaires Sociales, du Travail et de la Solidarité 2003; MISSOC 2003.

more generous, however, paying a means-tested allowance of up to €160 (£118, $180) a month to the mother from the fifth month of pregnancy until the child's third birthday.

At the time of writing, paid leave for fathers, paternity leave, existed only in France, where fathers are allowed to take up to two weeks of paid leave upon the birth of a child. However a similar provision was due to be introduced in Britain in 2003.

Parental leave is different to either maternity or paternity leave in that it can be taken by either parent, or in some cases by both, and extends beyond the first months of the child's life (see Table 31.4). All three countries have parental leave from employment but there are significant differences across nations. In Britain the statutory leave of 13 weeks is unpaid but it is a right of the individual worker, and hence available to both parents if they are employed. In Germany and France, as well as being paid the leave is constructed as an entitlement of the family rather than of individual parents. Of the three countries, France is the most supportive of parental caring. French parents are entitled to leave until the child's third birthday, compensated at the minimum at a rate of €516 (£380, $581) a month. The leave is more limited in Germany, although it is available to all parents rather than just those who were employed before becoming parents. A German parent can take leave for the first two years of the child's life for which they receive a flat-rate allowance of around €300 (£221, $338) a month. From the seventh month, the allowance is means-tested.

Table 31.4   Parental leave

	Britain	*France*	*Germany*
Duration	13 weeks, to be taken any time until the child's 5th birthday	Continuous extended leave until the child's 3rd birthday	Continuous extended leave until the child's 3rd birthday
Weeks paid	None	Entire leave period	First 2 years of child's life (means-tested from child's 7th month onwards)
Rates	–	€484.97 (£357, $545.59) per month	€307 (£226, $345) per month*

Note
* Parents have the option of taking a shortened benefit period of 12 months. In such cases the allowance amounts to €460 (£338.56, $517.50) per month.
Sources: Bundesministerium für Familie, Senioren, Frauen und Jugend 2003; CNAF 2003; DTI 2003; DWP 2003; Ministère des Affaires Sociales, du Travail et de la Solidarité 2003; MISSOC 2003.

Provision for lone parents

Lone parents *qua* lone parents are entitled to a particular cash payment in Britain and France but not in Germany (Table 31.5). Such a payment is in both countries dependent on means. However France has a payment specifically designated for lone parents (*Allocation de Parent Isolé*) whereas in Britain lone parents claim Income Support (the general safety net scheme). The payment rate is considerably more generous in France, but whereas in France lone parents are entitled to support from public funds only until their child reaches the age of three years, lone parents in Britain can (technically) claim Income Support as lone parents until their child reaches the age of 16 years.

France and Germany also have another provision for lone parents. Lone parents who are not receiving maintenance payments from the absent parent, and who fulfil certain conditions, are entitled to advanced child maintenance payment, a guaranteed maintenance allowance from the state for their children. In France the guaranteed maintenance allowance is automatically paid to lone parents when the other parent is dead or when paternity has not been established. In cases where the liable parent fails to pay child maintenance, the maintenance allowance takes the form of an advance payment which must later be reimbursed by the absent parent. In Germany, lone parents who are receiving insufficient or no maintenance payments for children from the other parent have the right to an advance on maintenance from the government for children up to the age of 12 years for a maximum of six years. As Table 31.5 shows, the amount is more generous in Germany.

Table 31.5 Cash provisions for lone parents

	Britain	*France*	*Germany*
Cash benefit for lone parents outside the labour market	Income Support	*Allocation de Parent Isolé*	None
Entitlement period	Up to the child's 16th birthday	Up to the child's 3rd birthday	–
Monthly rates (as at 1 January 2003)	£218.60 (€297, $334.24) for the parent plus £154 (€209.28, $235.47) for each dependent child	€521.20 (£383.60, $586.35) for the parent plus €173.84 (£128, $195.57) for each dependent child	–
Advanced child maintenance payment	No	Yes	Yes
Monthly rates	–	€78.23 (£57.58, $88)	€111 (£82, $125) for children aged under 6, €151 (£111, $170) for children aged, 6 12*

Note
* Old *Länder* only; a lower rate is applied in the new *Länder*.
Sources: Bundesministerium für Familie, Senioren, Frauen und Jugend 2003; Citizens Advice Bureau 2003; DWP 2003; MISSOC 2003.

Policy has a different cast in Britain. There the primary focus is on securing private maintenance. Set up in 1993, the Child Support Agency seeks to ensure that absent fathers contribute to the support of their children. Lone parents claiming certain state benefits are required to register with the Agency and provide information on the whereabouts of the absent parent. Failure to provide the information required (unless there is good cause for not doing so) is subject to penalties, including loss of benefit. Should the parent receive maintenance, he or she has their benefit reduced pound for pound, since any maintenance received counts as income when calculating the amount of the benefit to which they are entitled.

In addition to these payments, the relationship between lone parents and paid work has been the subject of policy reform, especially in Britain and France. A New Deal for Lone Parents was introduced in Britain in 1998, offering help and advice on job search, training, childcare and other employment-related matters. Part of New Labour's Welfare to Work strategy, it is designed to help lone parents on Income Support to find a job. The French government too has introduced a series of employment incentives for lone parents, especially by allowing an earnings' disregard of 100 per cent against benefits for a period of up to six months and a 50 per cent disregard for the following nine months.

Recent developments

Family policy is a dynamic area of policy within and across countries. While there is considerable variation in reforms being introduced in Britain, France and Germany, it is possible to identify a number of common trends. The most widespread of these is what can be termed a move towards a welfare mix whereby it is a policy goal to diversify the provision of services to families. Diversification has mainly taken the form of an increased role for the private sector in those countries that have traditionally adhered to a public service model.

A second widespread emphasis in recent policy is the reconciliation of work and family life. This has had two expressions in policy. On the one hand, employed parents are given increased incentives and support to take time off work to care for their children. Both parents can be targeted in this regard but there is increased interest in encouraging fathers to take (short periods of) time off work to care for their young children. This type of reconciliation policy is, by and large, EU-driven. On the other hand, there is a general move towards activating people to be employed. This could be said to have a certain reconciliation character in that male and female parents are increasingly encouraged to be economically active.

A move towards children's rights is a third identifiable trend in the policy landscape of the countries studied. This involves both improved access for children to services which are oriented to their social rights, such as pre-school and other educational services as well as health services, and the introduction of political rights for children, with a special emphasis on their right to participate in decisions which directly affect them.

A fourth identifiable trend is towards a closer focusing of state support on parenthood and parenting as against marriage. Parental or biological responsibilities are today emphasized over what might be termed more 'social' relations of partnership and marriage. The financial obligations of fathers are especially reinforced. There is also a move away from a tax privileging of marriage and a tendency to grant non-married couples similar rights and responsibilities as married couples.

Note: I am very grateful to Sara Clavero for excellent research assistance.

Sources

Bundesministerium für Familie, Senioren, Frauen und Jugend (2003), <www.bmfsj.de> [December 2003].

Citizens Advice Bureau (2003), <www.nacab.org.uk> [December 2003].

CNAF (Caisse Nationale des Allocations Familiales) (2003), <www.caf.fr> [December 2003].

I. Dingeldey, 'European tax systems and their impact on family employment patterns', *Journal of Social Policy* 30(4) (2001): 653–72.

DTI (Department of Trade and Industry) (2003), <www.dti.gov.uk> [December 2003].

DWP (Department of Work and Pensions) (2003), <www.dwp.gov.uk> [December 2003].

Famille (2003), <www.famille.gouv.fr> [December 2003].

German Embassy in the UK (2001), *Taxation Fact Sheet 2001*, <www.german-embassy. org.uk> [June 2002].

Inland Revenue (2003), <www.inlandrevenue.gov.uk> [December 2003].

S.B. Kamerman and A.J. Kahn (eds), *Family Policy: Government and Families in Fourteen Countries* (New York: Columbia University Press, 1978).

Ministère des Affaires Sociales, du Travail et de la Solidarité (2003), <www.emploi-solidarite.gouv.fr> [December 2003].

MISSOC (2003), 'Social protection in the Member States in the EU Member States and the European Economic Area. Situation on 1, January 2003 and evolution', <www. eu.int/comm/employment_social/missoc/2003/index_en.htm> [December 2003].

I. Montanari, 'From family wage to marriage subsidy and child benefits: controversy and consensus in the development of family policy', *Journal of European Social Policy* 10(4) (2000): 307–33.

C. O'Donoghue and H. Sutherland, 'Accounting for the family in European income tax systems', *Cambridge Journal of Economics* 23 (1999): 565–98.

Service-Public (2003), 'Le portail de la administration française', <www.service-public.fr> [December 2003].

Part VI
Other Policies

32
Culture
Clive Gray and Rolf Hugoson

Introduction

The role of the state in providing cultural policies and services has led to the creation of marked differences between the cultural policies of Britain, France and Germany. For example, spending on culture by all governmental bodies in Germany, at £56.50 (€76.92, $86.54) per capita, is significantly higher than in France, which spends £37.80 (€51.37, $57.80) per capita on culture, and in Britain, which spends just £16,60 (€22.56, $25.38) per capita (Feist 2001).

The nature of cultural policy

Government intervention in the field of culture is extremely wide-ranging and involves a large number of groups and individuals in both the public and private sectors of the economy. 'Culture' itself is a notoriously difficult word to define, and identifying a simple set of policy actions that make up the field of cultural policy is no simple matter. For the purposes of this chapter, and in accord with the view of cultural policy adopted by the Council of Europe (Council of Europe 1991: 228), cultural policy is taken to incorporate:

- support for the performing arts;
- support for museums and national heritages;
- the diffusion of national cultural products throughout the world; and
- the protection of uniquely cultural traits and characteristics.

Cultural policies are usually implemented through a fragmented set of organizations rather than by a single governmental organization. While Britain and France both have central ministries with responsibility for cultural affairs (the Department for Culture, Media and Sport in Britain and the Ministry of Culture in France) the actual provision of cultural policy in both cases is usually divided between governmental and quasi-governmental organizations operating locally, regionally, nationally and internationally. In Germany this multiplicity of actors is also present at the central level with the recently established (in 1998) Commission for Culture and Media located inside the Federal Chancellery, plus the Foreign Office and Federal Ministry of Education and Research as well as other international, national, regional and local actors (see Table 32.1).

The purposes of the funding that is made available to the *performing arts* by the state in each country are generally the same, being concerned with either subsidizing the costs of artistic production, investing in the creation of new works, maintaining performance spaces (for example theatres and concert halls), providing direct financial support to artists and companies, and encouraging private sector support for the performing arts (for example through tax incentives for investment in film production). The exact split between these forms of state support varies between the countries. The level of subsidy for orchestras producing 'classical' music in France and Germany, for example, often covers over 90 per cent of orchestral income, whilst in Britain it is more likely to cover about 50 per cent of income. State support also varies between artistic forms. Another example of the variability that exists can be seen in the case of taxation on the printed word. In all three countries books and periodicals are subject to a lower level of VAT than are other goods and services: in Britain there is a zero rate of VAT, compared with the usual 17.5 per cent; in Germany a reduced rate of 7 per cent, compared with 16 per cent; and in France a reduced

Table 32.1   Organizations responsible for cultural policy

	Britain	France	Germany
National	Department for Culture, Media and Sport Resource Heritage Lottery Fund	Ministry of Culture	Federal Commission for Culture and Media Federal Cultural Foundation Prussian Cultural Heritage Foundation
Regional	Arts Council of England Arts Council of Scotland Arts Council of Wales Arts Council of Northern Ireland English Heritage Commission for Architecture and the Built Environment Scottish Museums Council	22 Regions 98 *départements*	16 *Länder*
Local	Local Authorities	Communes	Local Authorities

rate for books of 5.5 per cent and for periodicals of 2.1 per cent, compared with 20.6 per cent for most other goods and services (European Commission 2000).

In the case of *museums and national heritages* there are many more similarities between the three nations concerned. The preservation of the national patrimony rests directly with the central state in France; with a combination of the central and regional state in Germany; and with national and local state actors, plus semi-autonomous agencies, in Britain. In each case museums are largely funded by local, regional and national governments (or some combination of all three) but managed by independent boards.

While a great deal of the exposure of national cultures to people and cultures that are located elsewhere in the world takes place through the medium of the private sector, for example via the sale of music, books and works of art, a semi-official *promotion and diffusion of these cultures* is also undertaken through the activities of bodies that rely heavily on state subsidy. The dominant bodies in this field are the Goethe Institute (85 per cent funded by the state), the British Council (33 per cent funded by the state), and the *Institut Française*, which is the French government's official cultural and linguistic centre (French Embassy London 2002). In addition, the embassies of the different countries are also used as mechanisms for the transmission of information and images about the respective countries and their cultures.

The *protection of national cultures* is largely a function of the dominant national actors in each state (the Department for Culture, Media and Sport in Britain; the Ministry of Culture in France; and the Commission for Culture and Media in Germany) and depends upon the self-images of the cultures concerned. While the state is also active in this field as a by-product of the operations of the education system, it can also be more explicitly involved in this area. Both France and Germany have bodies that act as guardians of the language, each of which is funded by the state, either national (in France), or federal and regional (in Germany). In the French case the formal acceptance of neologisms (or the creation of new words to do the same job) requires the imprimatur of the *Academie Française*. In Germany the independent but highly regarded *Gesellschaft für deutsche Sprache* dominates the process of determining the formal rules of grammar, spelling and punctuation. In Britain, by contrast, language is, if anything, subject to the anarchy of the linguistic marketplace and is clearly not accorded the same cultural significance as in France and Germany.

This concern for the content and character of national cultures is also shown by the doubts that are expressed about the influence and impact of imported media such as Hollywood films. France has played a major role in arguing that cultural industries deserve to be (and, indeed, *should* be) subsidized by the state to ensure their survival (see Padis 2002), and has introduced legislation specifying, for example, how much of the music output of French radio stations must be of French origin.

Specific comparisons

While there are broad patterns of similarity between how each component of cultural policy is undertaken across the three countries, there are also major differences between them. In general, national governments set the parameters of policy activity in the field of culture while the precise nature and detail of what is undertaken within these boundaries is determined by other actors, leading to significant policy variation both between and within states. This can be clearly seen in the cases of the performing arts, and support for museums and national heritages.

The performing arts

Central government spending on the performing arts is much higher in France than in Britain or Germany, even though overall government spending is highest in Germany and lowest in Britain (see Table 32.2).

In Britain support for the performing arts is divided. The major role of the Department of Culture, Media and Sport is to direct money granted by Parliament to a range of arm's-length agencies that have direct financial responsibilities. The dominant agency in terms of size and sheer financial clout is the Arts Council of England (Gray 2000), with counterparts in Scotland, Wales and Northern Ireland being funded by, and accountable to, the Scottish Parliament and the Welsh and Northern Ireland Assemblies respectively.

Local authorities are also a major part of the funding system for the performing arts throughout Britain. Although local authority support for culture and the arts is a statutory duty in Scotland and Northern Ireland, this is not the case in England and Wales (Gray 2002). The consequence of this has been that local authority support for the arts in England has varied significantly between

Table 32.2   Government expenditure on the performing arts

	Britain	France	Germany
National	€0.8 m (£0.6 m, $0.9 m)	€663.3 m (£488.2 m, $746.2 m)	€12.5 m (£9.2 m, $14.1 m)
Regional	€716.1 m (£526.9 m, $805.6 m)	€272.2 m* (£200.3 m, $306.2 m)	€1 249 m (£919.3 m, $1 405.1 m)
Local	€391.6 m (£288.2 m, $440.5)	€284.1 m* (£209.1 m, $319.6 m)	€1 560.6 m (£1 148.6 m, $1 755.7 m

Note
* These figures are estimates only.
Sources: Department of Culture, Media and Sport (2003a); Arts Council of England (2003); Scottish Arts Council (2003); Arts Council of Northern Ireland (2003); Arts Council of Wales (2003); Ministry of Culture (2003); Kulturfinanzbericht 2000 (2001).

authorities, with some being relatively generous and others being largely abstemious in terms of support.

In Germany there is a similar picture, with most financial support for the performing arts being generated below the national level. National support is divided between the Commission for Culture and Media and other central bodies, with none of them providing much direct support. The establishment in January 2002 of a new Federal Cultural Foundation (very approximately equivalent to the British system of Arts Councils) is intended to fund large arts projects at arm's-length from the Federal government.

The bulk of financial support within the German system is provided by the regional *Länder* and local authorities. The reunification of Germany served to highlight disparities between the *Länder* and has given the Federal government an opportunity to strengthen its own role as an agent of symbolic unity. The establishment of the Federal Cultural Foundation implies that the Federal government is likely to become more actively involved in this policy area than has previously been the case.

In France the central level clearly dominates funding, and the main central department directly funds some aspects of the performing arts, although others are supported by combinations of regional, *département* and local authorities. This has led to even greater disparities between local communes and areas than are present in Britain and Germany, as expenditure on the performing arts is massively skewed towards major cities with most communes spending little, if anything, in this area.

Museums and national heritages

Central government funding for museums and national heritages is highest in France even though overall government funding is lower than in Britain and Germany (see Table 32.3).

The protection and preservation of relics of the past is generally accepted to be a task that the state *must* have a dominating role in and, given the scale of

Table 32.3   Government expenditure on museums and the national patrimony

	Britain	France	Germany
National	£179 m (€242.3 m, $273.7 m)	€525.2 m (£386.5 m, $590.9 m)	€200.3 m (£147.4 m, $225.3 m)
Regional	£64.77 m (€88 m, $99 m)		€853 m (£627.8 m, $959.6 m)
Local	£1 435 m (€1 950.1 m, $2 194 m)		€652 m (£479.9 m, $733.5 m)

Sources: Welsh Assembly (2003); Scottish Parliament (2003); Department for Culture, Media and Sport (2003b); Resource (2003); Department for Transport, Local Government and the Regions (2002); Ministry of Culture (2003); Kulturfinanzbericht 2000.

expenditure that is associated with this function, is likely to remain an important state activity into the foreseeable future. Which part of the state is given responsibility for maintaining museums and architectural remnants of the past differs between the nations concerned and is a fair indicator of the significance and importance that are attached to cultural symbols by states and state actors.

In the German case much of the cultural heritage, and many museums, are strongly connected both to the specific regional histories of the individual *Länder* and to that of the German nation. In this respect both the Federal and *Land* governments have shown particular concern for the maintenance of the heritage of Prussia.

While France has just as strong a localist tradition as Germany, the preservation of a symbolic notion of what France actually is (the idea of *la France profonde*) is far more of a concern for the central state than is the case in Germany. The manipulation of national symbols (from Marianne to Asterix) is a common tool employed by the national state to manage both France itself and the image that it projects to the outside world, and the central state machinery is a far larger actor in this respect than it is in either Britain or Germany.

The British reluctance to become centrally involved with questions of culture is reflected by the hands-off or 'arm's-length' approach that is adopted towards museums and the national patrimony. While central government funds certain national museums and art galleries through a series of funding agreements, much of what is deemed worthy of preservation and exhibition is actually determined locally, predominantly by local authorities. The management of the system is almost entirely removed from direct political control through the use of relatively independent boards to oversee operations.

Recent developments

The field of cultural policy is marked by a great deal of continuity. The broad contours of the policies that have been pursued by governments in all three countries have remained remarkably similar for many years: the roots of British policy were laid in the late 1940s (Gray 2000) and French and German policies remain much as they were in the late 1950s (Ahearne 2003). While specific organizational mechanisms and managerial strategies have undergone change in all three countries, the basic thrust of policy has remained largely constant. It is possible that Germany may be seeing the start of a new era for cultural policy, with the Federal government beginning to develop a much more intrusive stance following the recent establishment of the Federal Commission for Culture and Media and the Federal Cultural Foundation. The implicit centralizing trend that this embodies is also present in England, where the takeover of the Regional Arts Boards by the Arts Council of England in 2002 marks a break with the decentralized structure of the system in the past. Whether these institutional changes can overcome the inertia that is evident within all three systems is open to debate.

What cannot be doubted, however, is that cultural policy remains a marginal policy arena for governments. However while 'culture' itself has been unable to generate a great deal of resistance to broader trends from patronization to radicalism to postmodernism to globalization, it has become almost obligatory for governments to take culture into account. This has become so regardless of what 'culture' might mean. While 'culture' continues to carry important symbolic resonances, states will continue to manipulate it for political reasons entirely of their own.

Sources

J. Ahearne, 'Cultural policy in the old Europe: France and Germany', *International Journal of Cultural Policy*, Vol. 9 (2003): 127–31

Arts Council for England (2003), <www.artscouncil.org.uk/funding> [12 November 2003].

Arts Council for Northern Ireland (2003), <www.artscouncil-ni.org/news/files/AR> [12 November 2003].

Arts Council for Wales (2003), <www.artswales.org.uk/aboutus/files/AnnReportfigures> [12 November 2003].

Council of Europe, *Cultural Policy in France* (Strasbourg: Council of Europe, 1991).

Department for Culture, Media and Sport (2003a), <www.culture.gov.uk> [12 November 2003].

Department for Culture, Media and Sport (2003b), <www.culture.gov.uk/heritage/index> [13 November 2003].

Department for Transport, Local Government and the Regions (2003), <www.dtlr.gov.uk/finance/stats/lgfs> [28 November 2003].

K. Eling, *The Politics of Cultural Policy in France* (London: Macmillan – now Palgrave Macmillan, 1999).

European Commission, *Inventory of Taxes* (Luxembourg: Office for Official Publications of the European Communities, 2000).

Federal Commission for Culture and Media (2002), <www.bundesregierung.de/Regierung/-,4562/Beauftragte-fuer-Kultur-und-Me.htm> [27 November 2003].

Federal Cultural Council (2002), <www.kulturrat.de> [18 February 2003].

A. Feist, *A Comparative Analysis of Arts Profiles for Selected Cities Around The World* (London: International Intelligence on Culture, 2001).

Foreign Ministry Cultural Policy Department (2003), <www.auswaertiges-amt.de/www/de/aussenpolitik/kulturpolitik> [18 February 2003].

French Embassy London (2002), <www.amba.france-uk.org/asp/service> [23 February 2003].

C. Gray, *The Politics of the Arts in Britain* (London: Macmillan – now Palgrave Macmillan, 2000).

C. Gray, 'Local Government and the Arts', *Local Government Studies*, Vol. 28(1) (2002): 77–90.

Kulturfinanzbericht 2000 (Wiesbaden: Statistiches Bundesamt, 2001).

D. Looseley, *The Politics of Fun* (Oxford: Berg, 1995).

Ministry of Culture (2003), <www.culture.gouv.fr/culture/min/budget2002> [14 November 2003].

M-O. Padis, 'France and cultural globalisation', *Political Quarterly*, Vol. 73 (2002): 273–8.

Resource (2003), <www.resource.gov.uk/documents/wrkplan2001> [12 November 2003].

Scottish Arts Council (2003), <www.sac.org.uk> [12 November 2003].

Scottish Parliament (2003), <www.scotland.gov.uk/library3/> [28 November 2003].

Standing Conference of the Regional Ministers of Culture and Education (2003), <www.kmk.org/kultur/home.htm> [18 February 2003].

Welsh Assembly (2003), <www.wales.gov.uk/keypublicstatisticsforwales> [28 November 2003].

33
Sport

Richard Giulianotti and Peter J. Sloane

Introduction

Britain, France and Germany possess three distinctive kinds of sports policy that reflect differences in their political and social history. In Britain, sports policy has been marked in recent years by the social control and free-market principles of Conservative government, followed by 'New Labour's' concern with issues of social exclusion and modernisation. In France, sports policy is marked by the State's comparatively extensive social presence, greater budget, and more elaborate framework for the administration of policy. In Germany, State involvement in sports policy is comparatively restrained, with an emphasis on private association and organization.

The nature of sports policy

The definition of what constitutes sport is far from straightforward. The 1980 European Sport for All charter suggested that there were four broad categories of sport: competitive games, outdoor pursuits, aesthetic movement and conditioning activity. A more concise definition is provided by the Council of Europe's European Sport Charter: ' "sport" means all forms of physical activity which, through casual or organized participation, aim at expressing or improving physical fitness and mental well-being, forming social relationships or obtaining results in competition at all levels' (Council of Europe website). Not all activities clearly fall within this definition. For instance, darts and snooker do not involve much physical activity, but are competitive. Here we adopt a broad perspective.

Given that sports expenditure is only about 2 per cent of household spending in the European Union, the extent of government involvement is perhaps surprising. But about 125 million EU citizens take part in one sport or another and this sector is growing rapidly. In Britain there are at least 112 recognized sports; in Germany there are 87,000 sports clubs and organizations; and in France there are 90 sport federations, 175,000 clubs and 14 million individual sport members.

Sports policy in Britain, France and Germany consists of a number of different components:

- Regulation of sports administrative bodies such as national sports councils and Olympic committees, commercial activities relating to sports-related goods, and the televising of sport, for example the regulation in Britain and Germany of the balance between subscription and free-to-air televised sport.
- Enforcement of prohibitions on doping and on violence among spectators and/or athletes.
- Provision of funding for major capital projects such as stadium refurbishment, the construction of national academies for elite athletes, and bids for major international events.
- The acquisition and disbursement of funding for sports programmes through national lotteries.
- Provision of education and publicity programmes either directly or through funding programmes provided by others to promote objectives such as increased exercise and participation in sport at grass-roots level as well as social inclusion and harmony in sport.
- Planning for the future in collaboration with sports organizations, for example in relation to new initiatives and bids for international events.

Some comparisons of government involvement in sport are given in Table 33.1.

Table 33.1   Methods of support for sport

	Britain	*France*	*Germany*
Gambling	National Lottery Sports Fund	Sports Lottery	Sports receive 12.5% lottery income
Spectator control	Extensive legislation	1993 *Loi Alliot-Marie*	1993 *Nationales Konzept Sport und Sicherheit* (NKSS)
Price regulation	Independent Football Commission	–	–
Regulation of televised sport	Listed events	–	Listed events
Promotion of elite athletes	UK Sports Institute	*La Commission Nationale du Sport de Haut Niveau*	Federal Institute of Sport Science

In Britain and France, there are dedicated Ministers for Sport, whereas in Germany sports policy is controlled by the Ministry of the Interior (see Table 33.2).

In Britain, the national government has an established Minister for Sport based in the Department of Culture, Media and Sport, which oversees the work of UK Sport and Sport England, the major agencies for disbursing government grants for sports projects. The separate regional parliaments and assemblies in Scotland, Northern Ireland and Wales enable a significant degree of sports policy to be controlled within these nations by elected representatives. Major agencies for implementing sport policies are the national sport councils within each of the four 'home nations'. These are independent of government with their own objectives and powers, but nonetheless are funded by the government through grant aid. They are also among the various distributors of the Lottery Sports Fund. The councils work alongside sports governing bodies, local sports councils, schools, health bodies, the local authorities and the private sector to finance grassroots and elite athlete projects.

A key role in sporting activity is undertaken by unpaid volunteers. Their number was estimated in 1995 to be in excess of 1.5 million and their contribution is valued at £1.5 billion (€2 billion, $2.3 billion) per year. Local authorities play a major role through their investment in sports facilities and by funding development officers and sporting events. The value of local authority investment in sport in 1998/99 was estimated to be over £970 million (€1.3 billion, $1.5 billion).

In France, the State's involvement in sports administration and development is rather more elaborate and formalized than in Britain. In May 2002 the national government of Jean-Pierre Raffarin created the distinct post of Minister

Table 33.2 Structure of sports organization

	Britain	*France*	*Germany*
Relevant central government department	Department of Culture, Media and Sport	Ministry of Sport	Federal Ministry of the Interior
Sports minister	Yes	Yes	No
Other bodies	Sports Councils Local government Voluntary sector	*Comité National Olympique et Sportif Français* (CNOSF) *Centres D'education Populaire et de Sport* (CREPS) Regions and *départements*	German Sports Federation *Länder*

for Sport. Since 1945 the French State has delegated authority to sporting federations to promote and organize their disciplines. The new sports law of 6 July 2000 differentiates between sports federations that gain state approval in their mission to provide a public utility, mainly through education within physical activities; and those federations that govern specific sports and thus control the relevant rule-books and organize competitions. The French State's major interface with sports organizations is through its permanent dialogue with the *Comité National Olympique et Sportif Français* (CNOSF). In 2002, the Sports Ministry held a budget of €538.7 million (£397.5 million, $606 million). In recent years this budget has been used to target specific 'priority' areas such as countering social exclusion, promoting employment and the development of young people; enhancing social dialogue with the young through sport, leisure and festivals; promoting social diversity and participation within and through sport, such as with regard to women and the disabled; developing grassroots education within and through sport; and taking stricter action against problems that undermine sport, such as doping. In addition, France's *régions* and *départements* have their own sports administrators to enact the Ministry of Sport's policies at local level, and the *Centres d'Éducation Populaire et de Sport* (CREPS) function mainly at regional level to promote sport through education, training, research and development.

In Germany sport is the governmental responsibility of the Federal Minister of the Interior. There are two basic principles that govern development policy. First, there should be an opportunity for everyone to use sporting facilities within easy commuting distance, at reasonable cost and in accordance with their abilities and interests. Second, government subsidies should be aimed at increasing the self-reliance of autonomous sports entities.

The German Sports Federation (DSB) was founded in 1950 as the umbrella organization for the German gymnastic and sports movement, and has both a co-ordinating and representational role in relation to the general public, government and international sporting bodies. The individual sports federations are responsible for the rules and regulations of their individual sports, the running of championships and the selection of players in international competitions. They are also responsible for the foundation of national training centres and the development of elite athletes.

As in Britain the sports system in Germany is characterized by a strong voluntary sector comprising numerous clubs and federations. The Federal Government, the *Länder* and local authorities provide the legal and material basis for the development of sports. All public support is, however, in accordance with the principle of subsidiarity, so that activities are only supported by the state where sports organizations possess inadequate staffing and financial resources. Most aspects of sport are in fact the sole responsibility of the sixteen *Länder* due to their being constitutionally responsible for cultural affairs, of which sport is one component. The *Länder* are responsible for the provision of recreational sports, particularly in schools and universities. Since the mid 1980s the DSB has adopted an active 'sport for all' policy designed to convince the political parties that sports activities have positive effects on public welfare and to convince sports clubs and associations that social inclusion would gain political approval. By 2000 membership of the DSB had reached just under 29 million or 28.5 per cent of the population, 38.6 per cent of whom were women.

Specific comparisons

A clearer view of the similarities and differences between sports policies in Britain, France and Germany can be obtained by examining four areas in more detail: support via gambling, regulation of stadia and spectators, the regulation of televised games, and the regulation of sports delivery.

Support via gambling

In each of the three countries there are provisions for the support of sporting activity from the proceeds of gambling. Britain's policy on community sport is based on the notion that local authorities should provide most public sector recreational facilities. Local authorities are assisted in this task by grants from the National Lottery's sport fund. In 1991 the government also established the Foundation for Sports and Art, which distributes about £40 million (€54 million, $61 million) per year for sports projects. Its income is partly derived from a tax on gambling on football pools and partly from voluntary contributions from the Pools Promoters Association. In the 1980s the Football Trust provided a further £10 million (€14 million, $15 million) to assist local authorities in improving the quality of pitches and changing rooms. Following the Hillsborough disaster it was merged with the Football Grounds Improvements Trust in 1990 to provide finance for all seated stadiums. Funds of £25 million (€34 million, $38 million) per annum are derived from a 2.5 per cent tax on football gambling and a contribution from the Football Association.

In France, 'coupon sport' helps to offset forms of social exclusion from sports participation in terms of affording equipment and sports club fees. The scheme is administered primarily at local level and has benefited young people in particular, notably the disabled. The Finance Law of 1985 created the Sports Lottery under the Ministry of Finance. The large sums derived from this persuaded the government to repeal a levy introduced in 1980 on parimutuel wagers at race tracks and off-track betting and to allocate a fixed sum of 20 million francs (€3.0 million, £2.2 million, $3.4 million).

In Germany lotteries are required to contribute 25 per cent of their income for non-profit purposes. Sports organizations receive 50 per cent of this money and thus are heavily dependent on this source of revenue.

Regulation of Stadia and Spectators

In Britain, sports policy has been distinguished from its European counterparts most markedly by its intensive concern with issues of public order and crime. Football hooliganism reached a peak in Britain in the mid-1980s and continues to occur in and around football grounds, particularly at smaller clubs and when England fans travel on the continent. Governmental legislative initiatives aimed at controlling disorderly fans have gradually yet profoundly reshaped the public experience of watching football and sport generally. Stadium facilities have improved dramatically, although ticket-prices have risen just as steeply and there is now no space for those who prefer to stand rather than sit during fixtures. Complex CCTV systems have been installed since the late 1980s to monitor spectators, while policing is increasingly based on 'intelligence', drawing heavily on databases compiled on disorderly fans.

Neither France nor Germany has anything like this long history of legislation aimed at combating fan violence. France, for example, was satisfied with the European anti-hooliganism measures introduced after the 1985 Heysel disaster. Its major national legislation was the 1993 *Loi Alliot-Marie*, which enables magistrates to fine drunken fans up to 50,000 francs (€7622, £5610, $8575). Violent spectators can be fined double that sum, coupled with a year in prison; those entering grounds with weapons or fireworks can receive three year sentences. This latter anti-missile measure was strengthened by a government decree of 13 March 1998 banning unauthorized manufacture or possession of certain medical equipment used in some incidents of fan violence. The 1998 World Cup in France featured exceptional security measures to deal with threats from outside the French supporter community. Elaborate CCTV systems were installed at each ground (although such surveillance remains much more circumscribed than in Britain), and magistrates were on hand at each game to issue warrants requested by police. The *Vigipirate* plan, co-ordinating all anti-terrorism forces, was also strengthened. Since then, French sports policy has emphasized the need to tackle many aspects of violence within sport. In February 2002 a national commission was established to prevent violence in all sports under the slogan 'Hors-Jeu La Violence' ('Offside Violence').

In Germany, a major policy aimed at controlling and reducing spectator violence has focused on the creation of 'fan projects'. There are now over 30 such projects, which are community-based initiatives that allow young supporters to meet and interact in a positive, non-violent context under different degrees of supervision.

Regulation of Televised Games

Due to the rise of subscription sports television channels, public access to televised sports events has become a major political issue. In Britain, the Broad-casting Act 1996 established a list of 'crown jewel' events that must be available on free-to-air terrestrial stations that are received by at least 95 per cent of viewers. These events include the Olympic Games, specific fixtures in football's World Cup and European Championship finals, the English and Scottish football Cup finals, Wimbledon, two major horse races, the world finals in rugby union, and rugby league's Challenge Cup final. The list excludes events such as Test match cricket and major golf tournaments such as the Ryder Cup and the Open, although satisfactory secondary coverage must be provided by free-to-air television. In France there are no comparable arrangements. However Germany has so designated the summer and winter Olympics, European Championship and World Cup football matches involving the German national team or the later stages of the competition, the semi-finals of the German FA Cup, the German national football team's home and away matches and the final of any European club competition involving a German club.

Regulation of Sports Delivery

The success of national sports in other nations (notably Australia) generated discussion regarding the need to establish a UK Sports Institute for elite athletes. The resulting institution has not been based at a single site but is instead founded on the principle of 'local service delivery'. Thus in England there are ten 'centres of excellence' with others located in Scotland, Northern Ireland and Wales. In France, elite athletics is controlled through *La commission nationale du sport de haut niveau* (CNSIIN) which is chaired by the Minister of Sport and has members from many sports organizations. In Germany the emphasis has been placed on the scientific support of elite sport, under the Federal Institute of Sports Science. This includes sports medicine, the prevention of drug abuse, the development of sports equipment and studies on training for competition.

French and German sports policies have shown themselves to be markedly more successful than British policies in securing the rights to host major international sports events. In football France hosted the 32-team World Cup finals in 1998 with notable success due to its modern infrastructure, an effective public/ private partnership in tournament development and the host nation's successful team performance. Germany won the bid for the 2006 World Cup finals, defeating England in part through the former's stereotypical reputation for efficient management and high quality infrastructure, and through the latter's weaker marketing skills, poorer infrastructure and reputation for fan disorder. England did host the 1996 European Championships, but a seemingly perfidious response from political leaders has undermined other British bids. The bid by Scotland for the 2006 European Championships was weakened by the Scottish Executive's reluctance to assist fully in stadium development, necessitating a weaker joint bid by Scotland and Ireland. At lower levels of sporting competition Britain has hosted international tournaments that feature a restricted number of nations (usually Commonwealth ones) such as the 'world cups' for rugby union, rugby league, one-day cricket and the 2002 Commonwealth Games in Manchester.

England's future chances of hosting a major sports event such as the Olympics have been undermined by the long-running saga over the future of a dilapidated Wembley Stadium and the question of where a new national stadium should be sited. Britain's position is not helped by its failure to place sports officials in major leadership positions within international sport governing bodies such as FIFA and the IOC. This reflects a long-term weakness within British sports policy, in that while Britain invented many modern sporting disciplines, it has failed to match that cultural influence politically by controlling the subsequent administrative and strategic development of these sports.

Recent developments

In Britain government policy has led to improved provision of sports facilities both for participation and spectator sports. This is seen most clearly in the provision of all seated stadiums. Attempts to control football hooliganism appear to have reduced if not eliminated the problem. French sports policy is, however, much more interventionist and corporatist; professional football clubs, for example, are often owned partly by local authorities and business leaders. By contrast, Germany has emphasized the independence of sporting organization from government control. Both France and Germany have recently been successful in hosting, or bidding to host, World Cup competitions through active government support. In the case of Britain, however, government support failed to attract this major world event.

While the EU accepts that sport is a 'special case' when assessing the implementation of European law, labour markets in sport have been transformed by EU directives. A landmark ruling by the European Court of Justice in December 1995 (the so-called Bosman Case) confirmed unequivocally that the Union's fundamental principle of free mobility of labour also applied to professional sports. Transfer fees in football, once a contract had expired, were declared to be unlawful. The implications have already had a major impact on football but are likely to spread to other sports such as rugby, hockey and basketball. The Union's competition policy rules have been applied to other areas too, such as the practice of giving tour operators exclusive rights to sell entry tickets as part of a package for the World Cup and the exclusive selling by league authorities of TV contracts for games of member clubs.

Sources

H. Dauncey and G. Hare (eds), *France and the 1998 World Cup* (London: Frank Cass, 1998).
European Commission, *The European Union and Sport* (Luxembourg: Office for Official Publications of the European Communities, 1996).

R. Giulianotti, *Football: A Sociology of the Global Game* (Cambridge: Polity, 1999).

C. Gratton and P. Taylor, *Economics of Sport and Recreation* (London and New York: Spon Press, 2000).

K. Heinemann, 'Sports Policy in Germany', in *National Sports Policies: An International Handbook*, eds. L. Chalip, A. Johnson and L. Stachura (Westport CT: Greenwood, 1996): 161–86.

B. Houlihan, 'Sport in the United Kingdom', in *National Sports Policies: An International Handbook*, eds. L. Chalip, A. Johnson and L. Stachura (Westport CT: Greenwood, 1996): 370–403.

B. Houlihan, *Sport Policy and Politics: A Comparative Analysis* (London: Routledge, 1997).

B. Houlihan and A. White, *The Politics of Sports Development* (London: Routledge, 2002).

A. Michel, 'Sports Policy in France', in *National Sports Policies: An International Handbook*, eds. L. Chalip, A. Johnson and L. Stachura (Westport CT: Greenwood, 1996): 139–60.

R. Naul and K. Hardman (eds.), *Sports and Physical Education in Germany* (London and New York: Routledge, 2002).

Useful websites

British Department of Culture, Media and Sport, <www.culture.gov.uk/sport>
British National Olympic Committee, <www.olympics.org.uk>
Council of Europe, <www.coe.int/T/E/Cultural_Co-operation/Sport >
French Ministry of Sport, <www.jeunesse-sports.gouv.fr>
French National Olympic Committee, <www.franceolympique.org>
German National Olympic Committee, <www.nok.de>
German Sport Federation <www.dsb.de>

34
Religion

John Madeley and Benjamin-Hugo LeBlanc

Introduction

The field of religion does not constitute a single public policy area in Britain, France or Germany, and none of these countries – unlike some others, particularly in Northern and Eastern Europe – have central government ministries or departments covering church or religious affairs. All three states, however, have historically been, and continue in a number of ways to be, committed to upholding particular principles and policy aims which have strong implications for religious organizations and practices. Thus, Britain supports two state churches, Germany makes generous provision for the support of some 60 different recognized religions while the French state, though constitutionally debarred from recognizing, remunerating or subsidizing any religion, owns all Catholic cathedrals built before 1905 and is committed to ensuring appropriate conditions for the free exercise of all religions.

The nature of public policy relating to religion

The widely accepted notion that liberal democratic states should remain neutral in matters of religion has not in any of the three countries entailed a complete mutual separation of church and state (Madeley and Enyedi 2003). Although religion as such does not constitute an acknowledged policy area in the way that social security, for example, does, there are a number of public policy concerns that do relate to and affect religious bodies. These include guarantees of internationally-agreed religious freedoms, arrangements for recognizing and occasionally regulating religious bodies, taxation issues and the funding of religious organizations, provisions for religious education, and access to public institutions such as hospitals, prisons and the armed forces.

More specifically, in all three countries public policies relating to religion comprise the following activities:

- enforcement of guarantees of religious freedoms;
- regulation of religious organizational forms eligible for state aid;
- tax concessions for religious organizations;
- funding the maintenance of religious property;
- regulation and funding of religious schools and welfare organizations;
- employment of chaplains in public organizations such as hospitals, prisons, and the armed forces.

In Britain and Germany, but not in France, the central state also grants legal powers to religious bodies, and provides religious education in state schools.

Finally, in Germany alone churches are granted specific tax-raising powers.

Specific comparisons

An idea of the substance of public policies relating to religion can be obtained by examining more closely those relating to religious freedoms, church property and finance, religious education, and ancillary services and organizations.

Religious freedoms

As signatories to the 1948 Universal Declaration of Human Rights and a number of other international covenants, conventions and treaties such as The European Convention on Human Rights and Fundamental Freedoms (1950), Britain, France and Germany are committed to upholding the rights of individuals to freedom of religion and belief (Boyle and Sheen 1997). Guarantees of these freedoms are to be found in all three states' national systems of law, in the case of France and Germany, respectively, the Constitution of the Fifth Republic (1958) and the Basic Law (1949). In Britain, which lacks a written constitution, the incorporation of the 1950 European Convention into British law in 1998 has finally introduced a positive legal guarantee for the first time. This shared subscription to the principle of religious freedom does not, however, involve common practice. In fact, quite distinct patterns of relationship exist between the state authorities and the churches, denominations, sects and other religious bodies in each country.

The only section of the 1919 Weimar Constitution of Germany directly incorporated into the Basic Law of 1949 declared that 'there shall be no state church' and further stipulated that 'each religious body regulates and administers its affairs independently', but this has not resulted in a complete separation of church and state. Over 60 religious organizations enjoy the status of recognized public corporations, which gives them access to a system of church tax collection operated by the public taxation authorities (*Kirchensteuer*). In addition it allows for cooperation in the provision of religious education in public schools, and the provision of various military, prison and other chaplaincy services in public service organizations. Other religious communities can in law achieve public law status, providing that they can prove that they are 'loyal to the state' and that 'their constitution and the number of their members offer an assurance of their permanency'. Religious groups and organizations which do not achieve this recognition, such as the Jehovah Witnesses and various Islamic sub-communities, can be registered as non-profit organizations and may thereby benefit from tax-relief.

By comparison, in Britain there is no formal separation of church and state: England and Scotland each have a single established church. The monarch still carries the title of Defender of the Faith and the office of 'Supreme Governor' of the Church of England and is barred from marrying a Roman Catholic or converting to Roman Catholicism. Twenty-six senior Anglican bishops sit as 'Lords Spiritual' in the Upper Chamber of Parliament, the House of Lords, where they can debate and vote on any issue along with the lay peers, or 'Lords Temporal'. Counterbalancing this privileged role in the highest councils of the realm, archbishops and bishops are appointed by the Crown on the advice of the Prime Minister and the Crown Appointments Commission, while all measures of the Church of England's General Synod have to be ratified by Parliament before they can be presented for Royal Assent. Non-established churches and religious organizations, on the other hand, are completely free and unencumbered by links with the state, although their privileged status as charities brings them within the sphere of the Charities Commission.

In France the leading principles governing church-state relations for almost 100 years have been complete disestablishment and outright separation. Within the framework of the Separation Act (1905) Protestants and Jews have been organized as *associations cultuelles*, and Catholics as *associations diocésaines*. Muslims, who constitute the second largest confessional grouping in France, typically avail themselves of the Law of Associations (1901) with its principle of freedom of association for non-profit purposes; their cultural associations typically support Quranic schools and often manage the mosques attached to such schools. While proclaiming the principles of freedom of conscience and the free exercise of religion, the 1905 Act determined that 'the Republic does not recognize, remunerate or subsidize any religion', but since the Second World War there has been a move towards a stance which involves the obligation of the state to ensure appropriate conditions for the free exercise of religion.

Church property and finances

In France, since the 1905 Separation Law put an end to the state's church budget, the payment of ministers' salaries and all other subventions from public funds, churches have had to rely on only two sources of finance: private giving and indirect help from the state. Because of the initial opposition of the Catholic Church to the 1905 change, ownership of many Catholic estates, including church buildings, was transferred to the *communes* (local authorities) and cathedrals became property of the state. This makes for the paradox that today the *laïque* state and *communes* own, and are responsible for maintaining, religious edifices built prior to 1905, while edifices built subsequently belong to the religious communities themselves and only receive the benefit of land-tax exemption.

In England, with its continuing church establishment, direct state financial support is equally limited: no payments are made by the state in respect of clergy stipends or pensions or of the operating costs of the churches. The bulk of resources have to be found instead by the Church of England's Church Commissioners, who distribute the revenues deriving from properties and investments for the maintenance of the clergy in relation to salaries, pensions and accommodation. Other sources of income include voluntary collections and fees for the performance of particular services. The churches are sole owners of their places of worship and are primarily – and often solely – responsible for their upkeep, although in recent decades some public funds have been made available for the maintenance of historic buildings. Thus the publicly-funded Churches Conservation Trust assists with the maintenance of redundant churches, and English Heritage makes grants for the repair of historic churches and cathedrals. In total, however, the state contributes less than 10 per cent of the Church of England's expenditure on its buildings.

In Germany the economic circumstances of the churches are considerably more solidly based since the churches can, as public law corporations, levy tax on the basis of the civic tax lists. This *Kirchensteuer* (church tax) system differs in some of its details from one *Land* to another, but its level as a percentage of income tax is fixed at 8 or 9 per cent (2 to 3 per cent of the taxpayer's income) in all *Länder*, and it is applicable to all taxable individuals who have been baptized and have not given up their Church membership by formal declaration. Employers collect the *Kirchensteuer* at source along with the income tax; the amount collected is then distributed by the tax authorities to the Churches against a small administrative fee. In 1999 the Catholic Church (27.2 million members) and Protestant Church (27.6 million members in 24 independent Churches) both received approximately €4.2 billion (£3.1 billion, \$4.8 billion) in taxes, representing 80 per cent of their annual budget. According to the German fiscal code, public law religious communities also qualify for other tax privileges, including relief from corporate income tax and inheritance and gift taxes. In addition churches can receive public subsidies for certain purposes, for example for the conservation of their buildings.

In the absence of such generous arrangements, tax concessions are of particular importance for the financing of churches in Britain and France. In Britain, centuries-old charity law provides some benefits; thus churches can enjoy certain advantages in respect of tax exemption. Alongside the Church of

England, many other religious bodies and institutions in Britain have achieved charitable status under the Charity Commissioners in England and a special section of the Inland Revenue in Scotland, which brings with it tax concessions. Charitable trust status has been granted to most of the well-known and long-established denominations, although some new religious movements have been refused.

Despite the French state's non-recognition of religions, French law also allows for the favourable taxation treatment of groups and associations not operating for profit, including religious ones. In addition, the law governing freedom of association permits subsidies from the state or public institutions insofar as they go to support charitable and/or cultural activities.

Religious education

All three countries are committed to upholding the rights of parental choice in the matter of religious education and accept the rightful existence of a private educational sector to cater for minority preferences, albeit subject to some form of public oversight. Nonetheless, contrasting histories of public policy development have led to markedly different patterns of provision of religious education, since the rightful place of religion in the education system, both in public and private schools – its character, scope, funding and control – has on occasion been a source of great controversy. The predominant role of established religion in educational provision in earlier periods has in each of the three cases been greatly modified and reduced; this is the case even in Britain where national, and in Germany where *Länder*, systems of actual, partial or virtual church establishment survive. In France public education has been almost completely laicized, and religious, particularly Catholic, education survives only in a small private sector. Table 34.1 provides details on religious education in Britain, France and Germany.

In Britain arrangements affecting religious education vary as between several different categories of state-funded schools and private schools. In addition to the regulation of publicly funded and managed *community schools*, the 1944 Education Act created a range of different categories of private schools. These had to choose one of the following statuses: (a) *independent* (with a great degree of freedom but no public aid); (b) *voluntary maintained* which should be either (i) *controlled* (entirely financed and controlled by the counties), or (ii) *aided* (less strict control, but also less funding), or (iii) *special agreement* (even more free and less financed). The 1988 Education Act further introduced a new *grant maintained* status, which opened the opportunity for some schools to be financed directly by central government instead of the local education authorities. Most independent schools promote a particular religious orientation by means of religious education classes and services. All the other categories of schools which receive at least some public funds are bound by the requirements that

Table 34.1   Religion in education, private and public

	Britain	France	Germany
Voluntary (private)	32% of all schools	17% of all students	5% of all students
Status of voluntary schools	Independent Controlled Aided Special Agreement	*'Hors-contrat'* (non-contract) Under contract (simple contract or by contract-association)	*Ersatzschulen* (Complementary schools: vocational) *Ergänzungschulen* (Substitution schools)
Public funding of voluntary schools	By contract From the counties or from the state	By contract From the state for current expenditure, and from local voluntary associations for capital expenditure	By law From the *Länder*
Religious education in public schools	Yes	No, except in Alsace-Moselle	Yes

the basic curriculum include non-denominational religious education and that there should be daily collective acts of worship, in both cases with opt-outs for parents and pupils who wish to be exempted. In 1988 an Education Reform Act ruled that the daily act of worship in all maintained schools must be 'wholly or mainly of a broadly Christian character'.

In France the role of religion in education has been a recurrent item of controversy for over two hundred years. A number of private educational institutions have developed alongside the formerly monopolistic state education system at all three levels. These private schools and colleges, which currently cater for approximately 17 per cent of all pupils, are overwhelmingly (90 per cent) Catholic. France's system of financing private schools is the most complex, consisting of many layers of regulations laid down at different periods. Overall there has been a general movement towards conciliation between the private and public sectors; for example, teachers' salaries in the private schools are paid by the state if the school is 'under contract', while non-teaching staff are paid by different organizations responsible for the administration of the private sector. Public schools at both primary and secondary levels are required by law to be secular or neutral, although chaplaincies are allowed if privately funded. No religious instruction may be provided within the schools themselves but traditionally there has been an arrangement allowing the release of primary school children on Wednesday afternoons to attend catechism classes.

In Germany, the Basic Law makes religious education in state schools a constitutional duty of the *Länder*. Most state schools are now interdenominational, with separate voluntary classes in the religion of choice. A significant number of Catholic and a smaller number of Evangelical (Protestant) state schools survive, and in some northern cities secular or non-denominational schools can now be found. A small, largely confessional private sector also exists at all three levels, including some recently-founded Muslim schools. Collectively the private schools currently cater for some 5 per cent of pupils and receive public subsidies to cover most of their current, but not capital, costs. The Basic Law also guarantees that religious education in all public schools (except those that are expressly non-confessional) will occur in accordance with guidelines set down by the religious communities themselves. Pupils in both private and public sectors must take a class on religion unless specifically exempted; parents may decide whether or not their child is to receive religious education or, instead, classes in ethics or philosophy, and students older than 14 may decide for themselves. The content of religious education is the responsibility of the churches, and religious education teachers are nominated by the appropriate church or religious community but paid by the state. The Islamic faith can be taught in public schools, but the lack of hierarchical structures in the Islamic community and the difficulty this raises in terms of nominating teachers and authorizing programmes of instruction has been an obstacle.

Ancillary services and organizations

In Britain, since 1945 social welfare provision, including health, has been overwhelmingly provided by a comprehensive system of state services. The role of non-profit religious agencies, which had been important earlier, was severely diminished as this system was progressively established. In the 1980s, however, there was a renewed emphasis on the role of voluntary agencies as service providers, and religious agencies have become significant providers of services in drug rehabilitation and childcare, in addition to the role of long-established organizations such as the Salvation Army. Many of these organizations receive public subventions. In France, healthcare and social services are also primarily provided by the state. However the law does permit churches to own and control their own caring institutions and allows them, as institutions recognized as being of public utility, to receive subventions from public funds. In Germany, free welfare associations, the largest of which are connected to the two major churches, are major deliverers of health and social services, ranging from 40 per cent of all hospital beds to 90 per cent of all employment for the handicapped. In this connection they receive significant levels of public subsidy.

In Britain the armed forces, the National Health Service and the prisons all employ chaplains recruited from the ordained clergy of the various denominations. Chaplains so employed are paid stipends or fees by the employing service. France's 1905 Separation Law also expressly allowed the organization of publicly-funded chaplaincies in hospitals and prisons and has been deemed to allow the survival of the parallel service provided at public expense by military chaplains representing the Catholic, Protestant and Jewish faiths. In Germany, law and contract assure the provision of religious services and assistance in the armed forces, hospitals, penal institutions and other public institutions. Military chaplains are given the status of state officials for the term of their service.

Recent developments

In both France and Germany issues have recently arisen around the display of religious symbols in schools. In France a major conflict erupted in late 1989 when three Muslim girls were expelled from a public secondary school for wearing the *hijab* (Islamic headdress). Over the next five years court decisions, declarations by the Council of State and directives by the Ministry of Education focussed on the issue without comprehensively resolving it. The outcome has been that some students have been prevented from wearing the *hijab* as an 'ostentatious political and religious symbol' while many more have not (Boyle and Sheen 1997). In Germany it was the use of a Christian symbol, the crucifix, by the education authorities that led to controversy. In Bavaria a law requiring the display of the crucifix in every state school classroom was successfully challenged after a series of failures in the lower courts. Finally in 1995 the Constitutional Court found the law unconstitutional, despite loud protests and demonstrations. The furore only died down when it became clear that only those crucifixes which were the specific objects of complaint needed to be removed (Robbers 1996). In Britain questions of this sort are not treated under the heading of religious freedom but of racial discrimination; on this basis the *hijab* and other religious symbols cannot be prohibited in schools.

In French law the freedoms of conscience and association imply the freedom of sects to exist so long as they are not deemed in some way to be contrary to law and good morals and do not undermine public order. However the attempts of many sects to have themselves recognized as *associations cultuelles*, with the advantages attaching to that status, have generally failed. Nor has any sect achieved recognition as an association contributing to public utility. There is a *Bureau des Cultes* within the Ministry of the Interior which deals with administrative matters arising in connection with the application of various laws to religious communities and maintains a general oversight of religious sects and cults. In Germany a number of high-profile cases, such as those that have resulted in the refusal to recognize Scientology as a religion as well as continuing problems connected with the provision of religious education for Muslims, suggest that regulations in this field await further development. In Britain religious groups and institutions (other than the established churches in England

and Scotland) enjoy no greater rights than those enjoyed by any other form of voluntary organization; there is no system of state recognition. Accordingly some of the difficulties connected with recognition procedures which religious groups (particularly new religious movements) have met in France and Germany have not arisen. On the other hand the Church of Scientology was prevented from registering a building as a place of worship, a humanist body was denied charitable status on the grounds that it did not exist for the purpose of advancing religion within the meaning of the law, and the Mormons were refused tax exemption for their main temple building on the grounds that it was not held to be a place of public worship. In addition, certain controversial religious figures have been excluded from entry into the country on public interest grounds.

Sources

K. Boyle and J. Sheen (eds), *Freedom of Religion and Belief: A World Report* (London: Routledge, 1997).

Catholic Church in France, </www.cef.fr/> [1 May 2003].

Catholic Church in Germany, </katholische-kirche.de/> [1 May 2003].

Charity Commission for England and Wales, <www.charity-commission.gov.uk/> [1 May 2003].

Church Commissioners for England, <www.churchcommissioners.org> [1 May 2003].

Church of Scotland, <www.churchofscotland.org.uk/> [1 May 2003].

Church Schools in England, <www.churchschools.co.uk/> [1 May 2003].

Evangelical (Protestant) Church in Germany, <www.ekd.de/> [1 May 2003].

French Interministerial Mission for Combating Sects, <www.reseauvoltaire.net/rubrique317. > [1 May 2003].

H. Judge, *Faith-based Schools and the State. Catholics in America, France and England* (Oxford: Symposium Books, 2002).

J.T.S. Madeley and Z. Enyedi (eds), *Church and State in Contemporary Europe: the Chimera of Neutrality* (London: Cass, 2003).

S. Monsma and C. Soper, *The Challenge of Pluralism; Church and State in Five Democracies* (Oxford: Rowman & Littlefield, 1997).

G. Robbers (ed), *Church and State in the European Union* (Baden-Baden: Nomos, 1996).

Index